EXPLAINING ECONOMIC BACKWARDNESS

EXPLAINING ECONOMIC BACKWARDNESS

Post-1945 Polish Historians on Eastern Europe

ANNA SOSNOWSKA

CEU PRESS

Central European University Press
Budapest–New York

First published in Polish as *Zrozumieć zacofanie: Spory historyków o Europę Wschodnią, 1947–1994* by Wydawnictwo TRIO, Warsaw, 2004.

English-language edition published in 2019 by
Central European University Press
Nádor utca 11, H-1051 Budapest, Hungary
224 West 57th Street, New York NY 10019, USA
E-mail: ceupress@press.ceu.edu
Website: www.ceupress.com

Main text translated by Jasper Tilbury.
Notes and bibliography translated by Anna Sosnowska.
The translation was funded by the National Program
for Development of Humanities, Republic of Poland.

ISBN 978-963-386-291-9

LIBRARY OF CONGRESS CATALOGING-IN-PUBLICATION DATA

Names: Sosnowska, Anna, 1969– author.
Title: Explaining economic backwardness : post-1945 polish historians on eastern Europe/Anna Sosnowska.
Other titles: Zrozumiec zacofanie. English
Description: New York : Central European University Press, [2019] | Includes bibliographical references and index.
Identifiers: LCCN 2018057270 (print) | LCCN 2018058649 (ebook) | ISBN 9789637326318 (pdf) | ISBN 9789633862919 (hardcover : alk. paper)
Subjects: LCSH: Europe, Eastern—Social conditions—20th century. | Europe, Eastern—History—1945–
Classification: LCC HN380.7.A8 (ebook) | LCC HN380.7.A8 S6713 2019 (print) | DDC 306.094—dc23
LC record available at https://lccn.loc.gov/2018057270

Printed in Hungary

Table of Contents

Introduction

It would be hard to disagree with the contention that the societies of Eastern Europe are poorer than those of Western Europe. There is no consensus, however, as to what caused this disparity in economic development. Nor is there any agreement about what should be done to enable the poorer countries to develop dynamically in the long term. In this book, I examine the economic backwardness of Eastern Europe from the perspective of the debate that took place among Polish social and economic historians in the postwar period.

The main points at issue in this debate concerned the extent to which the economic backwardness of Eastern Europe could be considered a special case, its origins, when exactly it emerged, and the course it took. No serious scholar disputed the very fact of the region's backwardness. The purpose of my analysis is to identify those elements of the debate that belong to the historical sociology of backwardness, particularly of Eastern Europe. I focus on several aspects of this debate: the historical geography of development, models of backwardness, and depictions of social stratification.

Very often the debate was conducted under the pressure of official communist ideology and Cold War divisions, the views of its participants inspired by Marxism. When answering the usual questions a scholar has to answer—what is your book about? How is the writing going?—I often have to explain my fascination with Polish postwar communist historiography, a fascination that in early twenty-first-century Poland many find incomprehensible. Indeed, I still find it necessary to clarify that my aim is not to show how the Polish People's Republic (PRL) stifled the freedom of academic thought and expression. On the contrary, what prompted me to undertake this analysis was the ideological and theoretical bias of sociology in East European societies *after* 1989. Treating the work of historians active during the People's Republic seriously, and not just as the product of their "captive minds,"[1] I question the idealized vision of the precommunist past that dominated academic and public life during the first postcommunist decade. At that time, the region's economic backwardness was solely attributed to state socialism, and the particular social structure was considered an outcome of central planning.[2] The debate within postwar historiography, albeit constrained by censorship, was where I found answers that were missing from sociological discourse. Firstly, I appreciate the attempts made within that debate to provide a causal explanation of economic backwardness. Secondly, the participants presented different ways of conceptualizing the issue, and these made for a genuine academic debate of an impressively high standard.

I should mention at this juncture that my serious, and not just ironic interest in the problem of backwardness means abandoning the postmodernist approach still so prominent in the social sciences. My approach assumes that measurable economic indicators do exist and that they can be arranged in a hierarchical order. In other words, in this book I assume that it is justified to speak of economic backwardness and that the sociology of backwardness is the sociology of economically weak societies.

[1] Miłosz, *The Captive Mind.* Written in Poland in the 1950s, the book by the Nobel Prize winner is one the most well-known accounts of intellectuals being attracted to, and then captivated by, communism.

[2] Domański, *On the Verge of Convergence*, Rychard, *Reforms, Adaptation and Breakthrough*, Sztompka, *The Sociology of Social Change*, Wnuk-Lipiński, *After Communism.*

Why is This Important?

The starting point for this book was an assessment of the discourse on the systemic changes that took place in Eastern Europe after 1989.[3] The most surprising feature of this discourse was the dominance of the modernization paradigm, which excluded any approach to social development that ran contrary to modernization theory. Although dependency theories, world-systems theory, and globalization were at this point in time discussed within the social sciences internationally, in Poland they were overlooked, usually without so much as an attempt at theoretical critique. In the social sciences, politics, and journalism, this tendency revealed itself in developmental optimism, in the division of political actors into reformists and lunatics, and in the division of social actors into dynamic achievers and inveterate losers. This was accompanied by a comparative perspective that was restricted to the most developed countries, an unspoken assumption about the "Europeanness" of Polish society and some of its neighboring societies, and an insistence that the period of state socialism was exclusively to blame for the region's economic backwardness. It was optimistically assumed that the introduction of liberal institutions into societies that—according to Samuel P. Huntington—were culturally synonymous with the West, would trigger the very same processes characteristic of developed countries.[4] The change that came after 1989 was to constitute either a deliberate imitation of the West or a return to social development rules that were universal or at least typical of Western civilization. According to the former, pro-imitative approach, those societies had to acquire civilizational competence, understood as: "deeply-rooted habits, impulses, and skills that are essential to take advantage of the institutions, forms of organization, lifestyles, and technologies which have developed within modern industrial civilization in its Western variant."[5]

---

[3] Sosnowska, "Tu, Tam—pomieszanie," Sosnowska, "Searching for a Theoretical Framework."

[4] Huntington, *The Clash of Civilizations*.

[5] Sztompka, "Teorie zmian społecznych." Throughout this book, works in English are quoted in the original version. Quotations from Polish works have been translated by Jasper Tilbury.

That Polish sociology was seduced by the theory of modernization can, in my view, be attributed both to political attitudes and to the changes taking place within the social sciences. Firstly, the treatment of national society as the primary unit of sociological analysis has deep roots within the tradition of social science. Sociology, which emerged as an academic discipline in the second half of the nineteenth century, was "concerned empirically, primarily, almost exclusively, with the core countries of the capitalist world-economy—indeed, primarily with just a few of them."[6] It regarded the populations of cohesive nation-states, characteristic of the modern West, as the main subject of analysis. Second, this fascination with modernization theory can be explained by global ideological attitudes in the years following the collapse of the Soviet bloc.[7] Third, the East European experience of the most active generation of the Polish intelligentsia at the turn of the last century is also important. I have in mind here the experience of dissent, especially after 1968, and of antisystemic opposition in the 1980s. Although this experience was mainly the preserve of liberal circles in Warsaw, thanks to their key role it also shaped the ideological profile of Polish social science in general.[8] Thus, the antipathy toward Marxism that typified the entire sociological community in Poland left that community with practically no choice, condemning it to different variants of modernization theory. For the latter is one of the few non-Marxist, pro-liberal, and pro-capitalist theories of social change and development. Another feature of the milieu responsible for the hegemony of modernization theory was that it widely endorsed the view—popularized by dissident literature in the 1980s and by the work of Samuel P. Huntington—that (Catholic) Central Europe, including Poland, was historically and culturally part of Western civilization. Consequently, one of the principal charges against modernization theory—the charge of Eurocentrism, which was eventually conceded even by its advocates, including East European sociologists—did not appear to threaten the quality of scholarship about societies in this part of the world.

The conditions under which the Warsaw sociological community operated, as recounted in the memoirs of its participants, inclines me

[6] Wallerstein, *Unthinking Social Science*, 20.
[7] Fukuyama, *The End of History*.
[8] Kovacs, "Praising the Hybrids."

to propose an even more far-reaching interpretation of its fascination with modernization theory.[9] The authors of those memoirs describe how, in the years following the liberalization of the post-1956 period in Poland, the community waged an intellectual struggle against the social dogmas of official ideology in areas as yet unrecognized and underestimated by the enemy—by analyzing the public perception of those dogmas through empirical and methodologically sophisticated research. In the long term, this led to the elimination from sociological debate of questions to which communist ideology had ready-made answers, and eventually to the conclusion that those questions were not even worth asking. Among the questions that threatened the official ideology were those relating to the theory of social development. In hindsight, one can see that the paradoxical outcome of that intellectual struggle between Party dogma on the one hand and empirical investigation on the other was that the historical approach was excluded from the main current of sociological discourse. The empiricism and rationalism of the Lviv-Warsaw School of Philosophy, which were supposed to guard against dogmatism, virtually became dogmas in themselves, unchallenged by other traditions in the humanities. The nature of intellectual and political resistance during the communist period thus led, on the one hand, to an asymmetry between the empirical and methodological (as regards empirical research) achievements of Polish sociology and, on the other, its weakness within, or even aversion to, research in the field of social theory.[10] That an important historical current in Polish sociology, as represented by Józef Chałasiński and Maria Ossowska, was entirely forgotten can also be seen as posthumous revenge by the guardians of political correctness in the Polish People's Republic.[11]

When analyzing the state of research on the changes in Eastern Europe after 1989, I reached the conclusion that it should consider three postulates. First, research should acknowledge the existence of competing paradigms in the approach to social development and

---

[9] Krzemiński, "Metodologia, jako filozofia pozytywistycznej równowagi," Hirszowicz, "Socjologia na Wydziale Filozoficznym UW," Kiciński, "Popaździernikowa socjologia."

[10] Krzemiński, "Metodologia," 118–19.

[11] Chałasiński, *Społeczna genealogia inteligencji*, Ossowska, *Bourgeois Morality*, Ossowska, *Ethos rycerski.*

change. Second, taking into account the interdependencies of the modern world, research should embrace a broad geographical perspective that is both comparative and global. Third, research should keep in mind the historical perspective. Although the historians' debate analyzed in this book does not provide immediate interpretations of the status quo, it is important both for development research and for East European studies. By offering diverse visions of the past, this debate—in the words of Witold Kula—"illuminates" both the subject of the sociological research and its theoretical challenges.[12] The third of the aforementioned postulates is not at all self-evident. For even if there was a general consensus as to the relevance of the social past and its impact on the present, it would still need to be decided which aspects of the past have been decisive in shaping the situation today. This would entail deciding which elements of the present deserve explanation in historical terms, and which elements represent the continuity of a given society. My assumption in this book is that the variable that can be explained genetically by reference to the social past is the economic backwardness of Eastern Europe. I do not assume, however, that backwardness is the unchangeable condition of East European societies; I merely observe that it has been to date.

An important distinction within the historical approach is the distinction between institutions and structures. Within the context of top-down social change—examples of which include the post-1989 transition and the attempts at reform in East European countries from the nineteenth century onwards—institutions incorporate clearly articulated rules, especially laws, as well as typical social attitudes that favor or hinder the introduction of change. Structures, on the other hand, may be seen as the international context for institutions, the representation of an unarticulated continuity in relations between regions at different stages of economic development.[13] Therefore, the difference between the institutional and structural approaches largely boils down to the chosen level of analysis: internal, often national; or external, often transnational or, ultimately, global. An example of the structural

[12] Kula, *Historia, zacofanie, rozwój*, 243–45.

[13] The classic of the institutional approach is Douglas Cecil North, a Nobel Prize winner in economics in 1993. North, *Structure and Change*, North, *Institutions, Institutional Change.*

approach would be to emphasize the persistence of international relations and civilizational boundaries where their disappearance is treated as a desirable phenomenon. Tony Judt wrote: "Is it enough to note the remarkable continuity between the outer limits of the Carolingian monarchy, the frontier of (some of the) Austrian and Hungarian territories in the Habsburg Empire, and the western edge of real existing socialism after 1947 in order to conclude that *tertium non datur?*"[14]

As regards the long-term and less advantageous forms of development in the eastern half of the continent, the countries within it "will never join the rest of the European Union on an equal footing. On the contrary, and offensive as it sounds, for the foreseeable future, it would be an act of charity, economically speaking, for the EU to absorb the countries to its east on such terms."[15]

In research on development opportunities and backwardness, the structural approach may be regarded as fundamentally more pessimistic than the institutional one. In reference to the problem of economic backwardness that is the focus of this book, the weaknesses—and indirectly, the strengths—of these two types of analysis are, to quote Andrew C. Janos, as follows: "If institutionalism ignores external constraints and the sheer weight of statistical evidence that dims the prospects of development, structuralists fail to account for obvious exceptions from the law of averages, ignoring the countries that, external constraints notwithstanding, have been successful in moving from poverty to prosperity."[16]

Traces of Debate

The main participants in the debate on East European backwardness were Marian Małowist and Witold Kula (who initiated it), their opponents—Jerzy Topolski and Andrzej Wyczański—and these historians' students and colleagues, notably Antoni Mączak, Benedykt Zientara, Ireneusz Ihnatowicz, Jacek Kochanowicz, Jerzy Jedlicki, Elżbieta Kaczyńska, Maria Bogucka, and Henryk Samsonowicz. I assume for

[14] Judt, *A Grand Illusion?*, 51.
[15] Ibid., 130.
[16] Janos, *East Central Europe in the Modern World*, 19.

the purpose of this book that the debate started with Witold Kula's postdoctoral lecture, "Social Privilege and Economic Progress" (Przywilej społeczny a postęp gospodarczy), delivered in 1947, and ended with Jerzy Topolski's book, *Poland in the Modern Age* (Polska w czasach nowożytnych), published in 1994.[17] The texts I analyze fall within one or more of the following categories:

1. they are comparative and transnational,
2. they make use of regional categories: Eastern Europe, Central Europe, etc.,
3. they conceptualize and interpret the circumstances of economic development and underdevelopment,
4. they analyze long-term, mass social and economic processes,
5. they put forward a development research methodology, thanks to which the authors' theoretical inspirations can be established.

I focus on the work of four authors of the older generation. The approach developed by this generation was sociological in the sense that it sought to explain and interpret East European backwardness rather than just to analyze its extent, as was done by traditional idiographic historiography. Małowist, Kula, Topolski, and Wyczański used sociological methods—a comparative perspective, analysis of social stratification and mobility, and attempts to find mechanisms linking various spheres of societal life. These authors' works on the history of Poland and the region were inspired by a particular kind of sociological curiosity: they asked questions about what had caused the state of affairs of which they were contemporaries. Since the aim of this book is to analyze a particular debate that took place within a specific genre of historical writing inspired by sociology, and not to analyze postwar social and economic historiography in general, I omit the considerable idiographic output of the latter as well as works that emerged within the four schools represented by the authors mentioned above.

A small number of social and economic historians outside those four schools went beyond the national level of analysis to consider development trends in the region. These included specialists in the

[17] Kula, "Przywilej społeczny," Topolski, *Polska w czasach nowożytnych*.

manorial economy based on the second serfdom, such as Jan Rutkowski, Władysław Rusiński, Franciszek Bujak, Kazimierz Tymieniecki, and Leonid Żytkowicz. The work of these authors played a significant role in the debate on the region's backwardness. The older generation, Rutkowski and Bujak, prepared the ground for this debate by creating the first economic studies centers in Poland before the war. All the aforementioned authors developed partial interpretations of the East European version of feudalism that were economic rather than social in approach. A comparative, transnational perspective was also adopted by historians of the nineteenth and twentieth centuries, such as Irena Pietrzak-Pawłowska in her work on the industrial revolution in the agricultural economies of Europe, and Jerzy Tomaszewski, who specialized in the post-Versailles history of the region. These historians did not, however, participate directly in the general debate on development and backwardness, and did not propose an overall view of Poland's place in Eastern Europe or indeed the latter's place in Europe.

Research Questions and Theoretical Inspirations

The main questions I ask in relation to the analyzed texts are as follows:

- What historical geography of development and backwardness and, more specifically, what boundaries and delineating criteria, and what name for the region do they propose, within which the Polish path of development should be analyzed?
- What historical model, theoretical assumptions, and method do they propose to interpret the Polish and East European path of development?
- What, if any, of the characteristics of East European societies do they regard as a cause or symptom of economic backwardness?

Terminology

The notions of "development," "underdevelopment," and "backwardness" frequently appear in this book. As is conventional in modern development economics, and in keeping with Kula and Małowist's intentions, I distinguish the first of these notions from growth understood in purely economic terms. Measured nowadays in terms of Gross Domestic Product (GDP) per capita, growth was calculated by historians in the past according to the volume of primary goods—grain or steel, for instance—produced during a given period. Development, on the other hand, implies characteristics such as an equitable distribution of social income or high average life expectancy within a society.[18] These indicators of sustainable development were proposed by Kula, among others. Development also has a fairly extensive metaphorical meaning. It describes the process by which certain trends are strengthened. In an extreme case, therefore, it is possible to speak of the development of backwardness; it occurs in this sense quite often. However, I have tried to ensure that this sense is clearly distinguishable from the principal meaning of development. I should also add that I have avoided using the term "progress," nowadays controversial, except where I directly refer to a fragment of text in which that term appears. The principal sense of the term "modernization" used in this book refers to modernization theory, which is characterized by specific assumptions about the conditions and criteria of development. However, it also appears in a more neutral sense. To avoid repetition, I use it as rarely as possible as a synonym for sustainable development, which is a positive consequence of profound social change.

I have also attempted to lend a neutral sense to the terms "underdevelopment" and "backwardness." I use them to describe the economic weakness of a country or area relative to the most economically strong country or area at a given time. Contrary to such notions as "dependency" or "delay," the terms "underdevelopment" and "backwardness" do not refer to the genesis or epistemology of a state of economic weakness. I am aware that the neutrality of the term "backwardness," in particular, is not self-evident. Indeed, in etymological terms, backwardness can be seen to be synonymous with something that suffers from stunted development, a term borrowed from child psychology, and treated as part of the vocabulary specific to a linear understanding of development and the classification of societies from primitive to civilized. Nevertheless, the use of this term in English has

[18] Srinivasan, introduction to *Handbook of Developmental Economics*, 12–15.

a fairly long tradition in studies on the specific development path and economic weakness of Eastern Europe. I identify with the tradition instigated by the works of Jacek Kochanowicz, Witold Kula, Andrew Janos, and Daniel Chirot.[19]

EASTERN EUROPE

Whenever I refer to the region itself, and not to its subsequent definitions, I use the term "Eastern Europe," as in the title of the book. I do so because that is the term that is most frequently used, which is a strong enough reason. But there is also another reason. When an author deliberately chooses to use the term "Eastern Europe" in their work, and not an alternative phrase, I see this as a meaningful act. Indeed, my own choice may be viewed in this way. Currently, the term "Eastern Europe" more or less signifies postcommunist Europe; the Europe that has recently joined the European Union or that still remains outside it. Public life in those countries revolves around terms of accession, economic migration, and the negative attitude of public opinion in the old EU. Those countries lie within the area formerly encompassed by state socialism; an area whose borders were established at Versailles in 1918 and whose quasi-colonial identity Małowist traces back to the sixteenth century.[20] In light of the fact that other terms are possible, my decision to opt for "Eastern Europe" is not an innocent choice.

[19] Kochanowicz, *Backwardness and Modernization*, Kochanowicz, "The Polish Economy and the Evolution of Dependency," Chirot, *Causes and Consequences of Backwardness*, Janos, *The Politics of Backwardness in Hungary*, Janos, "The Politics of Backwardness in Continental Europe."

[20] Małowist, "The Problem of the Inequality."

CHAPTER 1

In the Eyes of Others: Historical Sociology and its Image of Eastern Europe

The aim of this chapter is to present the image of Eastern Europe that has been created by historical sociology. This image began to take shape during the debate on the origins of modernity and the rise of the West. I therefore begin the chapter by introducing historical sociology itself, which was institutionalized as a separate discipline in the 1970s.

Historical Sociology: Generational, Political, and Theoretical Roots

Even the simplest definition of historical sociology, a field created from the convergence of history and sociology, must refer to the history of both disciplines. From the moment sociology emerged in the mid-nineteenth century, these two disciplines experienced periods of hostility and rapprochement. Scientism, which focused on identifying universal social laws, should be seen as one of the currents antagonistic to such rapprochement. It was represented by the classical Positivists, Auguste Comte and Herbert Spencer. Similarly ahistorical was the early twentieth-century functionalism of Bronisław Malinowski and Talcott Parsons, who tried to establish historically variable forms of the universal principle of social integration.[1]

---

1 Sztompka, *The Sociology of Social Change*, 202–22, Burke, *History and Social Theory*, 3–9. Bottomore and Mulkay, *Controversies in Sociology*, 15–23. See also: Szacki, "Early Positivism and the Beginnings of Sociology," and Szacki,

In historiography, the approaches hostile to sociology included idiographic history, whose narrative was organized around great events and personalities, and nationalist historiography, which took shape in the late nineteenth century and built a narrative around what it considered to be "eternal" nations.[2] Among the thinkers who symbolized the rapprochement between history and sociology, one should mention Alexis de Tocqueville, Max Weber, and Karl Marx (that part of Marx's *oeuvre* concerning the historical roots of capitalism).[3] Weber's works, such as *The Types of Legitimate Domination* and his essays on religion and economy, including *The Protestant Ethic and Spirit of Capitalism*, were particularly important for institutionalizing the convergence of sociology and history. They arose in an academic context, thus setting the criteria of sociological correctness, were relatively value-free, and eschewed the ideologies of the day.[4]

Dennis Smith, a British scholar of sociological thought and author of *The Rise of Historical Sociology*, traces the beginnings of the interaction between history and sociology to the postwar period.[5] He links the birth of historical–sociological sensibility to the state of consciousness—intellectual, moral, personal—of Europe's war generation. The continental experience of war and Nazism exposed the failure of traditional social science to explain major social events, and particularly to anticipate them. It also brought about an awareness of the bankruptcy of nationalist historiography. According to both Smith and Andrzej Grabski, a Polish historian of historiography, in the postwar years there was a shift away from the history of states and nations in favor of sociological tools and systemic and structural (as opposed to fact-based) ways of thinking. Among historians it created a tendency to think in terms of mass social phenomena and classes or groups (as opposed to individuals and great historical figures, but

"The Evolutionist Sociology," in *History of Sociological Thought*, vol. 2, and Janos, *Politics and Paradigms*, 17–24 and 36–44.

2 Burke, *Sociology and History*, 16–19.

3 Sztompka, *The Sociology of Social Change*, 202–22, Skocpol, "Sociology's Historical Imagination," Burke, "The Differentiation," 15–23.

4 Szacki, *History of Sociological*, 337–70, Weber, *The Protestant Ethic*, Weber, *Economy and Society*, Steinmetz, "Ideas in Exile."

5 Smith, *The Rise of Historical Sociology*.

also nations), and among sociologists it encouraged a thirst for historical knowledge and an identification of the barriers and opportunities entailed by the past.[6]

American historical sociologist Theda Skocpol and Polish historian of sociology Piotr Sztompka attribute the origins of historical sociology to the generational experience of another group.[7] In her introduction to *Vision and Method in Historical Sociology*, Skocpol presents the authors whom Smith considers to be the first modern historical sociologists (Talcott Parsons, Neil Smelser, Robert K. Merton, and Seymour M. Lipset) as merely the fathers of modern macrosociology. Sztompka notes that their approach to history was no different from classical European "sociology above history" or "historiosophical presentism."[8] Although historical sociology proper drew inspiration from those authors in terms of theoretical questions and an interest in social macrostructures, it essentially evolved in opposition to the functionalist model developed by Talcott Parsons. According to Skocpol and Sztompka, historical sociology arose as a protest against the dominant sociological tradition: the evolutionism and developmentalism of Auguste Comte, Herbert Spencer, Émile Durkheim, and Ferdinand Tönnies, which culminated in the functionalist model, and economistic, scientistic, and mechanistic Marxism.[9] I think that from the point of view of the emergence of historical sociology "as more than [just] historically rooted research" and as "a distinct theoretical perspective on the social world,"[10] the postwar years, and especially the 1960s and 1970s, should be seen as key to its institutionalization. These were preceded, following the death of Weber, by a period when the main trends in both disciplines diverged.

Before the "golden age" of historical sociology in the 1970s, new interdisciplinary forms of practising the social sciences appeared, although these did not lead to the institutionalization of the discipline. Such pioneering initiatives—not appreciated until several years later—included the work of the French Annales school created by

---

6 Grabski, *Zarys historii historiografii*, 189–99.
7 Skocpol, "Sociology's Historical," 2–4.
8 Sztompka, *The Sociology*, 202–06.
9 Ibid., 186–91, Skocpol, "Sociology's Historical," 2–4.
10 Sztompka, *The Sociology*, 206.

Lucien Febvre and Marc Bloch in the 1920s, "forty years before it became fashionable to combine history, sociology, anthropology, and economics";[11] Karl Polanyi's holistic, interdisciplinary approach to the social sciences most successfully realized in *The Great Transformation* that was published in 1944; and Schmuel N. Eisenstadt's functionalist and Reinhard Bendix's "Weberian" works from the 1960s.[12]

Thus, "around 1960," notes Daniel Grinberg from the perspective of a historian of historiography, "there appeared manifestos announcing the birth of new schools of historical thinking," including a "new social history" that postulated "giving a voice to the hitherto voiceless victims of history, the 'silent majority' who are virtually absent from classical historical texts,"[13] as well as the study of mass processes. The work to set the standard of this new social history was E. P. Thompson's *The Making of the English Working Class*, first published in 1963.[14] Alongside the history of conflicts, revolutions, and rebels, the book set out another of the new discipline's main areas of interest: the history of labor. Thompson offered an original interpretation of the process by which a self-aware working class was formed in England. He emphasized the role of culture (the Methodist church, traditional forms of communal social relations), conscious organizational effort, and moral choice, and argued against economism, which was still dominant within Marxism in the mid-1960s. As someone involved in left-wing political activity, a member of the Communist Party of Great Britain until 1956, and editor *Past and Present* and *New Left Review*, Thompson's voice was extremely important in the creation of a new historiography that was inspired by Marxism but that broke with it. His work set new standards for the analysis of other large social groups. Several other historians followed in Thompson's methodological footsteps: Eugene Genovese[15] in his work on American slaves, and

[11] Chirot, "The Social and Historical Landscape of Marc Bloch," 22.

[12] Bloch, *Feudal Society*, Polanyi, *The Great Transformation*, Eisenstadt, *The Political Systems of Empires*, Bendix, *Work and Authority*, Bendix, *Nation-Building and Citizenship*.

[13] Grinberg, "Problematyka przemocy," 155–56.

[14] Thompson, *The Making of the English Working Class*. See also: Trimberger, "E. P. Thompson: Understanding the Process of History."

[15] Genovese, *Roll, Jordan, Roll*.

Charles Tilly, Ira Katznelson, and Aristide Zolberg in their study of urban workers in the US.[16]

One can safely say that the renewed interest in social history during the 1960s was a stage in the transformation of historiography that convinced the (then) younger generation of sociologists of its merits and helped create historical sociology. The novelty of this historiography was that it rejected the nation-oriented approach prevalent in the nineteenth and twentieth centuries in favor of a "new history." Its leading lights would be Eric Hobsbawm and the British historians associated with *Past and Present*; Fernand Braudel and the French Annales school; and the Sozialgeschichte school in Germany.

At the same time, the 1960s was a period of crisis in functionalist analysis, which Jerzy Szacki described as "the theoretical superstructure of a solid, institutionalized academic sociology that was reconciled with the existing social order in a period when the United States witnessed no great ideological confrontations and the social world seemed perfectly stable."[17] American sociologists were now interested in the phenomena of conflict, revolution, and modern political change. "Between the 1950s and the 1980s, the implicit world views embodied in both static and developmentalist versions of structural functionalism were rendered less meaningful by the reverberations of political conflicts inside the United States and across the globe."[18] The newfound interest in groups and regions hitherto neglected by American social science led to a revision of views about history. In the 1960s and 1970s there appeared the first (now classic) texts by Barrington Moore, the Tilly family, especially Charles Tilly, and Theda Skocpol.[19] A common feature of these pioneering works in the new historical sociology and new social history was that they investigated aspects of communal life that traditional historiography had considered less important to world history than diplomacy, war, and politics. The authors analyzed the

---

16 Feagin, Tilly, and Williams, *Subsidizing the Poor*, Katznelson and Zolberg, *City Trenches*.

17 Sztompka, *The Sociology*, 204–06.

18 Skocpol, "Sociology's Historical," 3.

19 Moore Jr., *Social Origins of Democracy*, Skocpol, *States and Social Revolutions*, Skocpol, *Social Revolutions in the Modern World*, Tilly, Tilly, and Tilly, *The Rebellious Century*.

relationship between political regimes and their social environment, between social conditions and the course of political change. In contrast to traditional political history, in the 1970s the historical sociology of political institutions assumed that the political system or form of organization of the body politic was a consequence of changing social conditions rather than the diplomatic and military interventions of dynasties or "great historical figures."

The first "methodological manifestos" of historical sociology appeared in the early 1980s, the most radical being by Philip Abrams, who called for the full integration of sociology and history on the grounds that both disciplines had a common object of study: human society.[20] Sociology, he argued, should examine not social systems or activities but processes. "People make their own history—but only under definite circumstances and conditions; we act through a world of rules which our action makes, breaks and renews–we are creatures of the rules and the rules are our creations; we make our own world—the world confronts us as an implacable order of social facts set over against us."[21] Dialectical investigation of the circumstances offered by society at a given time and place on the one hand, and human agency on the other, should be common method of sociology and history. Peter Burke's less radical approach identified social history with historical sociology, and treated both as the study of the past with the aid of sociological methods and with reference to social theory.[22] The sociological methods that Burke believed should be introduced into historical research included: comparative studies; the application of a model understood as "an intellectual construct which simplifies reality in order to emphasize the recurrent, the general and the typical";[23] representative surveys of sources generated on a mass scale; the use of statistics; research on social stratification and mobility; and studies of mentalities and ideologies.

For the purpose of this book, the most important manifesto of historical sociology was Charles Tilly's *As Sociology Meets History*,

---

[20] Abrams, "History, Sociology and Historical Sociology."
[21] Ibid., 87.
[22] Burke, *History and Social Theory*.
[23] Ibid., 27.

published in 1981.[24] Tilly put forward the idea that historical studies are essential if we are to grasp the present. He argued that historical studies are key to understanding the changes that have led to precisely this and not another form of modernity. Tilly's premise was that we are much less likely to discover where a given aspect of social reality is leading us, or even what role it performs, than we are to discover its origins or what caused it. In other words, in the study of society, it is the genetic, historical, and causal explanations that make more sense than teleological or deductive ones. If, therefore, the task of sociology is to understand the key social forms of modernity, and these are "the two interdependent master processes of the era: the creation of a system of national states and the formation of a worldwide capitalist system,"[25] then the method of sociology should be to investigate the "long, slow, historically specific process."[26] In his 1984 book, *Big Structures, Large Processes, Huge Comparisons*, Tilly offered a detailed critique of the assumptions behind the classical sociology of modern change: the treatment of national society as a separate system, and changes to that system as a coherent, comprehensive, and gradual process of differentiation and specialization that served social integration. Tilly noted that sociology therefore treated everything outside this framework as anomie, dysfunction, and supposedly "illegitimate" violence, as opposed to state violence, which was "legitimate" because it led to integration. The sociology of modern change (mainly the formation of nation-states and the emergence of capitalism in different parts of the globe) should therefore take into account the specific historical context and the sequence and configuration of changes as well as the collective actions that produced them. It should assume that "the time and place in which a structure or process appears make a difference to its character, that the sequence in which similar events occur has a substantial impact on their outcomes."[27]

An unnecessary but nonetheless important circumstance for the image of historical sociology in 1970s was the fact that in American sociology departments—crucial to postwar sociology in general—

---

[24] Tilly, *As Sociology Meets History*.
[25] Tilly, *Big structures, Large Processes*, 147.
[26] Tilly, *As Sociology*, 39.
[27] Tilly, *Big Structures*, 79.

"radical sociology" had a chance to take shape. The latter emphasized its links with the New Left and was interested in groups and regions which sociology had previously neglected. It is this trend, I believe, that was responsible for the popularity of studies on phenomena that functionalist interpretations of social order regarded as "anomalies": revolutions, rebellions, and collective violence.

The generational experience and antiscientistic attitude of historical sociologists encompassed two more features that crop up in this book: internationalism (at least declared) and political engagement. The latter was associated with actual political activity or, more frequently, with lending a political context and message to intellectual work. A convincing New Left interpretation of the birth of the discipline by Skocpol and Grinberg presented a political and ideological portrait of its founders in the late 1960s and 1970s: the rejection of both "Western-style liberal democracy" and "Soviet-style socialism"; a desire to go beyond the ideological dispute imposed by the Cold War; anticolonialism; anti-imperialism and pacifism; antiracism; and, finally, antisexism.[28] The popularity of non-Soviet, humanist Marxism among historical sociologists in the 1970s had theoretical as well as political roots. As Perry Anderson argued, "it is the only thought which has rigorously united developmental and structural analysis, it is at once pure historicity (denial of all supra-historical essences) and radical functionalism (societies are significant totalities)."[29] One might say, however, that the decision to choose Marxism over Weberism, which undoubtedly also combined historiographical studies with a sophisticated holistic approach, was political and ideological more than it was theoretical.

The American Sociological Association finally recognized historical sociology as a separate branch of sociology in 1982, when it created its Comparative and Historical Sociology Section. As a discipline, historical sociology continues to grow, mainly in the US and UK. The most important forum for researchers is the Section's *Newsletter* as well as the *Journal of Historical Sociology*, which is edited primarily by scholars from American universities and has been published by Blackwell in the US and UK since 1988.

[28] Skocpol, "Sociology's Historical."

[29] Quoted in: Fulbrook and Skocpol, "Destined Pathways." Anderson, *Portugal and the End of Ultra-Colonialism.*

Historical Sociology as a Separate Discipline

The two main types of research activity characteristic of historical sociology are, first, the sociological analysis of past phenomena, and, more importantly from the point of view of this book, the study of processes of change that began in the past and whose consequences are a social phenomenon in the present. This distinction is almost exclusively analytical: research practice usually guides sociologists to the past, for it is there, and only there, that they can hope to answer the questions asked of modernity or provoked by the present state of affairs.

The first of these research activities is closer to social history. Among Polish authors, the finest examples of sociological studies of the past are Maria Ossowska's *Bourgeois Morality* and *The Chivalric Ethos* (Etos rycerski), Nina Assorodobraj-Kula's *The Origins of the Working Class* (Początki klasy robotniczej), and Józef Chałasiński's works on the social genealogy and transformation of Polish peasants, workers, intelligentsia, and émigrés.[30] A common feature of these books is their focus on the historical roots and transformation of particular social groups. Although these groups were crucial to determining the nature of the societies in which they lived, the authors stayed within the conventions of "micro" as opposed to "macro" research. An important area of historical microsociology is "everyday life." According to the model established by E. P. Thompson and Braudel for analyzing the "structures of everyday life," depending on social position and civilizational zone, the latter include: food, drink and stimulants, clothes and fashion, houses and dwellings, technologies for satisfying basic material needs, and the ways and means of exchanging goods.

When discussing this approach to historical sociology, the question arises as to whether it makes sense to distinguish it from social his-

[30] Ossowska, *Bourgeois Morality*, Ossowska, *Social Determinants of Moral Ideas*, Ossowska, *Ethos rycerski*, Assorodobraj-Kula, *Początki klasy robotniczej*, Chałasiński, *Drogi awansu społecznego robotnika*, Chałasiński, "Emigracja jako zjawisko społeczne," Chałasiński, "Związek z parafią," Chałasiński, *Młode pokolenie chłopów*, Chałasiński, *Rewolucja młodości*, Chałasiński, *Społeczna genealogia.*

tory. The terms "social history" and "historical sociology" are so close that they could be considered, following Burke, as equivalent ways of describing the research activities that have resulted from the convergence of sociology and history.[31] The best definition I can suggest of the boundary between social microhistory and historical microsociology is inductive and concerns the academic practice and self-identification of researchers themselves. Social history is a field practised in departments of history, while historical sociology is practised in departments of sociology, and both are subject to the academic principles in force at any given time in these areas. The point of departure for social history would be microhistorical or microsociological questions, beginning with a search for relevant sources and then for appropriate methods to analyze them, such methods being often but not necessarily sociological in character. Historical sociology, in turn, would start from research questions, an interpretative model, and a larger set of clearly defined assumptions, and would then search for materials—rarely and not necessarily source materials—in order to answer the research question and test the hypothesis.

The "micro" form of historical sociology was already dominant by the 1980s. That period, wrote Grinberg, "was marked by a retreat from large structures and long processes in favor of case studies, microhistory, and everyday life. . . . Diachrony and narrative made a triumphant return."[32] Feminist or "gender sensitive" historiography contributed models of reproduction and education, forms of family life, the perception of social roles, and the gendered division of labor.[33] Articles that employed any one of these sociological methods of conducting historical research came to dominate the *Journal of Historical Sociology* as well as two periodicals founded by and for social historians: *Comparative Studies in Society* and *Journal of Social History*, both published by Cambridge University Press (from 1959 and 1967, respectively).

---

[31] Burke, *Sociology and History*, 30.

[32] Grinberg, "Problematyka przemocy," 157.

[33] Nicholson, *Gender and History*, Zinsser, *History & Feminism*. Wyczański's school published within this field: Wyczański, "Die Frau in der Gesellschaft Polens," Kuklo, *Rodzina w osiemnastowiecznej Warszawie*, Kuklo, *Kobieta samotna*.

The second approach to historical sociology, which consists in identifying the origins of modern phenomena, is more different from social history than the first approach and more similar to sociology in its "macro" version. Ewa Morawska describes it as involving the use of "comparative methods of sociological analysis" and "the study of 'big structures and long processes' of societal transformations."[34] Skocpol saw it as an "ever-renewed tradition of research devoted to understanding the nature and effects of large-scale structures and fundamental processes of change."[35] Historical (macro)sociology understood in this way begins with a diagnosis of the current situation, identifying the key phenomenon that organizes communal life. It tries to answer the following questions: Where did this phenomenon come from? What historical circumstances contributed to its formation? Other such questions might include the origin of nation-states, capitalism, liberal democracy, and global inequality.[36] The most prominent examples of this approach are (some of) the works of Tilly, Moore, and Michael Mann, as well as the works discussed below that seek to explain the economic divisions of Europe.

In the case of "big" questions, the use of historical explanations almost automatically entails broadening the geographical perspective. History reveals differences in the timing, for instance, of the creation of nation-states in various parts of the world. This gives rise to another feature of historical macrosociology—the comparative or global perspective. In contrast to the comparative perspective, the global perspective juxtaposes societies not only and not so much in terms of their similarities and differences but in terms of their connections and interdependencies. A sensible approach is to combine both perspectives, adopting one or the other depending on how we assess the degree of interdependence between countries or regions in a given historical period. Thus, in his later works from the 1980s, Daniel Chirot compared Western Europe to other regions of the world in the period between the sixteenth and eighteenth centuries. For subsequent periods, however, he adopted a global perspective since he believed that that was precisely when the degree of interdependence between regions

---

[34] Morawska, foreword to "Historical and Comparative Sociology," 1–4.
[35] Skocpol, "Sociology's Historical," 4.
[36] See Kochanowicz, "Badania historyczno-porównawcze."

increased enormously.[37] Immanuel Wallerstein, on the other hand, used the term "world-system" even in relation to the sixteenth century.

To ask big questions and to produce a comprehensive picture of complex processes requires historical sociology to adopt an interdisciplinary perspective that combines not just history and sociology but usually also political science, economics, and anthropology. The Annales school also proposed to include research on social geography.

In the 1980s, historical sociology expanded its field of interest beyond the left-wing issues of revolution and persecuted groups. Currently, there is no point in associating it with any particular ideological position. In the last two decades of the twentieth century the most rapidly developing branch of macrosociology was the historical study on the origins of nationalism.[38] Thanks to Mann's *Origins of Social Power*, as well as the later works of Skocpol, Tilly, and Chirot, political structures became an important explanatory variable.[39] The institutionalism of C. W. North contributed analyses of law and custom to historical sociology. In the 1990s reference to national, cultural, or religious differences became a popular explanatory tool. An outstanding example of such an approach was *The Wealth and Poverty of Nations* by David Landes.[40]

---

[37] Chirot, *Social Change in the Modern Era*, Chirot, *How Societies Change.*

[38] This huge debate on the origins of nationalism was initiated by Ernest Gellner, who was opposed by Anthony Smith and Eric Hobsbawm. The debate continues within the framework set by these authors. On the one hand, there is an approach that treats nationalism as a modern phenomenon that was "created" in the nineteenth century, with ethnic groups as "immagined communities" or "constructed communities." On the other hand, the primordialist approach treats nations as "real beings" rooted in a remote, tribal past. The works from the initial phase of the debate include: Gellner, *Thought and Change*, Gellner, *Nations and Nationalism*, Hobsbawm and Ranger, *The Invention of Tradition*, Hobsbawm, *Nations and Nationalism*, Smith, *The Ethnic Revival*, Smith, *The Ethnic Origins of Nations*, Bhabha, *The Nation and Narration*, Anderson, *Imagined Communities*, Greenfeld, *Nationalism.*

[39] Mann, *The Sources of Social Power*, Tilly, *Coercion, Capital, European States*, Tilly, *European Revolutions*, Evans, Rueschemeyer and Skocpol, *Bringing the State Back In*, Rueschemeyer and Skocpol, *States, Social Knowle*dge, Chirot, *Social Change*, Chirot, *How Societies.*

[40] North and Thomas, *The Rise of the Western World*, Landes, *The Wealth and Poverty.*

Studies that I would categorize as belonging to historical sociology share the following features: 1. A tendency to understand history in terms of processes and cumulative change, however slow; 2. An interest in mass phenomena; 3. A tendency to organize historical material in the form of a model, as defined by Burke. Unlike fact-based history and the history of famous figures, historical sociology deliberately reduces reality to a set of phenomena that the researcher, on the basis of previously adopted assumptions, regards as key to explaining the problem. In contrast to historiography that is focused on the creation of states or nations, which also relies on a model of sorts, the best examples of historical sociology treat social phenomena relativistically as phenomena restricted to a particular time, place, and circumstance, and not as phenomena that are "natural" or a manifestation of some kind of "historical necessity." This applies to phenomena that are dominant in the contemporary imagination, such as the nation-state and nationalism, the market and capitalism, and socialism and Christianity. At the same time, studies that seek the origins of modernity run the risk of becoming somewhat teleological. This is particularly apparent in the approach taken by Anderson (discussed below), who traced the Cold War division of Europe to antiquity and the Middle Ages, or Wallerstein, who predicted communist revolution in the periphery of the global capitalist system.

Eastern Europe and the Rise of the West

Of greatest importance to the image of Eastern Europe that took shape within historical macrosociology were studies on the social origins of the rise of the West and the genesis of capitalism. This image arose in the context of attempts to answer the following questions: How was it that a small continent like Europe managed, over the course of four centuries, to expand its military and economic power and colonize or conquer most of the planet? Why was it precisely here that manufacturing technologies developed, culminating in Great Britain's industrial revolution of the eighteenth century? Were economic inequalities and political dependencies within national societies, and especially between societies, a necessary feature of capitalism? Posing such questions forced historians to loosen the traditional constraints of historiographical precision, and sociologists to accept that "history matters"—that the past has a bearing on the present.

In the following sections I discuss models of the historical sociology of Eastern Europe that were most prominent and influential in the postwar period. The originators of these models were: Fernand Braudel, long-time head of the Annales school of history in Paris; Immanuel Wallerstein, emeritus professor of sociology and founder of the Fernand Braudel Center in Binghamton, New York State; and the scholars Perry Anderson, Robert Brenner, and Iván T. Berend (a collaborator of György Ránki in the 1970s and 1980s), who, despite the great popularity of their ideas, did not create distinct schools. Anderson, Brenner, and Berend are professors of modern history at the University of California, Los Angeles, which shows that among university departments this is one of the friendliest toward historical sociology. Brenner is director of the Center for Social Theory and Comparative History. The name of the Center, which places a department of sociology side by side with a department of history, reflects the aims of this specific approach to historical material. Berend, a long-time professor at Budapest University of Economics, specializes in the history of Eastern Europe in the nineteenth and twentieth centuries and is head of the Center for European and Russian Studies at UCLA. He has used a modified version of the world-system model in his research since the mid-1970s, when he was still in Hungary. All these authors, therefore, appeal to similar traditions. They share similar intellectual interests and belong to research communities that remain in close contact.

The analysis that follows includes one more school of historical–sociological thought, initiated by István Bibó and Jenő Szűcs. Bibó, a Hungarian historian, became a legendary figure after the democratic transition Eastern Europe experienced in 1989.[41] This was due to his radically democratic views and his model of the Hungarian nation and state, which departed from the narratives dominant before the Second World War, during Hungary's wartime collaboration with Nazi Germany, and throughout the communist period. In the 1980s, Szűcs, a student of Bibó's, came up with the idea of a "Third Europe," an

41 See the political and intellectual biography of István Bibó in the introduction to Szűcs, *Trzy Europy*, 25–27.

intermediate region between the West and Russia. This idea tried to link Bibó's Central European perspective with the achievements of Western historical sociology.

Deciding in what order to discuss the aforementioned models presented something of a problem. I had to reject a straightforward chronological approach as most of the relevant works appeared at more or less the same time—the late 1970s and early 1980s. I therefore decided to group them according to ideological criteria. The models proposed by Wallerstein, Berend and Ránki, and Braudel and Brenner all relate to one another, while those of Anderson and Szűcs form a separate group.

The First Periphery of the World Capitalist System: Wallerstein

Immanuel Wallerstein's theory, although not meeting the criteria of good historical writing, was not only a novelty among sociological theories in the 1970s, but also revived the debate around the origins of capitalism. His three-volume history of modern world-systems and his numerous publications had "explicit political aspirations."[42] In the social sciences this was, in Wallerstein's view, inevitable. He believed that the social sciences were a cultural and political battleground between the supporters of capitalism and its whistleblowers, and he saw himself in the latter camp. The value of Wallerstein's work, therefore, predominantly lay in its theoretical and ideological contribution to ways of thinking about the development of capitalism. It illustrated, rather than verified, the model of capitalism he had adopted from the outset. Wallerstein believed it necessary to take a step toward history because he regarded capitalism as a phenomenon with specific geographical and historical roots whose expansion had been part of the process of historical change.

Beginning in the late Middle Ages when it started developing in Europe, the core of capitalism shifted in the sixteenth century from Italian cities to Amsterdam, and then in the eighteenth century to imperial Britain. In the first half of the twentieth century this central role was played by the United States, which today forms, along with

[42] Ragin and Chirot, "The World System," 279.

Japan, "the Pacific core." The system gradually incorporated new territories within its logic, usually as peripheral zones. These included Eastern Europe and the Latin American colonies in the sixteenth century, followed by successive European colonies, as well as other territories (the Ottoman Empire, Russia, Japan) that were made dependent by purely economic means, such that by the end of the nineteenth century it had become a truly global system.

Wallerstein's theory portrayed capitalism as a system that perpetuated and deepened existing inequalities. However, as it was subject to "cyclical fluctuations consisting of phases of expansion and contraction,"[43] it gave individual countries the chance to improve their fortunes. By introducing the category of semi-peripheries, world-systems theory tried to explain the shift in the core of capitalism from northwestern continental Europe to Britain, then to the United States, and more recently—as Wallerstein believed in the 1970s—to the Japanese–American Pacific region. It was also able to interpret the different developmental paths of individual peripheries, for example, the difference between the countries of Southeast Asia (industrial policy geared toward self-sufficiency and exports at a time when the West was experiencing recession) and Latin America (the opening of borders and debt, increasing in periods of global recession), and to explain the ways in which a country could move from the periphery to the semi-periphery and finally to the core (or the reverse).

The capitalist system, if it did not incorporate new peripheries, was in Wallerstein's view a zero-sum game. From the moment it incorporated all the regions of the globe in the nineteenth century, the capitalist system became a game in which there was a very small pool of high rewards to be won. These rewards could only be captured by depriving the enemy of everything it needed to win. The system relied on the exploitation of new territories. "The crucial fact about the expansion [European expansion in the Americas] was captured by Braudel: 'the gold and silver of the New World enabled Europe to live above its means, to invest beyond its savings.'"[44] The continuation of the system, especially after 1945 when the economy became truly global, was based

[43] Kochanowicz, "Teoria systemu światowego."
[44] Wallerstein, *The Modern World System*, 128.

on a struggle to maintain or reposition the core. "If in the next thirty years China or India or Brazil were in a true sense to 'catch up' [with the most developed countries], a significant segment of the world's population elsewhere in this world-system would have to decline as a locus of capital accumulation," wrote Wallerstein in 1988.[45]

When the system arose in the sixteenth century, territories incorporated as peripheries on the basis of their vulnerability acted as sources of food and raw materials. Such territories were, and continue to be, a source of cheap labor (in the past, often slave or serf labor) serving the internal agents of the global market. This international division of labor was advantageous to the core and its agents in peripheral countries. The creation in core countries of a so-called new middle class, and the almost complete disappearance of the working class and peasantry by the end of the twentieth century, was possible at the expense of exploitation of the periphery and immigration. Changes in social structure led to widespread prosperity. Profits were transferred from the periphery to the core and the wages of local producers were kept at a (too) low level. This international division of labor had political consequences. Small political and business elites in peripheral countries, who enjoyed an incomparably better standard of living than the rest of the population, were seen by Wallerstein as allies of the world powers. They allowed their economies to be exploited at the cost of keeping the masses, with their demands for equality, in check. The governments of dependent peripheral countries were often oligarchic and authoritarian.

The main contention of Wallerstein's theory was, let us repeat, the following: the capitalism that arose in northwestern Europe in the sixteenth century developed through the colonial or quasi-colonial exploitation of successive territories to become, in the nineteenth century, a truly global system.[46] In this model, Eastern Europe was one of the two oldest peripheries of the capitalist world-system. From the outset, the region was an easily accessible area for expansion. Just as the global capitalist system, the East European periphery arose in the sixteenth

---

45 Wallerstein, "Development: Lodestar or Illusion?"

46 The development of the capitalist world system is tackled in: Wallerstein, *The Capitalist World Economy*, Wallerstein, *After Liberalism*, Hopkins and Wallerstein, *The Age of Transition*.

century. The region developed in a different but complementary way to Western Europe.

Until the nineteenth century, Northwestern Europe remained largely agricultural. However, in the international division of labor that developed from the sixteenth century onwards, merchants and entrepreneurs in the region assumed the role of coordinators of international trade and manufacturers of processed goods, while Eastern Europe began a monoculture that was focused on the export of raw materials to the West. Whereas societies in Northwestern Europe developed social structures based on legally free-wage labor, East European societies relied on the labor of peasant serfs. Western Europe experienced the development of towns and cities, crafts, and trade, while Eastern Europe witnessed the growth of folwarks,[47] which monopolized trade and deprived local crafts of their raison d'être. "The inclusion of Eastern Europe and Hispanic America into a European world-economy in the sixteenth century not only provided capital (through booty and high-profit margins) but also liberated some labor in the core areas for specialization in other tasks [i.e., other than the production of raw materials]. . . . The trend in the core was *toward* variety and specialization while the trend in the periphery was toward monoculture."[48] In Wallerstein's model, the outcome of the economic division of Europe was the creation of two different but complementary paths of social development characterized by an organic, parasitic relationship between the core and the periphery.

According to Wallerstein, "even in the Middle Ages, it was not at all clear that Eastern Europe was destined to be the periphery of a European world-economy."[49] As a result of the emergence of the embryonic world-economy, the minor structural differences that existed between Eastern and Western Europe in the late Middle Ages were raised to the rank of factors that determined their different devel-

---

[47] A *folwark* was a serfdom-based, grain-producing agricultural enterprise owned by a lord. Since it was a specifically East European form of organizing production and society, I use the original term throughout the book. I write extensively about the *folwark* in all the chapters, focusing on its economic functions in Chapter 4 and its social and political functions in Chapter 5.

[48] Walllerstein, *The World System I*, 102.

[49] Ibid., 97.

opment paths and the interdependence of East and West. Wallerstein linked these initial sixteenth-century differences with the general law that governed the creation of inequalities within the system. "Thus, if at a given moment in time, because of a series of factors at a previous time, one region has a *slight* edge over another in terms of one key factor, *and* there is a *conjuncture* of events which make this *slight* edge of central importance in terms of determining social action, then the slight edge is converted into a large disparity and the advantage holds even after the conjuncture has passed."[50] This "slight edge," which became the key driver of sustained structural differences between Eastern and Western Europe, comprised three factors: 1. the relative weakness of East European towns and cities, which developed rapidly in the late Middle Ages but did not catch up with Western Europe in the sixteenth century; 2. higher population density and thus intensive farming in the West versus lower population density, favoring extensive farming and a system of coerced cash-crop labor, in the East; 3. the late medieval Turkish and Mongol–Tatar invasions of Eastern Europe, which brought destruction, weakened central authority, and led to emigration, especially in Poland and Hungary.

In the struggle for roles within the nascent European division of labor, some regions of Europe "could specialize in the activities essential to reaping this profit. They thus had to spend less of their time, manpower, land, and other natural resources on sustaining themselves in basic necessities."[51] Instead, these basic necessities were provided by the rest of Europe. This historical conjuncture, in which demographic factors proved key, assigned to Western Europe the remunerative role of merchant and organizer, and to Eastern Europe—the thankless role of peasant and woodcutter.

The high Western demand for products from the East, the low population density and scarcity of labor, the existence of as yet undeveloped areas and, indirectly, the inability of peasants to form associations and organize protest were the causes of the "feudal backlash" in Eastern Europe. A system of coerced cash-crop labor emerged that ensured the lowering of production costs. It was thus a means by

50 Ibid., 98.
51 Ibid., 98–99.

which landowners and European merchants and agents could increase their return and remain profitable, even at very low world prices. Agricultural work, not requiring any special skills, but requiring supervision, was the kind of work that was compatible with the system of serfdom and thus also with economies based on the export of raw materials. A classic example of this type of peripheral, open economy based on raw materials and coerced cash-crop labor was, from the sixteenth century, the Polish economy.

It was then, according to Wallerstein, that the large landed estates evolved into grain-producing agricultural enterprises, capitalist in nature because they produced for the market. The dominant economic mechanism was as follows: grain produced by serfs for the benefit of landowners and at the request of foreign merchants was transported by raft along the Vistula river to Gdańsk (Danzig), and thence through the Baltic Sea to the cities at the core of the world-economy. The trading network within the country was taken over by Baltic merchants. It was they who concluded contracts with the owners of folwarks, extended credit, organized the transport of grain, and distributed imported goods: spices, silk, salt, and wine. Following Małowist, Wallerstein described a trade technique worked out in the sixteenth century by merchants—primarily from Amsterdam—and developed over the next century: "What was the method? Very simple: it involved the purchase of goods in advance of their production, that is payments in advance for supplies to be delivered in the future. This prevented sale on an open market. It allowed the merchants rather than the producers to decide the optimum moment for world resale. And since the money lent tended to be expended by the time of delivery of the goods, if not overspent, the producer was always tempted to perpetuate the arrangement."[52] The volume of exported grain had to be so large (although Wallerstein did not provide any figures) that for centuries to come it determined the monocultural, dependent character of the Polish economy. On the other hand, the Polish economy made an important contribution to meeting the subsistence needs of the population of Northwestern Europe, releasing part of that population

[52] Wallerstein, *The World System I*, 122. He was following Małowist, "A Certain Trade Technique."

from agriculture and allowing it to undertake more complex and profitable ventures. Both directly (through the grain trade) and indirectly (through the development of non-agricultural sectors of the economy) it provided capital, which after being invested contributed to economic growth. "The surplus went overall disproportionately to supply the needs of the population of the core areas. The immediate profits of the enterprise were shared, as we shall see, between groups in the core areas, international trading groups, and local supervisory personnel," in other words—however much medieval historians might find that term jarring—between the owners of folwarks as well.[53]

The knowledge that Wallerstein used to produce his work covering four centuries of the history of Europe and its expansion was borrowed from the work of other authors. He drew on the publications of the Annales school, articles by Małowist that appeared in international journals, and the historical studies of the dependency theorists.[54] From the latter he borrowed the idea of the fundamental division between the core and the periphery as well as the Marxist understanding of the link between capitalism and exploitation. However, the ambition of Wallerstein's vision was that his analysis should pertain to the entire planet. This vision was also influenced by the knowledge and style of thinking of the Annales school. Daniel Chirot, a student and later a vehement critic of Wallerstein, pointed to still other relationships between the inspiration provided by the Annales school and the success of Wallerstein's model. The Annales community "strengthened his hand in three ways. By using their journals and expertise [Wallerstein] could tap a historical school that was highly respected by professional historians of all kinds and that was not tainted by ideological excesses. Moreover, despite the fame of the *Annales* school among specialized American historians, most American social scientists had never heard of them in the early 1970s. So, with legitimacy and easy access there was also novelty."[55]

---

53 Wallerstein, *The World System I*, 100.

54 Wallerstein dedicated the first, groundbreaking volume of *The World System* to Małowist and Braudel. In addition to the above-cited article by Małowist, "A Certain Trade Technique," Wallerstein frequently referred to Małowist, "Poland, Russia and Western Trade."

55 Ragin and Chirot, "The World System of Immanuel Wallerstein," 287.

The Most Durable European Periphery: Berend & Ránki

An outstanding example of the application of Wallerstein's model to the study of Eastern Europe was the work of the Hungarian historians Iván T. Berend and György Ránki.[56] To reconstruct their model of Eastern Europe, I principally relied on two books: *The European Periphery and Industrialization, 1780–1914*, written by both authors and published in 1982 in Budapest, and *Central and Eastern Europe 1944–1993: Detour from the Periphery to the Periphery*, written by Berend after he had moved to the United States and published in 1996. The terminology and theoretical perspective adopted in the authors' analysis paid homage to Wallerstein's method. As in the latter's model, the "core" and the "periphery" were essentially seen as historical categories with constantly changing points of reference. Certain peripheries would "catch up" and parts of the core would simultaneously decline, thus losing their "core" character.[57] The "core" of the capitalist world-system in the nineteenth century was Northwestern Europe, while in the second half of the twentieth century it was the United States and its European allies.

The region that in their 1982 book the authors referred to as "Eastern Europe," and in 1996 as "Central and Eastern Europe," was seen as one of the European peripheries. "Central and Eastern Europe" meant the areas that remained within the borders of the communist bloc in 1945, although sometimes Greece was also included. Although Berend placed the reasons for the region's backwardness in a wider context than the capitalist expansion of the West, the region's peripheral status within the capitalist world-system nevertheless remained the basis of his explanation. This is how he summarized the history of the

[56] Nowadays, Berend continues his studies on Eastern Europe in the United States. Berend was born, studied, taught, and published for several decades in Budapest. The posts he held in Hungary testify to his status in that country: he was Rector of the University of Economics in Budapest, President of the Hungarian Academy of Sciences, and Head of the George Soros Foundation. Since 1990, Berend has taught nineteenth- and twentieth-century Central and East European history at the University of California, Los Angeles.

[57] Berend and Ránki, *The European Periphery*, 9.

region: "Central and Eastern Europe found itself on the food delivering periphery of the Western core of a rising world-system. Declining to an earlier stage of serfdom, the region did not experience the rise of absolutist states, homogenizing different ethnic, linguistic, and religious groups and forming nations and nation-states out of multi-ethnic societies; instead, this 'unfinished part of Europe' . . . lost its independence, and all the countries of the region were absorbed by the Ottoman, Habsburg, and Russian multinational empires between the fifteenth and eighteenth centuries."[58]

In the late eighteenth and early nineteenth centuries, the region was still only one of many peripheries. "The ring of countries surrounding the core—Scandinavia, the countries of the Iberian Peninsula, the Italian states, the Balkans, the eastern region of the Habsburg Monarchy, and the Russian Empire—were all relatively backward, with no spontaneous domestic forces adequate for a transformation."[59] Attempts in the nineteenth and twentieth centuries to imitate the West and overcome peripheral status through economic means and state policies proved moderately successful at best. In contrast to Wallerstein, Berend and Ránki emphasized the role of the state in modernizing the periphery in the nineteenth century. They saw the creation and strengthening of the nation-state not as an ideology that served the bourgeoisie and made it difficult to control international capital, but as a way of mobilizing the masses in the interests of an autonomous state apparatus that was not necessarily connected with a particular social class. In Eastern Europe it was certainly not the bourgeoisie—"it was a peculiarity of the situation that it was precisely the ruling elite of the *ancien régime*, the great landowners, who had a stake in the answer that would be given to the economic challenge"[60] presented by Western Europe. Berend and Ránki also tried to establish why it was particularly at the end of the eighteenth century—and not sooner or later—that most countries of the periphery attempted to respond to the rise of the West through modernization. They found the answer in the political as well as in the economic sphere. "It was these parallel currents of prosaic economic interest and power politics on the one hand, and the

[58] Berend, *Central and Eastern Europe*, x-xi.
[59] Berend and Ránki, *The European Periphery*, 8.
[60] Ibid., 25.

exalted, abstract ideals of assuring the nation's future on the other, that determined the age in which the countries of the periphery answered the challenge of the West."[61]

Only certain countries, mainly Scandinavian ones, underwent successful modernization. Berend and Ránki avoided economic generalizations of the kind made by Wallerstein. They attributed Scandinavia's success to its geopolitical position, social structure, and the attitude of its elites—primarily the state, which promoted mass education.

> While at the beginning of the 'long nineteenth century,' these countries appeared as a unit in virtue of their backwardness and traditional economic structure, . . . by the end of the period, the similarities among them had largely ceased to exist. The Scandinavian countries had caught up, had become parts of the developed European industrial core; other countries, Italy and Hungary, but in part Russia, too, had started on the road to thoroughgoing economic change . . . Still other countries of Southern and South-Eastern Europe had hardly started on the road to change, or were bogged down at the very start.[62]

As a result, in the first half of the twentieth century, following the emergence of new nation-states in Eastern Europe, the region was still home to "backward economies, polarized societies, and authoritarian regimes."[63]

Berend regarded the introduction of state socialism in those countries as a result of the Yalta Agreement as another attempt to overcome backwardness. "The history of Central and Eastern European socialism is only a part of a centuries-long process. Its origin and characteristics are not understandable without the *longue durée* of the region's history. The communist experiment was part of a twentieth-century rebellion of the unsuccessful peripheries, which were humiliated by economic backwardness and the increasing gap which separated them from the advanced Western core."[64] Berend was willing to

---

[61] Ibid., 27.
[62] Ibid., 159–60.
[63] Berend, *Central and Eastern Europe*, xiv.
[64] Ibid., x.

accept the idea of (even enforced) socialist industrialization and modernization. He attributed its geopolitical failure to changes in the global economy, the ideologically determined inability of the Soviet model of modernization to react to those changes, and the system's resulting lack of legitimacy. The adopted plan and method of industrialization, the model of import substitution on which it was based, and the structural inability of the system to respond to changing economic circumstances meant that this latest attempt to overcome backwardness was doomed to fail.[65]

In the dispute over the nature of development in backward regions, Berend and Ránki adopted a position similar to that of most of my protagonists. Although the impetus for development came from a desire to catch up with the West, and the simplest way to achieve this was through imitation, industrialization in the periphery proceeded differently than in the core. The description of the process was very similar to that proposed by Kula.[66] In Eastern and Southern Europe, modern "reform generally came without a revolution, being executed from above by the ruling classes; accordingly, feudal relations were done away with only partially, the half-hearted solutions devised being fraught with contradictions. The failure to solve the land question and the problems of the peasantry, and the slowness of the development of bourgeois democratic institutions were other features common to all those societies."[67]

When it came to assessing the opportunities for development in the periphery, Berend and Ránki's attitude was closer to that of Fernando Cardoso and other theorists of "dependent development" than it was to classical world-systems and dependency theory.[68] The capitalist world-economy, though it exacerbated differences between countries, nevertheless provided growth opportunities to those dependent regions that were able to take advantage of them. "We find that

---

[65] Ibid., 153.

[66] See subchapter "A Model of Hybrid Development. Kula" in Chapter 4 of this book.

[67] Berend and Ránki, *The European Periphery*, 39.

[68] I discuss the dependency theory in the subchapter "Theories of Development in Non-Western Societies and Changes in the Post-War World" in Chapter 4 of this book.

although the process of integration into the world-economy was, by its very nature, an unequal one whenever unequal partners met, it did not preclude the possibility of—unequal—development. The integration of a more backward country did not necessarily and in all cases led to its 'peripherization'; nor, however, was it necessarily an opportunity for catching up."[69]

The European Periphery: The Second Serfdom and the Penetration of Capitalism: Braudel

Fernand Braudel's model was no less original than Wallerstein's. It also went beyond traditional thinking about capitalism. According to Braudel, any economic activity—agriculture, commerce, crafts, mining, manufacturing—could be an area of operation for capitalism. What characterized capitalist economic activity was the ability to respond to changing market conditions, to invest or disinvest, and to transfer capital from one sector to another in order to control supply. Braudel's school, like Kula's, was fascinated with capitalism, as was the modernization approach. However, it shared with world-systems theory the belief that, despite a tendency toward cultural homogenization, capitalist globalization exacerbated rather than blurred economic differences.[70]

Mischievous critics attributed the enormous popularity of Braudel's vision to his near marketing-style effort to meet the needs of a new paradigm. It was under the influence of Braudel's comparative studies, among others, that an approach took shape: "stimulated . . . by the contention that in Europe a 'miracle' of sorts had taken place (i.e., an accidental concurrence of many circumstances), whereas in other, often more advanced civilizations of an older pedigree (India, China, Islamic countries) there had been no breakthrough to modernity, capitalism, and a European-style economy. Through comparison, this approach searched for causes in various spheres—from ecology and geography, through political structures, to the role of religion."[71]

[69] Berend and Ránki, *The European Periphery*, 160.
[70] See Chapter 4.
[71] Kochanowicz, "Twórca i dzieło," 13.

Braudel searched for the origins of European industrial capitalism in the distant past and in the *longue durée*. Unlike Marxists, liberals, or Weberians, he did not treat capitalism as a phenomenon typical of modernity (as did liberals) or the post-feudal period (as did traditional Marxists) or of Protestant societies with their characteristic rationalization of activity (as did Weber). As in the liberals' interpretation, "capitalist tendencies" for Braudel were almost natural in character and not associated with any particular civilization, religion, or mentality. Such tendencies revealed themselves in all societies able to rise above the threshold of the natural economy, that is, an economy where production is oriented toward satisfying individuals' most basic needs. Wherever there was exchange and trade, there was an opportunity to stimulate the human tendency to generate profit, which was the foundation of capitalism. This approach situated Braudel closer to Marxist-materialists and further from Weberian-idealists in the debate over whether economy or culture, interests or ideas, had social primacy.

In Braudel's three-level interpretive model, capitalism occupied the top level. "The base, consisting of 'material life'—many sided, self-sufficient, and routine-bound; at the next level, 'economic life,' more clearly defined and as described here, tending to merge with the competitive market economy; and lastly, at the third level, the activities of capitalism."[72] On the first level, human activity consisted in simple interaction with nature in order to satisfy basic needs: ways of obtaining food, clothing, and shelter, ways of obtaining energy, and so on. Above this level, which Braudel termed "structures of everyday life," there was a second level: the market. Following classical economics, Braudel defined the market as a sphere where the free exchange of goods took place. In historical terms, the market took the form of itinerant trade, fairs, bazaars, and finally shops. It was usually local in nature, subject to competition, and prices were established through the free play of supply and demand. At the top of the structure was the elite level of capitalism: economic activity (commercial or productive) with "its unlimited flexibility, its capacity for change and *adaptation*," which was greater than on the other two levels.[73]

[72] Braudel, *Civilization and Capitalism* vol. 2, 455.

[73] Ibid., 433.

The origins of capitalism, according to Braudel, were to be sought in the activities of international merchants. "The indisputable superiority of *Fernandel*, long-distance trading, lay in the *concentrations* it made possible, which meant it was an unrivalled machine for the rapid reproduction and increase of capital."[74] The concentration and rapid growth of capital were the qualities that distinguished capitalism from the lower levels of the economic pyramid, where capital was fragmented, slowly reproduced, and its turnover was aimed at maintaining the status quo rather than stimulating rapid accumulation. Capitalism had the ability to surpass the cyclical, subsistence rhythms of everyday life and slow changes in turnover. It was able to subordinate markets and break free from their rules. The early capitalists, the elite of international commerce, "wanted to evade the free market, to eliminate competition by holding a virtual or actual monopoly, and to keep supply and demand so effectively separated that the terms of trade were entirely dictated by the middleman, who alone knew the state of the market at either end of the long chain."[75] Being a capitalist required special talent, accounting knowledge, creditworthiness, and the imagination to choose the right line of business or trade route because, as a rule, only certain undertakings (although it was not known which exactly) had a chance of going beyond the parameters of the traditional market economy. A successful merchant had to have the courage to invest and to take risks. "The minimum qualifications for entry to these extremely profitable circuits were: to have sufficient capital and local sources of credit, to be well-informed and well-connected, and to have associates at strategic points along the trade routes, who were a party to one's secrets." [76]

Thus, before the eighteenth century, capitalism was primarily a domain of exchange, distribution, and rarely or only to a minor extent, of production. "The capitalism [of Braudel] was above all the work of merchants and the work of towns and cities, where it developed from the thirteenth century onwards. He therefore mainly searched for the answer [to the question about the spread of capitalism precisely in Europe] in the freedom of the European towns and cities and in their

[74] Ibid., 408.
[75] Ibid., 416.
[76] Ibid.

opportunities for contact with other worlds. The rise of Venice, and later of other centers of the European economy, consisted in the fact that "they suddenly found themselves in an extremely favorable position on the great colonial trade routes, where it was possible to make vast profits quickly and reinvest them, and in the fact that Venetian merchants were able to take advantage of these opportunities."[77] If capitalism entered the sphere of production at that time, it did so casually, temporarily, and not transformatively; it merely subordinated production to its own system—the rapid circulation of goods and capital. Examples of merchant capitalism, "[which] was intended to dominate though not to transform craft production,"[78] were the merchant investments in European mining in the sixteenth century and in American mining a century later as well as the workshop system (*verlagssystem*) that gained popularity across Western Europe from the fifteenth century onwards.[79]

The difference between Braudel and Wallerstein was precisely their understanding of capitalism and the criteria they employed to determine what was capitalist and what was not. For Wallerstein, folwarks and *economiedas* were the institutions of capitalist agriculture, while landowners, just as Gdańsk and Amsterdam merchants or Portuguese agents, were capitalists. In Braudel's model, which allowed for the coexistence of different economic circuits and which did not seek the boundaries of socioeconomic stages of development, capitalism meant only the top level of trade and the only capitalists were international merchants. Sixteenth-century merchants were able to find economic niches to which local markets could not cater. Taking what Braudel termed capitalism with them, the great merchants abandoned regions and sectors of the economy when these ceased to produce spectacular profits. They found new trade routes and new areas of investment, because "the removal of investment is as characteristic of capital as investment: one kind of economic climate sees money put in, another sees it being taken out,"[80] and also because capitalism "was both *sufficiently informed* and *materially able* to choose the sphere of its

[77] Kochanowicz, "Twórca i dzieło," 13.
[78] Braudel, *Civilization and Capitalism*, vol. 2, 321.
[79] Ibid., 316–21.
[80] Ibid., 323.

action. . . . And more than the actual choices made—which might vary from century to century with changing circumstances—the very fact that it had the means to create its own strategy or to alter that strategy if necessary, defines capitalism as a superior force."[81]

In Braudel's model, the largest unit of economic division was something that he referred to as a "world-economy." It was self-sufficient, a world in itself, and isolated from the rest of the globe. "It only concerns a fragment of the world, an economically autonomous section of the planet able to provide for most of its own needs, a section to which its internal links and exchanges give a certain organic unity."[82] A "world-economy" was the start and end point of all economic circuits, which were limited by the transport possibilities particular to it. A "world-economy" was a product of economics and geography. Its borders did not coincide with the borders of political units or of civilizations defined according to cultural criteria.

The three-way division of economic activity in Braudel's model corresponded to a three-way division of space. At its center was a dominant city that determined the direction and rhythm of trade and imposed its conditions on the rest of its "world-economy." The center was surrounded by economic zones, among which Braudel distinguished intermediate zones, that is, "a fairly developed middle zone" (equivalent to Wallerstein's semi-periphery) and a "huge periphery, with its scattered population, [which represented] backwardness, archaism, and exploitation by others."[83] Outside the center of the "world-economy" life proceeded more slowly.

Within the division of labor in the European "world-economy" from the sixteenth to the eighteenth centuries, the small center occupied the best and most profitable position: "News, merchandise, capital, credit, people, instructions, correspondence all flow into and out of the city. Its powerful merchants lay down the law, sometimes becoming extraordinarily wealthy."[84] These same merchants or their emissaries organized production in "secondary zones" or used them as intermediate points in international trade. Braudel stressed that during

---

[81] Ibid, 400.
[82] Braudel, *Civilization and Capitalism*, vol. 3, 22.
[83] Ibid., 39.
[84] Ibid., 27.

this period, the penetration of capitalism—in terms of the number of actors involved, the flow of goods, and their impact on the life of the "world-economy"—was much lower than Wallerstein believed.[85] In the periphery, "the predominant social status is often serfdom or even slavery,"[86] with a small local elite taking care to ensure that economic life revolved around fulfilling orders from the center.

For Braudel, as for Wallerstein, the peripheries of the early modern European "world-economy" included East/Central Europe (Braudel used these terms interchangeably), southern Italy, and colonized Latin America. Of greatest interest to me is the first of these peripheries, which comprised Poland, Bohemia, and Hungary. "An economic conjuncture . . . was pushing East Europe back, in the early sixteenth century, toward a *colonial* destiny as a producer of raw materials, a development of which the second serfdom was only the most visible sign."[87] In contrast to Wallerstein, Braudel did not hold capitalism responsible for the backwardness of Central Europe. He tried to find a balance between internal and external causes. "From the outside there was the massive demand of West Europe which needed food and raw materials. . . . As for internal reasons, in the constant tug-of-war between state, cities and nobles, the latter were almost always the dominant group (except in Russia). The decline of cities and the urban markets and the weakness of the state corresponded to the takeover of the labor force (and also of the best land) which formed the drive behind the success of the feudal lords."[88] In Europe, the Kingdom of Naples and Sicily exhibited similar features.[89]

Unlike Russia and the Balkans, areas of Eastern Europe continuously remained within the European "world-economy" from the sixteenth century onward. In the Balkans, plunged into wars in the fourteenth and fifteenth centuries and then incorporated into the Ottoman Empire, the trade routes organized by Genoese and Venetian merchants were disrupted. Russia, in turn, remained outside the European system of dependencies until the eighteenth century, as in Wallerstein's

85 Kochanowicz, "Twórca i dzieło," 12.
86 Braudel, *Civilization and Capitalism*, vol. 3, 40.
87 Ibid., vol. 2, 267.
88 Ibid., 269.
89 Ibid., 265.

model. "When all is said and done however, there was no comparison between the Russian situation and the complete dependence of, say, Poland. When the European economy launched its assault on Russia, the latter had already embarked on a course of action which protected her domestic market and the development of her own artisan production, her own manufacturing enterprises created in the seventeenth century."[90] Although it had similar social structures, Russia differed from the East European periphery on account of its strong political structure. "But Russia did not follow the usual pattern. In Poland, Hungary, and Bohemia, the 'second serfdom' was established to the advantage of the nobles and magnates who stood between the peasants and the market and who controlled supplies to the towns, that is when the latter were not purely and simply their personal property. In Russia the leading role was taken by the state."[91]

In his dialogue with Wallerstein and Kula, Braudel tried to settle the status of the manorial economy not just in relation to the center of the "world-economy" but also in relation to the three levels of economic activity. In answer to the question whether the folwark was a capitalist enterprise, Braudel agreed with Kula that it was not. Folwarks and their owners were market players, participants in mid-level economic activity. The economic calculations of peasants were almost exclusively rooted in the "structures of everyday life" and rarely encroached on the market; if they did, they did so illegally. "Witold Kula's admirable study, which analyzes step by step what the 'economic calculations' of the serf-peasants and their masters might have been in Poland between the sixteenth and the eighteenth centuries," wrote Braudel of *Economic Theory*, "spells out why the landlords were not 'real' capitalists and could not be before the nineteenth century."[92]

Folwarks were nevertheless part of the circuit created and controlled by players at the highest level, which in the sixteenth century meant Amsterdam merchants. "The great landowner was not a capitalist, but he was a tool and a collaborator in the service of capitalism in Amsterdam and elsewhere . . . But it was the Polish noble who had the power—as he amply demonstrated—to set all the peasants and a good

90 Braudel, *Civilization and Capitalism*, vol. 3, 465.
91 Ibid, 446.
92 Braudel, *Civilization and Capitalism*, vol. 2, 267.

number of the towns to work for him, to dominate agriculture and even manufacture, virtually the whole of production in other words. When he mobilized all this power in the service of foreign capitalism, he was himself becoming an active participant in the system."[93] The chapters entitled "Capitalism and the 'Second Serfdom'" and "Capitalism and the American Plantations" provided "a few significant examples" of "how far capitalism was able to penetrate systems structurally very foreign to it, either by head-on assault, or by dominating production from a distance merely by controlling it at the bottleneck of distribution."[94] Like Wallerstein, or simply because he agreed with Wallerstein's comparison and interpretation, Braudel treated Eastern Europe and areas of Hispanic America in the sixteenth to nineteenth centuries as examples of agricultural economies where the rules of capitalism operated at a certain level. This view also prompted Kula to change his mind about whether the folwark was a capitalist enterprise or not.

Braudel's image of the "world-economy" was consistent with Wallerstein's model and was undoubtedly influenced by the fact that the two scholars cooperated closely. However, Braudel's image was more complicated, or perhaps simply more detailed, on account of his different research aims and interests. These interests were more in accordance with the academic traditions of historical research, and in *Civilization and Capitalism* he wanted to present an interpretation of economic life between the fifteenth and eighteenth centuries with all its permanent and changing elements.

Unlike Wallerstein, who was mainly interested in the expansion of capitalism and therefore sought to identify and emphasize social change, Braudel drew attention to its slowness and mystery. The author of the famous term, the *longue durée*, was more inclined to stress the persistence of social structures, and he searched for the most general rules to describe how these came about. Commenting on his many years of research on the Mediterranean economy from the sixteenth to eighteenth centuries, he wrote: "The basic distances, routes, delays, production, merchandise and stopping-places—everything or almost

[93] Ibid., 271–72.
[94] Ibid., 265.

everything had remained the same."[95] He offered a similar diagnosis when investigating the reasons for the success of a particular city or nation-state and the failure of other regions: structures were permanent in line with the principle, which Braudel took entirely seriously, that "a country is poor because it is poor, or to put it more clearly because it is poor to start with," while another "country develops because it is already developing, because it is caught up in a movement already under way which helps it."[96] According to Braudel, success, failure, and the distribution of power were somewhat mysterious, and the secret of success took a long time to reveal itself. "Success depends on seizing the opportunities of a given period, on doing so time and time again, and piling advantage on advantage," while "the inequality of the world is the result of structural realities at once slow to take shape and slow to take away."[97]

An Area of Normal Non-Development: Brenner

The view that backwardness was a "normal" state, and that development resulted from taking advantage of the small opportunity afforded by historical circumstance, was one that Brenner shared with Berend and Ránki. However, Brenner presented this view in a more radical form. Assuming, in contrast to evolutionism, that "historically speaking, non-development is the rule rather than the exception," he arrived at the conclusion that "if anything needs special explanation, it is the unprecedented breakthrough to sustained economic growth which took place in certain parts of Western Europe during the early modern period."[98] Brenner criticized both dependency theory and world-systems theory, describing their premises as "Neo-Smithian Marxism." He rejected the assertion that international trade played a key role and instead argued that classical Marxist studies of class relations within a given national society were fundamental to understanding development. His publications from the mid-1970s inten-

---

[95] Braudel, *Civilization and Capitalism*, vol. 3, 36.
[96] Ibid., 50.
[97] Ibid.
[98] Brenner, "Economic Backwardness," 15.

sified the historical debate about the origins of European capitalism and modernity, but they were also a reaction to the ongoing discussion in social science about the development opportunities of backward regions.[99] Brenner presented his most comprehensive picture of Eastern Europe in his article "Economic Backwardness in Eastern Europe in Light of Developments in the West," published in the 1980s, which restated his explanation of the birth of capitalism in England. His interpretation of late medieval and early modern European history divided the continent into four zones—not two or three, as was usually the case—according to the dominant class relations within them. The first region was England, where capitalism was actually born and where it spontaneously grew out of local structures; the second, Western Europe, was limited to France and western Germany, that is, regions with the oldest seigniorial structures; the third was northeastern Europe, comprising the sparsely populated eastern Germany and Poland; and the fourth was southeastern Europe, which fell under Ottoman rule at the end of the Middle Ages. Brenner's analysis did not include Russia, Scandinavia or southwestern Europe.

Each of these regions developed in their own particular way for a variety of reasons: different demographics, that is, primarily the size of the workforce relative to the amount of available land for cultivation; different relations between lord and peasant, and between lord and peasant vis-à-vis the state; different relations within the feudal estates; and distinct systems of land ownership. The seventeenth century, which marks the boundary of Brenner's analysis, witnessed the formation of various social, economic, and political structures that contributed to the further development of those regions. Western Europe evolved toward an economy based on small family farms that formally and *de facto* belonged to the peasants. The income peasants received from their production was used to satisfy their own needs, to buy goods in the prospering cities, and to pay taxes to a centralized absolutist state. The state, in turn, maintained the bureaucracy and the military. In Eastern Europe the nobility arose as the strongest social group and the economy was based on folwarks, which relied on the unpaid

[99] Brenner, "The Agrarian Roots," Brenner, "The Origins of Capitalist Development."

labor of peasant serfs. The owners of folwarks kept all the income generated from them and paid only a small portion of it in state taxes. The internal market disappeared and productivity declined. "The result [of these processes] was economic regression and social dislocation, the Northeastern European version of the 'general crisis of the seventeenth century'."[100] In southeastern Europe, which was incorporated into the Ottoman Empire, the economy, as in Western Europe, was based on small family farms that *de facto* belonged to the peasants but without any legal guarantees. Again, as in the West, these farms engaged in production to satisfy their own needs, pay taxes to the state and, to a lesser extent, sell to the market. In contrast to Western Europe, posts in the state administration were neither hereditary nor permanent, and the income of local representatives of central government came from the plunder of administered or conquered territories. When the territorial expansion of the Ottoman Empire ended in the seventeenth century, the ruling elites were deprived of their primary source of income and peasant taxes rose as a result. This, in turn, ruined the economic system, which had relied on the peasantry. It was only in England, and to a lesser extent in the Netherlands, that sociopolitical structures created conditions that were conducive to economic growth. Those countries' economies were based on tenant farms that belonged to a small group of lords. The rural social structure, which comprised aristocrats, tenants, and hired laborers, favored competition, specialization, efficiency, and production for the market. As a result, "only England and the Netherlands experienced no 'general crisis of the seventeenth century.' Instead, cheap agricultural products put a long-term downward pressure on wages, allowed for the rise of discretionary consumption, made possible the transfer of an increasing proportion of the population out of agriculture and into industry, and facilitated the emergence of a growing home market for industrial goods."[101]

For Wallerstein and Braudel, Eastern Europe's backwardness was a by-product of the development of capitalism in the Western core, whereas for Brenner this played a minor role. Conceptually, however, Brenner's analysis of social structures in the East was marginal to his

---

[100] Brenner, *Economic Backwardness*, 45.
[101] Ibid., 50.

attempt to explain the birth of capitalist social relations in England. It was also a protest against the bilateral division of Europe into East and West, in which the former was considered a victim of the latter—an interpretation that dominated Marxism in the 1970s. By questioning the main assumptions of the models proposed by 1970s Marxists, that is, that development was the norm and that backwardness or "non-development" was a deviation, Brenner's works were indirectly an attempt to "demystify" the image of Eastern Europe as a particularly backward region.

A Mixture of Primitivism and Imitation of the West: Anderson

The historian of ideas and political essayist Perry Anderson proposed very different criteria for the division of Europe. His model, like that of Jenő Szűcs, sought to explain the continent's inequalities in terms of the institutions and political traditions of ancient Rome and the Middle Ages. Unlike Szűcs, but similarly to Wallerstein and Brenner, Anderson identified himself as a Marxist and regarded class relations to be the basis of the political system.

In *Passages from Antiquity to Feudalism* and *Lineages of the Absolutist State*, both published in the 1970s, Anderson offered an interpretation of the history of European societies.[102] The division of Europe, whether two-part or four-part, had deeper roots than the previously discussed models suggested. Anderson traced these roots to two key moments in (West European) history: transition from antiquity to the Middle Ages, and the early modern period. He claimed that only the Romano-Germanic heritage could have formed the social, political, and economic basis of feudalism, then capitalism, and then strong, independent cities and a modern political system based on formal freedoms and the rule of law. Although this was a history of institutions and political ideas, Anderson inferred their existence from socioeconomic structures. *Lineages of the Absolutist State* was fundamental to the debate over the northern part of Eastern Europe because the political systems of early modern Prussia, Austria, and Russia represented "Eastern absolutism."

[102] Anderson, *Passages*, Anderson, *Lineages*.

Its absence in Poland supposedly confirmed the idea that without absolutism no European country was able to survive at that time. The Ottoman Empire—the southern part of Eastern Europe—was excluded from Anderson's analysis. He saw it as oppressive, and distinguished its Asian despotism from European absolutism. The latter, although like despotism associated with the abuse of central power, grew out of feudalism with its characteristic noble estate that enjoyed a hereditary right to land. Under Ottoman and Asian despotism, by contrast, the sultan was the sole landowner and a person's social position depended entirely on his whim. Anderson stressed that the seigniorial relations typical of Romano-Germanic feudalism "proper" did not develop in southeastern Europe. In *Passages from Antiquity to Feudalism*, in turn, he omitted northern areas of Europe that had not been part of Roman civilization. The analysis did, however, cover southeastern Europe, where, as in other parts of the Roman Empire between the end of antiquity and the feudal era, a system of slave labor was in force.

In both books, the East of Europe, whether its southern or northern part, represented that which it lacked to become part of Western civilization. Therefore, in the words of one historian of historical sociology, Dennis Smith, "the East/West contrast is central to the arguments of both *Passages* and *Lineages*. It provides a link between them."[103] According to Anderson, the two distinct developmental paths of East and West were already apparent when the Germanic barbarians destroyed and then appropriated the heritage of ancient Rome. He saw the "Romano-Germanic complex" as key to West European feudalism, absolutism, colonialism, and capitalism, and associated its absence in the East with even the communist revolution in Russia and the Cold War division of Europe. In the final sentence of *Lineages*, which I believe may be regarded as a kind of summary, Anderson wrote (in 1974) that "the consequences of the division of the continent . . . are still with us."[104] Social processes, resulting from a lower level of development already in antiquity, combined with later attempts to "catch up" with the post-Romano-Germanic countries of Europe, led in the twentieth century to Soviet and communist modernization.

---

[103] Smith, *The Rise of Historical Sociology*, 91.
[104] Anderson, *Lineages*, 431.

According to another interpretation—put forward by Mary Fulbrook and Theda Skocpol—the division between East and West did not fully capture Anderson's vision of Europe.[105] Its significance could only be appreciated in terms of the original division into the old (Mediterranean, Roman) and new (northern, barbarian) Europe. As a result, Europe was divided into four regions: (1) Old southeastern Europe, where a slave system existed in antiquity but where feudalism did not develop in the Middle Ages, the region being conquered by the Ottomans. (2) Old, "pure and universal" (a phrase used by the authors to debunk the image of the region) Western Europe, where feudalism was "the result of the fusion of elements resulting from the decomposition of the two previous production systems: the slave system of classical antiquity and the system of primitive tribal community of the peoples of the periphery. The slow Romano-Germanic synthesis during the Dark Ages eventually produced the new civilization of European feudalism."[106] (3) "New" northeastern Europe, where feudalism "expanded slowly and unevenly,"[107] was the result of imitation of the West, and "started chronologically later, without the benefits of the heritage of antiquity, and in more difficult topographic and demographic conditions."[108] (4) New Northwestern Europe (Scotland, Ireland, and Scandinavia), where the heritage of antiquity was absent, but which came to be dominated by Western structures. On this interpretation, the purpose of Anderson's argument was revealed with even greater force. His definition of feudalism and his model of the rise of the West were constructed in such a way as to explain the "naturalness" of the Cold War division of Europe into a developed and democratic West and a backward and authoritarian East. "For if Scandinavia ultimately produced a Western variant of feudalism *without* the benefits of the urban-imperial heritage of antiquity, the Balkans failed to develop a stable Eastern variant of feudalism *despite* the long metropolitan presence of the successor state to Rome in the region," that is, Byzantium.[109]

---

[105] Fulbrook and Skocpol, "Destined Pathways."
[106] Anderson, *Lineages*, 417.
[107] Ibid., 411.
[108] Ibid., 431.
[109] Quoted in: Fulbrook and Skocpol, "Destined Pathways," 188–89.

In terms of my own argument regarding Polish socioeconomic historiography, Anderson's *Lineages of the Absolutist State* is the more important of the two books mentioned here. It covered the history of the late Middle Ages and early modern era, hence the periods in which my protagonists specialized. Like them, Anderson devoted a lot of space and attention to Poland and its northeastern neighbors, and like some of them he excluded the lands of the Ottoman Empire from Europe. He did so because the Ottoman Empire was not subject to the seigniorial relations and estate-based divisions characteristic of classical feudalism. The main criterion Anderson used to classify European absolutism into its Western and Eastern forms was the existence or absence of serfdom, a phenomenon that has been analyzed in depth in Polish historiography.

As Anderson wrote in the introduction to his "Marxist study of absolutism," "the vertical division of the continent between West and East is here taken throughout as a central organizing principle of the materials discussed," since "the history of Eastern Europe is not merely a poorer copy of that of Western Europe, which can simply be added side by side to it . . . the development of the more 'backward' regions of the continent casts an unwanted light on that of the more 'advanced' regions, and often throws into relief novel problems within it, concealed by the limits of a purely Western introspection."[110] Unlike the other authors, and contrary to the trend of "history from below" that was fashionable in the 1970s, Anderson chose political history to reveal the difference between Eastern and Western absolutism. For in the premodern era, "secular struggle between classes is ultimately resolved at the political—not at the economic or cultural—level of society."[111] Anderson's analysis covered the countries of the West: England, Spain, France, and Sweden, the countries of the East: Poland, Austria, Russia and Prussia, and compared them to the territories of the Ottoman Empire ("The House of Islam") and Japan. Absolutism developed in all the European countries aside from Poland. Indeed, the Polish state collapsed precisely because it was unable to generate absolutist structures—the principal form of power in early modern

110 Anderson, *Lineages*, 9.
111 Ibid., 11.

Europe. The Eastern version of absolutism appeared later on, for other reasons (on a different social "base"), and assumed forms that were not the same as those in the West.

Anderson's image of the East had much in common with the stereotype of the region present in popular Western discourse in the eighteenth and nineteenth centuries. Describing the structures of East European feudalism, Anderson was not afraid to use such evolutionist terms as "more primitive," "backward," and "less developed." He cited Western visitors' impressions of the region's geography: "vast, sparsely populated tracts of land" and "a frontier character,"[112] and ironically referred to eighteenth-century Prussia as "this cabbage paradise."[113] Unlike in the West, social relations under East European absolutism were, in Anderson's view, devoid of freedom and honor. The monarch had greater power over the aristocracy, which was transformed into an obedient service nobility. The latter was tied to the state through the investiture of land, in return for which it provided faithful service. In contrast to the Western system of vassalage, the relationship between aristocrat and monarch was despotic due to the absence of reciprocity.[114] The peasant, in turn, was subject to the total and absolute power of his master.[115]

In Anderson's model, the process of historical development in Eastern Europe consisted of a series of attempts to imitate the more mature West. These attempts, made under different conditions and for different reasons, led to the creation of hybrid political structures, which were incomplete because they hardly resembled structures rooted in the "Romano-Germanic heritage" and because they stood in contradiction to the base. "The component elements of this feudalism were strangely re-shuffled into listing and asynchronous combinations, none of which ever quite possessed the completion or unity of the original synthesis. Thus the manorial system functioned both under nobiliary anarchy and centralized absolutism; dispersed sovereignty existed but in epochs of non-conditional tenure; conditional tenures appeared, but with non-reciprocal service bonds; feudal hierarchy was

112 Ibid., 223.
113 Ibid., 265.
114 Ibid., 220.
115 Ibid., 264.

eventually codified in the framework of state bureaucracy." The social system was, "in Western terms, a bizarre mixture of modern and medieval structures, [a] consequence of the peculiar 'squashed' temporality of the East."[116] Anderson noted that in various countries, absolutism was, among others, a reaction of monarchical elites to the international system emerging in Europe. In the monarchies of the East, it was the primary reason for the establishment of absolutism. Eastern absolutism, according to Anderson, gave the monarch even more independence from the aristocracy, but it also gave greater privileges to landowners vis-à-vis the peasantry.

Anderson's central argument sounds like a judgement of Eastern Europe, a region constantly trying to catch up with the West: Western absolutism was a system of power that aimed to maintain the privileges of the nobility, despite the abolition of serfdom and despite the freedom of the cities; in the East, by contrast, it emerged at the cost of extending the privileges of the nobility, intensifying serfdom, and restricting the freedom of the cities. The efforts of East European countries to imitate the West were doomed to fail because those countries lacked the appropriate heritage. From the moment they came into contact with Western civilization, without a social base to support successive social institutions imposed from the top-down (the adoption of Christianity, the introduction of feudal institutions, the Westernization attempts of Peter the Great, absolutism), East European countries formed structural hybrids.

A "Third Europe" between East and West: Szűcs

It was not just political arrangements and economic structures (as in Anderson's work), but also the social ties formed as a result of long-term processes, that became the basis upon which the Hungarian historian Jenő Szűcs designated different borders for Europe a few years later. Like Anderson and the medievalists of the Annales school, Szűcs attributed the origins of Western Europe's economic and political distinctiveness to the structures of vassalage—a specific form of (West

[116] Ibid., 227.

European) feudalism. Vassalage was to culminate in West European absolutism, with its appointed bureaucracy and guarantees of personal liberty and property rights. Szűcs's essay, "Three Historical Regions of Europe," was wide-ranging in character, referring to big concepts, intersubjective structures, and *longue durée* processes.[117] Initially published in Budapest in 1983 (as an article in English), it was one of the last great voices in the Cold War debate about the peripheral status of Eastern Europe. Szűcs commented on the work of Braudel, Wallerstein, and Anderson, and drew on the findings of Polish socioeconomic historiography. The bibliography contained works by Małowist, Kula, and Topolski, as the sole sources for the history of Poland, as well as works by Karol Górski and Karol Modzelewski, who analyzed medieval and feudal social relations.

Despite these similarities, Szűcs's essay differed in several ways from the work of both Western authors and most of "my" Polish protagonists. By participating in the Cold War debate, Szűcs went beyond its framework and became one of the first voices in the Central European discourse to herald the end of the Yalta division of Europe. His assertion was that Europe was divided into three, and not two, main parts. Although he referred to the principal subject of his analysis—Bohemia, Poland, Hungary—as "East Central Europe," it was precisely the latter's "centralness," its transience, its fluctuation between the two main blocks, between East and West, that was the main geographical and ideological message of Szűcs's book. In a similar vein to articles by Miłosz and Kundera, which I discuss in Chapter 3, Szűcs's book had an "emancipatory" purpose: it attempted to "liberate" East Central Europe from the East and presented the region as a victim of its powerful neighbors. Szűcs saw rising self-awareness as a source of liberation and urged intellectual revolt. In the introduction to the French edition of the book, Braudel described its message in the language of psychology: "Sometimes East Central Europe leans toward one neighbor, sometimes toward the other, she tends to betray one to choose another—although never voluntarily. This lack of balance affects her, . . . it makes her suffer and prevents her from being

117 Szűcs, "Three Historical Regions."

herself."[118] By establishing a separate identity and being aware of its roots, East Central Europe could bring about its desired "theoretical liberation," and this new perspective could also encourage the great Others—West and East—to look at themselves in a fresh light. Thus, because it entered the dominant discourse and was published at the right time politically, and because it took the form of an essay, Szűcs's text enjoyed popularity and recognition. It was published underground in Hungary in 1983, but four years later appeared in French with a foreword by Braudel, and in the early 1990s appeared in other Western languages. With the exception of Braudel, it is the only work so far presented here to have been translated into Polish, published by the Lublin-based Institute of East Central Europe.

Szűcs's approach to Western absolutism was very similar to Anderson's, which is why I do not describe it at length. The same was true of Russian absolutism, although its place in Szűcs's classification was unique. He identified it (and only it) with the "East European variant" of absolutism, while Austrian and Prussian absolutism were seen as intermediate variants. The fall of the Polish, Czech, and Hungarian monarchies (for Anderson, it was only the Polish monarchy) supposedly testified to the structural distinctiveness of the region, which in "early modern times produced . . . a number of variant models instead of one unified one, as if all the permutations and combinations were being experimented with."[119] Eager to maintain "anachronistic" structures, the nobility, which was the only actor in political and civic society, brought about the collapse of the state. For Szűcs, noble republicanism in Poland was an extreme example, but unlike Anderson he saw it not as an exception but merely as an extreme representation of what was typical for East Central Europe.

In a manner unique for historiography in the early 1980s, Szűcs elaborated on the question of the emergence of national communities and identities and treated Western absolutism as the first incarnation of the nation-state. He went beyond the ready-made "grand narratives" of historiography: the traditional national–patriotic narrative on the one hand, and socioeconomic historiography with its dislike of "idealistic"

[118] Braudel, preface to Szűcs, *Les trois Europes*. Translated from Polish edition: Braudel, preface to Szűcs, *Trzy Europy*, 9–10.

[119] Szűcs, *Three Historical*, 167.

categories on the other. Albeit unwittingly, and without theoretical exposition, Szűcs abandoned the paradigm that Michael Mann called the "single-factor explanation."[120] The great novelty of his book was that it offered a (nowadays popular) multifactor explanation and analyzed nationalism through the prism of social history.[121] In this respect it differed substantially from the work of Anderson and most other Marxist authors. Szűcs argued that the lack of experience of "national" absolutism in the countries of the "Third Europe" was significant for their national identity and attitude toward the state. Like his mentor, István Bibó, he treated the nation-state (a state organized according to the formula: one nation, one state) as a necessary condition of modern, democratic government.[122]

I imagine that Szűcs would agree with the view, expressed in a language slightly different to his own, that absolutism "got started" in a particular country when that country began to experience intensive economic development, and was replaced by another form of power when development stabilized. It flourished in countries that were "catching up" with the most developed and powerful nations, that is, England and the Netherlands. Indeed, even in the West it took on its most spectacular form not in England or in the Netherlands, which rejected absolutism in the seventeenth century, but in Spain, Sweden, and France. In the East, it assumed even more radical forms. The state became a political instrument in support of development, protecting the economy from competition at the hands of more powerful rivals. For the first time it gave expression to thinking in national categories, precisely in the area of the economy. What seems valuable, if idealistic, is Szűcs's observation that the absolutist state provided an opportunity to forge a solidarity that transcended feudal divisions: mercantilist policies and a central administration created a sense of community based on territory, laws, and tariffs, while a central army, and later state schools, created a community based on language.[123]

---

120 Mann, *The Sources of Social Power.*

121 East European nationalism from a historical perspective is discussed in: Seton-Watson, *Nations and States*, Sugar and Lederer, *Nationalism in Eastern Europe*, Sugar, *Ethnic Diversity*, Brubaker, *Nationalism Reframed.*

122 Bibó, "The Distress of the East European Small States."

123 Szűcs, *Three Historical Regions*, 161–67.

Therefore, even if, as Anderson claimed, by perpetuating the political structure of feudalism the absolutist state represented the nobility politically in the person of the monarch, it also aggregated the interests of the bourgeoisie within a territory controlled by a given monarch. A territorial community, a community of lands under the patronage of a monarch, became a community of manufacturing and commercial interests protected by tariff barriers. As Szűcs noted, following Bibó, absolutist states in the West "'administered together rather than annihilated' the colorful world of the traditional organizations [that] existed."[124] The absolutisms under which the countries of the "Third Europe" found themselves—the Austrian and the Russian—lacked this protonational character. Consequently, emphasized Szűcs, nation-states were shaped not by royal policies but by anti-imperial and anti-state uprisings. Opposition to absolutist power was secondary compared to opposition to the imperialism and foreignness of the state. Even if one were to agree with Anderson that, in terms of social structures, the most important division in Europe in the era of absolutism was the division based on the existence or non-existence of serfdom, and that the Prussian, Habsburg, and Russian variants of absolutism had more in common with each other than they did with any Western variants, it is nevertheless not possible to explain the multinational character of the absolutist monarchies in the East within the framework of Anderson's proposed model. Nor is it possible to deduce the "national" character of Western absolutisms from the fact that the peasants were, legally speaking, free. They built their empires overseas, but on the continent "created" nations. Anderson's model and classification of absolutism, although it started from the differences between East and West, ignored the key consequence of this form of power for both parts of the continent: the imperial nation-state in the West, which colonized overseas, and the multinational empire in the East, which colonized internally but was unable to create cultural uniformity. Szűcs, uniquely through the medium of social history, drew attention to this difference and explained it in terms of the natural and geopolitical possibilities for expansion and development. His model contained the seeds of Mann's multifactor explanation (from 1986) of the "European miracle,"

[124] Ibid., 164.

according to which the structures of the protonational state, nascent capitalism, and Christianity (the latter overlooked by Szűcs) supported each other on the path to rapid development.

Eastern and Western Europe: Between Peripheral Status and Imitation

The left-wing attitude of most historical sociologists from the late 1960s onwards meant that the main research problems in this field were, firstly, the origins of capitalism and the rise of the West and, secondly, the role of groups and regions "neglected" by traditional social science. In the West, the historical sociology of Eastern Europe was therefore a by-product of the search for answers about the origins of the rise of the West. The attractiveness of the models proposed by Wallerstein, Braudel, and Anderson for East European researchers is represented in this chapter by the historical schools in Hungary. Similarly, and often in reference to Polish historiography of the 1950s to 1970s, world historiography in the 1970s and 1980s created a very specific image of Eastern Europe. Its most important element—regardless of the period under analysis—was the region's weakness and backwardness compared to Western Europe. And this always meant economic weakness, since to speak of backwardness in the economic context was least problematic. When Russia was excluded from the region, the weakness was also political. In keeping with the left-wing attitude, this weakness was usually treated with understanding, and its causes were attributed to circumstances beyond the control of "the masses" in the region. In contrast to the "historiosophical presentism" of the evolutionist approach, historical sociology never presented backwardness as simply the delay of processes that had occurred earlier in the West. All the authors discussed here emphasized the uniqueness of the West's developmental path, which set it apart from other regions of the world, including Eastern Europe. "Backwardness" was conceptualized as: "peripheral status" (Braudel, Wallerstein, Berend, Ránki); normal "non-development" (Brenner); hybridity, that is, a mix of primitivism and failed imitation of the West (Anderson); and hybridity, that is, a mix of Eastern and Western development paradigms in the "Third Europe" (Szűcs).

	Eastern Europe developed independently of Western Europe			**Eastern Europe developed under the influence of Western Europe**
The rise of Western Europe was the result of its social and political institutions		Anderson: *Primitive hybridity in the 10th–20th centuries*		
	Brenner: *Normal "non-development" in the 16th–17th centuries*	Szűcs: *A mix of East and West in the 13th–20th centuries*		
The rise of Western Europe was the result of historical conjuncture				Braudel: *Peripheral status in the 16th–18th centuries*
			Berend & Ránki: *Peripheral status and crisis in the 18th–20th centuries*	
The rise of Western Europe was the result of the exploitation of other regions				Wallerstein: *Peripheral status and dependence in the 16th–20th centuries*

Figure 1. *Conceptualization of East European backwardness. Views about the rise of the We (y-axis) and the influence of Western Europe on the development of Eastern Europe (x-axis).*

As my overview attempts to show, the authors' detailed analysis of East European weakness depended primarily on their attitude toward capitalism and Western culture in general. Figure 1 illustrates the interdependence of views about the rise of Western Europe and the status of Eastern Europe. Located at one end of the scale is Wallerstein, who treated capitalism as a zero-sum game and the periphery as a victim of development at the core. The growing weakness of Eastern Europe was, therefore, a consequence of its exploitation by the slightly more developed northwestern Europe. The gap between the two regions of Europe and the weakness of its eastern part increased as capitalism developed and as the East became more dependent on the West.

Employing the same terminology (core versus periphery) to describe the relationship between East and West, Berend and Ránki were milder in their assessment of capitalism. Eastern Europe was one of Europe's peripheries primarily due to the policies of its local elites. By comparing different peripheral regions of Europe in the eighteenth and nineteenth centuries, Berend and Ránki concluded that the state had played a major role in the industrialization and modernization of underdeveloped countries. Such boldly reformist elites were lacking in Eastern Europe, and the region's development was not helped by the persistence of social structures that had taken shape over centuries.

For Braudel, the poverty and weakness of a region resulted from historical coincidence, a set of particular historical circumstances. These circumstances were diverse, however, and not just—as in Brenner's model—produced by class relations within a given society. Similarly to Wallerstein, Braudel linked backwardness, that is, the vast differences between various regions of the "world-economy," with the penetration of capitalist forms of economic activity. Although he appreciated the ingenuity of capitalism, he emphasized the undeserved nature, so to speak, of deepening poverty and backwardness on the one hand and wealth and power on the other.

Like Berend and Ránki, Szűcs treated East European backwardness as a consequence of both historical conditions and the bad choices made by political elites—a view popular in the region's historiography in general. Szűcs assessed the economic and political weakness of the "Third Europe" not only in relation to the rise of the West, but also in relation to the rise of the East, which had different origins and assumed different forms. Flawed social institutions were, for Szűcs, the outcome of a fatal mix of different institutional and civilizational paradigms.

Brenner attributed East European weakness solely to the nature of social structures and class relations in the countryside. He tried to adopt a neutral position. In the premodern period, development and stagnation were, according to Brenner, not so much the outcome of deliberate policies as of historical class-based coincidence. Demystifying backwardness as a specifically East European phenomenon, he placed it within the context of the general crisis of the seventeenth century, which affected every European country except England and the Netherlands. Brenner did not, however, attempt to explain the different development paths of Eastern Europe (Poland, eastern Germany), Western Europe (France, western Germany), and the European part of the Ottoman Empire in subsequent centuries.

Anderson's approach, which was the most radical on account of his attitude toward the "rise of the West," linked East European backwardness with the region's long-term exclusion from the sphere of Roman civilization and with the persistence of primitive social institutions. The imitation of institutional solutions that had been tried and tested in the West could not—in a different era and under different circumstances—produce anything other than an inefficient hybrid in the East.

The most frequently mentioned causes and manifestations of backwardness were the demographic, structural, and social characteristics of East European societies. These included the lower population density compared to the West and the lord-peasant relationship, determined by the unfree status of peasants and by serfdom. High population density was widely considered to be a factor conducive to economic and technological development in the pre-industrial age. "Demographic pressure" ostensibly shifted agriculture toward more intensive forms of land use, higher efficiency, and the cultivation of barren land, and in the long term—toward proto-industrial innovation, which gave employment to the "superfluous" section of the population. Low population density in the pre-industrial age led to precisely the opposite. Contrary to the predictions of classical economics, which was developed for the purpose of studying modern economies, in feudal agrarian systems the scarcity of labor did not lead to higher wages or to privileges but often to the restriction of rights and freedoms. Therefore, low population density in Eastern Europe not only perpetuated an extensive mode of production and lack of innovation but also tied peasants to the land.

Not all the authors linked the existence or persistence of serfdom in Eastern Europe to the demographic situation. However, they all saw it as the main cause of the region's stagnation and backwardness. Serfdom explained the slow pace of economic development. The restriction of peasants' personal and economic rights ostensibly led to low productivity because, after all, peasants worked on someone else's account and the quality of their work had no bearing on their income. On the other hand, the existence of unpaid labor was not conducive to technological innovation. In a system in which innovation could only come from the masters, there was no incentive to lower production costs in the long term. Another consequence of depriving peasants of economic initiative and access to the market was the decline of towns and cities, and local crafts, which had previously relied on production and trade on the local market.

Among the social consequences of serfdom, the most important and most negative were the acute social divisions, though these were usually seen as an indirect economic consequence of serfdom. Restrictions on personal liberty, which affected the overwhelming majority of the population, were for Anderson and Szűcs a sufficient reason to lament the despotic and anarchic political system of East or Central Europe. Even they, however, acknowledged the absence of a free town population and the polarization of society (a privileged nobility/ an enslaved peasantry) as a sufficient condition not only of political misery but also of economic stagnation. For the more economically-minded authors, that is Braudel, Wallerstein, Berend, and Brenner, social polarization entailed a lack of incentives for change and a lack of dynamism, which was necessary if more effective production methods were to be introduced. The nobility's social position relative to the peasantry and town population was so advantageous that it did not have to search for more effective forms of economic activity. The lower classes, in turn, did not undertake such efforts because they had no chance of social advancement, even if they were very enterprising.

CHAPTER 2

The Main Participants of the Debate: Sociological Historians in Postwar Poland

The main participants of the Polish postwar debate about the backwardness of Eastern Europe were four sociological historians: Marian Małowist, Witold Kula, Jerzy Topolski, and Andrzej Wyczański, as well as students of the first two authors in particular.[1] Their approaches differed according to the period studied, their authors' ideological position, and how they interpreted Poland's historical process, the country's place in Eastern Europe, and the latter's place in Europe as a whole. Witold Kula's school dealt with both Polish and, more generally, backwardness in the modern era, that is, from the emergence of capitalism in the West to the present day. Marian Małowist's school specialized in the birth of the modern era (thirteenth to sixteenth centuries), in other words, the initial period of European expansion and the key processes of modernity. Jerzy Topolski focused on the early modern era (sixteenth to seventeenth centuries), the genesis of capitalism, and the dualism of European development. Andrzej Wyczański presented a sociological analysis of Poland against the backdrop of

[1] I follow here the distinction between "sociological historians" and "historical historians" introduced by Dutkiewicz and Śreniowska, *Zarys historii historiografii*, 36–50. The former group sought to explain the causes of the phenomena they investigated, while the latter dealt with the archival details of past events.

sixteenth-century Europe—Poland's "golden age." The common elements in these four approaches, however, were robust enough to lay the foundations for a debate. They included the main research questions and an interest in sociology, which resulted in an interdisciplinary, comparative approach and a broad interpretation of the historical process with reference to the *longue durée*.

The authors' shared research interests included what they themselves described as an at times almost obsessive historical quest to identify the social circumstances that explained backwardness.[2] They all studied the social and economic history of Poland and, albeit to varying degrees, the social and economic history of the region, in the context of the formation of European modernity. They created an interpretive, as opposed to an idiographic, historiography, and readily embraced other disciplines within the social sciences, primarily economics and sociology. Their sociological approach was manifested in the use of models and theories or comparisons over time and space. Thus, in terms of methodology, they were closer to sociology, which sought interpretations and explanations, than they were to the traditional fact-based history still dominant in the postwar era. Their interests and approaches corresponded to the characterization of "sociological historians" presented by J. Dutkiewicz and K. Śreniowska in *An Outline of the History of Polish Historiography* (Zarys historii historiografii polskiej). According to Dutkiewicz and Śreniowska—strong advocates of this method of practising history—"sociological historians" are "historians who do not eschew generalizations or laws, who more frequently and willingly ask fundamental questions, and who see the bigger picture, whereas their opponents [historicist historians] often get bogged down in micro studies and historical curiosities and focus on the historical details of events and individuals without a solid foundation in theory."[3]

Another important step toward sociology that the authors discussed here took was to search for historical explanations to current problems. For all of them, the motivation to pose the question

---

[2] Małowist, "Marian Małowist o historii i historykach," 48–49.
[3] Dutkiewicz and Śreniowska, *Zarys historii*, 36.

about backwardness was very modern—they claimed it was still one of the most pressing problems of the contemporary world. In this way they crossed the boundary set by the founders of sociology between anthropology, history, and sociology, since only the latter was meant to deal with modern societies. The question why only certain societies "deserved" sociology, whereas others, the more backward ones, still failed to meet the criteria of modernity, proved to be especially important in the work of Małowist and Kula.

None of the research communities discussed here defined itself as a school of historical sociology, and their connections with this field, to the extent that these were noticed at all, have not been properly analyzed to date. However, the work of Małowist and Kula in particular was known to the international community of (historical) sociologists and "new" historians. Kula was quoted, albeit occasionally, by Braudel,[4] with whom he collaborated on research projects. For Wallerstein, the work of Małowist was a primary source of information about Eastern Europe, and his ideas—besides those of Braudel—were the main inspiration for world-systems theory.[5] However, none of this is sufficient reason to place the achievements of these Polish historians within the context of a field with which they never identified; it is only the nature of their scholarship which makes this possible.

They were historical sociologists when they dealt with socioeconomic macrostructures, when they advanced models and interpretations of development and social change with long-term consequences, and when they sought clarification of backwardness or economic development within historically-formed social structures. They were historians open to other, non-idiographic areas of social science when they used models and adopted a comparative perspective that was global or at least transnational, and when they placed the analyzed problem within the context of the creation of modern social and economic structures—processes which are also key to sociology.[6]

---

4 Braudel, *Civilization and Capitalism*.
5 Wallerstein, *The Modern World-System I*.
6 Stobiecki, *Historia pod nadzorem*.

Broad Interpretations—An Interdisciplinary Approach—A Comparative Perspective—Theoretical Innovation

BROAD INTERPRETATION—GLOBAL PERSPECTIVE: MAŁOWIST

Marian Małowist (1909–88) studied history at Warsaw University where, under the supervision of Marceli Handelsman, in 1931 he defended his master's thesis on the development of trade between Flanders and the Hanseatic cities in the thirteenth and fourteenth centuries, with particular emphasis on Poland. The subject of his PhD, defended in 1934, was the links between Stockholm's trade and Sweden's foreign policy in the years 1470 to 1503, based on archival research conducted in Stockholm. Up until the outbreak of the Second World War, Małowist worked as a secondary school teacher. At that time he also collected materials for a monograph about the Genoese colonies on the Black Sea in the fifteenth century. During the war, having escaped from the Warsaw Ghetto, he remained in constant hiding, teaching at a village school in the Podlasie region. He was also a correspondent for the magazine of the Polish Peasant Battalions (Bataliony Chłopskie),[7] and from 1944 worked for Polish Radio in Lublin after the city was liberated. Throughout the war years he also continued his research on Italian trading colonies, which led to his postdoctoral thesis on Caffa, a fifteenth-century Genoese colony on the Black Sea. From 1947 to 1979 he lectured at Warsaw University's Institute of History, where he was initially Head of the Department of General History and then, from 1955, Head of the Department of Medieval History. In 1955, he defended another PhD in history entitled *Studies in the History of Crafts in the Period of Feudalism in Western*

[7] The Bataliony Chłopskie was an underground army and resistance movement that operated in Nazi-occupied Poland during the Second World War. It was the second largest Polish military organization at that time, after the Armia Krajowa (Home Army). Unlike the Armia Krajowa, which was controlled by the Polish government-in-exile, the Bataliony Chłopskie was politically connected to the Polish Peasants' Party.

Europe in the Fourteenth and Fifteenth Centuries. In 1952 he became an associate professor, and in 1955, a full professor.

Małowist taught many outstanding students, such that one can probably speak of a "Małowist school."[8] Those students comprised a group of historians of the late medieval and early modern periods who were mostly associated with Warsaw University and, in general, with the Warsaw intellectual milieu. They included: Benedykt Zientara, Antoni Mączak, Maria Bogucka, Bronisław Geremek, Andrzej Wyrobisz, and Henryk Samsonowicz.

As Samsonowicz wrote of Małowist, "the main focus of his investigations was the uneven division of Europe's economic and social structure along the meridian."[9] Małowist devoted his life's work to the reasons for Poland's backwardness. Through decades of academic endeavour he developed his initial ideas on the subject. According to him, once it had achieved economic advantage over regions with which it maintained relations, Europe developed by expanding into those very same regions, the first of which was Eastern Europe. For this reason, Małowist conducted extensive regional studies in which he analyzed a given region's links with Europe. He began by looking at maritime issues.[10] The sea, regardless of whether it was the Baltic, the Black Sea, the North Sea, the Adriatic or the Atlantic Ocean always featured in Małowist's work as a strategic space which enabled contact between different lands, which was conducive to economic development based on trade, and which, in European history, also enabled political and military expansion. Małowist's main interest was the Baltic Sea region, in particular its trade, which until the fourteenth century was dominated by Upper German merchants in the Hanseatic cities, and later by Dutch and English merchants.[11]

---

8 Batou and Szlajfer, *Western Europe, Eastern Europe*.

9 Samsonowicz, "In Memoriam: Marian Małowist," 298.

10 Małowist, "Kwestia bałtycka," Małowist, "The Baltic and the Black Sea," Małowist, "Bałtyk i Morze Czarne," Małowist, "Baltic Affairs," Małowist, "Polish-Flemish Trade," Małowist "Riga und Danzig."

11 Małowist, *Handel zagraniczny Sztokholmu*, Małowist, "Historia gospodarcza Szwecji," Małowist, "Z problematyki dziejów gospodarczych."

It was precisely in the Baltic region that Małowist uncovered the inequality between its eastern and western areas. He researched the same problem—inequality in trade relations between East and West—in his studies on the Italian colonies.[12] He continued his studies on a more broadly defined Eastern Europe, the borders and thus the concept of which evolved in his work to finally encompass the area between the Baltic, Adriatic, and Black Seas.[13] In the 1960s he also conducted research on the Portuguese colonies in West Africa and Asia.[14] In the 1970s and 1980s his focus shifted toward empires, which he also analyzed in terms of expansion and exploitation. Besides the Portuguese empire he also studied the Asian empires, which had collapsed by the dawn of the modern era.[15]

Dependency and exploitation were the key phenomena in Małowist's model of trade relations between Western Europe and other regions. He confirmed their existence, principally by analyzing the structures and dominant groups within dependent societies, since it was these that determined the nature of those societies' relations with the stronger Europe. For Małowist, the most important and most interesting economic institutions were trade and crafts, as well as towns—the seat of both these institutions.[16]

In the final phase of his academic work, Małowist published together with Izabela Bieżuńska-Małowist a book entitled *Slavery* (Niewolnictwo).[17] This analysis of the medieval and modern history of the phenomenon adopted a regional and comparative perspective and, as in his previous works, referred to the problem of exploitation and conquest. After his death, Małowist's students published a collection of articles entitled *Europe and its Expansion in the Fourteenth to Sev-*

[12] Małowist, *Kaffa—kolonia genueńska*. English translation: Małowist, "Kaffa. The Genovese Colony."

[13] Małowist, *Wschód a zachód Europy*. English summary: Małowist, "East and West Europe."

[14] Małowist, *Wielkie państwa Sudanu*, Małowist, *Europa a Afryka Zachodnia*, Małowist, *Konkwistadorzy portugalscy*.

[15] Małowist, "Z zagadnień wzrostu," Małowist, *Tamerlan*.

[16] Małowist, *Rzemiosło polskie*, Małowist, *Studia z dziejów rzemiosła*, Małowist, "Z zagadnień popytu," Małowist, "Uwagi o roli kapitału kupieckiego," Bogalska-Czajkowska, "Od Antwerpii do San Salwador."

[17] Bieżuńska-Małowist and Małowist, *Niewolnictwo*.

enteenth Centuries (Europa i jej ekspansja w XIV–XVII wieku), comprising translations of earlier works published in foreign periodicals.[18]

Małowist was interested in the great global changes associated with the expansion of Europe, the beginnings of capitalism in the West, and the refeudalization of Eastern Europe in the late Middle Ages. The early modern era determined the future development paths of Eastern and Western Europe, which were separate yet complementary; it also determined the modern system of economic exchange and international division of labor.

Particularly during the period when he was producing wide-ranging studies, Małowist's approach to social change was global in character. In his view there was an obvious link between the working conditions of a Polish weaver on the one hand, and the structure of the grain trade in the Baltic and North Sea regions, the new trading opportunities for West European merchants following the conquest of West Africa and, consequently, the expansion of Europe and the evolution of the quasi-colonial character of the East European economy on the other. This was a very similar style of thinking to that of the historical sociologists (Wallerstein, Anderson, Moore, Skocpol) and the new historians (Braudel and Hobsbawm).

The model proposed by Małowist may be thought of as an implicit but very specific historical vision. His arguments, based on studies of the changes in urban craftsmanship associated with the evolution of the international division of labor in Europe at that time, emerged in the 1950s. They were not, however, systematically expounded until 1973, when the book *The East and West of Europe* (Wschód a zachód Europy) was published. Nor did Małowist ever claim that this collection of interpretive propositions was tantamount to a model.

Interpretive flourish and a global perspective allowed Małowist's implicit model to explain great historical change, whose consequence was the creation of separate yet interdependent social structures in the East and West of Europe. Unlike Kula, Małowist did not try to convince the reader that "events in economic history cannot be explained within the boundaries of a single country,"[19] nor did he become entan-

[18] Małowist, *Europa i jej ekspansja*.
[19] Kula, *An Economic Theory*, 132.

gled in the formal criteria for determining whether a model was correct and verifiable; he simply provided an interpretation of a great historical event.

AN INTERDISCIPLINARY APPROACH—THEORETICAL INNOVATION: KULA

Małowist's junior by a few years, Witold Kula (1916–88) studied history at Warsaw University and economics at the Free Polish University. Just before the outbreak of the Second World War he defended his PhD thesis on the demography of the Kingdom of Poland. During the occupation he was a member of the Polish Home Army's (AK) Bureau of Information and Propaganda, and editor of its Information Bulletin. He wrote his postdoctoral dissertation, *Social Privilege and Economic Progress* (Przywilej społeczny a postęp gospodarczy), at the University of Łódź in 1947. In the late 1940s and early 1950s he lectured at the Central School of Planning and Statistics (SGPiS) and at Warsaw University's Faculty of Humanities. He also wrote press articles, which in the 1950s were often propagandist in character. Nominated to an associate professorship in 1950, he became a full professor in 1963. In the years 1955 to 1975 he held the chair of economic history at Warsaw University's Department of Economics. Between 1953 and 1968 he led and then collaborated with a team affiliated with the Institute of History at the Polish Academy of Sciences (IH PAN) that researched social structures. At the end of the 1960s he was president of the International Economic History Association. Among the works of his students interested in the issue of backwardness, the most important were those by Jerzy Jedlicki, Elżbieta Kaczyńska, Janina Leskiewiczowa, Tadeusz Łepkowski, and Jacek Kochanowicz.

There were many currents within Kula's scholarship. Initially he dealt with the birth of capitalism in the Polish lands.[20] His studies on crafts and industry, the manufactories of the Polish magnates, and cot-

[20] The most important works in this area include: Kula, "Włościański przemysł domowy," Kula, *Historia gospodarcza*, Kula, "Manufaktura sukienna Radziwiłłów," Kula, "Rozwój kapitalizmu w rolnictwie," Kula, "Początki układu kapitalistycznego," Kula, *Kształtowanie się kapitalizmu*, Kula, "Zagłębie Dąbrowskie."

tage industries and workshops on church land led him to the conclusion that Polish capitalism emerged not in opposition to the feudal mode of production, but as an accompaniment to it, within the framework of the main economic institution of feudalism, that is, the folwark. This landed capitalism persisted and developed through economic and political cooperation between urban manufacturers and merchants on the one hand and large landowners on the other.[21] For Kula, these observations were a prelude to a new sphere of interest: the issue of the transition from feudalism to capitalism, particularly in backward countries. As Kochanowicz wrote, "the Polish case, tackled as an issue in itself, became an example of a much wider problem, namely, the initiation of growth and development within the context of economic backwardness."[22]

In the second half of the 1950s Kula carried out intensive studies of the Polish countryside, where delayed capitalism had taken on particular forms, as well as studies of the peasantry—the largest social group in a backward society. This current in Kula's scholarship found expression in the following works: *An Economic Theory* (Teoria ekonomiczna), *Emigrants' Letters from Brazil and the United States 1890–1891* (Listy emigrantów z Brazylii i Stanów Zjednoczonych), written together with Nina Assorodobraj-Kula, and *The Peasantry. An Intellectual Problem and a Social Science Issue* (Chłopstwo. Problem intelektualny i zagadnienie nauk społecznych), co-authored by Kochanowicz.[23] He described his intellectual journey from pre-industrial manufactory to peasant farm in almost personal terms.

> Having grown up during the greatest crisis in capitalism to date, my historical interests sprang from the history of industry. I studied the origins of industry in Poland, in other words, the eighteenth-century manufactories. My research soon showed that most of those manufactories belonged to large country estates, being an important element of their structure and how they oper-

[21] Kula, "Huta szklana w Cudnowie," Kula, *Kształtowanie się kapitalizmu*, Kula, "Przemysł włókienniczy," Kula, *Szkice o manufakturach.*

[22] Kochanowicz, "Czy tylko historia gospodarcza?" 135.

[23] Kula, *An Economic Theory*, Kula and Assorodobraj-Kula, *Writing Home*, Kula and Kochanowicz, *Chłopstwo.*

> ated. I therefore felt it necessary to study large-scale ownership—the dominant form of production in a backward country. Thus, having begun with the history of industry and the working class, my interest gradually shifted toward the countryside and the peasantry. I delved deeper into the issue that is nowadays referred to as the "agrarian question."[24]

Throughout most of the 1960s, Kula headed a team that researched social structures in eighteenth- and nineteenth-century Polish society. It included Janina Leskiewiczowa, who led the team after Kula's departure, Ryszarda Czepulis-Rastenis, Stefania Kowalska-Glikman, Elżbieta Kaczyńska, and Jerzy Jedlicki. Such research interests, as well as the style and methodology established by Kula in a series on social stratification and mobility, can certainly be described as typical of historical sociology.[25] The nine-volume series addressed typically sociological issues: it examined the changing stratification of Polish society in the period following the January Uprising of 1863, that is, after the abolition of serfdom, and the limitation by the Czarist authorities of the political and economic influence of part of the *szlachta* (nobility)[26] in the Kingdom of Poland.

---

[24] Kula, "Między Kordianem a Chamem," 419 and 455.

[25] Kula, *Społeczeństwo Królestwa Polskiego*, vol. 1–3, Kula and Leskiewiczowa, *Społeczeństwo polskie XVIII i XIX wieku*, vol. 4–8, and Kula and Leskiewiczowa, *Przemiany społeczne*. See also: Leskiewiczowa, "Program badania struktur społecznych."

[26] The Polish word *szlachta* is used throughout the book to refer to the Polish feudal upper class, which was defined by its inherited privileges. *Szlachta*, rather than "nobility" or "gentry" (the terms typically used in English-language literature), represents the difference between the Polish feudal upper class and its counterparts in England, France, and the German lands. The szlachta enjoyed a distinct position vis-à-vis the monarchy and was characterized by much higher internal economic stratification than the nobility of Western Europe. The proportion of szlachta in the general population was also higher than in the West. During the Polish–Lithuanian Commonwealth, the szlachta accounted for 10 percent of the general population. In addition, it included a variety of socio-economic groups: from fabulously rich magnates who owned huge landed estates and residences, particularly in the eastern part of the country, through the middle szlachta who owned smaller estates, to smallholders and landless individuals. However, all of them enjoyed the formal status of noblemen, equal to all other noblemen,

At roughly the same time Kula also undertook studies on historical metrology, which resulted in the book *Measures and Men* (Miary i ludzie), published in 1970 in Polish.[27] In the 1960s Kula also published his principal work on methodology, *The Problems and Methods of Economic History* (Problemy i metody historii gospodarczej),[28] reissued in 1983 with a new and expanded preface. In the chapter entitled "Historical Research on Social Structures," as in the "Introduction" to *Social Change in the Kingdom of Poland, 1815–1864* (Przemiany społeczne w Królestwie Polskim 1815–1864), Kula argued that the structure of employment and distribution of social income were part of the shared interest of economics, sociology, and economic and social history.

Throughout his active intellectual life, Kula also dealt with two other areas. The first of these, and the most important for my book, was economic historical sociology, the sociology of backwardness. Kula's interest in this area was already manifested in his articles written during the war. In cooperation with the Braudel school, Kula developed these investigations in *An Economic Theory*, in *The Problems and Methods of Economic History*, and in subsequent articles, some of which were collected and published in the 1983 volume, *History, Backwardness, Development* (Historia, zacofanie, rozwój).[29] The second area was current political events, which Kula acutely and critically commented on for his own benefit and that of his close friends. He was also a historical essayist and art connoisseur. His output includes many works of popular history and on the humanities in general: the early essays "Philomaths" (Filomaci), "Sorcery" (Gusła), and "Reflections on History" (Rozważania o historii) published in the 1988 volume, *The Rulers and the Ruled* (Rządzący i rządzeni) (1974), as well as his

with a right to vote in the *Sejm*, the *szlachta's* parliament. Between the late sixteenth century and the final partition of Poland in 1795, the parliament was not only the country's legislature but also was entitled to elect the monarch. This formal, legal egalitarianism combined with socio-economic differences resulted in both social and political clientage on a massive scale. See Wyczański, *Polska–Rzeczą Pospolitą Szlachecką*, Urwanowicz, *Władza i prestiż*, Mączak, *Money, Prices and Power*.

27 Kula, *Measures and Men*.

28 Kula, *The Problems and Methods*.

29 Kula, *Historia, zacofanie*.

journals, published posthumously in Polish: *Journal During the Time of Occupation* (Dziennik czasu okupacji) (1997) and *Short Chapters* (Rozdziałki) (1996).[30]

In the words of Kaczyńska, "for him, history was sociology, which did not end with the narrow backward reality of our times. It was rather sociology as a grand generalization of immense knowledge about societies and cultures."[31] The most important sociological elements of Kula's scholarship were his model of peripheral feudalism on the example of Poland in the sixteenth to eighteenth centuries, the delayed industrialization of nineteenth-century Poland (because the industrial revolution occurred later there than in Great Britain), and social development under the conditions of increasing backwardness.

Kula was a specialist in the practice of history, and it was he who introduced Polish historians to both the theoretical approach to historical research and the concept of the model.[32] His approach to creating research hypotheses, testing them, and determining the conditions under which his model of the Polish feudal economy could be verified, was more self-conscious (as shown by his use of figures, for instance) than Małowist's. At the same time, his conclusions had to be more specific and his interpretations had to be of lesser historical and geographical scope than Małowist's. As Kula himself explained, "the more elements we introduce into the model, the richer will be the theory we construct; but the number of societies to which that theory could be applied will decline commensurately."[33] His principal model, presented for the first time in 1962 in *An Economic Theory*, was meant to apply to the Polish economy in the sixteenth to eighteenth centuries. However, Kula also found it to be relevant to other economies, primarily in Southern Europe and Latin America. The difficulty, which Kula tackled in an innovative way, was the different economic rationality in feudal as opposed to capitalist economies, and the variety of rationalities used in feudal microstructures such as folwarks and peasant farms.

---

30 Kula. *Rozważania o historii.*

31 Kaczyńska, "In Memoriam: Witold Kula," 301.

32 Mączak and Tygielski, *Latem w Tocznabieli*, 167, Mączak, introduction to Małowist, *Europa i jej ekspansja*, 9.

33 Kula, *An Economic Theory*, 20.

The popularity of *An Economic Theory* in Italy, Spain, and Latin America shows that Kula was able to propose within it a model that related not only to the Polish economy of the sixteenth to eighteenth centuries.[34] The work presented more general evidence for the way in which economies based on agricultural production and with feudal characteristics (a free or unpaid workforce, ostentatious consumption by landowners) operated during a period when capitalism already existed in other areas and impacted them by creating sales markets, organizing trade, and supplying technological solutions. The terms "mercantile feudalism" and "landed capitalism" were an attempt to describe the specific character of backward countries in terms of their deviation from the models developed for countries that were the first to industrialize. *An Economic Theory* gave rise to the concept of capitalism in a backward country, a concept Kula would develop throughout the rest of his life.

Unlike Braudel's model of the origins of capitalism, Kula's interpretation did not treat the activities of powerful international merchants or huge centers of long-distance trade as elements of capitalism in the full sense of the word. Kula considered such activities and the associated accumulation of commercial capital more as a symptom that presaged capitalism but that still remained within feudalism.

The global character of Kula's approach was not as immediately apparent or as deeply internalized as Małowist's. As I will attempt to show in Chapter 3, the geographical scope of Kula's research did not equal Małowist's vision in terms of its precision or panache. At the same time, Kula, who was more involved in day-to-day academic life, criticized the division of history within Polish academia into national and general history.[35] Unlike Małowist, however, he used the language of this division, observed its rules, and only on the basis of a polemic would attempt to build a justification for his transnational approach. Nevertheless, Kula certainly remained more attached than Małowist to macroeconomic analyses at the national level. In *An Economic Theory*, the global perspective proved essential to his model only when he considered the decline of the feudal economy and the long-term

[34] A list of the foreign-language editions of *An Economic Theory* can be found in the bibliography on page 329.

[35] Kula, *An Economic Theory*, 132, Mączak, *Latem w Tocznabieli*, 113–15, 128.

process that led to its disintegration. In the chapter entitled "Long-Term Dynamics," Kula used other arguments than those based on the internal contradictions of the feudal system. What proved necessary was not just to identify the changing conditions on the external market, the principal recipient of Polish grain (which would have still made the division into internal and external conditions legitimate), but also to indicate general and global changes, that is, the emergence of a new capitalist economic system in Europe.[36]

A COMPARATIVE PERSPECTIVE—
AN INTERDISCIPLINARY APPROACH. WYCZAŃSKI

Andrzej Wyczański (1924–2008) studied history during the Second World War at the clandestine Warsaw University and Jagiellonian University under the supervision of Roman Gródecki, author of, among others, *The Emergence of Polish National Consciousness* (Powstania polskiej świadomości narodowej).[37] He wrote his PhD, *France and the Jagiellonian States, 1515–1529. A Study of French Foreign Policy during the Renaissance*, at Warsaw University in 1949 under the supervision of Tadeusz Manteuffel.[38] From 1953 he worked at the Institute of History at the Polish Academy of Sciences (IH PAN), first in the History of Modern Poland department and then the Economic History department. From 1974 he helped organize a branch of Warsaw University in the city of Białystok, and then a standalone University of Białystok. He lectured there for the rest of his professional life and set up a team that conducted research on the early modern Polish family. He sat on the editorial boards of two journals: *Acta Poloniae Historica* and *Renaissance and Reformation in Poland* (Odrodzenie i Reformacja w Polsce). Beginning in 1949, he helped found the National Library in Warsaw, where he set up the Microfilm Lab, which he led for the first ten years of its existence.[39]

---

36 Kula, *An Economic Theory*, 129–33, 151–52.

37 Grodecki, *Powstanie polskiej świadomości*. Biographies of Wyczański are included in Topolski and Kuklo, *Studia nad gospodarką*, Kuklo, "Profesor Andrzej Wyczański," Topolski and Kuklo, *Między polityką a kulturą*.

38 Wyczański, *Francja wobec państw*.

39 Wyczański, "Zastosowanie mikrofilmu," Wyczański, "Mikrofilm."

Similarly to Małowist and Kula, from 1956 Andrzej Wyczański collaborated with Braudel's school. Unlike them, however, besides social and economic history he also specialized in the history of diplomacy[40] and public administration as well as the domestic policy of the Polish–Lithuanian Commonwealth in the sixteenth century.[41] From the 1960s to the 1980s he published works on the social and economic history of Poland during its golden age. Wyczański was less involved than either Kula or Topolski in *The Methodology of History*. What is interesting nowadays, however—at a time when historiography is seen as an important source for analyzing the *zeitgeist* of the era from which it derives—is Wyczański's research on foreign historiography, particularly French writing on Poland,[42] as well as his articles on historical research in postwar Poland and on the Warsaw milieu of historians.[43] He remains the principal Polish authority on the court of the Jagiellonian king, Sigismund the Old (1467–1548).[44]

Wyczański's major works from the first phase of his research on the early modern Polish economy include monographs on the economic activities of the Polish szlachta, analyses of the effectiveness and organization of noble and peasant agriculture, and studies of food consumption.[45] All this research was summarized in a comprehensive

---

40 The works by Wyczański in this area include: *Francja wobec państw jagiellońskich*, "Polska w stosunkach politycznych," *Polska służba dyplomatyczna*, and a contribution to the debate in "Przedmurze?."

41 Important works by Wyczański in this field include: "Z dziejów reform," "Rozdawnictwo dóbr królewskich," *Między kulturą a polityką*, and "Polityka w Polsce."

42 Wyczański, "O francuskich badaniach," Wyczański (a contributor to the debate), "Obraz Polski w historiografii obcej."

43 Wyczański, *La Pologne au XIIIe Congres*, Wyczański and Topolski, "Badania historyczne w Polsce," Wyczański, "Czy istnieje polska szkoła historyczna?," Wyczański, "L'epoque de la Renaissance," Wyczański (with Groniowski, Leskiewiczowa, and Samsonowicz), "Warszawskie środowisko historyczne."

44 Wyczański, *Zygmunt Stary*, Wyczański, *Dogonić Europę*, Wyczański, *Między kulturą*.

45 The works in this area include: Wyczański, "O folwarku szlacheckim," Wyczański, *Studia nad folwarkiem*, Wyczański, "Uwagi o konsumpcji," Wyczański, *Plony zbóż*, Wyczański, *Studia nad gospodarką*, Wyczański and Mączak, "Folwark," in *Wielka encyklopedia*, Wyczański, *Studia nad konsumpcją*, Wyczański and Topolski, "Peasant Economy," Wyczański, "Przemiany organizacji wielkiej własności."

analysis of the institution of the folwark, which he presented in 1960 in *Studies on the Polish Folwark* (Studia nad folwarkiem szlacheckim).

Through his books, *Poland: A Res Publica of the Nobility* (Polska–Rzeczą Pospolitą Szlachecką) and *Poland in Europe in the Sixteenth Century* (Polska w Europie XVI stulecia), Wyczański became one of the principal and most original participants in the debate begun by Małowist and Kula on the economy, social structure, political system, and culture of pre-Partition Poland in the context of Europe. As Henryk Samsonowicz wrote: "His first overview of an important chapter in Polish history enjoyed the sort of recognition that is rare in historiography. The title of his book, *Poland: A Res Publica of the Nobility, 1454–1764* has entered the lexicon of the humanities as the definition of that period."[46]

Wyczański consistently opposed the idea that Poland was economically dependent on the West, pointing to the similarities rather than the differences in the social and political organization of Poland and its European neighbors.[47] He declared: "I do not believe in the uniqueness of Polish history in the sixteenth century . . . One cannot claim that against the backdrop of sixteenth century Europe the Polish economy was an exception, that the social structure had no analogy in other countries, that the political system was the opposite of what was happening elsewhere, and finally that the culture was completely different to that of other countries in our continent."[48]

Among the economic historians who took part in that discussion, Wyczański stood out in the 1970s and 1980s on account of his interest in education and symbolic culture, including religion.[49] He presented

---

[46] Henryk Samsonowicz, a fragment of the speech at the occasion of Wyczański's *Doctorat honoris causa* of the University of Białystok, Białystok 1999.

[47] Wyczański, et al., *Historia Polski*, Wyczański, *Polska–Rzeczą Pospolitą*, Wyczański, "Polska na tle Europy," Wyczański, *Wieś polskiego Odrodzenia*, Wyczański, *Polska w epoce Odrodzenia*, Wyczański, *Polska w Europie*, Wyczański, "The adjustment of the Polish economy," Wyczański, *Dogonić Europę*.

[48] Wyczański, *Polska w Europie*.

[49] Chapters on culture can be found in any of the main compilations. Works on education and Jagiellonian University include: Wyczański, "Uniwersytet Krakowski," Wyczański, "Rola Uniwersytetu Jagiellońskiego, Wyczański, "Oświata a pozycja społeczna." Works on mentality include: Wyczański, "Kultura polskiego Odrodzenia," Wyczański, "Uwagi o ksenofobii."

the relationship between the Polish–Lithuanian Commonwealth and Europe as one of conscious imitation and a shared set of values, in which Christianity, followed by Renaissance humanism and its institutions, particularly the universities, played a preeminent role. For this reason, and also because in comparative studies he restricted himself to Europe, the juxtaposition of Poland with countries in other continents was alien to him. Compared to other researchers he attached greater importance to institutional factors such as the political system, understood in legal terms, and the institutions of public administration. The only countries with which the sixteenth-century Commonwealth could be compared, therefore, were those that existed at that time, which in Eastern Europe meant the multinational Habsburg, Ottoman, and Russian empires.[50]

The activities of the team that Wyczański established in the 1970s to conduct research on early modern Polish society was an example of historical sociology par excellence. The book entitled *The Stratification of Polish Society* (Uwarstwienie społeczeństwa polskiego), which analyzed tax documents, looked at the most important social groups and social mobility in sixteenth-century Poland.[51] The four-volume *Early Modern Polish Society* [Społeczeństwo staropolskie] published between 1976 and 1986, edited by Wyczański, provided an overview of small structures (families, households, folwarks, rural communities) and macrostructures (occupational and property structures).[52] A project comparable to *Polish Society* (Społeczeństwo polskie), edited by Kula and Leskiewiczowa, *Early Modern Polish Society* contributed new issues to Polish historiography such as the organization of families and the social status of women and children. Wyczański's student, Cezary Kuklo, continued the project together with a team of scholars at the University of Białystok.[53]

---

50 An exception is: Wyczański, *Parallelisme des structures*. See also Chapter 3 of this book.

51 Wyczański, *Uwarstwienie społeczne*. Other important works in this field include: Wyczański, "The social groups," Wyczański, "Czy chłopu było źle?."

52 Wyczański, *Społeczeństwo staropolskie*, vol. 1–4.

53 A center for historical demography has been founded by Wyczański's students in University of Białystok: http://www.homoeconomicus.uwb.edu.pl/; Kuklo, *Rodzina*, Kuklo, *Kobieta*. Other Ph.D. students of Wyczyński include Alina Czapiuk, Anna Kamler, and Piotr Guzowski.

Wyczański was a staunch opponent of the colonial thesis vis-à-vis the Polish lands, and the "interpretive" part of his works often set out to dismantle it. He argued that the notion of "colonial dependency" "is . . . a straightforward misunderstanding. Firstly, capitalism did not yet exist in the West. Secondly, with not the best agriculture or—as in the Netherlands—with a very high population density, there was strong demand for grain in Western countries." He stressed the advantages that Polish merchants and Polish towns derived from the grain trade as well as the relatively good situation of the peasantry in the sixteenth century.

Along with Topolski, Wyczański certainly represented what he himself described as "an optimistic attitude in Polish historiography."[54] He endorsed the view that, in civilizational terms, the Polish lands and Central Europe simply lagged behind Western Europe until the fifteenth century. In the sixteenth century, which in Wyczański's model truly was the golden age of the Polish–Lithuanian Commonwealth, the Polish lands and society "caught up" with Europe in many areas of cultural and economic life. This success was nullified by an underdeveloped social sphere and by the inclusion into the Commonwealth in 1569 of lands that previously belonged to the Grand Duchy of Lithuania, which were more backward than those of the Commonwealth and proved to be a burden on the entire state.[55]

THEORETICAL INNOVATION—BROAD INTERPRETATION. TOPOLSKI

Jerzy Topolski (1928–98) is the only representative of the "Poznań school of economic history created by Jan Rutkowski" mentioned here.[56] Topolski studied history and sociology at Poznań University, which was reconstructed after the Second World War. He was a student, continuator, commentator, and publisher of Rutkowski's works.[57]

---

54 Wyczański, "In Memoriam."

55 Wyczański, *Dogonić Europę*, and Wyczański, *Polska w Europie*.

56 Topolski, "Kierunki rozwoju nauki," 21.

57 Rutkowski, *Wokół teorii ustroju feudalnego*, Rutkowski, *Wieś europejska*, Topolski, *Jan Rutkowski*, Topolski, "Podział dochodu narodowego." See also: Drozdowski, "Od badań regionalnych."

Having gained his PhD at the University of Toruń, "he supplemented his studies at the Institute for the Training of Academic Staff affiliated to the Central Committee of the Polish United Workers' Party (KC PZPR) in Warsaw."[58] Later he came to be permanently associated with Poznań University, where for many years he headed the Department of Modern History and the Institute of History itself. He established and led the journal *Studia Historiae Oeconomicae* and for several years was editor-in-chief of *Roczniki Dziejów Społecznych i Gospodarczych* (Annals of social and economic history), the oldest Polish journal devoted to this field. He also established contacts with Braudel's school.

Topolski published over a thousand major and minor works, a full list of which no one has yet dared to prepare.[59] His first works—his PhD and postdoctoral thesis (both written before the age of thirty)—are monographs on economic activity in the Gniezno Archbishopric from the sixteenth to eighteenth centuries.[60] His penchant for monographs and for Wielkopolska found expression in his studies on the history of the region.[61] This area of research was important for his more optimistic general view of the social and economic history of Poland. He identified characteristic economic phenomena of the prosperous region of Wielkopolska: small folwarks that produced for the domestic market in the sixteenth to eighteenth centuries; the early adoption of capitalism in agriculture compared to the other Partitions of Poland; and the development of industry around agriculture—all of which were usually ignored by the Warsaw historians.

Adapting the classification proposed by Wyczański, for the purposes of this book I distinguish four main currents within Topolski's oeuvre.[62] The most important of these are studies on the origins of

---

58 Wyczański, "In Memoriam," 139.

59 His bibliography until 1987 includes 805 entries. Topolska, "Bibliografia."

60 Topolski, *Rozwój latyfundium*, Topolski, *Położenie i walka*, Topolski, *Gospodarstwo wiejskie*.

61 Topolski, *Poznań*, Topolski, *Dzieje Gniezna*, Topolski, *Żnin*, Topolski, *Dzieje Wielkopolski*, Topolski, *Wielkopolski słownik*, Topolski, et al., *Dzieje Pleszewa*.

62 Wyczański classified Topolski's works as follows: 1. Modern socioeconomic history, 2. The theory of history and methodology of historical research, 3. Post-1945 history, popularization of history, historiography and social science. Wyczański, "In Memoriam."

capitalism in the West, and the origins of the manorial system based on the second serfdom in the East, in other words, as Topolski put it, the developmental dualism of modern Europe. This current includes *The Birth of Capitalism* (Narodziny kapitalizmu) and *The Polish and European Economies* (Gospodarka polska a europejska), both of which will be discussed in later chapters.[63] The second important current is the methodology of historical research and the theory of history.[64] Topolski's most popular work in this regard is *Methodology of History*. Two terms he coined ("non-source-based knowledge" and "axis of historical synthesis") have entered the lexicon of research methodology. Topolski advocated the use of modelling and theory in historical research. He was also known for popularizing new trends in Western historiography in Poland.

Another important current is overviews of early modern Polish and European history (the sixteenth to eighteenth centuries). These books are more traditional—chronological in form and narrative rather than analytical in style.[65] For my purposes, Topolski's final work of this type, *Poland in Early Modern Times* (Polska w czasach nowożytnych) is the most important; it is part of *Poland: A History of the Nation, State, and Culture* (Polska-Dzieje narodu, państwa i kultury), a series edited by Topolski. I regard this book to be a summary of the author's research, and also evidence of his ideological and epistemological change. Finally, several entries in Topolski's bibliography concern recent history. Many of these are examples of popular history, and some are propagandist in character.

Topolski argued with Kula "primarily over the person and achievements of Jan Rutkowski, whom Topolski vigorously defended,"[66] and

---

[63] Topolski, *Narodziny kapitalizmu*, Topolski, "Wskaźnik wzrostu," Topolski, "Causes of Dualism," Topolski, "Economic Decline," Topolski, "The Manorial–Serf Economy," Topolski, *Gospodarka polska a europejska*, Topolski, *Prawda i model.*

[64] Topolski, *Methodology*. The book was also published in Italian and Romanian. Topolski, *Narration and Explanation*, Topolski, *Historiography between Modernism and Postmodernism*, Topolski, *Marksizm i historia*, Topolski, *Prawda i model.*

[65] Topolski, *Zarys dziejów Polski*, Topolski, *Polska w czasach nowożytnych*, Topolski, *Historia Polski.*

[66] Wyczański, "In Memoriam," 140.

over the origins of the folwark and the way it operated. He argued with Małowist, in turn, over the causes of Europe's developmental dualism. In the early period of his activity (until 1965) Topolski criticized Kula and Małowist, arguing in favor of monographic works and against the construction of models based, in his view, on fragmentary data. However, he later abandoned criticism of his colleagues to become a fervent supporter of the theory and methodology of history, and from the end of the 1960s emphasized the advantages of modelling. He wrote: "To reconstruct economic history . . . [requires] linking four elements: human activity, the results of human activity, the establishment of historical facts, and the explanation of historical facts. The only method that can help to meet this challenge is, in our view, a model-based understanding."[67]

Topolski's students were researchers associated with the Adam Mickiewicz University (UAM) in Poznań and the University of Toruń: Krzysztof Brzechczyn, his successor in terms of theoretical temperament (creation of models, reference to the latest fashionable trends in Western social science) and focus on East European issues;[68] Gwidon Zalejko, Jan Pomorski, and Zbigniew Drozdowicz, all methodologists of history; and Andrzej Zybertowicz, a theorist of modern transformation and, from the 1990s, also of postcommunist transformation.[69] Topolski's methodological interests in the years leading up to his death were taken up by Wojciech Wrzosek and Ewa Domańska.[70]

Topolski was Kula's main rival in Poland as regards the methodology and theory of history. The two also differed on how to interpret the role of the folwark in the early modern Polish economic system. In *Truth and Model in Historiography* (Prawda i model w historiografii), Topolski defined the tasks of the modern historian as follows: "Historical narrative should not only be true to the 'facts,' but should also properly reflect the structure and dynamics of reality. To that end, what is necessary is an adequate (constantly verified) theory and its

67 Topolski, *Nowe idee*, 255.

68 Brzechczyn, *Odrębność historyczna*.

69 Zalejko and Zybertowicz, "Gospodarcza aktywność," Zybertowicz, "Materializm historyczny."

70 Topolski, Drozdowicz, and Wrzosek, *Swoistość poznania historycznego*, Topolski, Domańska, and Wrzosek, *Między modernizmem a postmodernizmem*.

application in historical research—a model, in other words, a historical picture that 'captures' the essential (and omits the secondary) elements (components) and factors (relationships between those elements) of past reality."[71]

Topolski's principal model is a theory that explains the origins and rapid development of capitalism in Western Europe versus the manorial-serf economy and stagnation in Eastern Europe. According to this interpretation, the early modern era resulted from a pan-European crisis in feudalism consisting of the emergence of a dichotomy between the imagined needs of the szlachta and their income. "[In] the long-term perspective the only way that the szlachta could increase, or at least prevent the decrease, of its income was through commercial activity."[72] The novelty of Topolski's approach was that it showed how grain-producing folwarks in Poland were equivalent to the enclosure of common land and sheep farming in England, sharecropping in France, Italy, and the German principalities west of the Elbe, cattle farming in Hungary, and fish farming in the Czech lands. Topolski summarized this key interpretation, which he repeated frequently and consistently for thirty years, as follows: "In our opinion, the expansion of farms by the East European nobility in order to produce for the market was one form of the pan-European phenomenon that was the growth in the economic activity of the nobility, which was especially apparent in the sixteenth century. That growth was a response to the crisis in the fortunes of the nobility, i.e., the increasing disparity between income and needs."[73]

Although, similarly to Małowist, Topolski spoke about the dualism of economic growth in Europe, he emphasized the internal causes—legal, economic, mental—of the emergence and disintegration of the manorial-serf economy. Like Wyczański but unlike Małowist, Topolski rejected those interpretations of East European development that depicted the region as a dependent quasi-colony.

71 Topolski, *Prawda i model*, 6.
72 Brzechczyn, *Odrębność historyczna*, 26.
73 Topolski, *Polska w czasach*, 321.

Marxism—Methodology, Intellectual Choices, Political Attitudes

Three of the four sociological schools of economic history analyzed here referred in their methodology to Marx's theory of social development. The exception was Wyczański, who, although he occasionally used Marxist terminology (base and superstructure, for instance), he saw Marxism neither as a genuine challenge nor as a political alternative.

Rather than discuss the ideological inspiration and political attitudes of the authors, in the following section I present those aspects of their biographies, attitudes, and beliefs that are currently a source of antipathy and distrust, and that—I suspect—could be seen as a reason for ignoring their work.

The Marxist leanings of Małowist, Kula, and Topolski may be attributed to the generational experience that was the Great Depression of the 1930s (which Małowist and Kula witnessed), the huge social inequality and unresolved agrarian question in prewar Poland, the intellectual atmosphere of the postwar years, the pressure from communist censors (particularly during the Stalinist period), and finally their relatively independent ideological choices. Looking back several decades later, in the wake of Martial Law when the intellectual elites had finally broken with the communist regime, Topolski had this to say about the impact of Marxism on historiography during the Stalinist period:

> . . . the research we conducted on the conceptual function of historical materialism in Poland in the years 1945–56 shows that what dominated back then was the selection of research topics (a preference for economic history, especially the history of agricultural production, and a preference for social history, especially the history of the class struggle) and—in regard to the history of the workers' movement, which was also favored—the examination of that history in terms of the history of the victorious Party or the victorious current within the Party. As far as explanations are concerned, no appreciable progress was made at that time. This is because the impact of theory did not manifest itself clearly enough.[74]

[74] Jerzy Topolski, *Teoria wiedzy historycznej*, 96–97.

On the whole, Małowist, Kula, and Topolski were Marxists out of conviction and rejected dogmatism. Only occasionally were they forced to refer to Marxism on account of it being the official ideology, and even then they stuck to the methodological rules established by their own or rival schools. They could do so thanks to the relative strength of the social sciences in Poland (compared with other countries in the communist bloc)[75] and to the relatively liberal regime in Poland (compared with the Soviet Union). Therefore, the Marxist character of their interests, the way they conceptualized problems, and their views, particularly those of Małowist and Kula, were neither opportunistic nor instrumental. For historians of their generation, the link between economic history and Marxism seemed obvious in the 1950s and 1960s, even if it does not so today.[76] Małowist said of himself: "I am a social and economic historian . . . My interest in economic history has to some degree been influenced by Marxism."[77] To study economic history was to declare that one recognized its importance as well as the primacy of the economy over other areas of life. However, Kula, Małowist, and Topolski's negative attitude toward capitalism—certainly in keeping with the spirit of their times—meant that, for them, Marxism was an almost natural choice.

Although Małowist belonged to a communist organization—the Communist Youth League—only in his teenage years, throughout his life he drew inspiration from Marx's theory of development, and politically he supported the communists' attempt to create an alternative to the capitalist economic bloc.[78] His interpretive model grew out of a vision of history whose participants were divided into the conquerors and the conquered, the exploiters and the exploited, the rich and the

[75] Keen and Mucha, *Socjologia Europy*, Kłoczowski, *Historiografia krajów Europy*.

[76] Leszczyński, *Skok w nowoczesność*.

[77] Małowist, "Marian Małowist o historii," 48.

[78] There is no explicit documentary evidence of Małowist's position. However, I base this claim on accounts where Małowist declared himself a Marxist and an opponent of capitalism and the legal privileges of the upper social strata. In 1987, he stated: "Our capitalism was backward because, among other things, there was no agrarian reform here. . . . The *folwark* harmed the internal market and was responsible for huge social inequalities." Małowist, "Marian Małowist o historii," 49.

poor. His economic, social, and general cultural views form a fairly coherent leftist system. More complicated was his attitude toward official Marxist organizations, especially in the early days of communism in Poland. When asked in an interview for *Res Publica* in 1987 about his political involvement during the Stalinist period, he said, "I never joined the Party, but I was a Marxist and as such had to fight on two fronts: on the one hand against old-school reactionary historians, and on the other against the Stalinists."[79]

Though neither was formally a member of the Polish United Workers' Party, Małowist's and Kula's views brought them closer to the revisionists—the pro-democratic, anti-Stalinist left, for whom the post-October thaw was a halcyon age. After 1968 they belonged to a group that Jakub Karpiński, writing in 1973, described as follows: "Sometimes it seems that the Party is willing to allow scholars to do research so long as they do not interfere with the ritualized ideological formulas that the Party is apt to repeat. Thus it is often better for scholars if they do not declare themselves to be Marxists, for then they cannot be accused of revisionism."[80]

In the Stalinist period, Małowist praised Marxist methodology as creative because "it allows one more properly to capture the relations and mutual interaction between the base and the superstructure . . . Older Polish historiography ignored this problem by placing the main emphasis on the struggle between different groups within the ruling class [between the szlachta and the magnates]."[81] At the same time he emphasized the dialectical nature of the relationship between what in Marxist historiography were termed the base and superstructure, especially after 1956. For instance, "trade developed in a form determined by the dominant social and economic relations within a given area and then transformed those relations themselves."[82]

---

79 IBID., 51.

80 Karpiński, "Marksizm w działaniu," 96. The history of revisionism in Poland between 1948 and 1973 is also discussed there, 86–96.

81 Małowist, *Miejsce Polski w świecie feudalnym*, 8. The bibliography of this text consists exclusively of works by Marx, Engels, Lenin, Stalin, and Soviet Marxists.

82 Małowist, "Poland, Russia and Western Trade," 38.

It was at that time, the late 1950s and early 1960s, that Małowist published articles that continued his prewar research on trade. This shift toward trade, especially international trade, as an important and "to some extent determining"[83] factor in the economic development of a region or country was a novelty for Marxist historiography. Though it was compatible with the neo-Marxist approach, often recalling the economic reasoning and vision of capitalism developed by dependency theory,[84] it was radically different from the Marxism of the Soviet classics. In Małowist's work, capitalism, and the rise of Western Europe that it caused, was clearly associated with trade, exchange, credit, purchase and sale, and not just with production. "While it is true that trade depends on the general state of productive forces and class relations, [it is also true] that trade can significantly affect them."[85]

In his model of the development and divisions of Europe, it was precisely trade, an area considered to be secondary to production, which had determined the dynamics of production as well as the distribution of social income in Eastern Europe from the fifteenth and sixteenth centuries onwards. According to Małowist, the period when East European production was dependent on Western markets and on the presence of Western merchants was not simply an age of commercial capital (or capitalism) that preceded capitalism proper. It determined the economic system and social structure as well as the balance of power in international politics for centuries.[86]

83 Ibid., 26.

84 See Chapter 4 of this book.

85 Małowist, "Poland, Russia and Western Trade," 26.

86 The only article which might call into question such an interpretation of Małowist's view of capitalism is a relatively unknown work of his, "Commercial Capitalism and Agriculture." In it, he wrote: "Commercial capital was only one of numerous elements that affected the agrarian revolution and one cannot credit it with a decisive role. A similar situation can be observed in central and eastern Europe between the sixteenth and seventeenth centuries, when the second serfdom began. We have known for some time that increased demand and higher prices paid for agricultural products from eastern Europe largely contributed to the massive exports of grain and other farming, breeding, and forestry products to western countries. Commercial capital had an important function in the organization of these exports, but it was certainly not the decisive cause of the generalized diffusion of serfdom in the rural areas of eastern Europe." Małowist, "Commercial Capitalism and Agriculture," 15–16.

Małowist's fascination with international trade and his geographically broad perspective on the world-economy had much in common with Braudel's vision, which was fully expounded in *Capitalism and Material Life*.[87] In the 1960s Małowist had already attributed the origins of capitalism to the international trade links subsequently identified by Braudel as the outcome of Europe's global expansion from the fifteenth century onwards. Yet in a review of the first volume of *Capitalism and Material Life*, Małowist challenged Braudel's idea that the metropolis had played a leading role, revolutionizing economic life. He pointed out that in the Middle Ages it was crafts, usually practised in the countryside and in small towns, that had played this role.[88]

The most striking feature of Małowist's vision was that he categorized economic entities in terms of the geographically defined economic area to which they belonged. This categorization was implicit and was not accompanied by a methodological commentary, but it remains very clear. Similarly to Braudel, for Małowist an economic area had to have some sort of objective creative force that was the outcome of its natural qualities—geography, climate, demography. This objective potential was then transformed (e.g., maximized or minimized) by history. The most important role in this process was played by the dominant social classes within the area in question. Małowist's world was divided into Europe—dynamic and prosperous thanks to its free and profit-hungry bourgeoisie—and the rest of the world, exploited by Europe, fragmented into political entities, and usually governed by a self-serving and snobbish elite. It was thus a vision clearly inspired by Marxism, one characterized by antagonistic forces in which the wealth and development of one group was conditional upon the impoverishment of another.

Let us recall that the key groups identified by Małowist were neither classes within a national society nor classes belonging to a transnational alliance. After all, West European merchants shared business interests with the noble elites of dependent countries. The strongest antagonism was in fact between the economic elite in developed countries and the most underprivileged groups in backward countries.

---

[87] Braudel, *Civilization and Capitalism*.

[88] Małowist, review of Braudel, *Civilisation materielle*.

As Małowist himself stated, these elements of his implicit model of Polish backwardness—a model also present in his vision of European expansion and the development of world capitalism—remained the focus of his life's work.

> I had long been troubled by the question of why Poland was backward. Straight away I was confronted by the problem of the folwark, the problem of serfdom. . . . In short, I began to study the folwark and Polish grain exports. I researched archives in the Netherlands and Belgium. However, since the Netherlands was not just the main consumer but also a center of international trade, we had to look at other regions too. This led to studies on England, northern France, and later—when I was giving annual lectures at the École Pratique in Paris—on Portugal as well. So you see the logic: I followed Polish grain all over the world.[89]

Kula's attitude toward Marxism was more spectacular than Małowist's; it is also better known thanks to the former's more extrovert personality. The best sources of information about Kula's Marxism are the texts collected in *Around History* (Wokół historii)—(in particular, "My Sentimental Education" (Moja edukacja sentymentalna) and "Sorcery" (Gusła)—*Journal During the Time of Occupation* (Dziennik czasu okupacji), and *Rozdziałki* (Short Chapters), as well as press articles he published in the early 1950s.[90] The methodological aspect of Kula's attitude to Marxism is also better documented than Małowist's and is found in numerous works on economic theory and social development.[91]

Similarly to Małowist, Kula linked his decision to study economic history with the idea of Marxism as a proposal for a desirable social order. He located the origins of his views in the period of the Great Depression, which coincided with his early youth. He considered the recession of the 1930s to be a formative personal experience

89 "Marian Małowist o historii," 49.

90 Małowist Kula, "Karol Marks," Kula, "Marks a sprawa polska," Kula, "O nowy, marksistowski," Kula, *Wokół historii*, Kula, *Rozdziałki*, Kula, *Dziennik*.

91 Kula, *The Problems and Methods*, Kula and Geremek, "Wstęp," Kula, *Historia, zacofanie*.

and believed that it disqualified capitalism as a social system. After the outbreak of the Second World War, anticipating the defeat of the West, Kula experienced perhaps his strongest fascination with communism in his lifetime. In November 1939, 23-year-old Kula noted the causes of the war: "I understood that there was no other way to avoid the possibility of war than to abandon the idea of the sovereignty of nations; we needed to form a union, equipped with an executive. Just as war between Azerbaijan and Georgia is unimaginable, so it must be unimaginable between Poland and Germany (to my mind this is probably the most important argument). . . . There is no other way to introduce a planned economy than by means of a Great Union State."[92]

Although he was a supporter of socialist democracy, Kula nonetheless had doubts about the desired scope of the planned economy. In a more moderate article from 1941, he struggled with the following question: "if democracy within society is to be maintained, who should decide about the usefulness of this or that good? The very principle of selection and the need to completely cease the production of certain goods cannot be seriously opposed. Were we to abandon that principle, we would maintain one of the most harmful phenomena of the capitalist system: the production of everything for which there is demand or for which demand can be manufactured (advertising)."[93]

Kula found a solution to the problem of backwardness in the most rationalistic and orthodox version of Marxism. The solution was industrialization, thanks to which the production of basic, low-quality goods for mass consumption could be increased. The necessary capital for this would come from savings, by "reducing the consumption of the middle and upper classes to that of industrial workers"[94] and, "in extreme cases"[95] by banning the import and production of luxury goods. Because, after all, "a person who earns more than others will not eat more bread than others do (assuming the latter are not malnourished), and when that person is unable to buy more cake, his higher income will essentially lose its meaning."[96]

92 Kula, *Dziennik*, 10–11.
93 Kula, "Podział dochodu społecznego," 20.
94 Ibid., 18.
95 Ibid., 19.
96 Ibid., 20.

Kula's output during the Stalinist period comprised, on the one hand, the academic works such as *Sketches of Manufactories* (Szkice o manufakturach) and *The Formation of Capitalism* (Kształtowanie się kapitalizmu), but on the other hand he also produced political articles such as "Marx and the Polish Question" (Marks a sprawa polska), the metaphorical "Sorcery" (Gusła), hidden from the censors until 1958, and his notes to *Short Chapters* (Rozdziałki). Both academic works bear the hallmarks of ideological dogmatism, which was probably a condition of their publication. In *The Formation of Capitalism*, Kula challenged Luxemburgism, stressing the importance of internal factors and arguing in favor of a national model of economy, development, and social change, although in 1947 he still clearly favored a colonial interpretation. In an article entitled "Social Privilege and Economic Progress" (Przywilej społeczny a postęp gospodarczy), he wrote: "The novelty of capitalism was that, in addition to benefiting certain social classes it privileged certain nations, and this was brought into sharp focus . . . By capturing their markets through production, technologically advanced nations acquired a permanent right to participate in the national income of backward nations. The latter may be called colonies, not in the legal sense, but in the social and economic one."[97]

Beginning in the early 1960s, in *Short Chapters* for instance, Kula criticized the bureaucratization of the labor movement, the ritualization of official political life, and the creation of Party mythology. He clearly expected socialism to be rational, and saw rationality as a value and advantage of the socialist system. At that time he began to mock, with increasing vigor, the language used by officials and journalists—their linguistic mistakes and "pointless complications and pretentious style,"[98] which, he felt, betrayed something more than just gaps in their education. These shortcomings testified to the increasingly hypocritical nature of official public life in Poland (as exemplified by the slogan of the nation's moral and political unity, often repeated in the 1970s when the system was experiencing a crisis of legitimacy) and to the formation of a bureaucratic oligarchy, which justified its existence by producing "refrigerators" instead of fridges. For Kula, the winks,

---

97 Kula, *Historia, zacofanie*, 44.

98 Kula, *Rozdziałki*, 377.

allusions, and euphemisms he noticed from the mid-1970s onwards, the overuse of the word "quite" before an adjective to avoid using a stronger, more appropriate epithet, were all signs that the system was in decline and losing public support.

Some of Kula's criticisms of the system, however, were purely political or purely economic in nature. The former included the Party's monopolization of public life and the ossification of the social structure, visible from the mid-1970s onwards. Indeed, the so-called minor stabilization of the 1970s was marked—as Kula put it in *Short Chapters*—by a silencing of ideology and by a focus on the self-reproduction of the system through an expansion of censorship, repression, and the power of the Party apparatus. Kula's economic criticism of Soviet-style socialism concerned the system's obsession with investment. He wrote: "Because the central planner has only eyes for one thing: investment. The task he sets himself (or that others set for him, silently but unambiguously) is: provide as many resources as possible, at any cost, in order to increase investment."[99] "Soon the bureaucracy will start to invest for its own sake, just to prove its worth, to justify its existence—as a matter of honor."[100]

In *Short Chapters*, one can detect Kula's ironic attitude toward the Party from as early as 1953; it later intensified. He made ironic remarks about the manipulation of the public's understanding of history (e.g., the celebration of the thousand years of the Polish state, the commemoration of obscure anniversaries at the expense of obvious ones), about socialist realism, and about the propaganda role of art and the officially promoted folk culture. Similarly, from 1953 onwards, Kula criticized both the social policy and international policy of the Polish People's Republic (PRL). However, there is a noticeable difference between Kula's attitude toward the PRL in *Short Chapters* from the mid-1960s and, for instance, that he presented in his article, "Economic Factors in the Polish Historical Process" (Czynniki gospodarcze w polskim procesie dziejowym), in which he comes across as a PRL patriot.[101]

99 Ibid., 369 (a note from 1974).

100 Ibid., 191–92.

101 In this article Kula wrote: "We should feel free to be moved when looking at the sudden and proud curves in the diagrams, as they are a mark of our generation's efforts." Kula, "Czynniki gospodarcze," 181.

Throughout his life, Kula wrestled with the fundamental questions of Marxism-Leninism: where revolution was likely to occur; the possibility of socialism in one country, especially in a backward country such as prerevolutionary Russia; socioeconomic stages of development; the inefficiency of the market mechanism and the purpose of investment; and the forms and protagonists of class struggle. Kaczyńska, an economic historian and Kula's student, wrote:

> Kula should be placed within the current of Marxist historiography. Witold Kula's Marxism—what kind of Marxism was that! . . . Taking a generalization as his starting point—whether it was accumulation, the class struggle, class interests as the motivating force of history, or the laws of the historical process—Kula analyzed and critiqued that generalization in such a way that ultimately he sowed more doubt than confidence in the "classics" . . . Starting from the classical Marxist theory of development, in the end Kula would show how much the economy depended on social systems, politics, and tradition.[102]

Janusz Żarnowski, a social historian of the twentieth century, assessed Kula's Marxism in a similar vein: "It was a Marxism that had nothing to do with the *History of the Communist Party of the Soviet Union (Bolsheviks)* and a lot to do with British Marxist historiography of those times . . . searching for new solutions, open to new trends in Western intellectual circles, intrigued by those trends; yet it was Marxism nonetheless."[103]

The term *Humanist Marxism* can, I believe, be attributed to Kula's understanding of the field in which he worked. He saw economics as a social science, not as mathematics. He claimed that "every economic problem has its—frequently encountered—social aspect, and

---

[102] Kaczyńska, "In Memoriam," 302–03.

[103] Żarnowski, "Historia społeczna," 18. In this article, published in 1997, Żarnowski ironically comments that in a collective volume entitled *Dziedzictwo Witolda Kuli*, "one of the authors decided to give Kula a posthumous lesson that he had used such terms as 'social class' and 'exploitation' too often, evidently because the author felt that [Marxism] discredited . . . Kula in the eyes of today's habitués of fashionable salons."

every social issue has an economic basis."[104] He understood social classes differently to "classical" theorists. As early as in 1947, observing the forms of capitalism in the West (managerial capitalism, the welfare state) as well as the new social structure emerging in a postwar Poland, he proposed a new criterion of class membership. This was not the relationship to the means of production, that is, property or its lack, but rather the level of consumption. He sought to define class as "groups of people with a similar standard of living rather than similar amounts of property."[105] Kula was also skeptical about the classless society that communism promised. He believed that diversity and social conflict were manifestations of life itself.

Unlike Małowist, Kula remained, I believe, a dogmatist of production. For him, modernity was associated with industrialization. Although the terms of trade became an important element in his model of the collapse of the Polish manorial economy in the eighteenth century, trade was never his favorite research area. His departure from the principles of the Marxist model was based on something different to Małowist's. Following Jan Rutkowski, a move for which he was often criticized, Kula focused on the distribution of national income rather than on the distribution of wealth.[106]

He abandoned the concept of universal development—popular in the social sciences in the 1950s and 1960s—especially when it came to the moment of transition from feudalism to capitalism. The processes of transition from feudalism to capitalism—the plural is important here because there were different paths rather than a single repeatable process—had elements common to all countries, but also elements typical of some of them as well as unique elements.[107] The way in which Kula defined the common elements of transition combined the approach of an economist with that of a sociologist. The necessary, definitive ele-

[104] Kula, *Historia, zacofanie*, 22.

[105] Ibid., 42.

[106] Kula, "Podział dochodu," 11–21. However, Kula criticized some aspects of Rutkowski's emphasis on the distribution of national income. In his 1956 introduction to Rutkowski's *Studia z dziejów wsi*, Kula insisted that it was the production of national income (which preceded distribution, after all) that should be thoroughly studied. He thus supported the Marxist emphasis on production contrary to Rutkowski's emphasis on distribution.

[107] Kula, "Przewrót przemysłowy."

ments of transition were: "the process of accumulation and a change in the structure of national income to one that favors accumulation over consumption. New technologies must be adapted to the traditional environment. Small rural groups must be broken up and big agglomerations must emerge. There must be greater social mobility in all its forms."[108]

Marxism remained Kula's most important methodological inspiration until the 1960s. It was during that time, too "[which] in any case seems characteristic of a certain stage in Polish intellectual history—the stage between October [1956] and March [1968]"[109] that methodological influences began to spring from elsewhere: not only from Marxism but also "from the achievements of Western, and especially French economic history, sociology, and anthropology."[110] Kula maintained an intensive contact with the Parisian Annales School. The fruit of this cooperation was Braudel's incorporation into his work of Kula's ideas about the manorial economy, capitalism in backward countries, and the calorie content of vodka.[111]

For Kula, the 1960s marked the beginning of an anthropological approach to economic history and economics in general.[112] Characteristic of this new sensitivity was the problem of universal economic rationality, which Kula tackled in many of his works. The changes in living conditions that accompanied the transition from a traditional (rural, peasant) to a modern (urban, worker) society were qualitatively so huge that most of the indicators proposed by researchers were inadequate as regards performing a "before and after" comparison. Kula considered average life expectancy to be the exception on the grounds that human life was the only universal, ahistorical value. At the moment

---

108 Kula, *Historia, zacofanie*, 82.

109 Kochanowicz, *Czy tylko historia*, 143.

110 Ibid. 143.

111 Braudel, *Civilization and Capitalism*, vol. 1: on vodka consumption, vol. 2: on the dispute over whether the folwark was a feudal or capitalist enterprise, vol. 3: Kula cited, as a theorist of economic history, on the interdependence between the capitalist economic system and other areas of social life, and on peasant economic behaviour in times of poor harvest. Braudel also cites a passage from Kula's *An Economic Theory*, which he regards as consistent with studies of the *longue durée*.

112 Kula, "Ekonomia a społeczeństwo."

of "feudal–capitalist" transition, the historical changes were so great that nothing, except the value of human life itself, could remain the same or even similar and therefore comparable.[113] According to Kula, all other indicators were to be rejected because they would fall within the rationality of this or that socioeconomic stage of development. In *An Economic Theory*, first published in 1962, Kula developed the idea that different eras were characterized by different rationalities. It was then that Topolski described Kula as a non-Marxist historian because he excluded "from his analysis any claims about human activity applicable beyond the feudal era."[114] Zygmunt Bauman, the future father of postmodern sociology, praised *An Economic Theory* for the same reason; in other words, that it relativized the rationality of economic activity on the basis of historical social conditions and dispensed with the view that capitalism necessarily followed feudalism.[115]

That Kula rejected the linear understanding of development characteristic of evolutionism and traditional Marxism is evidenced by his articles on the development of backward countries—those countries that entered the path of industrialization later than Great Britain.[116] Late industrial revolutions and delayed capitalisms, argued Kula, were different from the earlier ones, which were currently the most developed. In the 1960s, and subsequently, Kula elaborated his early concept of class hierarchy among nations.[117] During that period, this idea appeared in the new context of Third World countries attempting to industrialize.[118] For Kula, countries were the basic macroeconomic units, and nations (not classes within a given national society) were the principal economic actors. This idea certainly represents a modification of Marxism, though in falls within the neo-Marxist current to which dependency theory belongs.

113 Kula, *Historia, zacofanie*, 80.
114 Topolski, "Teoria ekonomiczna ustroju feudalnego."
115 Bauman, Review: "W. Kula, Teoria ekonomiczna."
116 Kula, articles in section "Underdevelopment and development" ("Zacofanie i rozwój"), in *Historia, zacofanie.*
117 Kula, *Przywilej społeczny.*
118 Kula, especially: "Sektory i regiony zacofane w gospodarce wczesnego kapitalizmu," in Kula, *Historia, zacofanie* 113–29, "Przewrót przemysłowy. Historia i perspektywy," in ibid. 130–57, "Zacofanie gospodarcze w perspektywie historycznej," ibid. 183–96.

Topolski was known both as a theorist of Marx's doctrine of social development and, up until the late 1980s, as a liberal proponent of Marxism trusted by the Party. This second aspect of his position within the Party brought Topolski popularity when, upon his intervention, the communist authorities allowed the well-known dissident Adam Michnik to finish his university studies and defend his master's degree in history.

Aware of the particular role of Marxism and the problematic position of Marxists in communist bloc countries, at the beginning of the 1980s Topolski described the situation of East European historiography in the postwar years. This description was not without autobiographical elements. "Although the general mechanisms of development also apply to the socialist countries of Europe . . . due to the . . . state's adoption of Marxism as an ideology that sets out the course of action and as a theory that provides a basis for choosing a strategy," it played a dual role.

> Firstly, one should mention the institutional support given to disseminating Marxism and studies associated with it . . . and, secondly, the preference that usually exists for this or that interpretation of Marxism considered to be correct in terms of the tasks and goals pursued by the centers of power. The first of these consequences had a positive impact on developing knowledge about the theory of historical materialism among historians. Across academia in general, however, it also meant that research choices could be dictated not so much by . . . theoretical reflection as by ideological conviction or a simple desire to participate in political life for one reason or another.[119]

In his theoretical studies, Topolski considered dialectical reflection "until it was given fullest expression by Karl Marx and Friedrich Engels,"[120] as an important achievement of historical research methodology. Until the late 1980s he pointed to historical materialism as the best theory and model for explaining the historical process and social

[119] Topolski, *Teoria wiedzy historycznej*.
[120] Topolski, *Metodologia historii*, 165.

development.[121] His works were not, however, aggressively doctrinaire. They were serious academic studies on methodology, as evidenced by the fact that translations of them appeared in countries beyond the communist bloc.[122] Though he was far from both Marxism and the theory of history, Wyczański, a friend and colleague of Topolski's, saw the latter's methodological works as a kind of Trojan horse: "*The Methodology of History* was a shield that protected us against attacks by hardliners and ideologists, since it introduced Western methods of research yet could not be regarded as contrary to rationally conceived Marxism. This, in turn, ensured a considerable degree of freedom when doing research and a common language with historians from the West."[123]

Associated with the Party's Institute for the Training of Academic Staff, Topolski enjoyed relative freedom to publish, and his books had large print runs. He published several extensive works on methodology.[124] These included works in which he presented "an approach to Marxism as an approach to one of many academic theories, and not a set of dogmas"[125]—principally *The Methodology of History* (Metodologia historii) and *The Theory of Historical Knowledge* (Teoria wiedzy historycznej) as well as works which dealt with the relationship of Marxism itself to the methodology of history.

Topolski's contribution to humanizing official, but also orthodox, deterministic Marxism was to raise the issue of the role of human consciousness in the historical process, a factor that was "integrated" in the "objective natural and historical reality."[126] This interpretation of Marxism was meant to be a continuation of the ideas of the young Marx as expressed in Topolski's favorite quotation from *The Eighteenth Brumaire*: "Men make their own history, but they do not make it as

---

121 Zybertowicz, "Materializm historyczny."

122 *The Methodology of History* was translated into Italian, English, Spanish, Romanian, Chinese, and "probably Russian, although it was never officially published in the Soviet Union." Wyczański, "In Memoriam,"142.

123 Wyczański, "In Memoriam," 142.

124 Topolski, *Methodology of History*, Jerzy Topolski, *Świat bez historii*, Topolski, *Marksizm i historia*, Topolski, *Nowe idee*, Topolski, *Prawda i model*, Topolski, *Teoria wiedzy historycznej*.

125 Wyczański, "In Memoriam,"142.

126 Topolski, *Prawda i model*, 6.

they please."[127] The emphasis in Topolski's interpretation fell on the first part of this sentence when he quarelled with the determinists and naturalists, and on the second when he criticized the historiography of famous figures.

The Theory of Historical Knowledge (Teoria wiedzy historycznej) seems to have been a breakthrough as far as Topolski's theoretical interests and sympathies were concerned. In it, he argued not only against fact-based history but also against evolutionism, Eurocentrism, and nationalism in historiography, as well as naturalist interpretations of Marxism, which brought him close to the ideas of Maurice Godelier and Louis Althusser.[128] He also expressed approval for the non-deterministic, Humanist Marxism of Antonio Gramsci.[129]

The role that Topolski assigned to the social context within which consumer needs develop was consistent with Gramsci's concept of hegemony. In this respect he was also similar to the neo-Marxist French sociologist Pierre Bourdieu. The rising incomes of townspeople and peasants in the fourteenth and fifteenth centuries were, in Topolski's model, an incentive for the szlachta to undertake new economic activities that would increase their own incomes. Hence, for the szlachta, the motivation to increase consumption was a matter of prestige, while for the town population and peasantry it was based on a desire to imitate the upper classes. In Topolski's analysis, human needs appeared to be relative and subjective, albeit objectively and non-materially conditioned by social norms characteristic of the given era and social group. This assumption became the basis for explaining the changes in modes of production in the late fifteenth and early sixteenth centuries, although Topolski considered it to be a universal law. Although not imposed by force or even propaganda, or the fact that no one consciously invents them, internalized needs nevertheless take over the minds of people, dictating aesthetic values, styles of consumption, and economic behavior, and thus determine the shape of the whole economic system. It was this phenomenon of indirect, impersonal, yet overwhelming cultural pressure exerted by the upper onto the lower

[127] Ibid.

[128] Godelier, "Objet et méthode," Althusser and Balibar, *Reading 'Capital'*.

[129] Gramsci, *Selection from the Prison Notebooks*, Foucault, *Archaeology of Knowledge*.

classes that Topolski attempted to describe as the relationship between the subjective and objective, the material and ideological. Gramsci called it hegemony; Bourdieu called it symbolic violence.[130]

Another taboo of deterministic Marxism that Topolski transgressed, if not broke, was to separate the criterion of the emergence of capitalism from the criterion of economic growth in the modern era. In line with classical Marxism, he regarded the commodification of labor and thus the abolition of serfdom to be the criterion for the transition from feudalism to capitalism. To this Marxist indicator of economic progress, however, Topolski added the growth rate of the economy, which to this day remains the most popular indicator of classical economics. He pointed out that different social arrangements such as rents, sharecropping, or serfdom could exist within regions that had similar rates of economic growth. The division of Europe based on the presence of serfdom (i.e., to the east or west of the Elbe) did not, therefore, correspond to the division based on the rate of economic growth.[131]

The situation of international social science and the intellectual atmosphere of the Polish People's Republic in the postwar years were conducive to Polish historians taking an interest in socioeconomic (as opposed to social and economic) issues. It was against this backdrop that a debate took place among researchers on the causes and symptoms of East European backwardness, which I refer to as the "East European debate." Its main participants—the sociological historians Małowist, Kula, Topolski, and Wyczański, together with their students—developed a new research methodology. This was characterized by a break with the paradigm of event- or fact-based historical writing and the historiography of famous figures in favor of a shift toward the methods of modern sociology. The sociological historians analyzed mass and recurring phenomena as well as long-term historical pro-

130 Bourdieu, *Language and Symbolic Power.*

131 See Chapter 4 of this book. Unlike Wyczański, I do not think that this tripartite division "questioned the orthodox Marxist emphasis on the importance of the border on the Elbe river." Topolski remained attached to that border in his thinking and treated the division into areas of economic growth as supplementary to the division of Europe according to the presence or absence of the second serfdom.

cesses that had consequences for the present. The principal actors in this narrative were big groups: social classes rather than outstanding individuals. Following the modern (as opposed to postmodern) sociology of their day, the founders of these four schools tried to paint a complete picture of the interdependencies within the socioeconomic unit they believed to be the most important, whether it was a national society, a region, a continent, or the world. It was thanks to them that the method and concept of the explanatory model was introduced into Polish historiography.

Three of the schools—Małowist's, Kula's and Topolski's—were directly inspired by Marxism. Janusz Żarnowski's view on the situation of postwar historiography and economic historians also relates to the group of historians discussed here, and to the East European debate that their works instigated:

> Historical materialism, proclaimed [in the late 1940s and 1950s] as the methodological basis of history, was understood in Party circles as follows: that one should always look for the economic causes of cultural and political processes and phenomena. For this reason, too, the advocates of "methodological reconstruction" paid particular attention . . . to economic history. But this state of affairs allowed some historians to withdraw into a field in which they could carry out more or less normal research work while minimizing their political servitude.[132]

[132] Żarnowski, *Historia społeczna*, 16.

CHAPTER 3

Eastern Europe Compared to Other Regions: The Historical Geography of Development

The aim of this chapter is to analyze the regional geographical categories used by the participants in the debate on East European economic backwardness. For the purposes of this book, interpreting the participants' choice of terminology is essential. Without defining the geographical area in question, the criteria by which it was considered distinct, and the other areas to which it was similar or fundamentally different, it is impossible to present fairly how the four historical schools viewed the development of the region and its social structure. Moreover, to adopt criteria that separate the region from the oldest and most popular name given to it in the postwar period, that of Eastern Europe, amounts to an interpretation of backwardness itself. I assume, for the purposes of this book, that naming the region "Eastern Europe," "Central Europe," "Slavic Europe" or "East Central Europe" is not an innocent linguistic endeavour but a political act. Following Iver Neumann, I believe that to use one of these terms and not another is an attempt to shape the region's identity, to choose one of the many identities that have historically been used, and to reject all other competing ones.[1] By analyzing the terminology, therefore, I will be able to interpret the views of the historical schools in the context of political conditions and changes in the social sciences in the second half of the twentieth century.

[1] Neumann, "Forgetting the Central Europe," 207.

I refer in this book to the Western tradition of analyzing regional cultural discourses. The architect of this tradition is considered to be Edward Said, an American literary scholar and the most famous spokesman for the Palestinian cause in the United States. First published in 1978, his book *Orientalism* gave rise to numerous studies that exposed Western discourse on the subject of this or that regional Other. *Orientalism* offered an in-depth view of the development of reflection and action vis-à-vis the Orient, a concept which, according to its author, "has helped to define Europe (or the West) as its contrasting image, idea, personality, experience."[2] Studies in this field treat historiography as a source of knowledge about the mentality of a given era. Social institutions and time-honored traditions are the outcome of random events, and the ones that survive are those that serve the dominant groups in society. Discourse analysis belongs to the tradition known as the hermeneutics of suspicion. Its principal tools are criticism of the sources of hegemonic interpretations of history, geographical images, and cultural classification as proposed by Antonio Gramsci, and analysis of the relationships between knowledge and power as proposed by Michel Foucault.[3]

The way in which regional discourse analysis has inspired me in this book is somewhat perverse. I analyze East European discourse about Eastern Europe—discourse about a region that is weak in the global division of power. At the same time, this discourse was created by insiders, scholars from the region. There is no question of any direct benefit of self-identity (in the Saidian sense) to be gained from the construction of an East European Other. At most, this historiography may be seen as testifying to a search for one's own identity. My main aim is not so much to expose but to rediscover the criteria for considering the region distinct. I also want to examine how consistently the authors used those criteria.

When I use the hermeneutics of suspicion as a method to determine whether geographical constructs conceal a hidden political agenda, I am more inclined to suspect the authors of:

---

[2] Said, *Orientalism*, 1–2.

[3] Gramsci, *Selection*, Foucault, *Archaeology of Knowledge*.

- seeking to legitimize the installation in Eastern Europe (an area beset by centuries of backwardness) of Soviet-style socialism (a remedy for this backwardness); the views of Małowist, Kula, and Topolski fall into this category;
- an ideological aversion to capitalism, which motivates their understanding of capitalism as a tool for the exploitation not only classes but also of regions, including Eastern Europe, from which the authors originate; the views of Małowist and Kula fall into this category;
- a willingness to conform to the dominant academic discourse; the views of Topolski fall into this category;
- a desire to incorporate the history of Poland into the West European mainstream; of this I suspect Wyczański, whose views anticipate the "Central European" discourse of the 1990s, and it is here that I am most faithful to the Saidian tradition of exposing the hegemony of the West.

I begin the chapter by presenting the genealogy and popularity in Polish historiography of the main terms describing the region to which Poland and its neighbors belong: "Mitteleuropa," "Central Europe," "East Central Europe," and "Slavic Europe." In the next four sections I analyze in detail the terms used by the four sociological schools of history—the main protagonists of this book.

"Eastern Europe" and Competing Terms

In historiography, it is assumed that the term "Eastern Europe" has been used in popular, journalistic, and literary discourse since the Enlightenment. According to Larry Wolff, one of the few modern historians specializing in Western perceptions of Eastern Europe, it was precisely during the Enlightenment that the term came to refer to this part of Europe, which was different from the "civilized" West.[4] Although one can criticize the image of a backward Eastern Europe

[4] Wolff, *Inventing*.

as the product of a purely imagined Enlightenment geography,[5] it seems that one should accept Wolff's contention that there exists a link between the rise of European modernity and the Enlightenment notion of civilization on the one hand, and the shift in Europe's lines of division on the other.

Both Wolff and other regional discourse analysts assume that the Enlightenment brought about a change in the geography of economic and cultural development.[6] Citing Machiavelli, the author of *Inventing Eastern Europe* writes: "in the Renaissance the fundamental conceptual division of Europe was between the South and the North,"[7] and Italian cities provided the model for material and symbolic culture. In the sixteenth to eighteenth centuries, "Europe's center of culture and finance had shifted from the treasures and treasuries of Rome, Florence, and Venice to the now more dynamically important cities of Paris, London, and Amsterdam."[8]

According to Enlightenment geography, the borders of Eastern Europe ran from the Baltic to the Ottoman Empire (the position of

[5] Wolff sees the divisions of the Enlightenment era as a source of the Western contempt for this diversified area. The eighteenth-century stereotype proved very durable and became an ideological justification for the Yalta division of Europe, which was treated merely as confirmation of the significant civilizational differences between East and West. The post-Cold War and post-communist vision of Eastern Europe essentially reflected the Enlightenment vision (backwardness and despotism), and Soviet communism was seen as the most recent incarnation of an Eastern and slightly Asian value system. Most likely, if the Cold War had lasted, this type of reflection on the place of Eastern Europe in European history would not have been possible. Only when criticism of the West was no longer associated with support for state socialism, and the arguments were no longer based on the Cold War alternative of liberal democracy or pseudo-socialist authoritarianism, did it become possible to see Eastern Europe in a context other than Soviet imperialism. Without fear that one was supporting the Kremlin, it became possible (both morally and intellectually) to see Eastern Europe as a subject of Western conceptualization and manipulation. In this sense, analyses of East European discourse draw on the cultural traditions of Western criticism, previously used by historians of postcolonial territories and in the Western historiography of those areas.

[6] Said, *Orientalism*, Todorova, *Imagining the Balkans*. Delanty, *Inventing Europe*, Mączak, *Odkrywanie Europy*.

[7] Wolff, *Inventing*, 4.

[8] Wolff, *Inventing*, 5.

Greece, the cradle of Western civilization, remained unclear) and from the western borders of Poland to Siberia. In the West, this area was deemed to have the following features: low population density; vast empty spaces symbolizing the untapped riches of nature; poverty; poor housing; bad roads; an absence of roadside inns; poor hygiene; and great social contrasts—against a backdrop of general misery, the residences and lifestyles of the elites appeared extravagant and incongruous with their environment. For those observers capable of formulating abstract conclusions, the salient feature of this great area was its position between the West and the Orient; an amalgam of Europe and Asia, of civilization and barbarism, of rationality and its opposite.[9] "Eastern Europe was located not at the antipode of civilization, not down in the depth of barbarism, but rather on the developmental scale that measured the distance between civilization and barbarism,"[10] argues Wolff, while Maria Todorova adds that the "Enlightenment idea of Eastern Europe . . . presupposed neither its definitive exclusion nor its unqualified inclusion" in Europe.[11]

In his essay, "East Central Europe in the Historiography of Countries of the Region" (Europa Środkowowschodnia w historiografii krajów regionu), Jerzy Kłoczowski points to a different, post-Versailles stage in the interpretation of the term.[12] The name of the region grew out of a need to define the area occupied by the new, postimperial countries of Europe. The historiography of the countries of the region, which was more active or even just emerging after 1918, used this name to denote the area previously belonging to the "three or actually four empires: Russian, Prussian-German, Austro-Habsburg, and Ottoman."[13] Eastern Europe encompassed, therefore, the new nation-states that were created in the second half of the nineteenth century in southeastern Europe as well as those that emerged from the Balkanization of the Habsburg, Russian, and to a lesser extent German

[9] I write about the "oriental" themes identified by researchers of historiography and East European political discourse in the following review: Sosnowska, "Europa Środkowo-Wschodnia a orientalism."

[10] Wolff, *Inventing*, 13.

[11] Todorova, *Imagining*, 153.

[12] Kłoczowski, *East Central Europe*.

[13] Ibid., 5.

empires.[14] The term "Eastern Europe" thus satisfied a need created by the new map of Europe, in which numerous small countries—a strange development by the standards of the postimperial age—occupied the area between Germany, Italy, and Soviet Russia. The countries in question were: Finland, Estonia, Latvia, Lithuania, Poland, Czechoslovakia, Austria, Hungary, Romania, the Kingdom of Serbs, Croats and Slovenes (known as Yugoslavia after 1929), Bulgaria, Albania, and Greece. Due to their standing in international politics, their recent history, as well as historiographical neglect, it was specifically these countries that constituted Eastern Europe. Although Kłoczowski, an advocate of the term "East Central Europe," argues that "Eastern Europe" was adopted in the "1920s evidently under the influence of Western scholarship," and that Polish academics used it "only in a geographical sense" without prejudging "the issue of more profound civilizational, economic, and political ties,"[15] there is much to suggest that the term was accepted by the historical community in Poland and elsewhere in the region. In 1927, on the initiative of Marceli Handelsman, the Federation of Historical Societies of Eastern Europe was founded, and in 1933 at the World Congress of Historians in Warsaw, a separate section devoted to the history of Eastern Europe was created. The area of interest for both research teams was "the lands stretching from the eastern borders of Germany and Italy and the western borderlands of Poland, Bohemia, and Austria to the European borders of the Russian and Ukrainian plains; Finland and Greece marked the northern and

[14] In historiography, political thought, and popular discourse in the second half of the nineteenth and beginning of the twentieth century, "Balkanization" meant the proliferation of national movements seeking to establish new nation-states. In the imperial political geography of the time, this meant "small" and numerous countries. Halecki, who supported the existence of small countries of free nations between the superpowers of Germany and Russia, saw the Balkanization of the northern territories of Eastern Europe (the Habsburg and Russian Empires) as a positive phenomenon. He therefore ignored the pejorative connotations of the term—the vicious conflicts between the Balkan countries in late nineteenth and twentieth centuries. See: Halecki, *The Limits and Divisions* and Todorova, *Imagining*.

[15] Kłoczowski, *East Central Europe*, 19.

southern limits of the area."[16] Terminological controversies notwithstanding, besides Handelsman two other Polish historians employed this concept during the interwar period: Oscar Halecki and Kazimierz Tymieniecki.[17]

After the Second World War, "Eastern Europe" became the dominant term in all forms of discourse—from political to academic. It denoted Russia or even the entire Soviet Union, along with all the European countries of the communist bloc.

SLAVIC EUROPE

The term "Slavic Europe" came to rival "Eastern Europe" in the nineteenth century. It originated from the linguistic and ethnographic studies initiated by Johann G. Herder. In the era of positivism and nationalism it was also used in historical and political discourse. In Russia, this category, with its racial connotations and political implications, was an important element of Slavophile ideology, which juxtaposed the culture and history of the peaceful and settled Slavs with the expansive traditions of the peoples of Western Europe.[18] "Slavic Europe" had a similarly political meaning in German historiography and political thought and practice, especially at the beginning of the twentieth century. The political boundaries of Europe in the nineteenth and early twentieth centuries and the fact that the Slavic peo-

---

[16] Ibid., 12.

[17] Halecki suggested varying the historical borders of "Eastern Europe." The latter would consist of the territories north of the Carpathian Mountains that were Christianized in the ninth and tenth century, including Kievan Rus', but not including the territory of the later Grand Duchy of Moscow. Halecki, "L'histoire de l'Europe orientale," quoted from: Kłoczowski, *East Central Europe*, 8. In other sources Halecki used this term to describe the territory stretching from the Balkans in the South to Russia in the North: Halecki, "Qu'est que l'Europe Orientale?," in Kłoczowski, *East Central Europe*, 23. Tymieniecki in *L'histoire sociale de l'Europe orientale* claimed: "Eastern Europe meant the regions east of the Elbe, excluding Scandinavia and the Southern Balkans," as well as Russia. The criterion of affiliation was the lack of Roman settlement in the early Middle Ages, and at the same time "the expansion of Germanic law to town and rural communities" in the late Middle Ages. Kłoczowski, *East Central Europe*, 10.

[18] Walicki, *A History of Russian Thought*.

ples were spread across several empires meant that, until the 1920s, "Eastern Europe as a whole had been the subject of Slavonic studies. The Western and American world was familiar with it from the work of German scholars."[19]

Thus, although the names of historians' associations contained the phrase "Eastern Europe," respecting the fact that the region included many non-Slavic peoples (Lithuanians, Latvians, Estonians, Hungarians, Romanians, and Albanians), *Słowiańszczyzna*, meaning both "the Slavic lands" and "the Slavs" as a people, remained the principal term used in post-Versailles historiography. According to Kłoczowski, in 1928, the Historical Society of Eastern Europe set up an editorial committee of the *Encyclopedia of Slavic Antiquity* (Słownik starożytności słowiańskich) under the leadership of Polish economic historian Franciszek Bujak. Toward the end of the 1920s Jaroslav Bidlo, a professor from Charles University in Prague, published his famous book, *The History of the Slavs* (Dějiny Slovanstva), according to which the Slavic nations had, with the exception of Russia, experienced common "waves" of historical rise and decline.[20] In later works, although he already used the term "East of Europe," Bidlo argued that there was a separate "Greco-Slavic, Orthodox world that we can contrast with the Romano-Germanic Western world." [21] Its roots "lie deep in Byzantium . . . The evolution of Western Europe and of Byzantine-Slavic Eastern Europe . . . should be seen from this perspective." Although Bidlo's understanding of the historical process was controversial, Kłoczowski, and to some extent Halecki, borrowed from him the term "Byzantine-Slavic Europe" or "Byzantine-Slavic civilization."[22]

The most obvious shortcoming of this term was that the area inhabited mostly by Slavs was also the homeland of non-Slavic nations. Handelsman pointed out that the Slavic lands were not even culturally homogenous as they had a varied political and religious history.[23] The term was also criticized because it was used in Russian and Russophile historiography, which treated the Slavic lands as a sphere of Russian

---

19 Kłoczowski, *East Central Europe*, 12.

20 Ibid.

21 Bidlo, "Ce qu'est l'histoire de l'Orient Europeen."

22 Kłoczowski, *East Central Europe*, 12.

23 Handelsman, "Quelques remarques."

influence. In German historiography the term "Slavic lands" signified backwardness, an incapacity for self-determination, and a region that could be easily colonized.[24]

But, despite the criticism, the term is still used in the names of institutions, periodicals, and books connected not only with linguistics and literary studies but also with history, politics, society, and culture.[25]

When referring to his 1984 work, *Slavic Europe in the Fourteenth–Fifteenth Centuries* (Europa słowiańska w XIV–XV wieku), nine years later, Kłoczowski wrote that he had used the term "strictly in the geographical sense." He distinguished three regions: "East Central Europe, South Eastern Europe and Kievan Rus'," [26] which were also home to non-Slavic nations. In Kłoczowski's understanding, these strictly geographical concepts did not overlap with the most important cultural divisions, primarily religious ones. This is probably why in his 1998 book (*Młodsza Europa*) he called the region the "Younger Europe."[27] The Slavic or Younger Europe was the Europe that had become "Europeanized," in other words that had adopted Christianity relatively late, that is, not until the ninth century. In Polish historiography, Kłoczowski was perhaps alone in making a distinction between the Westernized sphere and the Byzantine-Slavic sphere and including them in the same region. For him, awareness of the overlap between these two spheres was essential to understanding the history of the Polish–Lithuanian Commonwealth. Its Orthodox peoples were partly exposed to secondary Westernization after the Union of Brest in 1596. The latter created the Greek Catholic or Unitary Catholic Church, which respected Catholic dogmas and the authority of the Roman pope but maintained the Orthodox liturgical style. Kłoczowski's Polish, not to say early modern Polish perspective referred more to the ideas and era of Jagiellons than the Habsburgs. Moreover, although Kłoczowski represented the Catholic historiography associated with

---

24 Halecki, *The Limits and Divisions.*

25 There is the School of Slavonic and Eastern European Studies in London, which publishes *Slavonic and East European Review. Slavic Studies* is another relatively well-known journal. Both are concerned not only with studies of language and literature, but also with history and regional politics.

26 Kłoczowski, *East Central Europe.*

27 Kłoczowski, *Młodsza Europa.*

the Catholic University of Lublin (KUL), and his vision was the vision of a historian who understood culture as a manifestation of religion, his East Central Europe was only part of the "Younger/Slavic Europe" and did not bear the hallmarks of Catholic exclusivity. The "Younger Europe" was more an ecumenical project. Although it counted the Vatican as its patron, it was nonetheless Christian and Jagiellonian in outlook rather than Roman Catholic in the style adopted by the Counter Reformation. Kłoczowski's approach could be expressed thus: "Treating East Central Europe solely from the Western perspective fails especially from the point of view of the Polish–Lithuanian Commonwealth of many nations; there the meeting of both cultures [Latin and Byzantine] had enormous significance."[28]

In the early twentieth century, and especially during the interwar period, competing terms emerged to describe the area as a whole or parts thereof. One of these was the concept of "Mitteleuropa," used in German historiography; "Central Europe" arose in Polish historiography (mostly in its French version, "L'Europe Centrale," since French was the official language of the research teams mentioned earlier and the most popular language of historiography); "Slavic Europe" remained popular, especially in Czech historiography; and both "Europa Centro-Orientalis" and "East Central Europe" appeared for the first time in Hungarian historiography. In the next section I present a genealogy of these terms and the arguments that were used in favor of one term and not another.

MITTELEUROPA

This term gained popularity thanks to Friedrich Naumann's book of the same name, which was published in 1915.[29] For Naumann, Mitteleuropa signified an area of historical or potential German dominance. It represented a region that included Germany as well as countries with sizeable German populations that remained under the influence of German culture broadly understood. Besides Germany, therefore,

[28] Kłoczowski, *East Central* Europe, 44–45.
[29] Naumann, *Mitteleuropa.*

Mitteleuropa encompassed large areas to the east of Prussia's borders, into Russia and toward the Black Sea, as well as the former lands of the Habsburg Empire.

The postwar aversion to this term stems from its association with the slogans of Nazi foreign policy and an ideology that justified the annexation of Austria, the occupation of Czechoslovakia, and war against Poland and the USSR. The relationship between the claims of German historians and the war policy of Nazi Germany is a fact also emphasized in Polish historiography.[30] Here, Mitteleuropa signified the German "Drang nach Osten," a space to be conquered and developed so that it could become Lebensraum for the growing German nation. As one element in this triangle of phrases, the term Mitteleuropa is nowadays used less frequently in German historiography and since the 1980s has coexisted with the term Zentral Europa. It now refers rather to the area which I discuss below as "Central Europe."

CENTRAL EUROPE

The term "Central Europe" has been undergoing a renaissance since the early 1980s, a decade that marked the end of the community of communist states and the Cold War division of the world. The authors who use it reject the term "Eastern Europe" and instead refer to that region by juxtaposing Central Europe with Russia and sometimes with the Balkans. The term itself was previously used in Polish and Czech historiography both before and after the Second World War,[31] but it

30 Zientara, *Z zagadnień terminologii*, Ihnatowicz, Mączak, Zientara, *Społeczeństwo polskie od X do XX wieku*, Małowist, "Problems of Growth," and Halecki, *Historia Europy*. This fact is also stressed by Delanty, *Inventing Europe*, Todorova, *Imagining*, and Wolff, *Inventing*.

31 Rutkowski, "La genèse du régime." Halecki, "Europa Środkowa," Jędruszczak, "Europa środkowa," Żarnowski, "Stan i perspektywy," Żarnowski, "W sprawie genezy systemu," Tomaszewski, "Gospodarka krajów Europy," Tomaszewski, "Rewolucja w Europie," Balcerak, *Powstanie państw narodowych*, Balcerak, "Czynniki integrujące i osłabiające." Todorova claims that "'Stredni Evropa' was an expression of Czech political thought; it was Thomas Masaryk's peculiar zone of small nations extending from the North Cape to Cape Matapan," from the Sami people to the Turks, but excluding the Germans and Austrians (Todorova, *Imagining*, 150).

was never as significant back then as it has been since the 1980s. The authors who favored the term "Central Europe" in the 1980s argued that it had nothing to do with the legacy of Mitteleuropa. They emphasized the ideological and semantic difference between these terms.[32]

The term "Central Europe" and the controversy it produced in the 1980s and 1990s did not attract much interest from professional historians. However, its importance for East European discourse is enormous. The advocates of "Central Europe" were writers, intellectuals, and anticommunist dissidents, often in exile, who acted as (cultural) lobbyists for their countries—Poland, Czechoslovakia, Hungary, and, less frequently, Yugoslavia. They opposed the West's tendency to identify their countries with the Soviet Union and, historically, with Russia.[33] I present this debate here first because it used historical arguments, and second, because these arguments in regard to the history of religion, art, and political culture subsequently became, mainly after 1989, not only a part of political discourse but were also taken up by professional historians.[34] The war of words, just as the writers who provoked it had intended, changed the intellectual and political reality.

---

[32] Because it excluded the Balkans and Russia, there was no consensus even among opponents of the concept of "Central Europe" about its relationship to "Mitteleuropa." Delanty, who analyzed the stages of "the creation of Europe," treated the attempts to distinguish Central Europe as a *de facto* continuation of the idea of the German sphere of influence, which was deemed the "European" sphere of influence after 1989. Delanty, *Inventing Europe*. At the same time, the most convincing critic of the term, Maria Todorova, writes: "The Central Europe of the 1980s was by no means a new term but it was a new concept. . . . The debate of the 1980s was a new phenomenon with different motivations and goals." Todorova, *Imagining*, 151–53.

[33] Todorova, *Imagining*, 157.

[34] A classic example here is Szűcs, *Three Historical Regions*. Although he used the term "East-Central Europe," he referred to the historic territories of Poland, Bohemia, and Hungary, similarly to the propagators of the term "Central Europe" in the 1980s. Of the socioeconomic historians discussed here, Wyczański compared these countries according to their cultural and political traditions in the sixteenth century. Only Topolski decided to shift the borders in the 1990s due to cultural factors: Topolski, *Polska w czasach*, and Topolski, *Cywilizacje i kultury*.

The debate began in the mid-1980s with articles by Milan Kundera and Czesław Miłosz, the most famous Central European writers,[35] and "by the end of the 1980s, the arguments for an intrinsic difference between Eastern and Central Europe had already taken shape and was internalized by a considerable number of intellectuals."[36]

Miłosz's "Central Europe" was supposed to be a region which, "despite its many languages and nationalities," had been shaped over the centuries by a common culture. The common heritage of the region's nations was evidenced by cultural signs: the architecture of the cities, the traditions of the universities, the works of poets.[37] Miłosz saw the region as distinct on account of the "particular tone and particular sensibility" characteristic of its literature, which was not to be found anywhere else, "neither in West European nor American nor Russian writing,"[38] and on account of its features, "which distinguished it from its great neighbors to the west and to the east."[39] In the introduction to "About Our Europe" (O naszej Europie), Miłosz defines the region as an area where one speaks, and especially writes, "in Czech or Polish, Hungarian or Estonian, Lithuanian or Serbo-Croat"[40] but then he narrows it down: the special "rules of behavior to which intelligentsia adhered" were created throughout the history of the Czechs, Hungarians, and Poles, and were demonstrated in the resistance to the assimilationist intentions of "Moscow" in 1956, 1968, and in the 1980s.[41] The local literature was marked by "an awareness of history," and "the danger threatening the existence of the national community." "The nations of this part of Europe, even if some of them have enjoyed periods of splendour and prosperity, have long experienced foreign domination. . . . They have been oppressed by their enemies, whether Turks, Austrians, Germans, or Russians."[42]

---

[35] Miłosz, "O naszej Europie," was never published in English. Milan Kundera, "The Tragedy of Central Europe."
[36] Miłosz, "O naszej," 3.
[37] Ibid.
[38] Ibid., 3.
[39] Ibid., 5.
[40] Ibid., 3.
[41] Ibid., 10.
[42] Ibid., 4.

Another historically important feature of the region was its specific form of nationalism: "My Europe is a domain of fierce nationalisms, turned against external control but also turned against each another."[43] Miłosz's "Central Europe" was not the "hijacked West" as it was for Kundera and for the discourse of postcommunist transition in the 1990s. It was separate from the West, mainly for social and economic reasons. He wrote: "Then again, the countries situated between Germany and Russia were not that Western. . . . Pro-Western snobbery notwithstanding, we, from those predominantly agrarian marches, had more than one reason to quarrel with Western societies dedicated to trade and manufactories."[44] Miłosz's "Central Europe" was therefore a cultural community that was independent of existing Cold War divisions. The cultural criterion of the region's distinctiveness was not completely synonymous with the division between Latin West and Byzantine East, but at the same time it was not "an unfounded grievance on the part of nations proud of their affiliation to Western culture and now rendered Eastern by force."[45] Central Europe—particularly in its narrower definition, one can assume—was clearly different from Russia, and less clearly different from the West. For Miłosz, "in poetry, painting, and drama, Warsaw, Prague, and Budapest are more similar to Paris, Amsterdam, and London than they are to Moscow."[46]

The Polish poet's text was incidental and is in that sense utilitarian. In addition to general opinions such as the one cited above, Miłosz's judgements often relate to the state of cultural research, in which the cultures of the nations of the communist bloc are seen as homogenous and akin to Russian or sometimes Soviet culture. His general opinions appear balanced, and his utilitarian ones do not pretend to be otherwise. "Central Europe" is thus seen as a specific historical entity, neither Russian nor Western, and the dramatic need to distinguish it from Russia is a need intertwined with the post-Yalta environment.

---

[43] Ibid., 5.
[44] Ibid., 11.
[45] Ibid.,
[46] Ibid.

The same could not be said of Milan Kundera's article, "The Tragedy of Central Europe," published in 1984 in *The New York Review of Books.*[47] In it, Russia is portrayed as an alien civilization to the "Hungarian, Czech or Pole," on the grounds that the latter belong to "the part of Europe rooted in Roman Christianity"[48] and, what is more, those nations "have participated in every period of its history."[49] The division into Catholic West and Orthodox East is a fundamental and absolute division. It is Russia that is the symbol of the cultural Other in Kundera's text. "The countries in Central Europe feel that the change in their destiny that occurred after 1945 is not merely a political catastrophe: it is also an attack on their civilization."[50] Authentic cultural boundaries do not overlap with modern political boundaries—although on the higher moral plane from which Kundera speaks, they should. Since 1945 "the part of Europe [that is] situated geographically in the center [lies] culturally in the West and politically in the East."[51] Even though it is really "a West that, kidnapped, displaced, and brainwashed, nevertheless insists on defending its identity." The nations of "Central Europe" belong to the West, even though "their traditions of statehood have been weaker and less continuous than those of the larger European nations," even though they never managed to be "entirely integrated into the consciousness of Europe,"[52] and even though after the First World War they were only able to create a "region of small, weak states," forgoing the historic opportunity, given to them by the Habsburg Empire, to form a federation.[53] Although the Czechs "loved to brandish naively" in the nineteenth century their "Slavic ideology,"[54] and although "on the map of Europe, baroque Central Europe (characterized by the predominance of the irrational and the dominant position of the visual arts and especially of music) became the opposite pole of classical France (charac-

---

[47] Kundera, "The Tragedy."
[48] Ibid., 33.
[49] Ibid.
[50] Ibid., 34.
[51] Ibid., 33.
[52] Ibid., 34.
[53] Ibid.
[54] Ibid.

terized by the predominance of the rational and the dominant position of literature and philosophy),"[55] these countries nevertheless remained part of the West, albeit "its least known and most fragile part."[56]

In retrospect, it is clear that "the Central European idea of the 1980s was an emancipatory idea"[57] for it undermined the division of Europe imposed by the Yalta Agreements not only in the sphere of Realpolitik but also in the political imagination. The new terminology and new criteria for the region's distinctiveness were a metaphor of protest against the "'Yaltanization' of university programmes in America, manifested in their disregard for the countries that lay between Russia and Germany,"[58] and against an oppressive, authoritarian political system whose existence was guaranteed by the power of Moscow. It is for this reason that Central Europe was always described as the opposite of Russia.[59]

In terms of the region's borders and the criteria by which it was considered distinct, what is most important is that the term itself was entirely positive, in contrast to "Eastern Europe," which was synonymous with everything that was unwanted and bad. Thus, the region became a sphere of attractive linguistic, ethnic, and cultural diversity, and of original products or culture: the baroque and secession, the legacy of late-Habsburg democracy, and the intellectual and artistic atmosphere of Vienna, synonymous with a love of freedom and a stage

---

55 Ibid., 35.

56 Ibid., 34. It is interesting that Kundera "did not allow his essay to be published in" *In Search of Central Europe*, but it continued to be a leitmotif of the book. Iver B. Neumann, one of the authors, connected this fact with "the postscript to the Czech version of *A Joke* where he insisted that 'the essay falls into that part of his production which he disowns because it was tailor-made for Western consumption." See Todorova, *Imagining*, 145.

57 Todorova, *Imagining*, 147.

58 Miłosz, "O naszej," 3.

59 In the 1980s, due to the political geography of the region, especially in "Central Europe," many works were published both by East European émigrés and in *samizdat* editions: *Cross Currents*, *East European Reporter*, *Eastern European Politics and Society*, *Daedalus*, *Cadmos*, *The New York Review of Books*, *Svedečtvi*, *La Nouvelle Alternative*, *Nowa Koalicja*, and so on. A representative sample of these works was collected in the 1989 volume "In Search of Central Europe" in Todorova, *Imagining*, 147.

for civil society.[60] One must agree with Todorova that usually this notion "did not move out of the purported cultural parameters."[61]

Analysts of Central European discourse emphasize that the emancipatory attempt in the 1980s to distinguish Czechoslovakia, Hungary, and Poland from Eastern Europe played a strictly political role in the 1990s.[62] According to its "suspicious" critics, it created new divisions and became an ideology that privileged certain countries in the race to the European Union. Larry Wolff, the most measured and cautious of these analysts, wrote in 1994 that "the advocates of Central Europe today are committed to shattering intellectually the oppressive idea of Eastern Europe, to redeeming the Czech Republic and Hungary, maybe Poland, even perhaps Slovenia. Yet the rubric of Eastern Europe may still be invoked to perpetuate the exclusion of the rest [of the countries outside Central Europe], to preserve the distinction that nourishes our own [West European] identity."[63]

EAST CENTRAL EUROPE

This term, according to Kłoczowski, was first used in the name of the Hungarian historical society *Archivum Europae Centro-Orientalis* in 1935. In Polish historiography, its main proponent was Oskar Halecki. As an émigré in America, he continued to work as a historian and assumed the role of lobbyist for the region, which from 1943 he termed East Central Europe. His speeches and publications, as well as the terminology he proposed therein, aimed to combine the history of Europe's borders and divisions with current geopolitical solutions. Just as all other terms relating to the region's historical geography, this one was political too. Halecki, "in the dramatic circumstances of the war years, voiced his views on the fate of the small countries situated between Germany and Russia, combining strictly historical analysis

[60] Neumann, "Russia as Central Europe's Constituting Other," Schopflin and Wood, *In Search of Central Europe*, Feher, "On Making Central Europe."

[61] Todorova, *Imagining*, 148.

[62] Neumann, "European Identity, EU Expansion," Neumann, "Forgetting the Central Europe," Todorova, *Imagining*, Delanty, *Inventing Europe*.

[63] Wolff, *Inventing*, 15.

with a vision of the future of this area."[64] In 1950 he published *The Limits and Divisions of European History*, in which he set out in full his political and historical geography of Europe.[65]

Halecki's book was extremely important for the course of the East European debate, although the author seldom referred to socioeconomic history. Similarly to writers who advocated "Central Europe," the anticommunist school of Halecki and Kłoczowski used religious, ideological, and geopolitical criteria to win the discursive argument. Indeed, "East Central Europe," along with "Central and Eastern Europe," have become the principal ways of naming the region since 1989. These are the terms one uses when searching for information in library catalogs and via Internet search engines. It is thanks to the success of the discourse established by Halecki and Kłoczowski that the term "Eastern Europe," used by the protagonists of my book, is now considered passé.

The Limits and Divisions of European History is important here also because it "brings to a close the debate conducted in the 1920s and 1930s among Polish, Czech, and Hungarian historians, and their colleagues from other countries in the region, around such notions as Eastern Europe, Slavic Europe, Central Europe, and Central and Eastern Europe."[66] The protagonists of my book, even if they did not refer to Halecki (which would have been forbidden by the censors) were aware of that discourse and were aware that scholars of the older generation who had remained in Poland after the war had participated in it. First and foremost among these was Handelsman, "the finest of his generation" as Małowist[67] and Tymieniecki described him. Finally, Halecki's book is the most systematic geographical and historical analysis in Polish historiography to date.

Halecki's historical geography, although much more professional than Miłosz's or Kundera's, also had a specific political and symbolic

---

64 Halecki, "East Central Europe in Postwar Organization," Halecki, "The Historical Role of Central-Eastern Europe."

65 Halecki, *The Limits and Divisions*.

66 Kłoczowski, "Wstęp," *Historia Europy*, 7–8.

67 Małowist, "Marian Małowist o historii," 45.

objective.[68] The term "East Central Europe" was meant to convey the presence of historical links with two modern powers—Germany in the center and west of Europe and Russia in the east—and at the same time emphasize separateness from them. Halecki's articles written during the Second World War encouraged the Western allies to defend the borderlands of Western civilization, while *The Limits and Divisions of European History* tackled the post-Yalta order and the Nazi imperialism that preceded it. Similarly to the discourse of Central European writers, Halecki's proposals during the Cold War were addressed to Western audiences and sought to undermine the image of communist bloc countries (Eastern Europe) as an eternal and natural sphere of Russian influence. However, unlike in the 1980s, Halecki's terminological enemy was not only "Eastern Europe" but also "Central Europe," which treated the countries between Russia and Germany as a sphere of influence of one of these two superpowers. His criticism of thousand-year-old German imperialism was no less trenchant than that of Russian imperialism, which for émigré writers in the period leading up to 1989 was to become the exception.

Halecki applied religious, political, historiographical, and ethnic criteria—in that order of importance. In the first group (religious criteria), most important was the traditional division between Christians and non-Christians, especially Muslims (a distinction now only used by Christian thinkers). The division between Catholic and Orthodox believers was always present in Halecki's analysis, though it was supposedly the absence of Protestantism, or its marginal role, that determined the cohesiveness of East Central Europe. Unlike Kundera or Samuel P. Huntington, Halecki, an expert on Christian history and doctrine, said that "from the point of view of religious doctrine and even of ecclesiastical organization, the differences between Protestantism and both Catholicism and Orthodoxy are much greater than those which separate the two latter."[69] Although inhabited by both

68 Halecki was aware of the fluidity of cultural and political divisions and gave them primacy over conventional ethnic divisions. A unique example of such a dynamic approach was the differentiation between the "old" Kievan Rus' and the "new" Grand Duchy of Moscow.

69 Halecki, *The Limits and Divisions*, 106.

Catholic and Orthodox believers, East Central Europe was the smallest distinct region and was not divided along religious lines.

Among the political factors behind the formation of divisions in Europe, Halecki attached greatest importance to the international political strength and size of political organisms, and in the age of nations—to the nationalist criterion in Gellner's sense, that is, whether a nation did or did not possess a state.[70] Halecki's East Central Europe would have been an area of small states and nations without nation-states.[71]

The historiographical criterion was also very important to Halecki's concept of East Central Europe. European nations were divided into those that had a permanent position in world historiography and those that had been neglected by it. "All the other [except the Byzantine Empire, which "is duly considered in general historiography"] countries of that region are usually treated on the margin either of Western European history . . . or of Russian history."[72]

The ethnic criterion was revealed in Halecki's use of such terms as "Slavs," "Slavic element," and "Slavic character," and less frequently, the "Roman" or "Germanic" part of Europe. Referring to the chronicle of Jan Długosz,[73] Halecki claimed that "there was, as early as in the Middle Ages, a Slavic solidarity, either cultural through the community of the *nobile linguagium Slavonicum*, or political, in reaction to a common danger from the Germans and their empire. . . . Likewise threatened were the non-Slavic peoples . . . —the Hungarians, Lithuanians, Latvians, and Estonians—peoples whose history, like the history of the Orthodox Rumanians, is practically inseparable from Slavic history."[74] In an earlier work, Halecki determinedly tried to answer the question why East Central Europe, dominated numerically by the Slavic population and countries, had never been able to create a powerful pan-Slavic political unit.[75]

---

70 Gellner, *Nations.*

71 Halecki, *The Limits and Divisions*, 164.

72 Ibid., 118–19.

73 Jan Długosz (1415–1480) is considered to be the first Polish historian and the founding father of Polish historiography.

74 Halecki, *The Limits and Divisions*, 118.

75 Halecki, *The Historical Role*, 10.

His final definition of the region was as follows: "All these nations east of Germany, nations which in spite of their Catholicism and Western culture never receive sufficient attention in any separate treatment of Western European history, constitute together with their Orthodox neighbors, as far as these remained in the European community, the new, northern part of Eastern Europe, which in the European Age [which followed the Mediterranean Age in the Middle Ages, and due to the adoption of Christianity] appeared beside old southeastern Europe. "Eastern Europe would, therefore, be the region between the Holy Roman Empire, or the Teutonic and Roman nations, on the one hand, and Euroasian Russia, i.e., those Eastern Slavs who found themselves in certain periods of history outside the European community, on the other hand."[76]

From the 1970s, a group centered on Peter Sugar and Donald Treadgold at the University of Washington in Seattle also attempted to popularize the history of East Central Europe. The Polish émigré historian Piotr Wandycz collaborated with the group, as did Małowist's former students, Antoni Mączak and Henryk Samsonowicz, in the second half of the 1980s. Like Halecki, the editors "have taken as the limits of East Central Europe the territory between the German–Italian linguistic frontier and the political border of Russia, i.e. the USSR."[77] Within this area they distinguished two regions: north and south of the Danube and Sava, thus emphasizing, like other scholars, the importance of the internal historical border between the Ottoman and Habsburg Empires and between Catholicism and Orthodoxy. *The Price of Freedom: A History of East Central Europe from the Middle Ages to the Present* by Wandycz, and *East Central Europe in Transition: XIV–XVII Century* edited by Mączak, Samsonowicz, and Burke, appeared as part of the series.[78] Both books, in a manner typical of Polish historiography, are limited to presenting the history of three countries, Poland, Hungary, and Czechoslovakia, within their changing historical borders. "Accepting the arguments for applying the term East Central Europe in reference to the territories between the Baltic, Adriatic, Aegean and

[76] Halecki, *The Limits and Divisions*, 118.

[77] Kłoczowski, *East Central Europe*, 34.

[78] Wandycz, *Price of Freedom*, Burke, Mączak, and Samsonowicz, *East-Central Europe in Transition.*

Black Seas, [they] considered the selected area as the proper 'core'"[79] of the region.

The term "East Central Europe" emerged in Polish historiography in the late 1970s.[80] It was primarily used by social and political historians who worked for the Institute of History at the Polish Academy of Sciences (IH PAN). The term was not popular among economic historians, although Małowist and Wyczański sometimes employed it. In the late 1980s, and especially in the 1990s after the collapse of the USSR and the emergence of a new geopolitical order, "East Central Europe" became the mandatory, almost politically correct term to be used in the social sciences. Currently, the term is either a synonym for postcommunist but not post-Soviet countries that were admitted to the European Union, or it refers to a more distant, post-Versailles history. In the latter case it includes the countries between Germany and Italy to the west, Scandinavia to the north, Russia to the east, and Greece to the south. Since the war in Yugoslavia the term has come to mean the countries that are doing best economically, including the Baltic states, the Visegrad Group, and Slovenia and Croatia, in opposition to the Western Balkans (southeastern Europe) on the one hand, and Russia, Belarus, and Ukraine (Eastern Europe) on the other.

In the next section I present the geographical concepts used by the protagonists of this book. The order in which the material is presented is due to the fact that Topolski's geography emerged in relation to what Małowist and Kula had written about the region; Wyczański's, in turn, took shape in opposition to the regional approach adopted by the three other authors.

79 Kłoczowski, *East Central Europe*, 36.

80 Balcerak, "Czynniki integrujące," Balcerak, *Powstanie*, Żarnowski, "Stan i perspektywy," Żarnowski, "W sprawie," Tomaszewski, "Gospodarka krajów," Małowist, "Z problematyki wzrostu," Małowist, "The Problems of Growth."

Narrowly Specialized Development: The East of Europe: Małowist

FROM THE BALTIC ZONE THROUGH WESTERN AFRICA TO THE EAST OF EUROPE

Małowist scrupulously analyzed geography in his texts, although geographical terms such as "Eastern Europe" or "the East of Europe" appeared relatively late in the titles of his works. The notion of Europe's division along the meridian emerged in the 1930s when Małowist was studying maritime issues.[81] It crystallized during the postwar years with the formation of a new, non-bourgeois (as it was then called) interpretation of Polish history along with the study of crafts. It then matured in the 1950s and 1960s during a period of left-wing enthusiasm for decolonization. Małowist touched upon the concept of two, socially different but economically complementary, regions of Europe as early as in the 1950s. He set out the concept in greater detail in 1966,[82] before developing it in 1973 with the publication of *The East and West of Europe in the Thirteenth to Sixteenth Centuries. A Comparison of Socioeconomic Structures* (Wschód a zachód Europy w XIII–XVI wieku. Konfrontacja struktur społeczno-gospodarczych), which followed another decade of research on the role of the European economy in the late Middle Ages and early modern era.

The prototype of Eastern Europe was the Baltic zone. The characteristics it represented in Małowist's works from the late 1950s were identical to the characteristics of Eastern Europe in his works from the mid-1970s.[83] The Baltic countries became synonymous with a region

---

[81] Małowist mostly studied the Baltic region, but he also researched the medieval economic expansion of Italian cities—Genoa's expansion into the Black Sea, and Venice's into the Adriatic. Małowist, "Kaffa—kolonia," Małowist, "Bałtyk i Morze."

[82] Marian Małowist, "The Problem of the Inequality,." See also Batou and Szlajfer, *Western Europe.*

[83] Małowist, "Poland, Russia and Western Trade," Małowist, "The Economic and Social Development," Małowist, "Z zagadnień popytu," Małowist, "O niektórych cechach rozwoju."

whose social and economic development remained influenced by trade with the more developed West.[84]

> The expansion of the West toward the Baltic border regions, which manifested itself in the exploitation of their great agricultural and forest reserves, powerfully stimulated the development of agriculture, of the forest economy, etc. of those regions. . . . In all the Baltic countries which we have discussed here, the economic development of the fifteenth and sixteenth centuries followed a very definite line which showed itself in a one-sided development of agriculture and a feeble dynamic, sometimes even a strong decline, of industrial production. This state of affairs was probably the result of an excessive export of grain, timber, and raw materials, coupled with rather large imports of industrial goods.[85]

Małowist's postwar studies on the history of medieval crafts in Western Europe and Poland were also linked to his concept of the division of Europe into East and West. Referring to Rosa Luxemburg's theory of imperialism (opposed by the communist authorities) and to the theory of class struggle (endorsed by the communist authorities), in an article in 1953 Małowist presented his vision of the half of Europe, in which the East, with the collusion of its own governing elites, was exploited by the West.

> We should always bear in mind the increasing economic pressure exerted at that time by certain countries in Western Europe, which, having embarked upon the road to capitalism, began to exhibit a tendency to transform the lands of Eastern Europe into markets for their industrial products and into a source of food and raw materials. The latter development coincided with aims of the szlachta, who were hostile to the peasantry and town population. In an intense class struggle, the szlachta consigned the peasants to a life of near slavery, halted the development of towns and cities, thus contributing to their decline, and as a result of all

[84] Małowist, "The Economic and Social," 187–88.
[85] Ibid., 187.

> this pushed the country toward complete collapse in all aspects of communal life.[86]

Also key to Małowist's concept of Eastern Europe was his research on Europe in the thirteenth and fourteenth centuries and his participation in the debate on the crisis of feudalism in the West, an important debate in historiography at that time. In 1965 he wrote:

> The flourishing of trade and the influx of merchant capital to Eastern Europe (with the exception of Bohemia) persisted and intensified at a time when the West was experiencing a great economic crisis. . . . It should be noted that although German and Italian investment was an important driver of growth in many branches of manufacturing in Eastern Europe, it was accompanied by a massive influx of craft products and by the export of raw materials, which in time became very dangerous for local crafts, and hence for the economic base of many cities in Eastern Europe.[87]

At this stage of his research, Eastern Europe covered an area more extensive than the Baltic zone. Małowist also attributed the origin of the region's shared characteristics to a more distant past: the thirteenth to fourteenth as opposed to the fifteenth to seventeenth centuries.

To the Baltic zone he added those areas that had experienced the earliest (twelfth to thirteenth century) and "most rapid development . . . Bohemia, Silesia, the Carpathian countries, Małopolska, and in a broader sense and a little later, despite the Tartar invasions, also western and southeastern Rus' or Ruthenia,"[88] as well as the area

86 Małowist, "Rzemiosło polskie epoki Odrodzenia," 32.

87 Małowist, "Uwagi o roli."

88 Both Rus' and Ruthenia refer to the territory of the medieval Kievan state, located in today's Ukraine and Belarus, with its capital city in Kiev. As Halecki claims in *The Limits and Divisions*, the distinction between Rus'/Ruthenia and Russia is not reflected in any Western language, it is, however, cherished in the Polish historiography. Although the Kievan Rus' was Slavic and Christian Orthodox, it was not interested in Asian expansion and was not influenced by the Mongols and Tartars in the way that Muscovy later was. Halecki, *The Limits and Divisions*, 88–98.

"extending through central Poland, far to the east and north east."[89] As in previous articles, he consistently emphasized the separateness of the Russian lands.[90]

In another article published in 1966, in which Małowist argued that from the fifteenth century "Eastern Europe became for a long time a region complementary to the expanding West,"[91] the region remained within the same borders. However, in seeking to uncover the genealogy of backwardness, Małowist retreated to the tenth and eleventh centuries, paying particular attention to the Slavic dimension of Eastern Europe. "There was one institution among the Slavs of great interest which seems to me to prove that my supposition about the low level of productivity is correct. The embryonic states in Poland and Bohemia organized villages of service in which the population was compelled to do special and definite services."[92] This points to the subsistence and non-market character of the economy at a time when development in the West was already more advanced.

The structure of trade with the West remained the main criterion for distinguishing the region, although in addition to agricultural and forestry products exported from the Baltic zone there was also livestock and precious metals exported from the Carpathians. Another important criterion was the organization of trade and production by German colonists. Małowist also placed more emphasis on the importance of Western law in parts of Eastern Europe. "This law, imitated in Poland and Bohemia from the norms used in Germany, was here described as the privileges of German law"[93] and had an enormous influence on the development of those two countries as well as Hungary and Transylvania.

Małowist's detailed conceptualization of the "East of Europe" also took place within the context of research on Western Europe's colonial and overseas expansion and its extraordinary economic growth, unprecedented in world history. The mature version of Małowist's model of the division of Europe, in which the East was seen as the earliest and nearest economic colony of Western Europe, was influenced by the

89 Małowist, "Uwagi o roli," 221.
90 Ibid., 229–30.
91 Małowist, "The Problem," 15–28.
92 Ibid., 16.
93 Ibid., 19.

view, popular among left-wing intellectuals of the day, that colonialism had impacted negatively on the development of colonized areas.

Małowist's interest in the overseas expansion of the Iberian countries, and especially the Portuguese in West Africa in the fifteenth and sixteenth centuries, led in 1969 to the publication of *Europe and West Africa in the Age of Early Colonial Expansion* (Europa a Afryka Zachodnia w dobie wczesnej ekspansji kolonialnej).[94] It was here that Małowist found the economic and political key to describing the triangular relationship between the Iberian countries, the West, and Eastern Europe. "Portugal is an example of a feudal state which, despite a very weak economic base, began to conquer vast territories. Over time this exacerbated the country's economic and political problems and weakened its already not very cohesive social structures. We find a similar situation, albeit later on, in Castile and in certain East European countries. This contrasts with England, Holland, and even France, where colonial-type overseas expansion began on a large scale only when these countries had acquired considerable economic potential."[95] Here, too, Małowist analyzed the relationships between the structure of Baltic trade, organized during that period mainly by the Hanseatic League, and the West's capacity for organizing overseas expeditions. "We may assume that if no supplies had been forthcoming from Eastern Europe, the expansion of the Portuguese and Spanish fleets would have faced insurmountable difficulties. . . . Also, the supply of grain from the Polish territories to a certain extent ameliorated—over time, increasingly—the difficult situation of food shortages in the Ibe-

[94] Małowist, *Europa a Afryka*, 642. The outcome of this research was a comparative study: Małowist, "Europa Wschodnia i kraje iberyjskiein," Małowist, *Europa i jej ekspansja.*

[95] Małowist, *Europa a Afryka*, 51. On the similarities between the Iberian and East European countries, he wrote: "Did the trade with Africa foster the process of primitive accumulation in Portugal? For sure it increased the resources of the Crown, the nobility, and the townspeople for a longer time, Nevertheless, in Portugal, similarly to Spain and Eastern Europe at that time, another important part of this process hardly occurred—the separation of the people from their property and the means of production. There was thus a lack of labour. The internal markets developed only to a small extent. This is why the history of these countries did not lead them towards capitalism, but rather towards a petrification of feudalism," ibid., 246.

rian Peninsula. Undoubtedly, the overseas expansion of those countries in turn catalysed Polish–Lithuanian forestry and agriculture, although current research does not allow us to establish the magnitude of that impact."[96]

The analogy between early West European economic expansion in Eastern Europe and in Africa also proved significant.

> As previous studies have shown, there is no doubt that early colonial expansion in Africa was not tantamount to conquest and European political domination. Scholars agree that from the fifteenth century until the mid-nineteenth century, colonialism in Africa, with the exception of Angola, had an almost exclusively economic character. It is also assumed that European expansion was based on cooperation with the upper strata of West African society, and that this cooperation was an absolutely necessary condition of European activity in the Dark Continent. There are certain parallels here with Eastern Europe, where, during the same period—as I have often emphasized in previous works—the phenomenon of economic colonization was also present. It strengthened the old social structures and hampered further social and economic development, although of course both Poland and Russia, as well as their neighboring countries in the region, were much more civilizationally advanced than the territories of West Africa.[97]

The years immediately preceding the publication of *The East and West of Europe* introduced the concept of a wider geographical region divided into zones. The article entitled "Mining in Medieval Central and Eastern Europe as an Element of Socioeconomic Structures in the Twelfth to Fifteenth Centuries" (Górnictwo w średniowiecznej Europie Środkowej i Wschodniej jako element struktur społeczno-gospodarczych w XII–XV)[98] also included the Western Balkans (Serbia, Bosnia, and part of Macedonia) in the region. As in the Sudeten-Carpathian zone, in these areas German entrepreneurs orga-

[96] Ibid., 257.
[97] Ibid., 10–11.
[98] Marian Małowist, "Górnictwo w średniowiecznej Europie Środkowej."

nized the mining of coal and precious metals. An article published in the following year, "The Problem of the Economic Growth of East Central Europe" (Z problematyki wzrostu gospodarczego Europy Środkowo-Wschodniej),[99] included within this term the area from the Baltic to the Adriatic and from Saxony to the eastern border of the Grand Duchy of Lithuania, excluding Russia to the east, Prussia and Western Pomerania to the north, and Greece to the south.

Thus, between 1959 and 1973, the borders of "Eastern Europe" gradually expanded in Małowist's works, such that by the end of this period they corresponded to the borders of the Soviet sphere of influence in Europe as established at Yalta. One may assume that the reasons for choosing these regional boundaries were both political and historiographical. Małowist studied an area of Europe that was relatively little-known in Western historiography but which, due to the post-Yalta borders, was treated as a Russian sphere of influence. Lamenting the relative research isolation of historians of Eastern and Western Europe in the modern era, Małowist criticized the latter because they "tended to treat Eastern Europe as a single area without distinguishing sufficiently between the historically very different regions within it."[100]

FROM "INTENSIVE DEVELOPMENT ZONES" IN THE LATE MIDDLE AGES TO THE "EAST OF EUROPE" IN THE SIXTEENTH CENTURY

The fundamental division of Europe between East and West, which Małowist proposed in his 1973 book,[101] exactly followed the political division of the continent established at Yalta, although it concerned the distant past (the late Middle Ages) and referred to economic indicators. The area he analyzed "runs from the Baltic to the Adriatic and Black Seas, occupying a large part of the Balkan Peninsula. To the West it reaches the borders of Germany, and to the east it extends beyond the Urals."[102]

99 Małowist, "Problems of the Growth."
100 Małowist, "Poland, Russia and Western Trade," 26.
101 Małowist, *Wschód a Zachód.*
102 Ibid., 439.

Małowist identified three East European zones of rapid growth in the late Middle Ages. The first of these was the Baltic zone, comprising coastal areas and a hinterland. This zone, which experienced dynamic growth in the thirteenth and fourteenth centuries, encompassed "the southern shores of the North Sea and the entire Baltic Basin. Its axis was land and sea routes linking Bruges with Novgorod and smaller trading centers in northwestern Russia."[103]

The hinterland consisted of "part of eastern Germany, central Poland, Lithuania, and part of Kievan Rus'," which, "in the thirteenth century, experienced relatively weaker economic growth than the areas directly adjacent to the Baltic."[104] From the fifteenth century onward, its development resulted from the efforts of "countries in the Baltic hinterland to subjugate the coastal areas"[105] and thus gain access to the Baltic trade. Another area that underwent intensive development as early as in the fourteenth century was the Sudeten-Carpathian zone, whose "central axis" comprised "the mountains surrounding the Bohemian Basin and, further to the east, the arch of the Carpathian Mountains up to and including the Transylvanian Highlands. To the north of these mountain ranges the area included Silesia, southern Małopolska, and southwestern Rus', while to the south, in addition to Bohemia and Moravia, it included the Pannonian Plain."[106] This zone achieved "better results sooner" in political, cultural, and economic development than the second mining zone and third "intensive development zone"—the Balkan one. The latter comprised "the Balkan peninsula between the Adriatic, Black, and Aegean Seas, including Dalmatia, Bosnia, Serbia, Albania, northern Greece and, further to the east, Macedonia and Bulgaria."[107]

One suspects that Małowist's interest in areas belonging to the communist bloc was a projection of contemporary European divisions onto the history of the transition from the Middle Ages to the early modern era. It would be interesting to ask, therefore, what, according to Małowist, distinguished those areas from the lands directly adjacent

[103] Ibid., 25.
[104] Ibid., 98.
[105] Ibid., 136.
[106] Ibid., 138.
[107] Ibid., 139.

to them. For Germany and the Scandinavian countries to the north, and Greece to the south, did not lie within the area Małowist regarded as the East. Perhaps he doubted their affiliation to the East or saw them as less interesting than the areas behind the Iron Curtain, which had been neglected by historiography. In Małowist's model, two historic areas—Scandinavia and eastern Germany—performed the role of the western fringes of the East. The area occupied by present-day Greece was, in turn, almost entirely ignored. These areas shared certain characteristics with the East of Europe, while in other respects they were different. Identifying these characteristics should enable us to reconstruct the full set of features applicable to the East and its historical process as presented by Małowist.

For Małowist, the German duchies and Scandinavia, both geographically located in the Baltic zone, were usually placed in a Western as opposed to Eastern context. As regards the Germans (rather than "Germany"), the context was primarily their eastward expansion, which brought with it "Western" settlement law, more efficient manufacturing techniques, and trade, primarily Hanseatic trade, that was "dominated by German merchants."[108] At the same time, however, Małowist noted that eastern Germany played a similar role to that of Poland in the Baltic trade. From the fifteenth century onwards, "the local szlachta [in Mecklenburg, Brandenburg, and Western Pomerania] sought to take advantage of the higher demand for agricultural products. This is evidenced by the fact that they sold grain to the Dutch. . . . Already by that time, the szlachta was trying to force its peasants to sell their surplus grain, thereby cutting off the cities from rural producers."[109] For Małowist, the western border of the region proceeded "so to speak" through contemporary eastern Germany, through cities "located, so to speak, on the border between East and West, such as Vienna, Dubrovnik, Kotor, the Dalmatian centers of trade, Wrocław, Zgorzelec, and Leipzig,"[110] as well as Nuremberg.

As with Eastern Europe, Scandinavia was "penetrated" by merchants from the West,[111] and "the salient feature of Scandinavia and

108 Ibid., 125.
109 Ibid., 260.
110 Ibid., 249.
111 Ibid., 25.

the East European countries was the weakness of their towns."[112] Małowist also agreed with the opinion of Norwegian scholars, which sounded very much like his own colonial thesis on the history of Poland: "they hold the view that German economic dominance brought to an end the development of their country's cities, while the constant foreign demand for animal products led the Norwegian peasants to expand this sphere of production at the expense of their already weak agriculture."[113] Sweden, in turn, was an exporter of precious metals, rather like the Carpathian and Balkan zones. It, too, was under the influence of Western know-how: "Mining law standards were modelled on those used in Germany and then adapted to local conditions in Sweden, Poland, Bohemia, Hungary, and later in the Balkans,"[114] while "the export of German copper and iron . . . became an important factor of economic growth [in Sweden under Gustav I]."[115]

As Małowist stressed, Sweden was also an East European political player: "In the late sixteenth and early seventeenth centuries it competed with Poland, and especially with Russia, over Livonia" and "for political advantage in northeastern Europe."[116] However, unlike the countries to the east of Germany, Scandinavia was able to compete with the Hanseatic League in the Baltic; its fourteenth- and fifteenth-century rulers fought the privileges of the Hanseatic cities and waged war against them in the Baltic.[117] This changed the balance of power in the area, weakening the Hanseatic League and its ally, the Teutonic state, in the fifteenth century, while at the same time strengthening Danish and Dutch merchants.[118] From the seventeenth century Sweden followed a completely different development path compared to the East of Europe. Małowist attributed this to the expansion of the Swedish fleet and army, which made the country less similar to Poland and more similar to Russia. He also emphasized that Sweden's political institutions and social structure were different to those of both Poland and Russia.

---

[112] Ibid., 260.
[113] Ibid., 47–48.
[114] Ibid., 148.
[115] Ibid., 286.
[116] Ibid., 295.
[117] Ibid., 60.
[118] Ibid., 87, 90–91.

> Their *dominion Baltici Maris* was remarkably parasitic, yet it accelerated the economic development of Swedish cities, which in the second half of the sixteenth century remained weak; it also allowed the Swedes to maintain a powerful army and to pursue the politics of conquest until the second half of the seventeenth century. It seems to me that it was these circumstances that allowed Gustavus Adolphus and his successors to unite the aristocracy, which had previously been ill-disposed toward the centralizing ambitions of the Crown. The growing state apparatus, which was extremely efficient (particularly its military arm), as well as the administrations of subjugated provinces, created opportunities for the Swedish magnates to enrich themselves and satisfy their political ambitions. They could not achieve this inside the country due to the considerable power of the local peasantry, which had retained its freedom as well as a lot of land and its own representation in parliament (the Riksdag). An important factor behind Sweden's expansion was the development and modernization of its iron and copper industries.[119]

The centralization of power and the military distinguished Sweden in the long run from the smaller and politically weak entities in the region but made it similar to Russia. Yet, it was not only Sweden's military fortunes and political structures that determined its non-East European character. According to Małowist, what proved most important was that the country was characterized by different social structures. The peasantry remained independent from the lords, and central government was able to gain an advantage over the nobility.[120] Mączak argued that what made Sweden's developmental path different to that of other Baltic countries was, besides the mining of metals, its maritime expansion and the active role of the state in international trade, which in the sixteenth and seventeenth centuries was a common feature of Western policy.[121] For Anderson, the quality of Sweden's absolutist structures and the freedom of its peasantry were an argument in favor of regarding Sweden (which, after all, he had referred to as "the

[119] Ibid., 325.
[120] Ibid., 307.
[121] Mączak, *Między Gdańskiem a Sundem*, 165–67.

hammer of the East") as the youngest of the absolutisms in the West of Europe, not in the East.[122]

The position of Greece—situated in the East of Europe yet assigned to the West under the Yalta Agreements—was in Małowist's writings equally surprising. He did not devote much space to it. His analysis never ventured south of Thessaloniki, and thus Greece was for all intents and purposes excluded from the region. This decision was not clearly explained, and the only place where the reasons could be sought was in a subsection entitled "The South Eastern Part of the Peninsula from the Twelfth to the Fourteenth Centuries."[123] The existence at that time of Byzantium and then of the Ottoman Empire in the southern part of the peninsula (which was simultaneously the northwestern corner of both empires) was perhaps the reason why Małowist found it less interesting. The region developed quite intensively over a long period of time, completely apart from the future Western powers. The thirteenth and fourteenth centuries—an age of rapid development in adjacent areas—did not constitute a breakthrough in this part of the peninsula.

I think that Małowist's "East of Europe" is a term that is as much historical and geographical as it is related to the state of postwar historiography and the division of Europe. The declared criteria of belonging to the region were: intensive development, beginning in the twelfth to fourteenth centuries under the influence of Western technology and the export of raw materials to the West; sixteenth-century social structures, characterized by the elimination of local groups that organized trade and sometimes production; and often also serfdom. This structural element proved to be a more important criterion of East Europeanness than the political weakness from the end of the sixteenth century. Indeed, parts of Russia also belonged to the region. However, Małowist was of the opinion that the stability of the region, as his more detailed analysis demonstrated, was also ensured by political and ethnic factors. It is doubtful whether areas that had not been subject to Western settlement law (the territories of present-day Greece, Mace-

122 Anderson, *The Lineages*.
123 Małowist, *Wschód a Zachód*, 213–26.

donia, and Bulgaria) could have been included in Małowist's "East of Europe." Unequivocal membership of the region also required the population to be predominantly non-German.

The notion of Eastern Europe clearly made sense because, and only because, it stood in opposition to the notion of Western Europe, primarily represented by the pioneers of capitalism—the Netherlands and England. Eastern Europe was somewhat similar to the Iberian countries (as regards those countries' territorial expansion) in the sense that although they provided Western Europe with an example of profitable overseas expansion, they remained feudal and backward. Eastern Europe also bore the characteristics of colonial areas such as Africa (when one considers the relationship of those areas to the West).

Małowist's reflections on Europe appeared only in the context of its division into East and West, its uneven development, and the complementarity of socioeconomic and thus political processes, which occurred in different ways and under the intense and unequal conditions of interaction between the two parts of Europe. When it came to the internal affairs of Europe, the distinction between East and West was always present. Clearly, for Małowist, virtually no generalizations could be made of Europe as a whole. When it came to Europe's external relations (colonialism, above all, but also overseas trade), the term "Europe" appeared without an adjective, clearly referring to Western Europe only.

A Polonocentric "Eastern Europe": Kula.

Kula's interests were different to Małowist's. He did not focus on trade routes or trading areas, and geography did not feature prominently. In Kula's early research, the most important geographical terms were the Kingdom of Poland and, less frequently, the Commonwealth in its pre-Partition borders, within which there were areas (not even regions) comprising folwarks or manufactories.[124] In the 1960s and 1970s, national categories became Kula's dominant geographical categories.

[124] Kula's most important research published after 1956 includes: Kula, "Początki układu," Kula, *Kształtowanie się kapitalizmu*, Kula, *Szkice o manufakturach.*

One monographic work produced by his research team was devoted to the structure of "Polish society" and the "society of the Kingdom of Poland."[125] Methodological and theoretical works appeared at that time, and although they aimed to make universal claims, they mainly concerned Poland, for which the backdrop was Western Europe.[126] The examples Kula used to illustrate his claims originated mainly from Europe. Tadeusz Łepkowski, a student and colleague of Kula's, estimated that "at least 75 percent of the sources [Kula] drew upon in his works derived from only three countries (Poland, France, and Italy)."[127] England and Germany also played an important role in his arguments. Western countries served not just as a point of comparison but also as a model against which Polish problems could be judged. That Kula chose these regions was down to his methodology: "The choice of regions which are to be the subject of an analysis in depth should be made in the light of the objective. Furthermore, we maintain that the general tendency to study typical regions is not always correct; first because such regions do not exist, and second, because it is precisely the choice of atypical, extreme regions which often enables us to study the problem more effectively and rapidly."[128]

The geographical contexts into which Kula placed Poland were: Eastern Europe as a wider region of backwardness that shared the same features as Poland; Western Europe, which was the opposite of Eastern Europe; and the Third World—a region characterized by the greatest backwardness.

---

125 Kula, "Zagłębie Dąbrowskie," Kula, *Społeczeństwo*, Kula and Leskiewiczowa *Społeczeństwo polskie*, and Kula and Leskiewiczowa, *Przemiany społeczne.*

126 Kula, *The Problems and Methods*, Kula, *Measures and Men*, Kula, *Historia, zacofanie.* The fact that *An Economic Theory* was essentially an attempt at a model of the Polish economy in the sixteenth to eighteenth centuries was reflected for the first time in 1970 in the subtitle of the French edition, and later, in 1976, in the subtitle of the English edition. At the same time, the Italian and Spanish editions (Mexico 1974, Argentina 1976) kept the original title.

127 Łepkowski, "Wątki 'Trzecioświatowe,'" 197.

128 Kula, *An Economic Theory*, 161.

THE KINGDOM OF POLAND—POLAND—EASTERN EUROPE

The term "Eastern Europe" appeared only once in the title of a work by Kula—an article entitled "Notes on the Industrial Revolution in Eastern Europe" (Uwagi o przewrocie przemysłowym w krajach Europy Wschodniej) published in 1958.[129] It is no accident that this term was used in a work published in English for the first time. The article was for the benefit of foreign readers interested in the region as a whole rather than individual countries. Yet, here too, "Eastern Europe" was used interchangeably with "Poland" or "The Kingdom of Poland." Reading the article one gets the impression that, among Poland's neighbors, only Russia during its period of industrialization was of interest to Kula. At the beginning of the article he wrote: "I basically use material from Polish history. My aim is to show which of the aspects mentioned here that occur in other countries may be considered typical of Eastern Europe as a whole, or for a group of countries within Eastern Europe, and which are specific to Poland."[130]

In the article, the term "Eastern Europe" most frequently denotes the opposite of "Western Europe." "The mechanization of skilled and unskilled work was somewhat different in the East of Europe than in the West. Because unskilled labor was cheap in the East, unskilled work was mechanized very slowly."[131] Often, however, the difference between East and West is based only on the intensity of a given feature, for instance: "The role of the state . . . was not [during the nineteenth-century industrial revolution] at all smaller here. Indeed, it was perhaps even greater than in Western Europe."[132]

The term "Eastern Europe" appeared—often in juxtaposition to Western Europe—only when Kula wanted to make a generalization or present an overview of some aspect of economic history: "As we know, Eastern European countries were characterized by the persis-

---

[129] Kula, "Some Observations." Polish version: "Uwagi o przewrocie przemysłowym." The original Polish version of the article is referred to and translated here unless the differences between the two versions are indicated.

[130] Kula, "Uwagi o przewrocie," 64.

[131] Ibid., 71–72.

[132] Ibid., 67.

tence of the manorial economy,"[133] or "in East European countries, the role of the state in the process of primitive accumulation and industrial transformation was marked by certain specific characteristics."[134] Whenever he was talking about specifics, about source-based data on the economy of Eastern Europe, or when his generalizations needed an example, Kula would use the term "Kingdom of Poland" or "Russia" juxtaposed with "England" or, more rarely, "France." "To simplify: whereas in Western Europe it was the growing needs of light industry that caused the development of heavy industry, in Eastern Europe heavy industry came into being . . . because large landed estates needed to adopt capitalist methods of production. The first machine factories in the Kingdom of Poland produced not weaving machines but agricultural machinery."[135] Or: "An extreme example is Russia. In the eighteenth century, when England's biggest export was textiles, Russia's main industrial export was pig iron."[136]

Poland, in turn, served as an area where longer-lasting and more general processes occurred—processes that were neither as specific as when Kula was referring to the Kingdom of Poland nor as abstract as when he was referring to Eastern Europe. "The gradual . . . transition [from serfdom], dictated by economic necessity, . . . to hired labor on the folwark, combined with the extensive confiscation of peasant land—this time having the distinct character of primitive accumulation—created in Poland, in the first half of the nineteenth century, a sort of division within the country's existing labor force."[137]

The only point of reference for East European industrialization was the industrialization of Western Europe. The rhetorical function of this geographical term was similar to that of "Eastern Europe"; it appeared when Kula was formulating a general rule. In most of his comparisons, however, expressions of a lower, national level of generality were more typical: railways "emerged in the Polish Kingdom during a period when the steel industry was unable to build them—this

[133] Ibid., 65.
[134] Ibid., 67.
[135] Ibid., 68.
[136] Ibid., 67–68.
[137] Ibid., 66.

would have been unthinkable elsewhere, say in England."[138] The last part of the sentence quoted above, and the phrase "in other countries, as for instance in France," were omitted from the Polish version of the article. This, I believe, neatly illustrates Kula's approach in the late 1950s: not only a Eurocentric comparative perspective, which he himself criticized, but also the projection of phenomena characteristic of the most developed countries (England and France) onto the whole of Western Europe.[139] References to "elsewhere" and "other countries," though suggesting a broad comparative perspective, actually only applied to England or France.

Polonocentric Eastern Europe was, for Kula, an example of backwardness. It included "countries that had followed the so-called Prussian development path of capitalism in agriculture."[140] The sole geographical definition of the region, which appeared only in the English version of the article, was "areas situated east of the Elbe river."[141] More interestingly still, Kula did not, contrary to historiographical convention, define this border as one that separated lands with a free peasantry from those characterized by serfdom. The distinguishing feature of this region was, first and foremost, the large-scale and market-oriented character of production on the folwarks, which was unusual for classical feudalism.

"The concentration of a huge proportion of the country's productive forces in the hands of large landowners,"[142] which occurred in the sixteenth century,[143] was not, however, associated with primitive accumulation. These same characteristics were also true of Latin American plantations, established from the sixteenth century onwards. Kula did not mention this similarity, however, until the 1960s. Despite such geographical nonchalance, his proposed interpretation of the history of the region proved very attractive. Kula became renowned as an expert on Eastern European (and not just Polish) backwardness.

---

[138] Ibid., 70, Kula, "Some Observations," 243.

[139] See Chapter 4 of this book.

[140] Kula, "Uwagi o przewrocie," 64.

[141] Kula, "Some Observations," 240.

[142] Kula, "Uwagi o przewrocie," 64–65.

[143] Kula, "Some Observations," 240.

The most important collection of Kula's reflections on Eastern Europe (or, rather, the collection where the term appears most frequently) was a volume of articles from the 1960s published as *History, Backwardness, Development* (Historia, zacofanie, rozwój). The image of the region Kula presented here was not only geographically vague but quite frankly suspect: in a 150-page section entitled "Backwardness and Development," where eight of the nine articles were comparative and one even contained "Eastern Europe" in the title, and where the term "Eastern Europe" or its derivatives appeared on seventeen of the pages, only once did Kula mention a country other than Poland or Russia that conventionally belonged to the region. That country was Romania, which, alongside Russia and the Kingdom of Poland, was an example of an economic colony of the West: "Thus, the colonies were: the Kingdom of Poland when, in the last quarter of the nineteenth century, large-scale industry was created by foreign capital; Russia in the early twentieth century; and Romania in the interwar years."[144]

In effect, therefore, Kula embraced a Polonocentric image of Eastern Europe, as did subsequently the world-renowned historian Fernand Braudel. Responsibility for this image probably lies with the assumption that knowledge of the realities of Poland and Russia—as "extreme regions"—was enough to pass judgement on the whole of Eastern Europe. There is a small chance that Kula really did equate the borders of "Eastern Europe" with the borders of Poland and Russia. But if one accepts this possibility, then the following question also needs to be answered: the borders from which period in history? The nineteenth-century borders, which were the main focus of Kula's analysis? Probably not, because although Kula's research area was the Kingdom of Poland, his generalizations referred to "Poland," a country that did not exist in the nineteenth century. Another argument against this interpretation is provided by one of Kula's favorite examples of the center and the periphery: Vienna and the countryside around Kraków. The former did not belong to Eastern Europe, but the latter certainly did,[145] even though they lay outside the borders of

144 Kula, "Przywilej społeczny a postęp gospodarczy," 44.

145 Kula, "Sektory i regiony zacofane," 116, and Kula, "Przewrót przemysłowy," 155.

the Kingdom of Poland at that time. Perhaps, then, Eastern Europe was defined by the pre-Partition borders of Poland and Russia? But in that case, the dearth of examples from the Wielkopolska region is somewhat problematic.

EASTERN EUROPE AND OTHER REGIONS: LATIN AMERICA AND WESTERN EUROPE

In Kula's later works, Eastern Europe appeared in a more sophisticated form. Its characteristics had resulted from the course and consequences of the capitalist industrial revolution. Kula lent these characteristics a more extensive comparative perspective that was at once historical and geographical. The outcome of this comparative research was that he included the region in the category of "unsuccessful industrializations" along with Southern Europe and Latin America. The latter were, in the post-Second World War era, like the countries of Eastern Europe used to be before the war—"agricultural countries with a strong feudal legacy, large and formidable landed estates, and with massive overpopulation of the countryside."[146] According to Kula, Eastern Europe of the 1960s would have looked like the impoverished countries of Spain, Portugal, or Greece. It would have been characterized by the "insularity and extraterritoriality of major centers of industry owned by foreign capital"[147] as well as by great social, technological, and cultural inequality. "If anyone doubts that this structure had lasting qualities, let him look at today's Portugal, Spain, Greece, or the countries of Latin America."[148]

The earlier fate of Eastern Europe during the period of economic and colonial expansion by Holland and England was similar to the fate of the European colonies in the Americas. "If, despite low labor productivity and the considerable cost of maritime transportation over long distances, the products made by these 'colonies' (Eastern Europe on the one hand, the American colonies on the other) were successful and could be profitably sold on Anglo-Dutch markets, then this could only have happened thanks to the presence of a cheaper workforce.

[146] Kula, "Przewrót przemysłowy," 147.
[147] Ibid., 148.
[148] Ibid., 149.

This workforce was cheaper because it was unfree—in Europe characterized by serfdom, and in America by slavery."[149] Kula compared East European grain with American cotton. Given modest labor productivity, the low price of grain and cotton for West European consumers and the healthy profits made by local landowners were the result of the same system of exploitation—in America, the exploitation of "slaves, who later became free men in name only," and in Eastern Europe the exploitation of "serfs, later peasants, whose mobility was restricted by the possession of small, sometimes tiny farmsteads."[150]

The analogy between Eastern Europe and the European colonies in the Americas operates on many levels: raw materials (grain, cotton) are supplied to Western Europe, using an unfree and later "incapacitated" workforce (serfs, African slaves) on large private farms (folwarks, plantations), for the benefit of "local landowners" (the szlachta, plantation owners of European origin). This same juxtaposition is also found in another fragment. Although it is lengthy, I quote it here in full because it reveals Kula's unabashed Polonocentrism in his view of the region and his general geographical nonchalance, also with regard to "the West." Kula starts by reflecting on Poland's position in the international division of labor and identifies the mechanisms that governed the relationship between the Polish and Western grain markets. He then exemplifies "the West" with "England or Holland," and his conclusion, although based on an interpretation of Polish experience, concerns the position of Eastern Europe as a whole in the international division of labor.

> This issue is important because of Poland's position and role in the international division of labor. Soon after Poland took on the role of the "breadbasket of nations," yields began to stabilize. . . . Poland was the breadbasket of nations because any quantity of Polish grain could always be profitably sold in England or Holland. But it could be profitably sold there not because land and labor productivity in Poland were high, but precisely because they were low. It was a pre-colonial situation. The first coun-

[149] Kula, "Zacofanie gospodarcze," 187–88.
[150] Ibid., 192.

> tries to embrace capitalism set up sugar and cotton plantations overseas and found grain "plantations" for themselves in Eastern Europe.[151]

Kula contrasts Eastern Europe, sometimes in the company of other backward regions, with Western Europe. This juxtaposition is present in every moment of history he evokes. On the role of Eastern Europe in the sixteenth to eighteenth centuries, he writes: "Thus, the eccentrically located raw materials bases (Eastern Europe, America) could perform their role only to the extent that precapitalist forms of exploitation persisted there. Cheaply . . . sourced products could be expensively sold in Western Europe, which strengthened the economic, and in the longer term also the political power of the ruling classes in those countries."[152] In regard to a later period of history—the beginnings of capitalism outside Western Europe—the opposition between Eastern and Western Europe is used interchangeably with another opposition: the developed, advanced, industrialized nations on the one hand, and the underdeveloped, backward, and not yet industrialized nations on the other. To both sides of this equation non-European countries are added: Japan and the white dominions, where capitalist industrialization was a success, and the countries of the Third World, where it failed.[153]

Geographical nonchalance is the weakest aspect of Kula's vision of Eastern Europe. His writings contain an unjustified historical–geographical transition. Starting with Poland, the "breadbasket of Europe," Kula moves on to Eastern Europe—the exploited raw materials base of Western Europe. The important elements in this relationship are serfdom in Poland and Eastern Europe on the one hand, and developing capitalism in Western Europe on the other. At the time of attempted industrialization, Eastern Europe of the eighteenth and nineteenth centuries, illustrated with examples from the Kingdom of Poland and Russia, acquires the status of a group of countries marked by growing backwardness, a repository of "the coexistence of

151 Kula, "Czynniki gospodarcze," 164–65.
152 Kula, "Zacofanie gospodarcze," 188.
153 Kula, "Przewrót przemysłowy."

asynchronisms,"[154] that is, paradoxes. Thus, when these same terms appear in relation to the second half of the nineteenth century and into the twentieth century, the opposing pairs change. Now, not just Poland but also Third World countries are juxtaposed not only with Western Europe but also with other non-European developed countries (Japan, USA, Australia, New Zealand).

In this way Kula's geographically indeterminate Eastern Europe, which possessed the characteristics of Poland, became the prototype of a backward region. This feat was bolstered by the conviction that, since the model developed for the Polish economy was applicable to at least some non-East European backward countries (and the response to Kula's works suggested that this was indeed the case), it was all the more applicable to the whole of Eastern Europe.[155] In the 1970s, Braudel adopted Kula's idea of Eastern Europe, not Poland or the Baltic zone, as the grain plantation of the flourishing West. This idea was strengthened by the fact that it was similar to Wallerstein's vision,[156] and thanks to Braudel and Kula it became widespread in the social sciences.

Consequently, not only do we get a Polonocentric image of Eastern Europe but also an image—popular in historiography—of nineteenth and twentieth-century Poland dominated by the history of the largest Partition: the Russian one. Kula's comparative perspective, especially in its 1950s version, appears similar to the way in which Łepkowski described it, with some regret. Kula's analysis was fundamentally Eurocentric. "When it comes to the history of the last few centuries, among the colonial (later Third World) countries, Kula most frequently referred to India (following Marx and numerous British economic historians and economists) and to Africa, especially Black Africa (Ghana, West Africa in general, and Ethiopia). A great number of these references are simply a formal means of extending the analysis beyond Europe."[157]

---

[154] Kula, *Historia, zacofanie*, 120–21.

[155] Kula's works, especially *An Economic Theory*, became popular in Italy and South American countries. Kochanowicz, "Teoria ekonomiczna w oczach krytyków."

[156] Braudel, *Civilization and Capitalism*, Wallerstein, *The Modern World System I.*

[157] Łepkowski, "Wątki 'Trzecioświatowe'," 198–99.

From the Europe of Serfdom East of the Elbe to the Central Europe of the Jagiellons and Catholicism. Topolski.

One of Topolski's main areas of interest was the manorial economy and by extension the East European economy.[158] Besides the history of Poland and its most favored region (Wielkopolska for Topolski, the Kingdom of Poland for Kula), this was the only area where Topolski, like Kula, employed geographical categories. Yet, in his works, Topolski defined clearer borders and criteria for distinguishing regions. Similarly to Małowist, until the 1980s Topolski treated East Central Europe as a subregion of the bigger entity that was Eastern Europe.[159] In the 1990s, however, probably due to the change in geopolitical discourse, Topolski situated Poland within East Central Europe, and even within Central as opposed to Eastern Europe.[160] To the socioeconomic criteria he added civilizational criteria as understood by Samuel Huntington.

EAST OF THE ELBE

An early version of the concept of "Europe east of the Elbe" was presented most fully in Topolski's book, *The Birth of Capitalism* (Narodziny kapitalizmu), and its various summaries in English.[161]

Like Kula and Małowist, Topolski believed that the dualism of European development and the emergence of the socially and economically distinct region of Eastern Europe did not occur until capitalism had begun to form in the West. Unlike Kula and Małowist, however, Topolski felt that there was no significant relationship between the two economic systems—serfdom in the East and protocapitalism in the

[158] Zalejko and Zybertowicz, "Gospodarcza aktywność szlachty," 69.

[159] Topolski, *Narodziny kapitalizmu*, Topolski, "Causes of Dualism," Topolski, "The Manorial-Serf Economy," Topolski, *Gospodarka polska,* Topolski, "Modele teoretyczne."

[160] Topolski, *Polska w czasach nowożytnych,* Topolski, *Cywilizacje i kultury.*

[161] Topolski, "Causes of Dualism" and "The Manorial-Serf Economy." The theory was presented several times without significant changes, in e.g., Topolski, *Gospodarka polska.*

West. The starting point for Topolski's research was Małowist's colonial thesis, which for the time being concerned trade in the Baltic zone, particularly the Polish grain trade,[162] and Kula's *An Economic Theory* (Teoria ekonomiczna). Topolski rejected the former and gave credit to the latter without fully accepting it. As regards Topolski's economic geography—which is of interest to me here—also important were his studies on Jan Rutkowski's theory of the manorial economy based on the second serfdom.[163]

In contrast to Kula, and especially Małowist, but in agreement with Rutkowski, Topolski attributed the reasons for the different developmental paths of East and West to the different social structure and natural conditions in the two parts of the continent, rather than the relationship between those parts. "Topolski did not study the economic situation of many European countries in order to reconstruct the development dynamics of the continent as a whole. Instead, using a comparative approach, he wanted to gain a better understanding of the mechanisms of change in particular countries."[164]

The basic geographical distinction that Topolski used, beginning with *The Birth of Capitalism* until the end of the 1970s, was—in the context of sixteenth-century Europe—"Western Europe" and "countries east of the Elbe." The differences, though originating from earlier history were, according to Topolski, insignificant inasmuch as until the sixteenth century Europe could be treated as a single region. Despite "differences in the degree of urbanization, there were clear similarities in the economic development of most of Europe prior to the emergence, in the sixteenth century, of the aforementioned dualism in the agrarian system of countries conventionally labelled as being to the west or to the east of the Elbe. This applies to Bohemia, Hungary, Poland, Russia, as well as to other territories whose economic life in

[162] Małowist, "Poland, Russia and Western Trade," Małowist, "The Economic and Social Development," Małowist, "Z zagadnień."

[163] Topolski's works preceding the 1965 publication concentrated mostly on the folwark economy and class relations in the Archdiocese of Gniezno. His other works from this period discussed the methodology of Marxist historiography and the role of human intentional action in social change and development. See also Chapter 1 of this book.

[164] Zalejko, "Gospodarcza aktywność szlachty," 76.

the late Middle Ages we know something about."[165] The Elbe ostensibly marked the border between areas in which, from the sixteenth century onwards, the economic system was mainly characterized by the second serfdom and those in which it was not. The introduction of serfdom was only possible due to a law that already existed east of the Elbe, according to which peasants, in contrast to their Western counterparts, did not have the status of completely free people. However, in Topolski's view, it was not until the sixteenth century that this difference became fundamental to further development. An important factor in the creation of folwarks based on serf labor was the lower population density in the East and the vast tracts of unused land. In contrast to Rutkowski, whose model encompassed areas to the west of Russia and to the north of Turkey, Topolski—without fundamentally changing the criteria—included Russia in his model, referring to the region as Central and Eastern Europe.

In Topolski's model, the seventeenth century was a period when Europe's geography of development diverged further still. Areas of growth and stagnation did not form coherent geographical regions. The scene of dynamic development was the Netherlands, and increasingly during the seventeenth century also England, while the regions of stagnation and regression "must include primarily Spain, Portugal, Italy, Poland, and probably Turkey."[166] The only geographically cohesive area was a third, intermediate zone. It included France, Scandinavia, and the countries of Central Europe: Germany, Bohemia, Moravia, Slovakia, Austria, Hungary,[167] and Russia.

Following Rutkowski, the southern border of the region (although Topolski did not pay much attention to it) ran along the fifteenth- and sixteenth-century borders of the Ottoman Empire in Europe. According to this view, which in Polish historiography was also shared by Leonid Żytkowicz, the Byzantine Empire, and then the Ottoman Empire, were not characterized by the structures of feudalism, with its main division

[165] Topolski, *Narodziny kapitalizmu*, 40.

[166] Topolski, *Narodziny kapitalizmu*, 173.

[167] The term "Central Europe" appears in *Narodziny kapitalizmu* in relation to these countries on pages 165 and 170.

into nobility and peasantry. For this reason the territory of the Balkans had to be excluded from studies on the manorial economy.[168]

Thus, in Topolski's work of 1965, Central and Eastern Europe was a product of the fifteenth and sixteenth centuries, a consequence of the refeudalization of societies east of the Elbe. According to Rutkowski and Topolski, this process was made possible by the coexistence of "a strong nobility, which enabled serfdom to intensify, as well as favorable conditions for the export of grain"[169] from Poland or other agricultural and farm products (wine, fish, oxen) from neighboring countries. Sixteenth-century Central and Eastern Europe was undoubtedly meant to comprise Poland, Russia, Bohemia, and Hungary. The status of neighboring countries was not as evident. When Topolski referred to a non-West European section of the nobility with declining incomes, ostensibly "the Polish, German, Russian, Czech, Hungarian, and Moldavian nobility, etc.," he shifted the border slightly to the west, toward the east German territories, and slightly to the southeast, toward the future Romania.

For Topolski, however, the division of Europe into territories East and West of the Elbe was purely conventional. This line of division intersected with lines that split Europe into zones with different rates of capitalist accumulation and economic growth.

> Overall, one can say that the increased economic activity of the szlachta in the sixteenth century should be examined in various ways. It manifested itself in a different manner in different countries and had different economic consequences, not just in the economic life of those countries. In those places where it did not lead to greater capitalist accumulation . . . the development of capitalism also encountered difficulties and became delayed. This applies, in particular, to the countries of East Central Europe,

---

168 Rutkowki, "La genèse du régime," 211–17. Rutkowski himself never published extensively. His works were collected and edited by Jerzy Topolski: Rutkowski, *Wokół teorii*, Rutkowski, *Wieś europejska*. Likewise, Żytkowicz stressed the distinct character of the Ottoman agricultural systems. Zytkowicz, "W sprawie badań porównawczych," Zytkowicz, "Directions of Agrarian Development."

169 Topolski, *Gospodarka polska*, 74.

where the manorial-serf economy took hold and where refeudalization occurred as a result the new szlachta suddenly entering economic life. The emergence of capitalism was postponed until the nineteenth century even.[170]

FROM EASTERN EUROPE TO CENTRAL EUROPE

The best example of the development of Topolski's ideas in the later period is his collection of essays entitled *Truth and Model in Historiography* (Prawda i model w historiografii) published in 1982. This later version of his model is a response to the challenges presented by Western as well as national historiography. In the 1980s, Topolski engaged in polemics with Dobb, Anderson, Brenner, and Wallerstein first and foremost.[171] He also changed the terminology he used. I believe that it was precisely the influence of Western historiography that prompted Topolski to refer to the region consistently as Eastern Europe. The period of the region's formation was also substantially extended. Topolski's analysis went as far back as the tenth century, when feudal structures began to take shape in the East, later than they did in the West. The 1990s brought for Topolski a major shift in the way he perceived the main criteria of historical geography. His model of the region to which Poland belonged changed.[172] First, in his 1994 book, Europe east of the Elbe was once again referred to as East Central Europe or Central and Eastern Europe and was considered an economically backward region. The basic framework explaining the dualism of European development remained the same—its origins lay in the refeudalization of the East during the sixteenth century. However, even more forcefully than in *Truth and Model in Historiography*, Topolski stressed the earlier circumstances that had given rise to differences in the continent. "To explain the differences in the development of Europe west and east of the Elbe, one has to look to processes, still present in the Middle Ages, that changed the distribution of national

[170] Topolski, *Narodziny kapitalizmu*, 92.

[171] Anderson, *The Lineages*, R. Brenner, "Agrarian Class Structure," Dobb, *Studies in the Development of Capitalism*, Wallerstein, *The Modern World System.*

[172] Topolski, *Polska w czasach nowożytnych,* Topolski, *Cywilizacje i kultury.*

income and hence the position of various social groups and classes."[173] Besides the lower degree of urbanization and the legal dependence of peasants on their masters prior to the sixteenth century, Topolski also pointed to the lower level of commoditization and monetarization of the economy east of the Elbe.[174]

A new geographical element in Topolski's book of 1994 was Central Europe, which appeared in the title. It was a subregion of the lands east of the Elbe, of which the Polish–Lithuanian Commonwealth was part. Topolski distinguished this subregion according to political and to some extent cultural criteria, but not economic criteria. It was a sixteenth-century product of the dynastic policies of the Jagiellons and later the Habsburgs. Wherever the term "Central Europe" was used in isolation, that is, without "and Eastern," the context was the same. Here are some examples: "In the early sixteenth century, the Jagiellonian dynasty prevailed in Central Europe";[175] "the progress of the Jagiellons in Central Europe";[176] Zygmunt I the Old "already understood . . . that the area of Habsburg expansion would increasingly be Central Europe, which would require the support of the Jagiellons";[177] the Battle of Mohács erased "the possibility of the Jagiellonian dynasty's continued existence in Central Europe."[178]

Poland, Bohemia, and Hungary in their historic sixteenth-century borders were mentioned together, both as part of an implicit or explicit group and in other, economic contexts. "In East Central Europe Bohemia and Moravia were more urbanized than Poland, and even more so than the Hungarian lands, where, after the annexation of part of the country by Turkey (in 1526) the cities began to weaken"[179] and "In respect of this trade [of cattle] the Polish lands were part of a larger cattle-exporting region, which included Hungary . . . and Bohemia."[180] But, unlike in 1982, the commercial ties between

[173] Topolski, *Polska w czasach nowożytnych*, 20.
[174] Topolski, 21–23.
[175] Ibid., 12.
[176] Ibid., 216.
[177] Ibid., 219.
[178] Ibid., 219.
[179] Ibid., 48.
[180] Ibid., 57.

Bohemia, Hungary, and Poland were not, in 1994, sufficient to warrant these countries being regarded as part of a single, named region. Yet they were regarded as such on account of their common political and dynastic traditions. It was only these countries that constituted "Central Europe." The term "Eastern Europe" (without the "Central") was in turn reserved, as it originally had been in 1965, for areas to the east of that part of the Polish–Lithuanian Commonwealth that belonged to the Polish Crown. A typical context for this definition was as follows: from the seventeenth century, "cattle-breeding [developed] in areas of southern Poland, Ukraine, and even more so in the southernmost regions of Eastern Europe."[181]

Topolski presented an even more pronounced shift of emphasis from Eastern Europe to Central Europe in the 1998 book, *Civilizations and Cultures from the Fifth to the Twentieth Centuries* (Cywilizacje i kultury V–XX wiek), one of his final works. His interests also shifted away from economic history toward cultural history and the policies it fostered. In this late interpretation the world was divided not into areas of economic growth but, in the manner of Huntington, into geographically defined civilizational and cultural spaces. Each of these was composed of material and technological (including organizational) living conditions, that is, civilization, as well as culture (mentality, values, beliefs, ideologies, language) and its products (literature, science, art, religion). For European civilization, of greatest importance was "Latin (Roman) Christianity and the emergence of the political map of Europe, which defined the continent's political history for centuries to come."[182] Until the Ottoman conquest, the Orthodox Byzantine Empire and the Muslim world were civilizational and cultural spaces which, although separate from Europe, remained in contact with it.

Similarly to Perry Anderson, for Topolski the most important features of European civilization included social institutions formed through the interaction between Roman heritage, Christianity, and Germanic community structures: the barbarization of cities, the creation of new cities around abbeys, peasant farms as the main social unit and unit of production and, most importantly, feudalism defined

181 Ibid., 23.

182 Topolski, *Cywilizacje i kultury*, 5.

as a system of seigniory. The latter determined the position of every person (from peasant to king) in the complex social hierarchy.

Topolski emphasized that not all the European institutions took root in East Central Europe.

> The system of seigniory and benefices did not develop in East Central Europe. The outcome of granting immunities to the szlachta (and the Church) was a direct transition from a situation in which the ruler . . . regarded the whole territory of the state . . . as his dynastic *patrimonium* to a situation in which the ruler exercised full ownership over his own domains and nothing else. In the absence of vassals obliged to perform military service, the raising of an army involved a mass appeal to the szlachta (rather than to powerful lords who could lead their knights into battle) and the monarch's own troops.[183]

East Central Europe appears as a domain of Catholicism, and it is precisely Roman Christianity that identifies the region culturally with Europe. But, as the above quotation suggests, in civilizational terms East Central Europe does not entirely belong to the same space as post-Roman Western Europe.

Topolski changed the geographical terminology he used in line with his interests and under the influence of trends in world academia. Initially he argued that although Western Europe and Europe east of the Elbe had developed from the sixteenth century according to different social systems (with either a free peasantry or serfdom), this had not predetermined their economic future. What was equally important was the capacity for economic growth, which was relatively independent of social structures. Influenced by world academic discourse, in the 1980s Topolski gave a new name to the area east of the Elbe that encompassed the lands of the seventeenth-century Commonwealth, Russia, eastern Germany, the Habsburg Empire, Transylvania, Moldavia, and Wallachia—Eastern Europe. Back then, too, he had stressed the importance not only of purely economic factors (economic growth) but also of formal and legal factors (political and social organization) which had shaped the region since the tenth century. After 1989 he referred to the combination

[183] Ibid., 95.

of these two features as "civilization." In the 1990s, he characterized the region according to its civilizational and cultural features associated with the dominant religion. East Central Europe was restricted to the Catholic countries, where the introduction of feudal institutions was delayed and where in the sixteenth century serfdom re-emerged. On this interpretation the region became the "younger sister" of Western Europe—culturally identical, but with a less advanced civilization.

From Antiregionalism to Central Europe: Wyczański.

Wyczański's works are atypical for postwar socioeconomic historiography in terms of the geographical categories he uses in relation to the sixteenth-century Polish–Lithuanian Commonwealth.

I call Wyczański's early approach—which lasted until the mid-1980s—"antiregionalism," because the author did not accept the dominant classification into East and West and employed geographical categories (including North and South of Europe) in a purely descriptive manner. His main geographical categories were countries and provinces, and not supranational regions.

The period Wyczański dealt with was marked by a change of perception about the main dividing lines of civilization. The juxtaposition—still dominant at the beginning of the sixteenth century—of the civilized South versus the primitive North had to change during that century on account of the spectacular rise of Amsterdam and its neighboring cities. Aware of the relative nature of such divisions, Wyczański did not quite accept as self-evident the division between East and West that began to emerge in the sixteenth and seventeenth centuries.

POLAND IN THE SIXTEENTH CENTURY: A MIDDLING EUROPEAN COUNTRY, NOT A COUNTRY IN THE MIDDLE OF EUROPE

Wyczański's antiregionalism was more pronounced in his earlier works, which placed the Polish–Lithuanian Commonwealth in the context of other European countries of the time.[184] In his 1973 book, *Poland in*

[184] Wyczański, "Polska na tle Europy," Wyczański, *Polska w Europie.*

Sixteenth-Century Europe (Polska w Europie XVI stulecia), Wyczański presented an antigeopolitical view of history that was much more radical than Małowist's. While the latter believed that explanations that relied on geopolitical arguments absolved the elites of responsibility for the fate of their country, he nevertheless considered regional differences to be an objective product of historical experience, whereas Wyczański seemed to reject the existence of the second relationship altogether. I write "seemed to reject" rather than "rejected" because Wyczański's methodological utterances on the theory of history were, in this work and in others, even more tentative than Małowist's.

Wyczański's Europe did not, at the beginning of the early modern era, possess any robust divisions that could be termed regions. Rather, it was a collection of countries that had similarities based on various phenomena measured by indicators such as the state of education, the prevalence of the arts, urbanization, population density, etc. Wyczański's comparisons revealed that

> Poland in the first half of the sixteenth century belonged in terms of its size to the group of middling European countries, being somewhat overshadowed by its great neighbors to the east, north and south, and even to the west, if we consider the Reich to be a country. . . . The lands of the Polish Crown were similar in size to the territories of Italy, Austria (after 1526) and England of that time, and much smaller than those of France and Spain—the largest and most powerful countries in the west of Europe.[185]

When, after the union with Lithuania in 1569, Poland found itself among the three largest European nations, as the illustration in his book shows, Wyczański did not interpret this to mean that the country belonged to the same group as the Grand Duchy of Moscow, "Turkey in Europe," and Sweden.[186] Instead he emphasized that Poland "found itself among the largest European nations, surpassing in this regard all the *Western* countries of Europe."[187]

---

[185] Wyczański, *Polska w Europie*, 15.
[186] Ibid, 17.
[187] Own emphasis added. Ibid., 18.

When discussing other indicators whose purpose was to establish the position of the Polish–Lithuanian Commonwealth in Europe, Wyczański emphasized the distinctiveness of the Polish Crown lands on the one hand and the new lands of the Grand Duchy of Lithuania on the other. Yet he did not do this for the territories of other empires: Bohemia and Hungary, not to mention Croatia and Slovakia, were not treated independently but simply as a part of Austria. The same was true of countries conquered by the Ottoman Empire. Thus,

> Poland, with its 7.5 million inhabitants or thereabouts, and that's after the union with Lithuania, found itself within the group of medium-sized European countries."[188] "Population density . . . lowers the position of Poland, i.e,. the Crown plus Lithuania, still further. . . . On the other hand, the Crown proper, i.e., without the Lithuanian provinces, had an average population density of approximately 20.6 inhabitants per square kilometer" and "was more similar to the relatively densely populated Western countries.[189]

As regards the level of economic development in the sixteenth century, measured by urbanization, prices, and grain yields, then "Poland, in the sense of the Crown, of course"[190] belonged to the group of countries with an averagely developed economy, along with England, France, Spain, Portugal, and the German Reich, being second only to the Netherlands and Italy. However, "Lithuania's economic level . . . diverged significantly from that of the Crown . . . and was more similar to the economic level of the less populated countries of Eastern and partly of Southern and Northern Europe."[191] Intellectual life, for which a network of universities was essential, divided Europe into yet more groups. "The university network, which developed during that period [fourteenth to sixteenth centuries], mainly encompassed Italy, France, and parts of Spain and Germany. More distant countries in the north and east of Europe, in turn, had very few universities: England (2), Netherlands (1), Switzerland (1), Bohemia (1), Austria (1), Poland (1)

[188] Ibid., 19.
[189] Ibid., 21.
[190] Ibid., 78.
[191] Ibid., 82.

Sweden (1). Hungary even failed to maintain for any length of time its only university founded at Pécs,"[192] while Russia and Turkey had no universities at all. Constitutionally, it was not until the late sixteenth century that the Polish–Lithuanian Commonwealth became the exception in a centralizing Europe. "This process of centralization and concentration of power in the hands of the monarch occurred in most countries in the west, and even in the east of Europe, for instance in Russia under Vasili III and Ivan IV."[193]

Wyczański's indicators distinguished a group of countries characterized by the second serfdom. It was the same group that Topolski and Małowist had identified. Interestingly, unlike in other contexts, where "Northern and Eastern Europe" or "Western Europe" were the dominant geographical terms, here Wyczański opted for "Central and Eastern Europe." While he agreed with the facts, and even used the same term, he did not consider the restoration of serfdom to be either a negative phenomenon or indeed the most important one that would generate social and political structures and determine a future development path. The countries mentioned in this context characterized by the second serfdom did not, therefore, constitute any sort of lasting region, and the same was true of countries that were similar in terms of other indicators.

> In sixteenth-century Poland, and indeed in eastern Germany, Denmark, Livonia, Russia, Bulgaria, Bohemia, and Hungary, the serfdom that developed had a different character and different causes [than the serfdom of medieval Europe]. It was precisely the development of the monetary economy that caused [serfdom] to develop and the amount of peasant labor to rise. At least nominally, serfdom was intended to increase surplus agricultural production that could be sold on the market.[194]

Wyczański argued that "if we exclude the problem of serfdom as specific to Central and Eastern Europe, it turns out that most social phenomena of that era were the same across Europe.[195]

---

[192] Ibid., 195.
[193] Ibid., 130.
[194] Wyczański, *Polska na tle Europy*, 151.
[195] Ibid.

POLAND IN CENTRAL EUROPE

Several years later, in 1987, there appeared a popular, illustrated book entitled *Catching up with Europe* (Dogonić Europę), which is key to my discussion here.[196] In it, "Europe" acquired a clearer normative meaning—as a paradigm of economic, social, political, and cultural development (the book was divided into chapters thus named). Now Wyczański's antiregionalism was not so obvious as in his previously discussed works. Scandinavia, the Ottoman Empire, and Russia—which in *Poland in Sixteenth-Century Europe* were at least present in the statistics—had almost completely disappeared, along with the formal constraints of an academic work. At the same time, however, the geographical terms Wyczański used for parts of Europe took on a normative character. Development zones, regions of "backwardness," and countries that were "catching up" were grouped geographically. Poland was included in the group of "backward" countries. "Inevitably, the long-delayed entry into the European arena of the countries of Central, Eastern, and Northern Europe necessarily created a gap in relation to the West and South of the continent; a gap which, over the centuries, those countries attempted to bridge with varying speed."[197]

Wyczański combined the Renaissance and modern geographies of development. Similarly to the north Italian commentators of the fifteenth and sixteenth centuries, the author of *Catching up with Europe* found a model of this civilizational race south of the Alps, and like those commentators he had in mind the Italian cities. However, in keeping with the modern geography of development he also juxtaposed the West, and especially France, with the backward East. Thus, thanks to an injection of Renaissance perspective on Europe, with its focus on the North-South divide, Wyczański's Eastern Europe was only one of three geographically defined areas of "backwardness": the Center, the East, and the North. Backwardness was related to the date of adoption of Christianity, which did not take place in these non-Western and non-Southern parts of Europe until the tenth and eleventh centuries. It was only then that the nascent political entities joined the institu-

196 Wyczański, *Dogonić Europę*.

197 Ibid., 1.

tional "system of European civilization," a system that was multifaceted (legally, economically, culturally) and conducive to development.

More clearly than in Wyczański's earlier works, the social structure associated with Central Europe's manorial economy was a symbol of social backwardness. Yet it represented only one form of social backwardness, different to those characteristic of the East and North. "In Poland and in other Central European countries the szlachta were mainly concerned with agriculture, and specifically with their own folwarks."[198] Serfdom and the lack of "vagabonds and dispossessed people"—"therein lay the major difference in the social structure compared to the West. It was a gap that neither Poland nor any of its neighboring countries was able to bridge to any significant degree."[199]

In Wyczański's 1987 work, Central Europe meant the Polish–Lithuanian Commonwealth and its neighbors—countries dominated by the manorial economy, which, despite their cultural proximity, were unable to catch up with Europe. Both the terminology and the model recalled the Central Europe that Czesław Miłosz had proclaimed three years earlier: culturally rather Western, but economically backward and socially different from the West. Wyczański's work also anticipated the East Central Europe of the 1990s as understood by Topolski and Mączak. This consisted of countries that were more European than Russia but more rural than Western Europe, and economically and socially backward. We can only surmise that, besides the Polish part of the Commonwealth, what was meant was Bohemia and Hungary together with Slovakia and Croatia. Wyczański never precisely explained why Poland and its neighboring countries were "unable to bridge [the gap to Western Europe] to any significant degree." The word "unable," however, would seem to suggest the elites of those countries rather than external forces, which, in Kundera's conception of Central Europe, had kidnapped them and torn them away from the West.

Poland and its unspecified "neighbors" belonged to one of the three backward regions: Central Europe. For Wyczański it was an area characterized by the manorial economy, which he treated as a manifes-

[198] Ibid., 14.
[199] Ibid., 15.

tation of "backwardness." Thus, backwardness had geographical and neighborly connotations (the manorial economy prevailed in a cohesive, geographically defined area), while catching up with Europe had no such connotations. In this new understanding, Poland became a partner of the Eastern and Western powers on account of its non-economic characteristics: geographical size, diplomacy, culture, education, and lifestyles of the nobility. In this way, during the sixteenth century, Poland freed itself from a region defined by economic and structural indicators and entered a category of its own.

Wyczański's epistemological antiregionalism derived, I believe, from a hostility toward the notion that Poland belonged to a region fraught with negative connotations—Eastern Europe. Firstly, Wyczański opposed Małowist's colonial thesis and the treatment of Poland exclusively as a passive object of the activities of foreign centers of power, whether political or economic: "To see Poland as a mere tool of international machinations is absolutely misplaced."[200] Rejecting the notion of dependency, he also rejected the concept of "Eastern Europe," the salient features of which were precisely weakness and dependency.

Second, his research focused on the sixteenth century, the golden age of Polish history, so he had less reason to consider the ultimate failure and partition of the Polish–Lithuanian Commonwealth in the eighteenth century. It is also apparent that his choice of this particular period was inspired by the belief that a historic opportunity for dynamic development had existed at that time.

Third, Wyczański's interests were wide-ranging but geographically narrow. His historical models had neither the geographical depth of Małowist's nor the ideological motivation of Kula's or Topolski's, which would have made it theoretically necessary to consider the region distinct. Wyczański dealt in parallel with various aspects of public life—diplomacy, politics, the history of education, especially the history of the Jagiellonian University, and not just with society and economy. His method consisted of exploring issues connected with Poland and narrowing his geographical field of interest. Wyczański's bibliography leaves us in no doubt: the only geographical terms used in

---

[200] Wyczański, "Przedmurze?," 6.

the titles of major works, apart from Poland, are Europe and Franco–Polish diplomatic relations.

Fourth, perhaps as a result of his fascination with Western culture, particularly French culture, Wyczański emphasized the similarities between Polish society and the culturally dominant societies of England and France. Consequently, he also had to emphasize the differences between the Polish Crown on the one hand and the eastern part of the Commonwealth and Russia on the other. Finally, more noticeably than the other three authors, Wyczański represented an evolutionist approach to social processes taking place within a developmentally homogenous European space. In the sixteenth century, the farther from the southwestern center of civilization a country lay, the more backward it was, yet it was not without hope of catching up with the leading European nations.

CHAPTER 4

Development Studies: Sociology and History. Models of Backwardness

In this chapter I reconstruct, analyze, and compare competing models of social development that postwar Polish historiography used to describe the historical process in Eastern Europe. The analysis is based on works that either presented models directly, or from which views about development or about Eastern Europe can be deduced. I also consider methodological and theoretical works in which the authors commented on the international debates over development conditions, particularly in backward regions. This type of material is principally offered by the texts of Witold Kula, which is why the section on Kula is the longest.

I present the mature versions of: Małowist's model of colonial development; Wyczański's model of "catching up with Europe"; Topolski's model of "unfortunate historical coincidence"; and finally Kula's model of hybrid development, that is, the development of an agrarian society under the strong influence of mature capitalism in Western Europe. When commenting on each model, I discuss how it changed and its affiliation with the sociology of development.

By presenting the models in this order, I reveal the relationship between them and the main theoretical and ideological currents that still set the framework of the debate on development. The sequence therefore reflects to a lesser extent the chronology of the dispute over East European development. Małowist's colonial development model was the main stimulus and constant point of reference for postwar economic historiography in Poland. His model of Eastern Europe's dependence on Northwestern Europe was also consistent with dependency theory, which emerged at roughly the same time, mainly in Latin America. There is no reason to believe, however, that Małowist was aware of it. His articles, together with the historical studies of the dependency theorists, were the main historical material used by Wallerstein, whose ideas, in turn, inspired the present-day antiglobalization movement. Through this ideological and theoretical affinity, Małowist's model formed one extreme of the international academic and public debate on East European development.

The views of Wyczański marked the other extreme of the development debate and anticipated the theory of modernization and the "catching up with Europe" approach, which became popular in Eastern Europe at the turn of the last century. This theory is based on the assumptions of social evolutionism, although Wyczański, in accordance with a trend still popular today, restricted its originally universalist pretensions to a particular cultural zone—Europe. Poland's catching up with Europe, though unsuccessful beyond the sixteenth century, was aided by the fact that the country belonged to the same cultural and political (though not economic and social) European community. This attitude is characteristic of liberal theories of development found nowadays in academia and represented by both economic neoliberalism and by cultural explanations of the development of certain regions and the backwardness of others.

In the later phase of their work, Topolski and Kula represented a midway approach. Starting from the classical Marxist theory of development, in their later work they abandoned the idea of the necessarily linear nature of development. They accepted that in Eastern Europe, the modern historical process had proceeded differently than in the most advanced countries. Likewise, they rejected the idea of the necessary and "natural" character of economic progress. There were major differences between Topolski's and Kula's models, but they both adopted an intermediate position in the debate on development.

Theories of Development in Non-Western Societies and Changes in the Postwar World

After the Second World War, social science was presented with a new set of challenges: previously unknown social and political phenomena that needed to be described and interpreted. Key components of the global social order, which changed how the world was perceived, included the new form and mode of operation of capitalism in the West and the emergence of a communist bloc and new postcolonial countries.[1] These changes forced scholars—not only anthropologists—to rethink the meaning of terms such as "development," "growth," and "progress." The postwar years shifted social science's interest toward issues that had previously been tackled only by ethnology: the universality versus the variability of human nature, and the diversity of social orders and their associated values. The societies of the Soviet bloc, where modernization was controlled by the state and was not the result of market processes, did not fit within the framework of classical sociology and its distinction between traditional and modern societies.[2] Another anomaly was Japan, which underwent capitalist modernization but within its own and not Western culture.

One of the most important challenges for social science in the postwar years was the attitude toward non-European cultures. All the social sciences—not counting anthropology, which had already been evolving since the early twentieth century—attempted to meet this challenge. In the introduction to his seminal book about Africa, Małowist wrote:

> It seems that it is time to go beyond the confines of the limited sources concerning early medieval Europe and abandon what is, after all, obsolete Eurocentrism. In defending the right to use a comparative method in such cases, I would like to distance myself categorically from those researchers who treat the history of Africa as something essentially different from the history of

[1] See Kula, *The Problems and Methods*.

[2] Janos, *Politics and Paradigms*, 17–24 and 24–30, Ziółkowski, "O różnorodności teraźniejszości," Sosnowska, "Teorie zmiany i rozwoju."

> Europe. At any rate, in the case of Africa one cannot accept the claim made by Claude Lévi-Strauss about the ahistorical mentality of the first inhabitants of America. . . . Sources on both the history of medieval Europe and the history of Africa show that, very often, similar economic and political impulses elicited similar reactions in people on both continents. Therefore, the differences are often more to do with the chronology of the phenomena under comparison than with their essence. I believe that this entitles me to use the comparative method.[3]

An important question for social science was the compatibility of the modernization project—previously only carried out in Western countries—with social conditions in the rest of the world. The emergence of the communist bloc, and its economic competitiveness until the 1960s, changed the understanding of modernity. It deprived modernity of its hitherto compulsory component: capitalism. Unlike in classical social science, and unlike today, the most important components of the concept of modernity until the mid-1970s were industrialization, mass production, urbanization, the severing of traditional ties, and geographical and social mobility. The question about traditional versus modern society, which played a key role in classical sociology, was in the half-century following the Second World War gradually replaced by a question about the diversity of traditions and the possible forms of modernity that could arise from those traditions.[4]

The sociology of social change and development in non-Western societies fell somewhere between the debates in the field of general social theory and historical debates about the origins of modernity (which I discuss in Chapter 1). It asked questions and drew conclusions at a lower level of generality than social theory and often made use of detailed case studies. Historical explanation and the incorporation of historical material, although sometimes used, was not as crucial for this discipline as it was for historical macrosociology. By asking

[3] Małowist, *Europa a Afryka*, 12.

[4] The most important works on modernity as a sociological project include: Habermas, *The Structural Transformation*, Giddens, *Capitalism and Modern Social Theory*, Giddens, *The Consequences of Modernity*, Bauman, *Modernity and Ambivalence*.

about the opportunities and threats to economic development, the sociology of change was closer to economics and applied social science. Within its framework attempts were made to create models of development and social change in backward regions. These approaches were Popperian interpretations or, as Wallerstein described them, "organizing myths," rather than theories in the positivist sense whose claims could be fully verified.[5] The appeal to the general laws of the historical process, and the (albeit limited) possibility to verify and falsify using historical data or contemporary empirical data, meant that in the social sciences these approaches were called theories of social development, while in *The Methodology of History* they were referred to as models.

THEORIES OF MODERNIZATION, CONVERGENCE, AND MARXIST HISTORICAL MATERIALISM

The oldest of these theories, which gave rise to the debate over the conditions and opportunities for development of non-Western societies, are the theory of modernization and the theory of convergence. These were the result of reflection, mainly by American scholars, on the changes in postcolonial societies, which in the late 1940s and early 1950s were termed the Third World (modernization theory), or on the changes in societies of the Second World—the Soviet Union having been joined at that time by societies in Central and Eastern Europe and Asia (convergence theory). Both theories drew on the traditions of social evolutionism and classical sociological thought, which were reprocessed by functionalism (then dominant in American sociology) and by Talcott Parsons' idea of social harmony.[6] They "put the emphasis on endogenous, immanent causation [of change]," and treated modernization and convergence as "necessary, irreversible, endogenous, and ultimately beneficial."[7] The most famous advocate of the theory of modernization was Walt W. Rostow. In 1960 he summa-

[5] Popper, *The Poverty of Historicism*, 150–152, Wallerstein, "Economic Theories and Historical Disparities of Development," 32.

[6] Parsons, *Societies: Evolutionary and Comparative Perspectives*, Parsons, *The System of Modern Societies*. See also: Janos, *Politics and Paradigms*, 44–54, Martin, "Modernization in Crisis."

[7] Sztompka, *The Sociology*, 131.

rized his view of the transformation of traditional society into modern society in a work entitled, somewhat revealingly, *The Stages of Economic Growth. A Non-Communist Manifesto.*[8] This process had three main phases. The first was the creation of appropriate preconditions for the growth of innovation and investment: the achievement of a certain level of education, a favorable legal environment, and auspicious cultural and political circumstances. The decisive phase was called "take-off." The positive growth effects of the shift toward mass consumption during take-off would then multiply during the mature phase. Thus, the theory of modernization provided "less developed countries with guidance on how to proceed in order to effectively mimic the more developed countries."[9]

In the Soviet Union and Eastern Europe, the dominant model for interpreting the historical process was the Marxist theory of development. As Kochanowicz wrote, "the Marxist theory of development is difficult to recreate, since classical Marxist theorists never formulated it explicitly, while later commentators interpreted and continue to interpret it in many different ways," among which the version codified by Stalin acquired a "dogmatic and doctrinaire character."[10] It would not be wrong, I believe, to sum up the theory's assumptions—which also applied to the versions developed in the Soviet Union—in terms of evolutionism, developmental optimism, and technological reductionism. A brief description of it was provided by Jeffrey L. Anderson, a researcher of the theory of long-term economic change. The model assumed that the "historically continuous process of improvement in technology leads to tension between classes which are defined by their members' degree of control over the means of production. The development of new techniques means that the political and social 'superstructure' is no longer appropriate to the way goods and services can be produced. This tension is resolved by a revolution which establishes a new power structure in society appropriate to the new ways

[8] Rostow, *The Stages of Economic Growth*. A few years later the results of the debate around Rostow's work were published: Rostow, *The Economics of Take-Off*.

[9] Kochanowicz, *Spór o teorię*, 22.

[10] Ibid., 16.

of production."[11] Like modernization theory, historical materialism assumed that "transformations are autodynamic, immanent, endogenous," but also, which was its specific feature, "they are instigated by endemic contradictions, strains and tensions within the structure."[12]

The Soviet modification of classical historical materialism justified the possibility and appropriateness of socialism in backward countries. Its appeal boiled down to the assumption that revolution and socialist industrialization could—because social change followed technological change—"guide" agricultural societies directly toward modern socialism.[13]

A source of optimism for the theories of modernization, convergence, and the Marxist theory of development, regardless of whether their recommendations were liberal or socialist, was the assumption that technological change (i.e., industrialization), once triggered, led to changes such as urbanization and the emergence of mass society, the growth of prosperity, a rise in the average level of education, social differentiation, and specialization (modernization and convergence theory) or the intensification of class conflict (Marxism). All these theories linked modernity to the rejection of traditional mores and to changes in the social structure; the main differentiating factor was achieved, and not inherited status. These changes would result in the gradual but nevertheless permanent and irreversible convergence of societies, despite their different development levels at the outset (modernization theory, the Marxist theory of development) or—as the ideologically midway theory of convergence assumed—irrespective of how these changes were introduced, whether through capitalist or centrally planned industrialization.[14] Regardless of which side of the ideological barricade their advocates stood, "the core of the conceptions of growth among development economists of the 1950s was increasing produc-

[11] Anderson, *Explaining long-term*, 8. See also: Sztompka, *The Sociology*, 169–173, and Janos, *Politics and Paradigms*, 11–17.

[12] Sztompka, *The Sociology*, 172.

[13] Batygin and Deviatko, "The Metamorphoses of Russian Sociology," Janos, *Politics and Paradigms*, 33–36.

[14] Convergence theory, which emerged in the 1960s, was not developed at universities in the Soviet Union until the 1970s and 1980s. Batygin and Deviatko, *Metamorfozy*, 28–29.

tion and consumption, but also increasing employment and improved standards of living."[15]

Both the Marxist theory of development and the theories of modernization and convergence saw change as a process immanent to national societies, and progress as both a historical necessity and a reward for the effort of modernization. The Eurocentrism of development theories in the nineteenth and first half of the twentieth centuries lay in the assumption that all societies would develop similarly to the most advanced societies of the West, and that economic growth would lead to political and economic democratization (whether liberal or socialist) in both national societies and the world in general.

In the late 1960s and early 1970s, these optimistic theories underwent a crisis, which in the sociology of development, as in sociology in general, led to the emergence of new interpretations.[16] "Precisely this question of distribution became of central concern among development economists from around 1960. This new interest was also prompted by the fact that, at this time, figures began to appear which indicated that growth was frequently very unevenly distributed socially, geographically and between the different economic sectors."[17] This theme, as well as the identification of external, global factors governing the development of non-Western societies, distinguished the dependency and world-systems theories that emerged in the 1960s and 1970s from older theories.

DEPENDENCY AND WORLD-SYSTEMS THEORIES

Dependency theory, and later Wallerstein's world-systems theory, questioned the assumption about the internal nature of factors of development, stagnation, and backwardness, and referred to the nineteenth-century theory of imperialism. Both theories offered a different perspective on the origins of capitalism, the rise of the West, and the history and future development opportunities of non-Western societies. They rejected the evolutionist, universalist epistemology of change and the terminology of classical Marxism. Non-Western societies, argued

[15] Martinussen, *Society, State and Market*, 36.
[16] Janos, *Politics and Paradigms*, 68–72.
[17] Martinussen, *Society, State*, 37.

the most radical versions of these theories, were not areas of "backwardness" that followed the well-trodden path left by the development avant-garde, but societies that were "dependent" on economically stronger ones: "the periphery of the world-system" exploited by the core. Ideas that were later to be popularized by dependency theorists appeared in reflections on the economy of Latin America already in the 1940s;[18] in relation to backward countries, including those of Eastern Europe, they appeared even earlier—in the theories of imperialism of Lenin and Rosa Luxemburg.[19] In the 1960s, these ideas were developed by radical groups of Latin American Neo-Marxists in response to the failures of US economic aid in the region. Since the latter was based on the premises of the modernization school, dependency theories constructed their approach in opposition to it, "frequently attacking it as a rationalization of imperialism."[20]

In contrast to modernization theory and classical Marxism, dependency theory, in its extreme version, is a rather pessimistic way of looking at the development of underdeveloped countries. The studies of dependency theorists, although based on an ideological conviction about the exploitative nature of capitalism and the primacy of economics over politics, are quasi-historical and comparative in nature. They compile data from the colonial and postcolonial periods in order to show that, despite political changes (decolonization, the shift of the capitalist core from the European empires to the US), Latin America's economic dependence on the "advanced" countries has not diminished.[21]

---

[18] The precursors of dependency theory are regarded to be Hans W. Singer (1910–2006) and Raul Prebisch (1901–1986), an Argentine economist, professor at the University of Buenos Aires, organizer of the central banks of Argentina (1948) and Mexico (1963), as well as Advisor to the Economic Commission for Latin America. Prebisch, *Change and Development*, Singer and Roy, *Economic Progress and Prospects*, Singer, *Growth, Development, and Trade.*

[19] Luxemburg, *The Industrial Development*, Lenin, *The Development of Capitalism*, vol. 3.

[20] So, *Social Change and Development*, 169.

[21] The most important works in this field are: Frank, *Capitalism and Underdevelopment*, Amin, *Unequal Development*, Dos Santos, "The Crisis of Development Theory," Evans and Stephens, "Development and the World-Economy."

A feature common to all studies on dependence is the tendency to emphasize the destructive influence of the links between postcolonial countries and the West. The basic explanatory model of dependency theory is the opposition between a developing, rich, internally democratic, and externally imperialist core on the one hand, and a dependent, poor, authoritarian, and internationally impotent periphery on the other. In the latter, "there is foreign control of export enclaves, and industrialization is under the control of multinational corporations, which repatriate profits more than they reinvest them. Urbanization is accompanied by increasing social inequalities and the marginalization of the masses. The pursued industrialization strategies are inflationary, and this causes international capital to support repressive, bureaucratic–authoritarian regimes."[22] The main obstacles to the development of the periphery, therefore, are its position in the international division of labor, the terms of trade imposed by the core, and authoritarian national governments, supported by the core in order to guarantee the profitability of its operations. On this interpretation the periphery is condemned to supplying raw materials, whose prices are kept low by buyers in the core, and to importing technology and highly processed products whose prices are kept artificially high by monopolistic big corporations. According to dependency theorists, capitalism develops in a completely different way in the core compared to the periphery. "Dependence affects the character of industrialization, urbanization, processes of social change, and the nature of political systems."[23] Under the influence of capitalism, not only do societies not converge, they actually diverge even more. As a way out of this vicious circle, radical dependency theorists recommend weakening contacts with the core and building an alternative socioeconomic system.

A more optimistic (in Piotr Sztompka's words) version of dependency theory, more conciliatory toward capitalism, was developed by the long-time President of Brazil, Fernando Cardoso, together with Enzo Falletto.[24] They postulated "an analysis of concrete processes of development" in the periphery and they did "not aspire to build an

---

[22] Kochanowicz, "Teoria systemu światowego."

[23] Ibid.

[24] Cardoso, "Associated-Dependent Development," Cardoso and Faletto, *Dependency and Development.* See also: Morawski, *Socjologia ekonomiczna.*

alternative . . . theory of development applicable to all the periphery and at all times."[25] Their concept of dependent development assumed that although, as classical dependency theorists claimed, the influx of foreign capital created islands of highly-advanced modern enterprise in a sea of backwardness, in the long term these could (though not necessarily) contribute to genuine economic development. Indeed, such islands could serve as an example for local entrepreneurs, promote local accumulation, and trigger spontaneous growth. "The global economic interconnections appear as the means toward ultimate emancipation [from colonial dependence] rather than an instrument of continuing subjugation."[26]

In the mid-1960s, in the face of the failure of US policy toward Latin American countries, the belief that there existed different development paths within the periphery became part of development economics, a field that emerged after the Second World War and flourished in the United States in particular. The work and recommendations of Albert Hirschman and Celesto Furtado in Latin America were situated within the critical trend of mainstream economics. What their approaches shared was an openness to competing schools of economic thought: classical economics, Marxism, Keynesianism. They rejected the orthodox versions of those theories and adopted a moderate political attitude, revolutionizing the canon of economic advice for undeveloped countries rather than rejecting it wholesale.[27] In his research on the Brazilian economy, Furtado linked economic history with the theory of economic growth.[28] His views and his theory of dependency emphasized the different development paths of the first capitalist countries compared to backward countries and the generally negative impact for society of the links between the periphery and the core. Furtado advocated far-reaching state intervention, but not the nationalization of the means of production.[29] He stressed the importance of the penetration of old, non-capitalist social structures

25 Palma, "Dependency," 803.
26 Sztompka, *The Sociology*, 90.
27 Hirschman, "A Dissenter's Confession," 87, Furtado, *Development and Underdevelopment.*
28 Furtado, *The Economic Growth of Brazil.*
29 Furtado, *The Myth of Economic Development.*

by modern capitalist enterprises and attributed less importance to international commerce and the terms of trade. In *Development and Underdevelopment*, he wrote: "The economic structure of the region into which the capitalist enterprise has penetrated . . . does not necessarily become modified as a result of that penetration. . . . The level of real wages is determined by living conditions prevailing in the region in which the new enterprises are set up, without any precise connection with the productivity."[30]

Hirschman, the author of a work that analyzed "the politics of foreign trade, the possibility of using trade as a means of political pressure" in relations between Nazi Germany and southeastern Europe,[31] called himself the "frequently unacknowledged founding grandfather" of studies on dependence.[32] His subsequent approach to Latin America's economic problems was founded on a belief in the "originality and creativity in deviating from the path followed by the older industrial countries, in skipping stages, and in inventing sequences that had a 'wrong way around' look," which was far removed from the two dominant paradigms.[33]

The 1970s were marked by the "coexistence of contrasting perspectives in the field of development,"[34] that is, modernization theory and dependency theory. The explanatory potential of the latter was weakened by the success of "dependent development" in postcolonial regions of Southeast Asia. Besides Japan, the Asian Tigers emerged. In the mid-1970s, "East Asia (Japan, Taiwan, South Korea, Hong Kong, and Singapore) continued to experience a remarkable rate of economic growth."[35] It turned out that, contrary to what classical dependency theorists had assumed, international trade and the international division of labor were not (always) a zero-sum game, and in crisis situations the core could generate profits not just for itself but also for certain peripheries able to develop under the conditions of

[30] Furtado, *Development and Underdevelopment*, 130.

[31] Hirschman, *National Power*, v–vi. See also: Hirschman, *Journeys Toward Progress*, Hirschman, *Underdevelopment and Dependence*.

[32] Hirschman, *Essays in Trespassing*, 27.

[33] Hirschman, "A Dissenter's Confession," 96.

[34] So, *Social Change*, 169.

[35] Ibid., 170.

dependence. The Dependencia school also came in for criticism on account of its revolutionary, socialist recommendation to detach the economies of Third World countries from the capitalist system. These criticisms were linked to the crisis in the communist bloc, which was already in evidence by the early 1970s: the Sino–Soviet split (shortly followed by the disengagement of the less geopolitically important Romania from the Soviet Union) and the opening up of communist countries to capitalist investment. Western loans and the importation of technology were seen as evidence of the failure of development outside the capitalist system and the secondary "peripheralization" of the communist bloc.

The response to this empirical and ideological challenge was Wallerstein's world-systems theory, the historical aspects of which I discuss in Chapter 1. Here, I merely wish to emphasize the theoretical significance of Wallerstein's proposal to change the unit of analysis from the national to the global as well as the contribution of world-systems theory to the study of economic change in the modern world.[36] In contrast to earlier theories of development, this model assumed that due to the nature of capitalism and its key role in organizing the modern world, historical development could be understood by abandoning the study of individual societies and even comparative analysis, and instead accepting that capitalism, in spite of political boundaries, was a single, global system of relationships and inequalities, a totality. By creating and maintaining relations between various regions, capitalism determined whether those regions belonged to the core or to the periphery. Economic ties and dependencies were more powerful than any political divisions. "The secret of capitalism was in the establishment of the division of labor within the framework of a world-economy that was not an empire rather than within the framework of a single national state."[37] Social classes were therefore transnational. "The upper classes are situated primarily but not exclusively in the core, and peripheral societies contain the most exploited and the majority of the world's proletariat."[38]

---

[36] Janos, *Politics and Paradigm*, 76–80.
[37] Wallerstein, *The Modern World System I*, 127.
[38] Ragin and Chirot, "The World System," 277.

By introducing the category of semi-peripheries, world-systems theory tried to explain the shift in the core of capitalism from Europe to Great Britain and then to the United States and Japan. It was also able to interpret the different development paths of individual peripheries in the 1970s and 1980s, primarily the difference between the countries of Southeast Asia (self-sufficiency and export-oriented policies when the West was in recession) and Latin America (the opening of borders and debt, increasing in periods of recession), and to explain the ways in which a country could move from the periphery to the semi-periphery and finally to the core (or the reverse).[39] Among the limited opportunities for development, Wallerstein identified two courses that were open to relatively industrialized peripheries: "seizing by chance" (when the core is in crisis: the substitution of imported products, but the importation of technology; expansion into the internal market and into other peripheral national markets interested in products and technologies regarded by the core as obsolete; intensive industrialization and urbanization; reduction in the political influence of the rural population), and "development by invitation" (when the core is expanding: incentives for foreign investment; a close relationship with the core by opening up to its products).[40]

In Eastern Europe in the 1960s and 1970s the official version of historical materialism became theoretically marginalized. Among intellectuals, faith in socialist ways of overcoming backwardness also decreased.[41] The perspective and dilemmas of dependency theory thus became, especially in Poland and Hungary, an attractive intellectual proposition—more so in economics and historiography than in sociology. In the 1970s, the Polish economists Marian Ostrowski and Zdzisław Sadowski used elements of dependency theory to interpret the growing development gap and indebtedness of communist countries compared to the West.[42] The Polish historians Marcin Kula, Tadeusz Łepkowski, Henryk Szlajfer, and Ryszard Stemplowski also adopted a position similar to that of the Dependencia school on the

---

[39] Wallerstein, *The Capitalist World Economy*, and Wallerstein, *Geopolitics and Geoculture*.

[40] Wallerstein, *The Capitalist World Economy*, 66–95.

[41] See Kula, *Rozdziałki*, notes from the 1970s, e.g., 236, 369, 415–17.

[42] Ostrowski and Sadowski, *Wyzwania rozwojowe*.

development opportunities of undeveloped countries.[43] They primarily studied Latin American societies and made use of studies on dependence carried out by scholars in the region. Sometimes they simply searched for analogies between the region and Eastern Europe.

Małowist, who was working during the same thirty-year period on Eastern Europe's colonial path of development, came to similar theoretical conclusions as the dependency theorists. Although he probably did not read their work, and his interests were strictly historical and academic, he drew on the same theoretical and ideological sources. Małowist dealt with other regions, but his model of the relations of Eastern Europe and West Africa with Western Europe is strikingly similar to that of the dependency theorists. They held similar views about the origins of capitalism, the mechanisms by which dependence was reproduced, and the narrowly specialized nature of economic development as a cause of stagnation. Despite the similarity of their arguments, however, it is not possible to uncover the precise link between the Dependencia school and Małowist's research.[44] Kula, on the other hand, made direct use of the Dependencia's research, to which he was introduced by the younger generation of Polish researchers mentioned above. His categorization of Eastern Europe and Latin America as "raw material supply bases" for the West was an idea he developed from the mid-1960s.[45] Kula also collaborated with Iván T. Berend and György Ránki, who from the late 1970s were influenced by world-systems theory. Despite the clear similarities in their understanding of the region's history, and their similar ideological inspiration, Małowist, unlike Kula, did not establish contact with the Budapest milieu.

---

43 Kula, *Początki czarnego niewolnictwa w Brazylii*, Łepkowski, "Słowo końcowe," Kula, *Zamachy stanu, przewroty, rewolucje*, Łepkowski, *Historia Meksyku*, Łepkowski, and Kula, *Dzieje Ameryki Łacińskiej*, Szlajfer, *Modernizacja zależności*, Stemplowski, *Ameryka Łacińska.*

44 Asked by Stemplowski why he had not studied Latin America in the sixteenth century, which he could have tackled via his knowledge of Portuguese history, Małowist answered that he became interested in Africa, "especially that this was the moment of its emancipation, the 1960s." Małowist, "Marian Małowist o historii," 50.

45 See the subchapter devoted to Kula in chapter 3 of this book.

THE NEW MODERNIZATION THEORY

After the criticisms made by dependency theorists in the 1960s and world-systems theorists in the 1970s, in the 1980s modernization theory was reformed and experienced a renaissance.[46] It changed its hostile attitude toward tradition, which it no longer regarded as an obstacle to modernization, and instead treated it as a positive or negative factor of development depending on the nature of the tradition concerned. It treated in a similar fashion the external conditions of development, which had been neglected in the 1950s. The new theory of modernization was less Eurocentric and less convinced about the linear nature of social development; it was also less optimistic about the possibility of stable democratic governments in the Third World. The analyses carried out within the framework of this new paradigm resembled case studies. In contrast to the classical perspective, the new approach did not deal with the general theory of development but instead focused on specific local conditions—historical, political, social, etc. The empirical findings of comparative studies provided specific examples of different development paths.[47]

Modern approaches to economic development—those embraced by the international organizations that monitor and support development, and which therefore cannot really be seen as an expression of political radicalism—have incorporated much of the social criticism levelled at economism and determinism. "In the construction of explanations of long-term economic change in large systems, attention is increasingly being paid to the restraints on growth rather than to the more traditional search for causes."[48] Since the early 1990s, the United Nations Development Programme has used the terms "human development" and "sustainable development," which—surprisingly, if one compares them with the strictly economic recommendations for developing countries—include criteria relating to life expectancy and the quality of life, the distribution of education, the social structure, and political institutions.

---

[46] Sztompka, *The Sociology*, 136–40, So, *Social Change*, 50–80.
[47] So, *Social Change*, 50–80.
[48] Anderson, *Explaining long-term*, 69.

> With the first Human Development Report from 1990 . . . [the UN] presented a more comprehensive concept of human development. . . . The report defined human development as a process of enlarging people's choices. At first, attention was concentrated around the choices in three essential areas: the opportunity to lead a long and healthy life; the opportunity to acquire knowledge; and the opportunity to have access to resources needed for a decent standard of living. . . . To these were later added considerations regarding political freedom and human rights; human development for women as well as for men; environmental and other aspects of sustainability; and themes regarding citizens' participation and opportunities to affect the political decisions in society.[49]

The term "underdevelopment" has also changed in post-Cold War discourse. It is no longer just GDP per capita and other "average" data that are taken into account, but also structural factors. "Third World countries (i) tend to have a larger agricultural than industrial workforce; (ii) tend to rely on a limited number of raw material products for export; (iii) have relatively poor diets and high levels of illiteracy; (iv) have often experienced a colonial past."[50] At the same time, both the terminology and paradigm of modernization theory—with its division into traditional undeveloped societies and modern developed societies, to which the former must conform in the course of development—are still used, particularly by economists oriented toward policy-making and empirical research.

However, the work of East European research communities in the 1990s testified to the attractiveness of the modernization paradigm not only for politicians. The disgrace of the Soviet project gave rise to a mood popularly expressed in Fukuyama's claim about the end of history and the victory of the liberal-democratic order.[51] This theoretical mood was conducive neither to dependency theory nor to world-systems theory, which saw liberal democracy as immoral and oppressive and argued for it to be replaced. The theoretical assumptions and emo-

---

[49] Martinussen, *Society, State*, 38.
[50] Webster, *Introduction to the Sociology*, 23–24.
[51] Fukuyama, *The End of History*.

tional attitudes behind the new approach were reflected in the opinion of Piotr Sztompka, a theorist of social change and an advocate of neo-modernization or postmodernization theory in the study of postcommunist societies: "Once the artificial blockades were lifted, the pre-modern, ugly face of Soviet and Eastern European societies appeared in full clarity."[52] Sztompka argued for the concepts of modernity and modernization to be associated with capitalism and rationality, and not with industrialization, as was the case in traditional studies.

The disputes around the opportunities and threats to development in non-Western societies also took place within the framework of the East European debate. The arguments presented within it did not always exhibit the discipline required in sociological debates. Kula and Topolski "revealed" their method of conceptualizing historical material, but such deliberations were largely absent in the work of Małowist, and especially Wyczański. As I will try to show, however, all four schools managed to produce coherent and competing models of development and underdevelopment.

A Model of Colonial Development. Małowist

Małowist's views constituted an implicit model of the development of Eastern Europe as an economic colony of the West. This model attributed the refeudalization of the region to its intensive trade links with the more economically advanced West. Małowist pointed to the negative structural impact of serfdom on development and to the "regressive" nature of the folwark and other economic phenomena from the sixteenth century onwards. He analyzed the long-term structural effects of this type of economy, as opposed to short-term effects, which were measured by the trade balance and income from production.

Małowist's research temperament was such that he never engaged in theoretical reflection. His views on meta-research were almost exclusively conveyed through his colleagues and collaborators.[53] A book by

[52] Sztompka, *The Sociology*, 138.

[53] Małowist, "Marian Małowist o historii," Mączak, introduction to Małowist, *Europa i jej ekspansja*, 5–12.

Wallerstein,[54] which was based on Małowist's work and dedicated both to him and Braudel, provoked Małowist into "disclosing" his theoretical assumptions. The introductions to Małowist's major works also gave the reader some insight into the basis of his model.[55] Despite the lack of theoretical deliberation, his implicit model of the emergence and development of economic dependence was suggestive; its mature version, which covered the whole of Eastern Europe, was presented in *The East and West of Europe* (Wschód a zachód Europy).

Economic dependence, which was colonial in nature, arose in the late Middle Ages and was subsequently to determine the narrowly specialized development of the eastern part of the continent. In this model, East European backwardness was a consequence of the European division of labor, within which East and West played different but complementary roles. The East was a producer and exporter of raw materials as well as a recipient of luxury goods manufactured in the West or imported from outside Europe by West European merchants. The West, in turn, was a producer of processed and increasingly sophisticated goods and also the place where the centers of industry, trade, and colonial expansion were located.

Małowist's detailed analysis covered the period from the late Middle Ages until the early seventeenth century. He argued that the demographic, economic, and structural-legal backwardness of the East relative to the West was already in evidence when the first East European monarchies were created between the tenth and twelfth centuries. The key period when this imbalance was transformed into dependence was, according to Małowist, the crisis of the thirteenth and fourteenth centuries in the West. In the fourteenth and fifteenth centuries the East of Europe witnessed intensive development at a time when the West was in crisis, which helped to reduce the economic gap between the

54 Wallerstein, *The Modern World-System.* Małowist elaborated on the differences between his own views and those of Wallerstein in an article published posthumously: Małowist, "Podziały gospodarcze i polityczne," 233–44. English translation: Małowist, "Economic and Political Divisions," 229–45.

55 Małowist, *Wschód a Zachód*, Małowist, introduction to *Konkwistadorzy portugalscy*, 11–15, Małowist, introduction to *Europa a Afryka*, Małowist, "Kapitalizm handlowy a rolnictwo," 31–34.

two parts of the continent. The close links with the West (primarily trade), which had already existed since the thirteenth century, intensified during the crisis as Western merchants sought new markets. Eastern Europe proved to be a wellspring of cheap raw materials that were needed in the West: timber and other building products, grain, flax, oxen, and minerals.

To meet this demand, the economies of Eastern Europe developed in a narrowly specialized manner, focussing on the export of raw materials. Comparing the region to Western Europe, Małowist wrote:

> In the East, which was economically backward due to its unfavorable starting conditions, trade with the West meant civilizational progress and the enrichment of local and foreign merchants and feudal lords. But it also caused the economy to become somewhat narrowly specialized, despite the fact that in certain periods it even helped to temporarily enhance the power of wealthy state organizations, as can clearly be seen in Hungary during the Angevin dynasty, in Bohemia during the thirteenth and fourteenth centuries, and in Serbia under Stefan Dušan.[56]

The structural division of Europe, which was long-lasting and constituted an objective condition independent of institutions, took shape in roughly the fifteenth century. Western demand for raw materials from Eastern Europe had a direct impact on the establishment of folwarks in the Baltic zone, mines in the Balkans, and the organization of picking and animal farming in Russia and Central Europe. Competitive prices could only be achieved by keeping production costs low, and this was possible thanks to the introduction and then intensification of serfdom. An auspicious circumstance for this structural solution was the scarcity of labor associated with low population density. According to Małowist, but contrary to the assumptions of classical economics, scarce labor, under the conditions of personal serfdom at that time, had the effect of tying peasants to the land.

The architects and beneficiaries of this economic system were the East European nobility. They used their export revenues to pur-

[56] Małowist, *Wschód a Zachód*, 375–76.

chase craft products imported from the West, which despite the crisis of the thirteenth and fourteenth centuries were of higher quality than local products. "In the period between the thirteenth and late fifteenth centuries a distinct form of trade relations between the East and West of Europe took shape, which consisted in exchanging raw materials for craft products and luxury goods. In the sixteenth century it was precisely this type of trade between the two sides that greatly intensified."[57]

Already by the sixteenth century, local crafts and trade and their urban centers, which were in any case weaker than in the West, had begun to decline, even though they had experienced growth from the fourteenth century onwards. The incomes of peasants gradually fell because their land was incorporated into folwarks, and serfdom intensified. With the rise of serfdom and the decline in peasant incomes, demand decreased for low- and medium-quality goods hitherto produced by local artisans and distributed through local trade. "From the fifteenth century, and particularly later, circumstances which were so favorable for Eastern European agriculture led to the introduction of labor services and the second serfdom. This phenomenon enriched and strengthened the nobility and, in Russia and for a certain period in Poland, those merchants linked with agricultural interests. Urban industry . . . struggled against the competition of foreign products and the difficulties caused by the smallness of interior markets and either remained insignificant or, as in Poland, was destined to disappear."[58]

Beginning in the sixteenth century, the disappearance of the internal market returned the economy to a natural state, even though—as emphasized by earlier historiography, which regarded the sixteenth century as the golden age of the Commonwealth, and by later critics of Małowist's model—the trade balance was still positive during that period.

> It is well known that the huge export of grain and forestry products meant that in the sixteenth century the balance of Poland's maritime trade with the West was very positive. In Russia this

[57] Małowist, *Wschód a Zachód*, 379.
[58] Małowist, "The Problem of the Inequality," 28.

> had been a continuous phenomenon since the early Middle Ages. We know that in the sixteenth century, also in Hungary and then in the Balkans, cash flowed in from the West. However, it was rarely used for productive purposes and was mainly assigned to consumption. Various factors were responsible for this. The intensification of serfdom and the peasants' rapidly increasing workload as well as their lack of access to urban markets meant that the purchasing power of the vast majority of the population began to decline, especially in the late sixteenth and early seventeenth centuries. This impacted unfavorably on the situation of small and later medium-sized towns that relied heavily on local and regional markets. One can see evidence of this in Poland and Hungary, and much later on in Bohemia and the Balkans. It seems that in Russia the steady expansion of arable land and the exploitation of riches in the north rescued the situation for quite some time.[59]

Simultaneously, raw materials exported from Eastern Europe, mainly ores and products needed in the construction of ships (timber, tar, wood tar), supported West European overseas expansion. Cheap food allowed the societies of Northwestern Europe to specialize in more profitable lines of business. The Eastern demand for luxury goods also supported the development of West European crafts, while the capital amassed by merchants and rulers allowed them fund overseas expeditions.

For Małowist, participation or non-participation in colonial expansion was another element that testified to the separate, very different, but nonetheless complementary ways in which the East and West of Europe developed. No country of the East engaged in overseas colonization. The East also differed in terms of social and political structures from the Nordic countries and Germany, which had likewise not participated in early colonization.[60] The consequences of overseas expansion proved extremely important not just for the development of capitalism in the West but also for East-West relations. In the seventeenth

[59] Małowist, *Wschód a Zachód*, 383.
[60] Compare the fragments on Małowist in chapter 3 of this book.

century, when ores, food, and other raw materials from the European colonies came into circulation and productivity in the West increased, East European products became less attractive. Małowist suggested that due to this narrow specialization and the sociopolitical structures on which it was based, the economy could no longer extricate itself from the crisis of the following centuries, which had different causes.

The novelty of Małowist's approach was that he showed how the negative effects of the manorial system based on the second serfdom had already begun to appear by the end of the sixteenth century. His thesis ran contrary to the 1950s fascination with Renaissance culture and economy, which supposedly flourished until the mid-seventeenth century. Later, the thesis was accepted, having been confirmed in detailed studies undertaken by Małowist's students[61] on the negative consequences of the manorial economy for domestic crafts and towns. Antoni Mączak, inspired by his mentor's argument about the negative impact of serfdom and grain exports on the economic structure of Baltic coastal areas, carried out extensive research on the free peasantry in the Żuławy region.[62] The research confirmed the export-oriented character of their production, which was connected more with Dutch merchants than with the internal market, and also the better economic performance of their farms compared to folwarks. In his book, *Between Gdańsk and the Øresund* (Między Gdańskiem a Sundem), Mączak presented his findings on the goods trade between Gdańsk and the Western ports.[63] The results apparently confirmed the idea that the Baltic zone was home to phenomena "reminiscent of modern forms of colonialism, in which the colonial areas are both a source of raw materials and, perhaps even principally, a market for industrial products exported from the metropolis."[64]

---

[61] Zientara, *Dzieje małopolskiego hutnictwa*, Samsonowicz, *Rzemiosło wiejskie*, Mączak, *Sukiennictwo wielkopolskie.* Wyczański remained the exception in this regard. On the reception of the thesis and the dispute around it, see Mączak's introduction to Małowist, *Europa i jej ekspansja*, 8–10, Wyrobisz, "Zagadnienie upadku rzemiosła," 132–38.

[62] Mączak, *Gospodarstwo chłopskie.*

[63] Mączak, *Między Gdańskiem a Sundem.*

[64] Ibid., 156.

Maria Bogucka and Henryk Samsonowicz conducted a historico-sociological study of the situation of towns in the Polish–Lithuanian Commonwealth.[65] Their findings confirmed Małowist's claim that Baltic trade had played an important role in shaping the economic division of Europe between the fourteenth and seventeenth centuries. They also pointed to the economic extraterritoriality of Gdańsk and the significance of the exports and interests of Western merchants (first the Dutch, then the English) for the development of the Vistula towns and the decline of other towns that were reliant on the domestic market.[66] The huge interest among historians in the 1960s and 1970s in Baltic affairs and in the development of Gdańsk and other towns may be seen as a further attempt to test Małowist's hypotheses.[67]

The radicalism and rhetoric of the colonial thesis changed over time, reaching its apogee when Małowist was studying Iberian expansion in West Africa. In contrast to Kula, in whose works the colonial analogy did not appear until the 1960s and not without the influence of Latin American dependency theory, Małowist, from the early 1950s onwards, linked Poland's underdevelopment to the capitalist development of Northwestern Europe. His subsequent research revealed Poland's development path to be a prototype of the Baltic zone, and later, of Eastern Europe in general.

When compared to the current paradigm of multifactor explanations of social processes, Małowist's model appears radically economistic. It assumed the primacy of the economic sphere over other spheres of communal life. The latter merely expressed the interests of

[65] Bogucka, "Merchant's Profits in Gdańsk Foreign Trade," Bogucka, "Handel bałtycki w życiu Polski," Bogucka, "Obcy kupcy osiadli w Gdańsku," Maria Bogucka et al., *Warszawa w latach 1526–1795*, Bogucka and Samsonowicz, *Dzieje miast i mieszczaństwa*, Bogucka et al., *Studia nad dziejami miast.*

[66] Samsonowicz, *Badania nad kapitałem mieszczańskim*, Samsonowicz, *Późne średniowiecze miast nadbałtyckich*, Mączak and Samsonowicz, "La zone baltique."

[67] See: Małecki, *Studia nad rynkiem regionalnym*, Gierszewski, *Statystyka żeglugi Gdańska*, Molenda, *Górnictwo kruszcowe*, Molenda, "Miasta górnicze," Zins, *Anglia a Bałtyk*, Małecki, *Związki handlowe miast polskich.* Research review: Bogucka, "Les dernieres recherches," Samsonowicz, "Recherches polonaises sur l'histoire de la Baltique."

the ruling class. This premise was reflected in the following passage from *The Portuguese Conquistadors* (Konkwistadorzy portugalscy): "The basic trend of history is, above all, the desire of humanity and of individual groups to secure a decent standard of living and economic success. This affects political and cultural phenomena as well as ethical concepts. We also know that all these areas of life interact with one another, determining the attitudes of societies and individuals toward reality."[68] For Małowist, man was primarily *homo economicus*. "Man acts under the influence of various impulses, of which the economic impulse is paramount, although it often manifests itself in a highly sublimated form."[69]

Małowist believed cultural factors to be of marginal importance. If he considered the impact of culture on the development opportunities of a given society, he looked for that impact in the ideals of a good life and, unlike modern researchers, never linked these ideals to religion. According to Małowist, the set of values embraced by the Polish elite of the sixteenth century epitomized a culture that was not conducive to capitalism, and therefore, in the circumstances of the time, was not conducive to economic development either.

> Poland gradually acquired an economy which, at bottom, is close to the classic colonial pattern. This came about partly as a result of the country's culture, or even its national character. Land became the only important source of wealth. The wealthy nobleman, exploiting his serfs, and thus able to acquire a standard of living suitable to his social station, became the only man worthy of respect. . . . What were the ideals propagated by the two great Polish poets of the sixteenth century, Rej and Kochanowski,[70] two men, who, though they differed both in education and talent, nevertheless championed patterns of life which were to remain influential among many subsequent generations? The style of life of which they dreamed was that of retirement in the countryside, far from the storms of the world. The social

[68] Małowist, *Konkwistadorzy portugalscy*, 14.
[69] Ibid., 48.
[70] Mikołaj Rej (1505–1569) and Jan Kochanowski (1530–1584) were the most prominent Polish writers of the era.

groups in Western countries, whose members blazed the trail of rapid economic development, had far different . . . ideals in life.[71]

Wallerstein's idea of Eastern Europe as the first victim of European economic and colonial expansion and one of the first peripheries of the capitalist world-system led Małowist to refine his position. In 1987, when asked for his opinion about Wallerstein's model, Małowist stressed that Eastern Europe had not been a passive victim of capitalist expansion and that its economic dependence on the West had resulted from the behavior of its elites, the closed nature of its social structure, and the lack of structural balance between territorial expansion and economic development. These aspects of Małowist's model are, I believe, still relevant today. They anticipate the modern concept of sustainable development, which is measured by structural and not just financial indicators.

For Małowist, what characterized the whole of Eastern Europe—from Poland to the Ottoman Empire—was the unnecessary weakness or absence of political institutions that could defend local economic interests; a weakness, moreover, that was not based on an overwhelming difference in development levels as in the case of African and Latin American societies. Małowist repeatedly emphasized that in the thirteenth and fourteenth centuries the entire region grew much more rapidly than the West of Europe, aided by similar social institutions. He believed that the lost opportunity was down to the attitude of the local elites and ruling classes at the moment they encountered and later traded with the more efficient West. In an interview with historians with whom he was on friendly terms, including the dependency theorist Ryszard Stemplowski, Małowist emphasized the difference between his position and that of Wallerstein and the dependency school.

Małowist: . . . unlike Wallerstein I think that these [social] institutions [adverse from the point of view of long-term develop-

[71] Małowist, "Poland, Russia and Western Trade," 32–33. Małowist paid attention to "the feudal mentality" and the concept of a good life while researching the colonization of West Africa. Małowist, "O społecznych aspektach wczesnej ekspansji kolonialnej," 20.

> ment] arise not only due to the impact of the core but also the impact of local conditions.
> **Tymowski:** Which of those internal factors do you consider to be especially important?
> **Małowist:** The social structure. . . . Asymmetry [in international trade] can hamper the development of the weaker party in the relationship. It seems to me that this was the case regarding Eastern Europe's contact with the West. However, nineteenth-century Japan provides a different example. In both cases, was the determining factor not the different economic and political orientation of the dominant social groups?[72]

According to Małowist, positive development impulses could, in the long term, arise only from within a society. He categorized "areas incapable of dynamic development" as those characterized by "a highly restricted internal market and total dependence on more developed countries."[73] This claim, made during the most radical phase of his colonial thesis, linked the progress of some countries to the regress of others but nonetheless stressed the importance of internal reactions to external influences. Dependence was only possible in the absence of an adequate response to the development and expansion of other societies. The exploitation of others, in turn, as Małowist showed in *The Portuguese Conquistadors* and *Tamerlane and His Times*, could not be the sole basis for long-term development. Predatory empires—the term he used to describe the Portuguese and Timurid empires—did not last long as they failed to develop an internal market, bring innovation to the social structure, and make the political system independent of the personality of the ruler. Małowist thus set limits to his economic determinism.

The factors favoring development were not only the growth of the internal market but also the flexibility of the social structure and the rationalization of power structures. In the political sphere, a pro-development system could not be despotic because in the long term, despotism was not conducive to development; its social consequence was the passivity of major groups in society. Passivity, in turn,

72 Małowist, "Marian Małowist o historii," 50.
73 Małowist, *Europa a Afryka*, 589.

was the opposite of change and innovation. What was conducive to development, however, was a social structure whose flexibility was legally guaranteed (and not just by the decrees of this or that ruler, for instance).[74] A structure of this kind provided opportunities for social mobility and innovation in all areas. An open structure within a non-despotic system of power was the opposite of a structure based on social polarization and the entitlement of one group versus the discrimination of other groups.

A social system that made intensive economic development possible was one that had the ability to generate change. For this reason, Małowist attributed the inefficiency and transience of the Portuguese colonial empire and the Polish–Lithuanian Commonwealth, and the problems of the Russian and Ottoman empires, to the disharmony between territorial expansion and economic underdevelopment. "In the late sixteenth and early seventeenth centuries . . . Turkey entered a phase when it experienced difficulties similar to those that later led Poland to ruin and caused so many problems for Russia. The Ottoman state apparatus was too big in relation to its economic potential."[75]

Economic exploitation and territorial expansion in other regions, however, could be a component of long-term power. Małowist's most extreme depiction of this problem was nonetheless milder than Wallerstein's. In *Europe and West Africa in the Age of Early Colonial Expansion*, he wrote: "It is hard to resist the temptation to see the sixteenth and seventeenth centuries not just as an era when several countries in Northwestern Europe experienced rapid progress but also as an era when the already slow development of huge parts of the world ground to a halt, became distorted, and consequently led to regression,"[76] and "the colonial exploitation of Africa, America, and to some extent Eastern Europe as one of the factors behind the emergence of Western capitalism, especially in the sixteenth and seventeenth centuries, in my opinion deserves far greater attention than historians . . . have hitherto given it."[77] For Małowist, colonial exploitation was one of the many reasons for the West's power, and not its foundation, as in Wallerstein's model.

---

[74] Małowist, *Tamerlan*, 83–119.
[75] Małowist, *Wschód a Zachód*, 369.
[76] Małowist, *Europa a Afryka*, 10.
[77] Ibid., 589.

A Model of Catching up with Europe: Wyczański

Wyczański's model, like Małowist's, was implicit. I reconstruct it here primarily on the basis of Wyczański's book, *Catching up with Europe* (Dogonić Europę), which was published in 1987. Similarly to Małowist's *The East and West of Europe* (Wschód a zachód Europy), it summarized many years of research and presented a more mature version of the author's views.[78]

In Wyczański's historical model, Poland and its neighbors were seen as a group of countries that, although backward, had a large development potential, measured by their ability to imitate the institutions of the West. The model assumed the evolutionary nature of development, understood as a march toward a clearly defined goal, set by the standards of the most developed countries. Commenting on the differences between the Polish Crown lands and the Lithuanian-Ruthenian lands in the sixteenth-century Commonwealth, Wyczański wrote: "Their social structures were distinct, and the dynamics of those structures even more so. By 'distinct,' I do not mean that they were dissimilar; rather, that they were at a different stage of historical development. Lithuania, a country with a poorly developed, more primitive economy did not *yet* have the kind of social structures that the [Polish] Crown and *particularly* Western countries had in the sixteenth century." What Lithuania experienced in the sixteenth century was "processes similar to those that had previously occurred in other countries, only that these were *delayed*."[79]

In the late Middle Ages, claimed Wyczański, Polish society attempted to catch up with the most developed parts of Europe, which at that time included northern Italy and France. The differences in de-

[78] Wyczański, *Dogonić Europę*. Similar arguments in: Andrzej Wyczański, *Wschód i Zachód Europy*.

[79] Own emphasis added. Wyczański, *Polska w Europie*, 113–14. In the 1999 edition the evolutionist approach is still present, albeit toned down: "the Commonwealth consisted of two quite different organisms—the Crown and the Lithuanian–Russian territories, which differed economically, socially, politically, and culturally. These differences should not be seen as contradictions but rather as different development stages," in Wyczański, *Polska w Europie*, 201.

velopment levels were due to how early or how late Christianity had been adopted, for this allowed entry into the "system of European civilization," which was conducive to development. In this sense Poland and its neighboring countries lagged behind. Bridging the gap, or catching up, were understood by Wyczański to mean an institutional desire, fostered by the governing elite, to achieve "the same level . . . similar values,"[80] as in developed countries. Usually this was done by attempting to imitate pioneering societies, although the ingenuity of local elites sometimes allowed the same goals to be achieved in a slightly different way. In any case, Wyczański's model assumed that backward countries could either effectively catch up or fail in their ambition. "Catching up was therefore an intentional act, often imitative, but always a step forward. 'Catching up with Europe' implied both the deliberate adoption of foreign ideals, goals and experiences, and the achievement of similar results through native development."[81]

As shown by the methodology of his subsequent comparative studies, notably *Poland in Europe in the sixteenth century* (Polska w Europie XVI stulecia),[82] Wyczański assumed that societies formed national or state systems and that these totalities could be compared to one another using key criteria. His was therefore a multifactor model. In addition to economic, social-structural, formal-legal, and demographic indicators he took into account the conduct of diplomacy and the international position of states. He also considered culture (which clearly distinguished his model from the others presented here): educational institutions, the level of education, art, and, indirectly, religion. Wyczański's comparison of all the European countries that existed at the time showed that Poland's efforts to imitate the West in the sixteenth century achieved considerable success. "Poland . . . was neither a front-runner storming ahead of the pack nor a laggard struggling to keep up. She was an equal partner for all the major European countries."[83]

---

80 Wyczański, *Dogonić Europę*, 79.

81 Ibid.

82 The comparative works published prior to *Polska w Europie* include: Wyczański, "Polska na tle Europy," Wyczański, "Społeczeństwo polskie,."

83 Wyczański, "Polska na tle Europy," 173.

Wyczański's analysis of Polish institutions in the sixteenth century revealed positive similarities to Western institutions and very few negative differences. The former included, first and foremost, the level of economic development. Wyczański measured it using indicators such as grain yields, the level of material culture, the growth of the monetary economy at the expense of the natural economy, the increase in labor productivity,[84] and the percentage of the population not engaged in agriculture. Economic development measured in this way placed sixteenth-century Poland within the group of medium-developed countries, which included England, France, Spain, Portugal, and Germany.[85] During that period the Polish economy was able to enter the European economy on favorable terms. The balance of trade was definitely positive and the structure of exports attested to the commercialization of agricultural production. Poland thus became specialized in agriculture and animal farming within the European economy,[86] and "the export . . . of raw materials does not necessarily imply . . . economic backwardness or international trade on unfavorable terms."[87] Imports, in turn, included essential products that the country lacked (e.g., scythes, cloth, pepper) and there was no irrational import of luxury goods during that period. "While exports were specialized and comprised not so much raw materials as agricultural products, imports did not differ from the normal imports of most European countries, especially when it came to products nowadays considered luxuries."[88]

Another measure of catch up during the first half of the sixteenth century was the ability to imitate Western legal norms and Western political and public institutions. The former included mainly the feudal rights of the szlachta and town population and the provisions of German town law, which set the rules for the establishment of towns and settlements. State structures and the way in which they pursued international policy also came to resemble the Western model. The treaties of the first half of the sixteenth century testified to the "maturity of Polish political concepts and, at the very least, placed them on

---

[84] Wyczański, *Polska Rzeczą–Pospolitą*, 13.

[85] Wyczański, *Polska w Europie*, 78–79, "Polska na tle Europy," 151.

[86] Wyczański, *Dogonić Europę*, 3.

[87] Ibid., 3.

[88] Wyczański, *Polska w Europie*, 53.

a par with the arrangements that existed in other European countries, including France."[89] The similarity in terms of both institutions and values manifested itself in culture and education. The network of parish schools "in Poland at that time—'in four [Polish] Crown provinces (not including the Ruthenian territories' in Lithuania)—was as robust as it was in France or in England."[90] There was also the Jagiellonian University, which allowed the national elites to connect with cultural centers in Italy and France. An important element of this "borrowing of the ideals of culture and learning from abroad"[91] was the relatively large number of Poles who studied there. "Poland, together with the countries north of the Alps, tried to emulate Renaissance Italy, from which it got humanism and Renaissance art. Poland sent its sons to Italy to be educated, and evaluated people according to Italian criteria."[92]

Thus, according to Wyczański, due to its imitation of cultural and educational institutions, its institutional policy arrangements, and, to a lesser extent, social and legal solutions, combined with its strong economic performance and advantageous position in international politics, Poland caught up with Europe during the first half of the sixteenth century.

Catch up measured by the degree of imitation did not, however, bring similar success in the social sphere. The latter, according to Wyczański, remained backward, that is, it maintained earlier arrangements that were already disappearing in the West; it was burdened by a more powerful medieval legacy. Poland achieved economic performance comparable to that of the West within the framework of other institutions of production. "This is because, formally, there were major differences between the economies of Poland and other developed countries in Europe. Whereas folwarks and serfdom were the rule in Poland, tenant farms and sharecropping prevailed abroad."[93] Changes to the feudal organization of society in Europe had little impact on peasant strata in Poland. "The only things happening in Poland that

89 Wyczański, *Dogonić Europę*, 79.
90 Ibid., 37.
91 Ibid., 79.
92 Ibid.
93 Ibid.

were mirrored in the developed countries of the West were the economic, social, and cultural mobilization of the szlachta, the growing importance of at least part of the town population, and the replacement of elites. The gap between Poland and Western Europe was due to the stronger feudal legacy among Polish peasants and the expansion of serfdom."[94]

Wyczański's model seemed to suggest that imitation was more attractive for the elites and thus that is where it was most effective. The policy of imitation affected the various social strata at a rate commensurate with their place in the social hierarchy—the higher up they were in the hierarchy, the faster they accepted Western models. This evolution encompassed society, beginning with the elites and often not reaching the lower strata. "As regards the magnates, szlachta, and town population, similar phenomena could be observed in Poland and abroad. The situation of the peasants, despite some analogies, was very different. This is most likely because the evolution of social relations in Poland was delayed in comparison with the West."[95]

Wyczański's model appeared to indicate that imitation was most effective when it concerned the establishment of institutions that not only did not threaten the position of the elite but actually strengthened it: schools, universities, bodies representing the szlachta estate, as well as manorial and diplomatic organizations. Imitation did not, however, include Western solutions that required the upper strata to forgo, at least in the short term, some of their privileges in favor of the lower strata, primarily the replacement of personal serfdom with land-based serfdom—sharecropping or rent.

Wyczański drew attention to the fact that the changes in the sociocultural sphere were not only elitist but also piecemeal. Whereas the szlachta learned from its European counterparts how to be economically and educationally active, it did not, according to Wyczański, participate to any major degree in the European religious struggles of the early sixteenth century. The Reformation "was accepted . . . in Poland locally and sort of reluctantly."[96] Wyczański tried to explain this phenomenon by pointing to the superficiality of the Poles' Christian faith.

[94] Ibid.
[95] Ibid.
[96] Ibid.

He constantly referred to Polish backwardness in the religious sphere too—in all likelihood Christianity was poorly internalized, such that it could not arouse similar passions as in Western societies. "Perhaps they [the Poles] looked upon the Church as a human institution—an important, even necessary institution, but nonetheless composed of people."[97]

Hence, the early sixteenth century was the period when Poland was most effective in catching up with Europe and thus experienced intensive development. The crisis in subsequent centuries was due to the country's inability to imitate the West completely. In terms of the social system, the following decades saw the gap between Poland and the West increase as "the folwarks gained a position of absolute dominance in their competition with the peasantry . . . the negative consequences of this gap did not fully reveal themselves until later."[98] The second half of the sixteenth century and subsequent centuries witnessed another failure to imitate the West—this time in relation to the political system. During the golden age, "the scope of royal power and its tendency to grow, and forms of representation and deliberation, were similar to Western Europe, and the political aspirations of the szlachta did not challenge this similarity, since parliamentarism in various forms . . . played a greater or lesser role in almost all European countries."[99]

In later periods, however, the gap between Poland and Western Europe increased. Poland remained a *Res Publica* of the Nobility while absolutism became the dominant political system in the West. In both spheres—the social structure and the political system—the attempt to catch up with Europe was delayed by the Lithuanian and Ruthenian lands of the Commonwealth, which lagged behind the West even more than the Polish lands did.

Wyczański's model took shape in opposition to Małowist's colonial thesis and the image of East European backwardness in Western historiography. In challenging the colonial thesis, Wyczański used logical arguments in addition to factual and theoretical ones. Most prominent among the factual arguments were the findings of his research, cited above, on the structure of imports and economic performance

97 Ibid.
98 Ibid.
99 Ibid.

of the Commonwealth. Among the theoretical arguments the most important were: Wyczański's treatment of raw materials exports as evidence of specialization within the framework of the European economy (and not of narrowly specialized development as Małowist argued), and the positive trade balance (a factor ignored by Małowist) as evidence that Poland conducted international trade on favorable terms. The most important logical argument against the colonial thesis worthy of consideration was that "there were other countries with a similar economic structure that did not pay for their economic handicap by suffering partition or total collapse." Russia and the German principalities in the East—because it is probably those that Wyczański had in mind—despite having manorial-serf economies, and despite exporting raw materials and importing highly processed goods, not only avoided collapse between the sixteenth and eighteenth centuries but actually grew into world powers, if not in an economic sense then certainly in a military one. Their example showed that there did not exist a necessary relationship between folwarks and serfdom on the one hand and political disintegration on the other.

In my view, Wyczański's model was an example of the incursion of modernization theory into Polish historiography, although it differed from modernization theory primarily in terms of the historical epoch to which it related. Wyczański's concept of development, specifically the development of Poland in the fifteenth and sixteenth centuries, referred to a premodern period, hence a period to which the original theory of modernization did not apply. The similarity consisted in the fact that, first, Wyczański adopted the evolutionist view that development implied following the trail blazed by the most developed societies of the West. This meant that it was imperative for backward societies to imitate Western societies. Second, Wyczański's model, similarly to modernization theory in the 1950s and 1960s, treated national communities as virtually closed and autonomous systems. On the other hand, by narrowing the comparative perspective to European societies and placing Poland within the context of Western civilization understood in cultural terms, Wyczański's model was similar to the modernization perspective adopted by Polish sociology in the 1990s.

The concept of traditional societies "catching up" with modern societies, introduced by modernization theory, was in Wyczański's model applied to societies that he felt belonged to Western civilization.

It was also extended to the premodern era. Catching up through imitation entailed the wholesale acceptance of institutional arrangements from as early as the Middle Ages, that is, feudal arrangements. I should emphasize here that Wyczański did not treat Poland's catching up with the West in the sixteenth century as a prelude to it becoming a modern capitalist society, which, he argued, only happened in the eighteenth and nineteenth centuries.[100] Rather, he saw it as the choice of the most beneficial development model during that period. That Wyczański made such a distinction—between feudal catch up and modern, capitalist catch up—is shown by his concept of capitalism and by the fact that his model societies were located in the sixteenth century, namely in France and northern Italy, and not in the great powers of the modern age. Attachment to the evolutionist idea of unilinear development was stronger, even in Wyczański's more mature model, than in the three other interpretations presented here. Although this element became less prominent in Wyczański's views as well, it never weakened to the extent that he could regard Polish development as fundamentally different to West European development.

Social evolutionism, understood as the attribution of varying degrees of sophistication to observed organizational forms, is part and parcel of any economically sensitive social thought—one that regards the size and distribution of social income as a factor in the organization of society. Such an understanding of evolutionism means little more than an acceptance of the idea that the societies of the world form a hierarchical structure according to their degree of affluence, even if simple ones are never meant to resemble more complex ones. On such a narrow definition of the term, all the historians described here remained evolutionists in all of their works—they used phrases such as "developed societies," "backward societies," and so on. However, a basic element of evolutionism in the social sciences is an assumption about the universal social progress of humanity and the necessary replacement of simple organizational forms with more complex ones, that is, with more mature social institutions. This approach assumes that wherever simple forms still exist, they will be ultimately replaced

[100] Wyczański, *Polska na tle Europy*, 149–50

by more complex ones that are already known from elsewhere.[101] In historical and economic research, this attitude can manifest itself in the assumption that organizational forms other than the most progressive ones are anachronisms or accidental mutations which should give way to the latter. Wyczański seemed to acknowledge that the laws of development were universal within a given sphere of civilization. His attitude toward social evolutionism changed in a manner characteristic of the transformation within modernization theory itself. Starting from optimistic evolutionism, his approach later shifted to assisted evolutionism. Imitation was to be controlled by a rational elite. This is evident when one compares his works from the 1970s with *Catching up with Europe*, published in the late 1980s.

Over that same period Wyczański changed his interpretation of the history of Polish society. Whereas initially he had searched for the similarities between Polish and Western European society in the sixteenth century, later on he identified areas where catching up through imitation had brought success and those where it had not. His earlier view was that European countries, which shared the same ideals, developed in a manner similar to each other, differing only in the degree of advancement of the same processes. Poland in the sixteenth century developed just as other European countries did, including those that would play a key role in the future, such as England. The author's credo from the 1970s was as follows: "Without questioning the so-called specificity of Polish society during that period, I wish to refer here to a claim I made several years ago, namely, that the vast majority of the phenomena that occurred in sixteenth-century Poland could be described as 'normal' for European countries at that time. This position also inclined me to search for phenomena in Poland that were regarded as typical of other countries, rapidly developing countries included."[102] This was evidenced by Wyczański's conviction, expressed elsewhere, that "it should be sufficient for us to conclude that the direction of change in the economy was generally similar and that in this respect Poland was not backward compared to the rest of Europe; that qualitatively and quantitatively there occurred in Poland quite

[101] Sztompka, *The Sociology*, 107–12.

[102] Wyczański, *Uwarstwienie społeczne*, 6.

similar phenomena to those in France, Spain, Italy, and Germany."[103] It was during that period that Wyczański most strongly opposed the colonial interpretation of the history of Poland and her neighbors. He saw it as an unjustified projection of the principles of modern capitalism onto a precapitalist age.[104]

Toward the end of the 1980s, while still rejecting the idea of the country's capitalist dependence on the West in the sixteenth century, Wyczański acknowledged not only that there were differences between Poland's social structure and that of the West but that these differences had played a key role in Poland's negative future development. By dividing the catch-up criteria into the material and the social, he argued that backwardness in the social sphere, combined with the simultaneous success of imitation (measured by purely economic criteria), had been the cause of future decline and political disintegration. The idea that the polarized social structure was one of the reasons for the collapse of the Commonwealth and, less frequently, of other Eastern European states, also appeared in the models of Małowist and Kula. However, those authors tended to see polarization as the result of economic phenomena. The analytical separation of the economic sphere, whose basic phenomenon was growth, and the social sphere, whose salient feature was equality or equilibrium (or their absence), was clearly only present in the works of Wyczański.[105] On the other hand, Wyczański shared with Topolski a quasi-Weberian understanding of the impact of cultural values (not necessarily religious values, hence "quasi"-Weberian) and an emphasis on endogenous mechanisms of development and stagnation.

---

103 Wyczański, *Polska na tle Europy*, 151.

104 Wyczański declared that he "would be afraid to discuss capitalism, even in its early stage in the sixteenth and seventeenth centuries," in Wyczański, "W sprawie oceny gospodarki europejskiej," a review of the book *Narodziny kapitalizmu* by Topolski, 618. He developed this position in Wyczański, "Polska na tle Europy," 149–50.

105 Kula wrote at length about division of social income as being equivalent to the Wyczański's "social sphere." Kula, "Podział dochodu społecznego," and Kula, "Przywilej społeczny a postęp gospodarczy." Research on the division of national income as the main socioeconomic indicator was initiated in Polish historiography by Rutkowski, *Badania nad podziałem dochodów*.

A Model of Unfortunate Historical Coincidence: Topolski

Topolski's view of East European development in the early modern era consisted of three analytically distinct models. "Those theories basically concern three closely related aspects of the issue: the causes of dualism in the economic development of Europe; the causes of the development of the manorial system based on the second serfdom; and the causes of economic decline in many parts of Eastern Europe that, in addition to the differences between the socioeconomic systems of the East and West, also deepened the disparities in the level and pace of economic growth."[106] The first of these models—the emergence in the sixteenth century of a developmental dualism in early modern Europe—was meant to explain the birth of capitalism in Northwestern Europe and the refeudalization of Eastern Europe.[107] The second model, maintaining the assumptions of the first, explained the way in which the manorial–serf economy operated—from its inception in the sixteenth century, through its contraction in the seventeenth century, to the attempts to surmount it in the eighteenth century. Recovery from the crisis was captured in greater detail in a sub-model relating to the economy of eighteenth-century Wielkopolska—"an example of a developing region."[108] The third model proposed by Topolski aimed to explain the differences in economic growth across seventeenth-century Europe—the crisis in Southern and Eastern Europe, the dynamic development of Northwestern Europe, and the slow development of other areas. Both the second and third models—the manorial–serf economy and the crisis of the seventeenth century—were presented in their most detailed form in the latter stages of the Polish debate.[109] Topolski's models were characterized by straightforwardness and precise exposition. Unlike other models presented here, his were accom-

106 Topolski, "Modele teoretyczne," 295–96.

107 Topolski, *Narodziny kapitalizmu*, Topolski, "Wielki przewrót w gospodarce europejskiej," Topolski, "Causes of Dualism."

108 Topolski, "Model gospodarczy Wielkopolski."

109 Also: Topolski, "Economic Decline," Topolski, "The Manorial–Serf Economy," Topolski, "Założenia modelu gospodarki polskiej," Topolski, *Polska w czasach nowożytnych*, 561–83.

panied by theoretical reflection on the usefulness of models in historical research. In the 1970s, Topolski became an ardent promoter of this method of historical research.

Over the next thirty years, despite changes in geographical terminology and chronology, Topolski's explanation of the refeudalization of Eastern Europe in the sixteenth century remained essentially the same. However, he broadened the set of factors that were to cause the economic decline in the Commonwealth in the seventeenth and eighteenth centuries and yet only stagnation in other areas of Europe where serfdom existed.

In the words of Piotr Wandycz, a sympathetic commentator on Topolski's methodological achievements, his vision of East European development went through "a significant evolution from sophisticated Marxism to an attempt to reconcile individual and social freedom of choice with the conditions governing that choice and the role of chance."[110] In its more mature version, Topolski's vision was one variant of the model of historical coincidence. This was a multifactor model in which different development paths were seen as unforeseeable configurations of circumstances and factors and in which cultural factors (mentalities) played a preeminent role. It is this last, the most complex version of the model of East European development that is the subject of my analysis.

In Topolski's model, the culminating moment when the development paths of East and West diverged was the end of the Middle Ages and beginning of the early modern era. During that period the internal market expanded due to the rising incomes of the lowest estates across Europe. At the same time, the difference between the incomes of the szlachta and the lower estates decreased. This difference had previously ensured the former a level of consumption high enough to underscore its privileged status. "At the end of the Middle Ages the relationship between the needs and incomes of the szlachta changed: these two quantities moved in opposite directions, and this encouraged the szlachta to develop activities aimed at increasing its income. This process occurred in both Eastern and Western Europe."[111] Faced

[110] Wandycz, "Polska," 44.
[111] Topolski, *Gospodarka polska*, 75.

with a relative decrease in its income, the nobility in each country responded in a similar way, that is, it "simply developed its own economic activity."[112] Although the desire to raise income was common to the whole European nobility, and its reaction was rational from the point of view of its own economic advantage, the realization of this desire had different macroeconomic consequences. The specific form of economic activity undertaken by the nobility "could either result in an increase in domestic output or simply in the increased exploitation of the peasantry with no positive impact on economic growth."[113]

In the countries east of the Elbe, the legal dependence of peasants on their masters encouraged the latter to take up economic activities based on serfdom. "The general . . . phenomenon characteristic of Europe east of the Elbe was the transition from a rent economy, i.e., the collection of money rents and contributions in kind from the peasants, toward the organization of independent agricultural production. . . . [This was possible thanks to the fact that] in the countries east of the Elbe the peasants were not formally free as in Western Europe, and besides, the position of the szlachta was . . . stronger than in the West."[114] The incentive to establish grain-producing folwarks in eastern Germany and Poland, livestock farms in Hungary, Moldavia, and Wallachia, and fish farms in Bohemia was therefore—and here Topolski was in agreement with Rutkowski—the development of the internal market and the favorable conditions for the production and sale of those goods. In Topolski's model, a condition for the expansion of folwarks was the unfree status of peasants, and the reason why serfdom could intensify without any major protest was that in the sixteenth century peasant incomes also increased.

The high and rising incomes of all groups in the sixteenth century began to decline in the first half of the seventeenth century. Topolski's model attributed this fall in incomes principally to lower yields and the ravages of war, which affected the entire manorial–serf economy across Europe. "In the economic sphere the crisis was caused by lower motivation and productivity among the peasants, associated with the institution of serfdom; it was also caused by the weakening of the towns,

[112] Ibid., 76.
[113] Topolski, *Narodziny kapitalizmu*, 106.
[114] Topolski, *Polska w czasach nowożytnych*, 23.

which was in turn due to the contraction of the internal market caused by the economic weakness of the peasants. These processes were the opposite of what was happening in Western Europe at that time: we had refeudalization, and they had the growth of capitalism."[115]

The crisis in the manorial economy that emerged in the seventeenth century was, in Topolski's model, mainly due to the decline in the productivity of serf labor, "and taking only this factor into consideration," argued the author, "we can explain the decrease in the productivity of the serf system. . . . The most negative effects of serf labor were seen in crop cultivation, especially grain."[116] This explained why the crisis was particularly acute in areas where there existed grain-producing folwarks, that is, the Commonwealth and eastern Germany. Yields fell, and so did the incomes of rural groups—szlachta and peasants alike. As a result the domestic market shrank, which in turn led to a decline in craft production. However, it was only the szlachta, using its political advantage, that could attempt to reverse its falling income. "The owners of folwarks mainly relied on two methods. Firstly, they increased the amount of land under cultivation and, secondly, they intensified serfdom."[117] This led to a further decline in efficiency, productivity, and the size of the internal market. It also changed the income structure, primarily to the detriment of the peasantry and also the town population and middle szlachta. However, it also allowed the owners of large folwarks to maintain high incomes for quite some time. "Bigger properties had an automatic advantage over smaller ones. Indeed, as far as the incomes of their owners were concerned, the latter were protected against falling productivity by the fact that they held reserves of both land and serf labor."[118] The cumulative effect of these negative economic phenomena was more social inequality and a further increase in the political dominance of the szlachta, especially the magnates. This was expressed in the concentration of land ownership and in the magnates' absolute political dominance. Its manifestation was a system of oligarchy among the magnates and the weakening of

[115] Ibid., 5–6.
[116] Ibid., 564.
[117] Ibid., 565.
[118] Ibid., 566.

royal power in Poland, and absolutism "in the class interests of feudal owners" in neighboring countries.[119]

The wars of the seventeenth century affected the Commonwealth particularly badly. They were waged on its territory and lasted longer in the Commonwealth than elsewhere, bringing towns and cities to ruin.[120] Indirectly, therefore, these wars were a result of the political system (the Khmelnitsky Uprising of 1648 and the subsequent conflict in the eastern borderlands) and the weakness of the state (the Swedish invasion of 1655–60).

Topolski regarded the crisis of the seventeenth century, which was so detrimental to the Commonwealth, to have been caused by changes in mentalities and political structures. The falling demand for grain on Western markets was a secondary factor. Topolski agreed with Małowist that in the late seventeenth and early eighteenth centuries, changes took place on foreign markets that were damaging to the grain trade. In the colonial model, the import of craft products and export of raw materials was a result of trade relations with the West. In Topolski's model, by contrast, it was a result of the internal relations of production and internal class relations as well as professed economic values and ideologies. An important factor behind the crisis was thus the growing dominance of the magnates and their ethos, their contempt for productive activities, and their belief that an autarkic economy was superior to one based on commerce and industry.[121] Topolski emphasized that the manorial economy's mechanism of decline took the form of a vicious circle: falling productivity, yields, and incomes among most groups in society, and the increasing power of the magnates, which in turn led to a greater burden on the peasants, a shrinking domestic market, lower productivity, and so on.

According to Topolski's model, at the end of this period the szlachta found new ways to increase its income. In areas dominated by large estates this usually involved the magnates organizing itinerant

---

119 Ibid., 23.

120 Ibid., 573–76.

121 Ibid., ch. "Ewolucja modelu i myślenia gospodarczego. Rozwój gospodarczy kraju." A forerunner of this cultural explanation can be found in Topolski, *Narodziny kapitalizmu*, 173–78.

trade as well as the production, sale, and licencing of alcohol.[122] Manufactories located on folwarks, which made use of serf labor, aimed to reduce expenditure through local production. In areas where the folwarks were smaller, "autonomous," and not oriented toward export—mainly in the regions of Wielkopolska and Pomerania—the economy was modernized through rents, the cultivation of crops other than grain, the expansion of non-agricultural forms of production, and the influx of new settlers who operated as smallholders.[123]

In the second half of the eighteenth century, therefore, the whole of Eastern Europe was, according to Topolski, characterized by slow but steady economic growth. What determined the future development of the region was the political system and the power of the state. The Partitions of the Commonwealth and the rising power of neighboring countries were a consequence of political solutions. "Therefore, the Partitions did not hit a Poland that was economically failing, but a Poland that was developing and overcoming the vicious cycle of poverty. Yet the state remained weak."[124] At the same time, in neighboring countries (Russia, Prussia, and the Habsburg Empire), which also had manorial–serf economies, absolutist power structures took shape, with their characteristic expansionist policies and centralized armies.

The most enduring element of Topolski's model, which he perfected over thirty years, was its emphasis on the internal—national or even local—conditions that governed development. These included:

- the social structure,
- the economic motivations of individuals and classes, together with their cultural and political determinants, and their unforeseen macroeconomic consequences,
- the impact of the natural environment.

In Topolski's model, the influence of external markets was limited.

Similarly to Kula's model, the originality of Topolski's model, already in its earliest incarnation, lay in the fact that it sought the roots of capitalism in the social structure of the European countryside

[122] Topolski, "Założenia modelu gospodarki polskiej," 39–40.
[123] Topolski, "Model gospodarczy."
[124] Topolski, "Założenia modelu gospodarki polskiej," 43.

in the early modern era. Topolski's belief that the lord-peasant relationship was key to economic development in the sixteenth and seventeenth centuries anticipated Brenner's model, which I discuss in Chapter 1. Indeed, Topolski later engaged in a polemic with Brenner. What was unique in Topolski's approach was that he focused on the economic activity of the szlachta. "Previous interpretations of the origins or beginnings of European capitalism have generally focused on the development of those groups in society, mainly town populations, which became stronger as the monetary economy took hold. In this study, by contrast, we concentrate primarily on the activities of a social class which, unlike other social classes during that period, was losing . . . its footing, that is, the szlachta."[125]

Another element of continuity in Topolski's approach was his relationship to the colonial model. Topolski remained opposed to the colonial model on the grounds that it overestimated the role of foreign markets. In 1977, he wrote:

> We believe that the colonial thesis, which, as its starting point, evaluates the role of foreign trade in isolation from the rest of the economy, cannot form the basis of a model of the Polish economy between the sixteenth and eighteenth centuries (or even part of that period). It fails to take into account facts which, in our view, are more important than trade relations between the East and West of Europe. . . . Mechanisms of change and processes should be sought, first of all, within the economy itself, i.e., within the structures that motivate the activity of individuals, groups, and classes under specific objective conditions. Only by looking at the whole picture can one try to establish the impact of external factors, determined by foreign trade, on economic life.[126]

Some aspects of Topolski's model did change, however, such as the reasons why the crisis of the seventeenth century took a different course in Eastern Europe and the ways in which the crisis was overcome in subsequent centuries. By altering this element of his expla-

125 Topolski, *Narodziny kapitalizmu*, 179.
126 Topolski, "Założenia modelu gospodarki polskiej," 15.

nation, the late version of his model downgraded the importance of the manorial–serf economy as a reason for Poland's backwardness. The backwardness and decline of the Commonwealth were now seen as an extreme case, in which various negative processes overlapped, and not as a direct consequence of the system created in the sixteenth century.

The seventeenth-century differences within the Europe of serfdom were ostensibly due to the level and rate of economic growth. Topolski's comments on three separate zones of economic growth during that period—intensive development in England and the Netherlands, regression and stagnation in Poland, Spain, Portugal, Turkey and southern Italy, and slow development in other parts of Europe (including those that had a manorial–serf economy)—allow us to reconstruct his list of causes of the crisis and the changes he made to it.

In the 1960s—a period in which his views could be described, following Wandycz, as "sophisticated Marxism"—Topolski tried to identify the single most important factor that would differentiate areas of stagnation and development. Equating the latter with economic growth, he regarded the possibility "to develop accumulation (and therefore investment)"[127] as a necessary condition for growth to occur. The introduction of such an extremely economistic definition of development can be understood as an attempt to find a common denominator between liberal and Marxist analysis, and indeed this was Wyczański's interpretation. However, I believe that Wandycz's interpretation was more accurate than Wyczański's. It seems to me that in the 1965 version of his model, Topolski argued that the possibility for accumulation and investment was exclusively determined by the class relations within a given society.[128] It was precisely class relations that were the single most important reason for growth or stagnation. In the seventeenth century, societies which had the greatest potential "to develop accumulation," claimed Topolski in 1965, were those in which "the decomposition of feudal relations in the countryside" had advanced the furthest, that is, where the position of the nobility had relatively weakened, where there was the greatest separation of land (ownership) from work, and where the use of hired labor was most

[127] Topolski, *Narodziny kapitalizmu*, 165.

[128] Ibid., 165–78. See: Wyczański, "In Memoriam: Jerzy Topolski," 139–42. Compare the excerpt and the accompanying footnote in Chapter 2.

common. This encouraged the prudent use of hired labor and thus boosted technological innovation, which in turn contributed to an increase in production and a lowering of production costs. The second indicator of development—both chronologically and in terms of its importance to Topolski's understanding of capitalism—was the spread of the industrial mode of production. In the seventeenth century this was evident, above all, in England and, to a slightly lesser degree, in the Netherlands and northwestern Germany, although in the sixteenth century these countries were economically stronger than England. Economic growth was lower, argued Topolski, the more feudal and less capitalist the "structure of social relations" and the stronger the position of the nobility. "In countries marked by stagnation and decline, the victory of the nobility was complete. . . . Because it did not affect economic growth (unlike in England and in some countries of the second group), the nobility's economic activity hampered the development of the towns and town populations. What remained for investment was only a relatively small amount of feudal accumulation, as accumulation from small-scale production (peasant farming, crafts), especially in Spain and Poland, was almost non-existent."[129]

One can deduce from Topolski's essay, "Premises of a Model of the Polish Economy in the Sixteenth to Eighteenth Centuries" (Założenia modelu gospodarki polskiej XVI-XVIII wieku), published in 1977, that mentality—"factors of consciousness," "incentive structures,"[130] "social tradition and routine"[131]—became increasingly important in his model. Direct economic factors lost significance. More than previously, Topolski highlighted the impact of economic ideology on development. He introduced the idea of the "granary dogma" to describe the dominant economic ideology in Poland between the sixteenth and eighteenth centuries. The attachment of folwark owners to grain production explained their unjust and pernicious belief in the West's reliance on Polish grain and in the superiority of the autarkic Polish system over the Western one. The structure and policies of the state became a new variable in the model. "The main cause of the slowdown was the process of refeudalization, in relation

[129] Ibid, 178.
[130] Topolski, "Założenia modelu gospodarki polskiej," 15.
[131] Ibid., 27.

to which the state played a catalysing role; it made itself felt not only in the social and economic sphere but also in the sphere of mentalities. Spain, Portugal, Italy (especially southern Italy), and the Balkan countries suffered economic stagnation and decline, as did Poland, devastated by war and [ruined by] its manorial–serf economy."[132]

The Polish–Lithuanian Commonwealth was apparently the only country with a manorial–serf economy to experience a profound crisis in the seventeenth century. The influence of local magnates on state policy supposedly explained (in the late 1970s) the difference between the decline of the Commonwealth and the moderate growth of other manorial–serf economies "east of the Elbe." The state and the dominant mentality acquired a relative autonomy in Topolski's model.

The impact of the external market and exploitation by the more developed countries also became autonomous, albeit less important, conditions. The same was true of natural conditions, such as good harvests. Under the influence of Kula's research, Topolski accorded more weight to this factor than to prices. Likewise under Kula's influence he introduced into his model the factor of the profitability of the peasant economy.

In the next incarnation of his model,[133] a mere five years later, mentality—the "incentive structures" and "value systems" that appeared in his jargon in the 1980s—now took on a fundamental importance. Topolski extended the list of factors that contributed to the backwardness of Eastern Europe and the birth of capitalism in Northwestern Europe. "To explain this one has to specify . . . the conditions that had a positive impact and not just those that created an 'environment' for that impact to happen. For capitalism to emerge there had to be towns, agricultural production, accumulation . . . but also the absence, in the sixteenth century for example, of plague, which would have killed off most of the population. The absence of a particularly severe plague, therefore, was essential to the emergence of capitalism. You might call this an obstructive condition. For a given consequence to occur, the absence of obstructive conditions is, of course, essential too."[134]

---

132 Ibid., 35.
133 Topolski, "Modele teoretyczne."
134 Ibid., 314.

Topolski's somewhat abstruse deliberations suggest that, to a greater extent than previously, he considered underdevelopment to be the outcome of many different factors, and he attributed less importance to the class structure and class struggle. I believe that this change was to some degree influenced by the numerous studies that offered attractive but nonetheless single-factor explanations. When taking issue with authors who pointed to a single key factor that explained backwardness (Anderson, Wallerstein, Brenner), Topolski juxtaposed it with other factors that were just as likely. Commenting on the position taken by Brenner, who, like Topolski in 1965, linked the emergence of different development paths in Europe to class relations in the countryside, he wrote: "His class struggle hangs in a vacuum. . . . It is simply that, for Brenner, the class factor is merely a necessary but not a sufficient condition."[135] Topolski highlighted the differences within Europe of the folwark and the (albeit limited) importance of foreign trade. When, in turn, he analyzed Wallerstein's model, who treated international trade as the basis for economic inequalities in early modern Europe, Topolski emphasized the importance of social factors. Despite his ornamental allegiance to Marxism, he no longer asked about the first cause, the only sufficient condition. He accepted the importance of various factors and emphasized the non-material ones. He tried to determine the proportions and degree of interaction between different historical circumstances.

In the early 1990s version of his model, Topolski saw both the development and the decline of the Polish economy as the result of historical coincidence. In his list of explanatory factors, now enriched with new entries, wars were clearly demoted as a cause of the seventeenth-century crisis in the Commonwealth. Systemic factors and policies, including economic policies, acquired greater significance.

Topolski's approach, therefore, changed from trying to identify the principal cause of development and backwardness to viewing economic development as a configuration of numerous circumstances that influenced each other. Among the new factors in his model of backwardness, cultural and political factors gained most in importance. The evolution of his model may therefore be seen as a transition from economic reductionism, through the inclusion of an increasing number

---

135 Ibid.

of factors, to a vision of history as coincidence, and in particular the growing importance of cultural factors.

Topolski's model evolved almost in parallel to the changes that took place in mainstream historical research on the origins of Western power. The 1980s witnessed, as Andrew Janos tried to describe it in 1986, a paradigm shift in the social sciences from economistic structuralism to cultural explanations.[136] I would add that this shift also changed expectations about how major social phenomena could be explained. The diminishing interest in the 1990s in major processes and skepticism as to whether they could be explained at all, which Janusz Żarnowski emphasized,[137] was preceded in the 1980s by a tendency to understand historical processes as a result of coincidence or contingency.[138] In the field of historical studies on development, ideas about the birth of capitalism as a European miracle, an unforeseeable mix of natural, institutional, and social coincidences, emerged in the 1990s and became hugely popular.[139] Much more so than the other authors portrayed here, Topolski was fascinated by, and responded to, the paradigm shift in historical research. To a lesser extent than the other models, his vision of development was related to the debates taking place within sociology.

I should emphasize that what has remained fresh and interesting in Topolski's model is the assumption, maintained in successive versions of the model, that it was precisely the behavior of the szlachta,

[136] Janos, *Politics and Paradigms*.

[137] Żarnowski, "Kryzys i perspektywy historii społecznej," 383–92.

[138] Important works that adopt this perspective are cited in Chapter 1: Mann, *The Sources of Social Power*, Chirot, *Social Change*. In the first work, the source of European dynamism is sought in the accidental conjunction of political, religious, and socioeconomic phenomena. The second work stresses the favourable coincidence of geographical, political, legal, and religious circumstances that established Europe's dominant position in the world. An earlier explanation which classified the events as a "miracle" was proposed by the Noble Prize winners North and Thomas, *The Rise*. See also: Kochanowicz, "Twórca i dzieło."

[139] Jones, *The European Miracle*. As I wrote in Chapter 1, Braudel's *Civilization and Capitalism* and, to some extent, R. Brenner's *Economic Backwardness*, with which Topolski was familiar, can be classified within this paradigm. More information about the debate over the origins of capitalism and the rise of the West—but only in context of East European backwardness—can be found in Chapter 1 of this book.

a group associated with the old regime, that played the key role in the revolution of the sixteenth century. That explanation is all the more interesting because it arose despite the author's best efforts to remain loyal to the Marxist theory of transition from feudalism to capitalism.

A Model of Hybrid Development: Kula

In this section I discuss two separate models that relate to historical periods in which the criteria of economic rationality were different.[140] The first of these, presented in detail in 1962 in *An Economic Theory* and modified over the next two decades, sought to establish the mechanisms by which the manorial–serf economy operated and then collapsed at a time when capitalism was developing in the West. It was based on research on the Polish economy between the sixteenth and eighteenth centuries.[141] The second model was implicit, being the result of theoretical studies and attempted comparisons (rather than research, per se, as I showed in Chapter 3). It aimed to determine the laws governing the transition from feudalism to capitalism as well as the course of the industrial revolution and the functioning of capitalism in Poland—a backward country—and then extend these laws to Eastern Europe. The model attempted to generalize the processes behind failed industrial revolutions in countries where these had occurred in the nineteenth century. Kula included the countries of Southern and Eastern Europe and Latin America in this category.[142] For the purposes of this chapter, I consider the late version of Kula's model.

---

[140] The differentiation of feudal and capitalist rationality, and the determination of their criteria, is one of Kula's most important arguments. W. Kula, *Początki kapitalizmu w Polsce w perspektywie historyczno-porównawczej*, 78–81, Kula, *An Economic Theory.*

[141] Kula, *An Economic Theory*. Kula writes about the role of theory and model in the introduction and conclusion. Kochanowicz and Mączak noted that Kula's model explained the decline and not the origins of the manorial–serf system, Kochanowicz, *Spór o teorię,* 116–19, Mączak, "O przydatności modeli ekonomicznych."

[142] Kula presented this implicit model of the beginnings of industrialization and capitalism in *Historia, zacofanie.*

Unlike Topolski and Wyczański, but somewhat similarly to Małowist, Kula explained backwardness not just in terms of internal social and economic structures but also in terms of external influence. However, unlike Małowist, and similarly to Wyczański and Topolski, he treated national society as the primary unit of his analysis. Kula attached as much significance as Małowist did to the influence of Western capitalism on East European development. He wanted to establish the ways in which "the threads originating from those centers spread throughout the entire country,"[143] that is, what this meant for the economy and society of a backward country. In keeping with the author's theoretical intentions, one can interpret Kula's vision of the development of a backward society that remained in contact with advanced capitalist societies as a hybrid of classical development.

Overlapping with the course of natural development that "resulted from the passage of time,"[144] as Kula described it, were influences from the outside world. The effect of these influences in Kula's model was similar to that of cultural diffusion. It was "an exogenous change of external origin that modified rather than fundamentally transformed the cultural system," and the rule was that "intense diffusion in one cultural sphere may be accompanied by the absence of change in other spheres."[145] For Kula, however, the outcome of such influences was a mix of non-harmonized elements from various epochs (not cultures)—feudalism and capitalism, or socialism.[146] Starting from the assump-

---

143 Kula, "Przewrót przemysłowy," 148.

144 Kula, *Kształtowanie się kapitalizmu*, 50.

145 Ewa Nowicka, "Dyfuzja kulturowa," 152–54.

146 The term "hybrid" became popular in social theory in the 1990s under the influence of criticism of the concept of modernity. According to the critics, modernity was rather a project of classical sociology than an adequate description of historical reality. The term "hybridity"—understood as a mix of elements belonging to different categories—describes various social phenomena and at the same time deconstructs the paradigm of modern social theory. It is used most often in cultural studies on postcolonial societies, immigrants from postcolonial countries, or "marginal" groups, similarly to the term "creolization." There is even a category of "Hybridity (Social Science)" in the catalogue of the U.S. Library of Congress. See: Brah and Coombes, *Hybridity and Its Discontents*, Werbner and Modood, *Debating Cultural Hybridity*, Aparicio and Jáquez, *Musical Migrations*, Young, *Colonial Desire*, Zarifian, *L'émergence*

tion that the transition from feudalism to capitalism as represented by the Marxist theory of development should be considered a model of "normal" or "classical" development,[147] Kula described the successive stages of development of a backward society as the "coexistence of asynchronisms" and structural paradoxes.[148] Elements of the new era appeared under different conditions (determined by the fact that capitalism already existed in other countries), in a different order, and at a different pace. Coexisting with "vestiges of feudalism" that were more durable than in advanced countries, they formed other, hybrid configurations that were usually less conducive to economic development. To describe Kula's model as one of hybrid development also alludes to the author's theoretical dialogue with two major interpretations of social change—the Marxist theory of development and dependency theory.

HYBRID FEUDALISM

Kula's model of Polish feudalism from the sixteenth to the eighteenth centuries had just one element that was characteristic of feudalism in general, and it was not its defining feature because it was also present in other systems: "(1) The overwhelming predominance of agriculture

d'un peuple monde. In a similar manner and with similar theoretical intentions, the term "mixed economy" was used in reference to Third World countries in the period of decolonization and increased interest in the economies of those countries. See Tajerowa, *O gospodarce mieszanej*. The term "hybridity," although Kula never used it, seems to fit his tendency to describe underdeveloped countries in terms of paradoxes and a mix of elements from different eras.

147 Kula, "Przewrót przemysłowy," 143–44.

148 The term "coexistence of asynchronisms" was introduced in Kula, "Sektory i regiony zacofane" in *Historia, zacofanie*, 120–21. In underdeveloped regions or countries "there is a coexistence of forms which have never occurred synchronously in developed countries, because for new forms to exist, old ones had to be eliminated. The discussed phenomenon, which may be called 'the coexistence of asynchronisms,' is characteristic not only of Poland [before 1945]. It can also be observed in the history of the Russian Empire and is currently very much in evidence in the colonial, semi-colonial, or recently decolonized countries." Previously Kula chose to explain the phenomenon in terms of paradox, mix, and "dislocated" path: Kula, "Początki układu kapitalistycznego," 74–75, 81.

in the country's economy."[149] The other elements introduced into the model were either associated with aspects of the East European version of feudalism, which was based on serfdom, or with local characteristics that were specific to the Polish manorial-serf economy.[150] These were as follows:

> (2) The fact that land is not a commodity, primarily because only the nobility can own it, but also because the rate of interest on loans is higher than the yield from landed property. (3) The division of all the forces of agricultural production solely between the village and the lord's demesne. (4) The existence of actual institutional barriers which limit social and geographical mobility, above all for the peasants (serfdom). (5) The obligation upon all peasants to pay most of their rent in the form of labor power (corvée). (6) The fact that industrial and artisan activities are carried out within the confines of the large landed estates or the guilds. (7) The absence of juridical restrictions upon the liberty of the nobility in the economic area. (8) A strong tendency among the nobility toward the consumption of luxury products (a tendency conditioned by the characteristics of the socioeconomic system). (9) The existence, not far from Poland, of economically more advanced countries at a distance accessible by the means of transportation. (10) The absence of all state intervention in economic life (even in the form of protectionist custom duties).[151]

Most of these characteristics related to the social and political conditions of economic activity; one of them was systemic-legal (7), and another was what we would nowadays refer to as cultural (8), although Kula saw it as systemic. Item no. 9 suggests backwardness

[149] Kula, *An Economic Theory*, 26.

[150] In *An Economic Theory*, Kula left the decision about differentiating between the underdeveloped, East European and Polish features of the system to "further research." Among the societies to which his model could be usefully applied, he mentioned Hungary and Russia. Kula, *An Economic Theory*, 26.

[151] Kula, *An Economic Theory*, 26.

and a hybrid form of development. The nature of this development was hybrid because Polish feudalism was subject to influences from beyond its borders, not only in a geographical but also in a systemic sense: these influences originated from the new capitalist system. And this had to do with backwardness because when capitalism appeared in England and the Netherlands, with which Eastern Europe, including Poland, maintained economic relations, "there was a causal relationship between the development of certain regions and the weaker development of other regions."[152]

In Kula's model, the principal institutions of the Polish version of feudalism were folwarks and peasant farms, while crafts and towns played a marginal role.[153] Between the sixteenth and eighteenth centuries this system underwent both internal and external changes. The internal changes concerned the typical economic activities of lord and peasant resulting from their economic rationality consistent with their status. The external changes primarily concerned Poland's terms of trade. What was hybrid about the period was the fact that the structural effects of feudal privilege were different than in the more advanced countries. Whereas in the latter, privilege temporarily led to accumulation, investment, and "spontaneous growth," in Poland the income the szlachta derived from its privileged status was used to purchase "luxury" imports; it thus flowed abroad without contributing to growth.[154]

The internal changes were "constant tendencies and the accumulation of the consequences of phenomena of a 'conjunctural' nature [that] lead, in point of fact, to a change in structure."[155] Among the phenomena that "occur periodically or continuously and the course of which is irreversible . . . [and whose] effects build up and bring about a change in structure"[156] the most important in Kula's model were those relating to the assets held by the main groups in society and their contact with the market. First, the average size of the peasant farm decreased due to the confiscation of land by folwarks and the split-

---

152 Kula, "Zacofanie w perspektywie historycznej," 184.

153 Małowist was critical about this approach. Discussion of Kula's *An Economic Theory, 693.*

154 Kula, "Przywilej społeczny."

155 Kula, *An Economic Theory*, 201–02.

156 Ibid., 118.

ting up of farms on account of the rising peasant population; at the end of the eighteenth century it was even "below the optimal point at which it may be regarded as the minimal area of land sufficient to feed a peasant family and reproduce the forces of production."[157]

Second, in connection with this, and due to the cultivation of barren land and the taking over of smaller folwarks by larger ones, there was a "tendency to unify and isolate economically large landed estates."[158] Third, peasant farms, followed in the second half of the eighteenth century by folwarks, strove toward an autarkic model, that is, the ability to satisfy all needs within the confines of their own feudal enterprises. Kula's research showed that the declining productivity of peasant labor was more pronounced on folwark land than on peasant farms. This led to "the opposing tendency on the peasants' part to produce, at whatever cost, a commercial surplus and to develop a market relationship," and also, particularly in the second half of the eighteenth century, to "the tendency of the large landed estate to 'naturalize' the activities involved in production and transportation" in order to capture that surplus.[159] To this end, the szlachta created monopolies on the sale of alcohol and on trade in craft products made on folwarks. Indeed, at the end of the eighteenth century the first manufactories appeared on Polish soil—folwark manufactories. Technologically modelled on the protocapitalist French manufactories, these were essentially feudal institutions that relied on serf as opposed to hired labor and used their own means of production rather than buying them commercially. This meant that their economic rationality calculations were typical of a "feudal enterprise" and not a capitalist one.[160]

According to Kula, however, the aforementioned structural changes were incomprehensible if one did not consider the global economic changes that were taking place at that time, above all the emergence of capitalism in the most developed countries. To illustrate these external impacts Kula distinguished two economic sectors and intro-

---

157 Ibid.

158 Ibid.

159 Ibid.

160 Ibid. See also Kula, "Początki układu kapitalistycznego," 55–75, Kula, *Szkice*. These two works summarized the research on Polish manufactories which Kula conducted between 1950 and 1956.

duced an index describing the international terms of trade available to different social groups.

Kula's model assumed that between the sixteenth and eighteenth centuries the manorial economy based on the second serfdom was a dual economy.[161] The commercialized sector produced for the market, while the natural sector was oriented toward subsistence and survival. Big landowners and direct producers (the latter being personally dependent on the former) waged an uneven struggle for participation in the commercialized sector—for access to the market.

Kula showed that the way in which the commercialized sector operated was determined both by the internal market and, increasingly, by the accessibility of the foreign market in more advanced countries. The latter was especially attractive because it was a much more absorptive market and the terms of trade it offered for goods produced in Poland (i.e., mainly grain) in exchange for imported goods increasingly favored the former right up until the eighteenth century. In the sixteenth century, "the terms of trade in international commerce shifted to the 'advantage' of Poland: the latter was able to import a greater amount for the same quantity of commodities exported."[162] There was "a very rapid increase at first (sixteenth century), then slower (from about 1660), and then after a brief decline at the end of the seventeenth century, a slow but virtually constant increase for all the eighteenth century."[163] The beneficiaries of this situation were therefore producers who were able to get their goods

[161] Kula modified the dual economy model introduced by Lewis, "Economic Development" and Lewis, *Theory of Economic Growth*. In this model, the division into commercialized (capitalist) and natural (subsistence) sectors reflected the division by enterprise type, which in the case of the Polish economy in the sixteenth to the eighteenth centuries meant the folwark and the peasant farm. Unlike Lewis, however, Kula claimed that "the division into two sectors did not reflect the division by enterprise type but actually encompassed virtually every enterprise." Moreover, he argued that the rationality of the "large landed estate" under "dual economy conditions" was fundamentally different to that of the capitalist enterprise. He also noted that the rationality of the peasant enterprise could not simply be reduced to subsistence and survival. Kula, *An Economic Theory*, 62–75. It was also in *An Economic Theory* that Kula wrote about two distinct rationalities of enterprises operating under feudalism and capitalism.

[162] Kula, *An Economic Theory*, 132–33.

[163] Ibid., 119–20.

as close as they could to this attractive market and in the largest possible quantities. Participation in the market, and especially participation in the lucrative Gdańsk market, was also a social indicator in Kula's model. The group that profited hugely from it was the magnates—the owners of the largest estates, which were still growing between the sixteenth and eighteenth centuries, who had at their disposal the greatest amount of serf labor. Thanks to this, the volume of grain they produced on their folwarks was sufficiently large that its transportation to the Vistula ports and on to Gdańsk, while expensive, remained profitable. It was the magnates, too, who purchased the majority of luxury goods offered by foreign suppliers. Over the course of two centuries their terms of trade—Kula equated these with Gdańsk's terms of trade—improved more than eightfold. They began to worsen, and thus folwark revenues began to decline toward the end of the eighteenth century. This led to more cash being drained from the peasantry through increased pressure to buy alcohol (over whose production and sale the szlachta enjoyed a monopoly) and through the setting up of manufactories during this period.[164]

The middle szlachta—that is, the owners of smaller folwarks and fewer villages compared to the magnates—formed an intermediate group. Their access to the market was limited to domestic urban markets. Those with folwarks located in the Vistula basin or who could deliver their goods to the Vistula towns were in a more favorable position. Their typical terms of trade, Kula assumed, were those that were offered in the country's interior, in Kraków. Between 1550 and 1750 these terms improved by roughly 50 percent. In the second half of the eighteenth century, the amount of assets held by the middle szlachta was in decline.[165] The group that lost the most in the long term from the economic changes of the sixteenth to eighteenth centuries, but which found it easiest to survive the recession of the second half of the eighteenth century, was the peasants. Their terms of trade, calculated on the basis of Kraków prices, improved in the second half of the sixteenth century and then declined, by the mid-eighteenth century reaching a level that was lower by half compared to 1550, the base year.

---

164 Ibid., 135–48.
165 Ibid., 150–59.

Kula argued that the system, despite its macroeconomic inefficiency, lasted for as long as it remained beneficial to the ruling class, that is, the magnates.

> This is, in appearance, a favorable situation, the opposite of the one in which countries exporting raw materials find themselves today (countries that are generally underdeveloped). In these countries the terms of trade have been worsening for the past century, exacerbating already existing economic difficulties. . . . The shifts in the terms of trade, which were seemingly favorable to Poland, in reality undermined Polish economic development, although they brought great economic advantages to a single social stratum. Due to the concurrence of great worldwide changes, the Polish nobility, and particularly the upper nobility, found themselves in the position of rentiers, "coupon clipping" and profiting from the process of economic retrogression in the country.[166]

The collapse of the folwark system in Poland at the end of the eighteenth century was, according to Kula, associated with the declining opportunities for export and, more broadly, with the proliferation of industrial and colonial capitalism in the West. Weighing up the causes of the system's collapse in the seventeenth to eighteenth centuries, Kula argued that "the industrial revolution took place outside this system. . . . Outside it there arose a powerful, expanding system with which it could not compete. A secondary effect of this fact was a drastic and lasting limitation on the export of Polish agricultural produce."[167] "[It was] impossible to return to the state of affairs of the sixteenth to the eighteenth century. . . . It is necessary therefore to construct a new model. Here, then, is an example—certainly not the only one—of changes external to the model which deprive it of validity."[168]

The new model—industrialization and the rise of capitalism in a backward country—showed that the long-term effects of the system were very unfavorable to the economy and that its social and economic consequences would prove very resilient.

---

[166] Ibid., 133.
[167] Ibid., 185.
[168] Ibid., 183–84.

FROM HYBRID CAPITALISM TO HYBRID SOCIALISM

In Kula's model, the transition from feudalism to capitalism took Eastern Europe from backwardness (i.e., the gap separating it from the pioneers of industrialization and capitalism) embedded in a feudal social structure to backwardness embedded in a mixed feudal-capitalist structure.[169] Kula described the trends of that period as "development under the conditions of increasing backwardness."[170]

In Eastern Europe, claimed Kula, just as in the majority of backward countries, the capitalist modernization of agriculture followed the so-called Prussian path,[171] which entailed "adjusting the folwarks to capitalist production methods and transforming the peasant economy, even the partially rent-based economy . . . into an appendage of the great landed estates."[172] The first of these processes involved the intensification of production, commoditization, and the concentration of land ownership. Due to the introduction of rents, undertaken in response to rural overpopulation and excess serf labor, the internal market expanded and the peasantry became stratified. From the point of view of the attempts at industrialization during this period, what was important was the creation of a group of superfluous, landless people.

Kula attributed the industrialization attempts in Eastern Europe to the influence of the powerful and unrivalled West European model of capitalist production.[173] He presented these attempts as the effect

169 Kula, *An Economic Theory*. This is why Kula argued that research on "the shaping of capitalism," "social mobility," and "social change" in the Kingdom of Poland should have focused on the period prior to 1864, the year which marked the abolition of serfdom and the commercialization of labor. Kula, *Kształtowanie się kapitalizmu*, Kula, *Społeczeństwo Królestwa Polskiego*, Kula and Leskiewiczowa, *Społeczeństwo polskie*, Kula and Leskiewiczowa, *Przemiany społeczne.*

170 Kula, "Rozwój gospodarczy," 11–23. Łepkowski interprets nineteenth century economic development in Poland in a similar way. Łepkowski, *Polska—narodziny nowoczesnego narodu.*

171 Kula, "Początki układu kapitalistycznego," Kula, "Początki kapitalizmu w Polsce."

172 Kula, *Kształtowanie się kapitalizmu*, 97.

173 In the discussion on *An Economic Theory* organized by *Kwartalnik Historyczny* in 1963, Kula posed a question that was not at all rhetorical: could capitalism have emerged in Poland (or, for that matter, in any other

of economic cooperation between the feudal lords, who had excess land and labor at their disposal, and the domestic and foreign bourgeoisie—cooperation that in the Kingdom of Poland during the first half of the nineteenth century was largely financed by the state treasury.[174] The research conducted by Kula's team confirmed that these industrialization attempts did indeed lead to accumulation. However, they resulted in higher consumption and imports rather than increased investment.[175] As it failed to bring about economic growth, "the Polish etatist experiment of the nineteenth century was extremely costly," wrote Jerzy Jedlicki.[176] His research also bore out Kula's claim that industrialization in the Kingdom of Poland during that period had proceeded by a series of "leaps" and essentially failed; it also indirectly corroborated Kula's argument about the persistence of feudal structures and the lack of continuity of social change. "Observing these 'leaps' one can make two general observations: a) none of them was a continuation of the previous one, and b) none of them was on a scale comparable to the 'leaps' that occurred in more developed countries. What is most striking is the lack of continuity."[177]

---

country which at some point in its history had been underdeveloped) without "external intervention (i.e., without the intervention of a pre-existing capitalism from elsewhere)? . . . At this point in the discussion it would seem that the answer to this question must be negative. And if it is, then the modern economic history of the entire world boils down to a single question: the origins of capitalism in England. Everywhere else, capitalism was the product of more or less effective imitation and was an attempt to escape backwardness." Discussion of Kula's *An Economic Theory*, in *Kwartalnik Historyczny* 3 (1963): 690–96. More far-reaching conclusions, presenting the beginnings of capitalism in underdeveloped countries in terms of cultural diffusion, were drawn by Jedlicki on the basis of his studies of industrialization in Poland. He stressed the role of "foreign institutional influences (promissory notes, civil codes, notarial services, mortgages, accounting, budgets, commissariats, etc.), consumption habits and technological inventions and, above all, paradigms of economic behaviour," in Jedlicki, "W sprawie automatycznego krachu," 246.

[174] Kula, "Uwagi o przewrocie."

[175] Kula's students also tackled the beginnings of industrialization in Poland. Kowalska, Jedlicki, and Jezierski, *Ekonomika górnictwa*, Kula, *Badania nad dziejami przemysłu*, Jedlicki, *Nieudana próba*.

[176] Jedlicki, *Nieudana próba*, 373.

[177] Kula, *Początki kapitalizmu w Polsce*, quoted in: J. Jedlicki, *Nieudana próba*, 5.

The hybridity (the mixing of phenomena from different phases of the "classic" model) of the first attempts at industrialization consisted in the fact that these were undertaken within a feudal social structure. Firstly, industrialization was largely the brainchild of the szlachta and mainly served its consumption needs. Secondly, coerced (serf) labor was often used.[178] Generally speaking, the various phases of industrialization occurred in a different order and at a different rate than in the first industrial countries. They were determined by different needs. One example is the role of the machine-building industry, which Kula believed to be important. Whereas in Western Europe the machine-building industry arose in order to meet the needs of light industry and reduce expenditure on unskilled labor, in Eastern Europe, argued Kula, it mainly served "the needs of large landowners, who were introducing capitalist production methods during that period" and performed the functions of a skilled workforce, which did not exist at that time. The low cost of unskilled labor, in turn, meant that there was little incentive to replace it with machines.[179]

In Kula's model, the formal emancipation of the serfs in Eastern Europe in the nineteenth century was not seen as a breakthrough. While it led to the intensification of economic development and social change, East European societies remained a venue for "the coexistence of asynchronisms."[180] Kula's diagnosis of the development of the Polish economy the second half of the nineteenth century, as well as the language he used and the way in which he conceptualized it, were shared by Łepkowski.

> Poland . . . was an example of an agrarian, semi-feudal country that was, as it were, "crowned" by capitalist industry. . . . Indeed, various forms of decaying agrarian feudalism essentially coexisted with the capitalist structures in the strict sense. A form of capitalist agrarian relations combined with major remnants of the serf

[178] Kowalska, Jedlicki, and Jezierski, *Ekonomika górnictwa*, Władysław Rusiński, "W sprawie struktury gospodarstw chłopskich."

[179] Kula, "Uwagi o przewrocie."

[180] Kula, *Historia, zacofanie*, 120–21, Kula, *Kształtowanie się kapitalizmu*, 96–97. See also: Pietrzak-Pawłowska, "The Industrial Revolution and Asynchronism," 101–18.

> system emerged. Added to this multiplicity of systems was huge regional variation, which, although typical of capitalism (the gulf between England and Scotland), was much deeper in Poland, being already very strong in the eighteenth century and even stronger in the second half of the nineteenth century.[181]

External influences increased in the century following the top-down agrarian reforms in Eastern Europe and continued to involve the selective adaptation of Western methods. A novelty was foreign investment. Internal trends boiled down to the dual nature of the economy being maintained and greater polarization between economic sectors and regions. It is worth noting that, according to Kula, the period from the emancipation of the serfs until 1939 was uniform as far as developmental trends were concerned. He appeared to believe that the creation of the Polish state, as well as the land reform it carried out and its attempts at industrialization, did even less than the Partitions of Poland in 1795 to change the rules behind the creation and distribution of social income, which were key to development.

Kula described the East European economies of that period within the framework of a model of economies of a medium degree of backwardness, that is, those which experienced an industrial revolution in the nineteenth century but in which industrialization was unsuccessful.[182] He presented such economies as hybrids. On the one hand they represented the characteristic features of early capitalism and industrialization in general: the fragmentary nature of both, the predominance of agriculture, a dual economy, and the regionalization of economic growth.[183] On the other hand the coexistence of different forms of production—island-like, fragmentary industrialization and economic sectors subject to capitalist rationality versus small-scale craft production and an almost natural peasant economy—proved more durable and resulted in greater social and cultural polarization than in the West. This polariza-

181 Łepkowski, *Polska—narodziny*, 120.

182 Kula, "Przewrót przemysłowy," 146–48. See also: Kula, *Kształtowanie się kapitalizmu*, 94–96, 101.

183 Kula, "Sektory i regiony zacofane." See also: Pietrzak-Pawłowska, *Gospodarka przemysłowa*.

tion was especially sharp due to the presence of phenomena that were completely unknown in early industrialized countries: the import of technology and goods from more advanced countries, competition from more developed countries,[184] the possibility of risk-free investment in those countries,[185] and the role of foreign investment.[186]

Until 1945, claimed Kula, Eastern Europe was composed of

> agricultural countries with very few powerful landowners and peasant overpopulation. The overpopulated countryside, which provided the folwarks with extremely cheap labor, allowed those countries not to invest and not to mechanize their production. On the other hand, overpopulation of the countryside, which was a burden on the labor market, depressed average wages, especially for unskilled work, to a level that was attractive for foreign capital. . . . As a result, the period of the industrial revolution led to emergence of "islands" of industry in a still predominantly agricultural country. . . . Because it belonged to foreign capital this industry was not, so to speak, self-sufficient. . . . [This phenomenon] made it possible to export profits in the form of costs even when, in a given country, there were legal obstacles to the export of profits.[187]

By comparing, on the one hand, the prerequisites of normal development toward an industrialized capitalist society and, on the other, the state of pre–Second World War Polish society, Kula concluded that the latter had a "mixed" nature. "Capitalism and industry 'should' dramatically: (1) get people moving (in Poland in 1939, two thirds of the population lived in rural areas); (2) force them to raise their skills; (3) expand people's horizons; (4) greatly increase productivity; (5) people only develop in contact with other people (urbanization, industrialization, the workers' class struggle). . . . Poland in 1939: undoubtedly

[184] Kula, "Uwagi o przewrocie."
[185] Kula, "Sektory i regiony," 116–17.
[186] Kula, "Przewrót przemysłowy."
[187] Kula, "Przewrót przemysłowy," 147–48. See also Mieszczankowski, *Struktura agrarna Polski*.

capitalist, but how feudal! . . . The country as a whole is an object of exploitation."[188]

A comparison of Kula's model descriptions of successful and unsuccessful industrializations in countries that followed the Prussian path shows that what principally differentiated the latter from the former were the inconsistent attempts to solve the agrarian question and the huge share of foreign investment in the absence of an interventionist state.[189] According to Kula, although in Eastern Europe folwarks were opened up to hired labor, unlike in Prussia, this did not reduce the number of peasant farms or siphon off "superfluous" people to industry.[190] Peasant farms were maintained as "subsistence plots" because other sectors of the economy were not able to absorb the newly formed mass of potential hired workers. In contrast to Germany, argued Kula, industrialization in Eastern Europe did not compete with the agrarian nature of society; it supplemented it in an island-like fashion, providing employment in periods when there was no agricultural work. "Capitalism in Poland was largely island-like and semi-colonial. It was 'semi-colonial' because Polish land was treated as an investment for foreign capital that was often short term, even transient in nature. . . . And it was 'island-like' because it was surrounded by a sea of semi-feudal peasant poverty."[191]

This was confirmed in Kochanowicz's comparative studies on the impact of Prussian and East European modernization on the peasant economy.[192] Kula emphasized that in contrast to Eastern Europe, in Prussia/Germany and Japan, which fell within the same model of industrialization, "state intervention was huge" and was served by an ideology of nationalism that was not only economic.[193] Kochanowicz also drew attention to factors ignored by Kula, which differentiated the course of modernization in Eastern Europe from that of Germany—the

188 Kula, *Rozdziałki*, 402–04. See also: Orczyk, "Conditions and Extent," 241–50.

189 The industrialization model of Prussia/Germany and Japan is presented in Kula "Przewrót przemysłowy," 139–42.

190 Ibid. Kula, "Zacofanie w perspektywie."

191 Kula, *Wokół historii*, 423. Kula, "Sektory i regiony zacofane."

192 Kochanowicz, *Spór o teorię*, 168–70.

193 Kula, "Przewrót przemysłowy," 140–41.

extra-economic role of the nation-state and popular attitudes toward entrepreneurship. "The high level of education" financed by the state, and consequently "the high standard of science, which was quickly implemented into manufacturing . . . as well as the major role of the banking system [including cooperatives] in financing investment, were development factors specific to the Reich."[194]

Kula's vision of socialist modernization in Eastern Europe can be similarly interpreted using the category of hybrid development. Despite the opportunity afforded by socialist industrialization—as Kula believed until roughly the mid-1960s—Eastern Europe continued its hybrid model of development. Soviet modernization failed, according to Kula, because it was not structural; it was not a harmonized change of the entire social system. The vestiges of feudalism proved to be very durable. "Stalinism in the Soviet Union built huge industrial facilities, but it did not make corresponding changes to the social structure. It failed to make society more flexible, as was required by an industrialized economy. Instead of opening society up, it did the opposite. The socialist countries experienced stunted growth because the methods used were only good for quantitative growth. . . . The development of the forces of production led 'upwards,' while the organizational and political superstructure led 'downwards'—toward the manifestations of feudalism."[195]

The originality of Kula's model lay in the fact that it transcended the dilemma formulated by social science at that time. Kula questioned the need to choose between the Eurocentric concept of universalism in development and the relativistic concept of a multiplicity of equal development paths. I believe this was the most interesting theoretical aspect of Kula's model, and one which is still relevant today.

That advanced and backward countries followed different economic development paths was a problem that Kula tackled in his early works. Until the mid-1950s the theoretical tool he used to analyze it was the Marxist theory of development, tailored to the needs of undeveloped societies. He presented the origins of capitalism in Poland as a mixture of feudalism and capitalism. Hybrid organizational forms were apparently unknown in the history of developed countries, which Kula

[194] Ibid., 153, 149.
[195] Kula, *Rozdziałki*, 258–60.

equated with England and France. Kula attempted to conceptualize underdevelopment in all its aspects during the 1960s, when the Eurocentric paradigm hitherto dominant in the social sciences came into conflict with the new, relativistic paradigm.

Kula's views on this matter sometimes lent themselves to unequivocal interpretation. "Witold was in my opinion much closer to those who promulgated European norms and unilinear development than to those who advocated multilinearity and untranslatability," stated Łepkowski with some regret.[196] My own bibliographical review suggests that Łepkowski's claims, including those about Kula's reluctance to recognize "Poland's membership in a particular community of backwardness,"[197] stemmed from his unfamiliarity with the texts included in Kula's 1983 volume, *History, Backwardness, Development* (Historia, zacofanie, rozwój), and were based on only one of many possible interpretations of *The Problems and Methods of Economic History*. Jedlicki and Kochanowicz, in turn, emphasized that Kula was aware not only of the economic and social but also the cultural aspects of the "uni- or multilinear development" dilemma. From this perspective, the tension in Kula's views was between "the idea of the equal value of all cultures and the theory of progress."[198] This kind of general assessment is warranted in regard to those of Kula's works that attempted to challenge the "anthropological point of view" in economics. He presented this dilemma in *The Problems and Methods*:

> And so we have, on the one hand, unilinear evolutionism, which poses as the fundamental issue of our times that of the unification of the world in the framework of industrial civilization, implying, it would appear, that the historian's task today is to examine the past for forces making for that unity. And, on the other hand, there are the multilinear theories, intellectually plausible and yet inevitably leading to a scientific impasse that threatens abdication; for how are we to study foreign civilizations if we are, almost by definition, unable to comprehend them, having no criteria but

---

[196] Łepkowski, "Wątki trzecioświatowe," 201.
[197] Ibid., 206.
[198] Jedlicki, "Witold Kula jako historyk cywilizacji," 97, Herling-Bianco, "Jedno- i wielokierunkowość rozwoju."

> those of our own civilization? . . . Nothing could be more calculated to repel the historian than the extreme formulation of either thesis.[199]

Kula's late model was an attempt to respond to the onesidedness of both these approaches. In relation to his theoretical texts, I see Kula's ideas as an attempt to create a model that takes into account diverse development paths but also permits international, cross-cultural—universal (!)—comparisons. "[A historian's] professional training and values should incline him to resist all ahistorical reductionism that measures past and present civilizations by the norms suited to our own criteria. And yet the uncompromising 'multilinearity,' insisting on the 'untranslatability' of cultural values, arouses his resistance, too. The practice of history, the results which it yields, and their verifiability (if only in the light of ever newly discovered evidence), set him at variance to either polar view."[200] Thus formulated, this theoretical goal was, I believe, responsible for Kula's categorization of East European development as hybrid. The region's development path, just as the social configuration of its successive stages, was "the same, but also very different" to that of developed societies.

In the 1960s, Kula abandoned what he referred to as the "naïve evolutionism" of classical social thought in favor of "multilinear theories."[201] One example of his rejection of evolutionist assumptions was his attitude toward the notion of "progress." In a seminal article published in 1947

[199] Kula, *The Problems and Methods*, 406–07.

[200] Ibid., 407.

[201] Kula rejected "naïve" evolutionism as represented in his work by Adam Smith and Karl Marx, as well as extreme cultural relativism, which assumes the equality of all cultures and economies and opposes any attempt to assess or compare them. Although it is not directly related to the model of socio-economic development in Eastern Europe, it is worth noting that Kula deconstructed the radical cultural relativism that questioned *any* criteria of development as a defensive reaction to decolonization ongoing at the time: "the 'multilinear' revival hints at a loss by the Western white man of his unshakeable faith in his 'rights' and hints at something like an inferiority complex . . . And why is it that the 'multilinear' theories have found more propitious soil in the more advanced rather than the so-called 'underdeveloped' countries?" Kula, *The Problems and Methods*, 406

he took the appropriateness of this term for granted, including it in the title and defining it as "the growth of social income per capita in a given society."[202] Twenty-five years later, in an unpublished note to *Short Chapters* (Rozdziałki), he completely rejected the notion on the grounds that it was related to social evolutionism: "We should be employing concepts other than 'progress' and 'reaction' because these derive too directly from an approach that depcits history as linear progress."[203]

Ultimately, Kula preferred the "humanistic" dimension of progress to the purely economic one. He claimed that "any criteria of progress that the researcher uses are debatable. However, the positive evaluation of human life as a criterion, which is implied by the adoption of this particular indicator, is perhaps the least controversial, for it is hard to imagine any social research without it."[204] The cross-cultural indicator in question—life expectancy—has lost none of its attractiveness nowadays.[205] It is used by international institutions that monitor development, such as the UN Development Programme, the World Bank, and the OECD. In addition to reflecting an economy's performance, it also reveals the principles by which income is produced and distributed, that is, the social structure in which the economy is embedded. It is thus similar to the concept of sustainable development.

Kula retained from the Marxist theory of development a belief in the key importance of social structure and class conflict as well as a naïve evolutionism.[206] In addition to that theory, the theoretical tools he used to conceptualize backwardness included Braudel's notion of *longue durée* structures, studies of underdevelopment in economic theory, and studies on the development of postcolonial countries—

202 Kula, *Przywilej społeczny*, 27.

203 Kula, *Rozdziałki*, 330.

204 Kula, *The Problems and Methods*, 462.

205 Ibid., 458–62.

206 In Kula's private notes, especially those from the 1970s, one can observe an intellectual stubbornness in defence of the original Marxist theory of development and in opposition to Lenin's "weakest link" theory, i.e., communist revolution in a backward country, with later Soviet modifications—"socialism in one country." Not without regret, Kula returned to evolutionism in the sense that he believed it was impossible to skip any development stage. Kula, *Rozdziałki*, especially the years 1970–1971 and 1974–1975. See: Lenin, *The Development of Capitalism in Russia*.

anthropological ideas about the equal value of all cultures, and dependency theory. The expansion of Kula's theoretical interests was part of a deeper trend in Poland during the post-1956 era of political liberalization. "The synthesis of Marxist inspiration and openness to international humanities seems . . . characteristic of [this] stage in Polish intellectual history," wrote Kochanowicz in 1985. He placed Kula's later works in the context of the changes taking place at that time in economic thought, literary theory, and intellectual history.[207]

Despite his wide-ranging interests, I believe that it was Kula's conviction about capitalism in other countries influencing domestic social structures of a backward society that had the greatest impact on his attempts to conceptualize social change in backward countries. An approach that charted the course of this influence, codified by dependency theory, responded to the demand to consider numerous development paths, Braudel's demand to appreciate the revolutionary nature of international trade, and Gerschenkron's demand to take into account international competition.[208] Dependency theory, in accordance with Kula's inclinations, treated backward national societies as the basic unit of analysis. The Dependencia school did not, however, satisfy Kula's condition that a backward society should be treated as having agency, that is, characterized by its own internal contradictions. Kula's model was richer than that of the Dependencia school in that it appreciated the dual nature of the economy and the island-like character of modernity in a backward society.

Notwithstanding the scope of Kula's interests, I propose to see his late model of East European development in terms of his theoretical struggle with on the one hand the Marxist theory of development, and

---

[207] Kochanowicz stressed the generational, environmental, and even social character of the changes in intellectual attitudes and the dialogue with Marxism, which crossed the boundaries of the academic disciplines. Among the economists from the same "circle," Kochanowicz mentioned Kalecki, Lange, and Sachs, among historians of literature he mentioned the founder of the Institute of Literary Research of the Polish Academy of Sciences, and Kula's friend, Żółkiewski, and among philosophers and historians of ideas, like Baczko and Kołakowski. Kochanowicz, "Czy tylko historia gospodarcza?," 143.

[208] Gerschenkron, *Economic Backwardness.*

on the other, the various approaches to international impacts on a backward society.

When seen from the perspective of dependency theory, Kula's views on development seem, in the words of one of its advocates, Tadeusz Łepkowski, consumed by "an obsession with feudalism."[209] The idea that backwardness was manifested by the presence of vestiges of feudalism distinguished Kula from researchers who were sensitive to capitalist "dependence"—the dependence that capitalism brought to underdeveloped countries. Similarly, from a Braudelian point of view, Kula's belief that feudalism held primacy over capitalism in Poland's economic system prior to the Partitions, and his theoretical linking of capitalism and industrialization, appear to show that he accepted the Marxist theory of development.[210] On the other hand, from Topolski's 1960s perspective, Kula's model of feudalism lacked certain features of the Marxist theory of development—the automatic mechanisms of feudal decay and the formation of a new capitalist economic system.[211] For Jedlicki, this same element seemed to prove that Kula had happily abandoned the idea of the "automatic collapse of feudalism" predicted by the Marxist theory of development.[212] Many years later, Topolski criticized Kula for attaching too much importance to the role of international commerce and the terms of trade. In this way he identified, or at least associated, Kula's position with Małowist's colonial thesis.[213]

Kula's ambiguous sympathy for and indifference to the Marxist theory of development and dependency theory can also be seen in the language he used and in his chosen vantage point. He borrowed terms from both theories and, significantly, also omitted terms that were key to those theories. His proposal to treat the terms of trade as an important analytical category brought his views closer to classical theories of economic imperialism and to dependency theory from the late 1950s and early 1960s. At the same time, Kula employed the terms "delay" or "backwardness" (the former mainly in the 1950s, the latter in the 1960s) and consistently avoided the term "dependence." Łepkowski

209 Łepkowski, "Wątki trzecioświatowe," 199.
210 Braudel, *Civilization and Capitalism*, vol. 2, 270–72.
211 Topolski, "Teoria ekonomiczna."
212 Jedlicki, "W sprawie automatycznego krachu."
213 Topolski, *Polska w czasach nowożytnych*, 26, 562–67.

drew attention to this. "A dichotomous division clearly pervades Kula's work. On the one hand, we find countries that are 'delayed' or 'backward' or—and this is an important caveat—'so-called backward' or 'postcolonial' (because they are not 'dependent,' a term which he does not use at all), and on the other, countries that are 'developed.'"[214]

The importance that Kula attached to "backwardness"—and this was the key word in his model—is an example of how torn he was between the Marxist theory of transition from feudalism to capitalism and dependency theory. In the 1960s, when he was in the process of repudiating the unilinear model of development, and even in an article of 1969 whose message was closest to dependency theory, Kula still defined "backwardness" as a condition that could be determined by comparing the development levels of different countries, as if those countries represented different stages of the same journey. As before, the opposite of "backward countries" were "advanced countries."[215] However, Kula emphasized that in the former, capitalism, in the sense of a stage of socioeconomic development, not only arrived later but in a different manner: it was imported, thus exacerbating backwardness (as in dependency theory). On the one hand, backwardness implied an economic gap between one country and another country or group of countries that were most advanced in capitalist development. On the other hand, claimed Kula, it was only possible to speak of backwardness in the age of capitalism, for only then did we find "a causal relationship between the development of some regions and the weaker development of other regions"[216]—he was referring here both to regions of a country and to regions of the world.

There was also an ambivalence in the way Kula used the term "capitalism." Backward countries, that is, countries that were not fully industrialized and thus poor, did not qualify as capitalist but rather as feudal or semi-feudal.[217] Nor did they become capitalist, despite the fact that they traded with capitalist countries and were part of the same

214 Łepkowski, "Wątki trzecioświatowe," 199.

215 Kula even used this differentiation in his article "Zacofanie gospodarcze" from 1969, whose general message is closest to dependency theory.

216 Kula, "Zacofanie gospodarcze," 184.

217 Compare with Foster-Carter, "The Modes of Production Controversy," and Taylor, *From Modernization to Modes of Production*.

international division of labor. For dependency theory and world-systems theory, this was a sufficient condition to treat capitalism as the dominant, structurally determined order, and those countries as dependent or peripheral capitalist countries. For Kula, this was not self-evident. That he wavered between two understandings of capitalism—as a method for organizing a national economy or as a method of economic exchange—is attested by the following remark: "All the long-term tendencies discussed here are [also] paths leading to capitalism. But the question arises: paths to capitalism in Poland, or to capitalism elsewhere?"[218]

A characteristic feature of Kula's views on the development of backward societies is that he adopted a variety of vantage points. Even when, in keeping with dependency theory, he divided nations and countries into the exploiters and the exploited, he never abstained from analyzing class relations within national societies. Anticipating the criticisms made of dependency theory in the 1970s and 1980s, Kula argued that acceptance of the unfavorable rules set by international capital did not simply mean that these rules were imposed from the outside. Rather, such acceptance resulted from the struggle for dominance between social classes at the local level. Ultimately, it was local elites who decided whether to accept or to reject those rules. Using the categories proposed by Janos, one could say that Kula accepted the new international method for analyzing social change, in which the unit of observation was the world-system and its actors were countries and national societies. He did not, however, give up classical analysis, in which the unit of research was a national society and the actors were domestic social classes.[219]

So, on the one hand, Kula's model was close to dependency theory. Like the latter, it ascribed great importance to the negative impact of international trade on backward economies. On the other hand, Kula's description of backward economic systems in terms of the "coexistence of asynchronisms" and "vestiges of feudalism" demonstrates that he was committed to a vision of what the Marxist theory of development and the classic process of transition from feudalism to

[218] Kula, *An Economic Theory*, 151.
[219] Janos, *Politics and Paradigms*, 147–49.

capitalism should look like. A mixture of economic arrangements of varying degrees of commercialization was, in Kula's view, the salient feature of backward countries and early capitalism, whereas a few years later, Braudel, who was not an adherent of the Marxist theory of development, considered it to be the rule of the modern world.

Eastern and Western Europe: Between Catching up and Dependency

All the models presented above—let me emphasize once again that these were the main contributions to postwar historians' debate on the nature of Polish and East European development—conceptualize East European development by juxtaposing it with West European development. Regardless of the period to which they related, all the models showed that development in the East proceeded differently and less favorably than in the West. They also concurred that the most important, or one of the most important factors behind this difference, that is, backwardness, was Eastern Europe's social structure, which was characterized by serfdom and a polarized structure of rights and incomes. Where the models differed was in regard to other factors of economic backwardness. Among such factors, which could not be attributed to the social structure, Małowist and Kula mentioned economic relations with the West. In Małowist's model it was the "asymmetry of international trade" with a stronger West European partner, while for Kula it was the terms of trade. In a manner characteristic of the communist period, all the models gave less prominence to political and cultural factors than would be the case today. The late models of Wyczański and Topolski gave greater consideration to political and cultural factors than Kula's and Małowist's did, although the latter two authors did not ignore such factors either. Wyczański pointed to the possible role of the state in promoting the imitation of beneficial institutional models, while Topolski and Kula drew attention to the role of mentality when taking economically important decisions, such as how much to invest and how much to consume. The general trend in the postwar decades was to abandon single-factor explanations and the search for a "first cause," and instead to take multiple factors into consideration. Topolski's 1994 model went furthest in this direction, no doubt because it was the latest of the models presented here.

My assumption is that the differences between the models had more to do with theoretical premises than with facts. Although the models concerned different historical periods, I believe that they all contributed to the theoretical debate. Given that the models analyzed different systems—the economic and social structures of Europe (Małowist), national societies or the inhabitants of countries (Topolski, Wyczański), the production and distribution of national income in the Polish lands (Kula)—one might ask whether it is legitimate and reasonable to compare them. I believe that, ultimately, it is. First, all the models cover the sixteenth century, and their conceptual differences are most clearly revealed in their assessment of the social and economic achievements of that period. Second, the unit of analysis each author chose did not so much result from the factual material available as reflect his theoretical assumptions about which historical data were key to explaining development.

The graph below attempts to summarize the various models of East European development through historical epochs. The first dimension—an assessment of West European impacts as either favorable or unfavorable—illustrates the perceived strength of these impacts. However, it does not consider whether the impacts were economic or not. The second dimension illustrates the perceived similarity of Poland/Eastern Europe's development path to that of the West; the two extremes of the y-axis are: "a completely different path" and "the same path." The graph presents the development differences between Poland/Eastern Europe and Western Europe over successive historical periods, as represented by the four models, but it does not reflect the different ways in which the region was conceptualized in each model.

Figure 2 presents the four models in terms of their *method* of conceptualizing East European development compared to that of the West. I use the following differentiating features: the level of analysis (national or transnational/global) and the role attributed to the economic impact of Western Europe (the most developed countries) on social change and the direction of development in Eastern Europe in the sixteenth century. The decisions about the unit of analysis, and about the historical period from which one should start to consider the

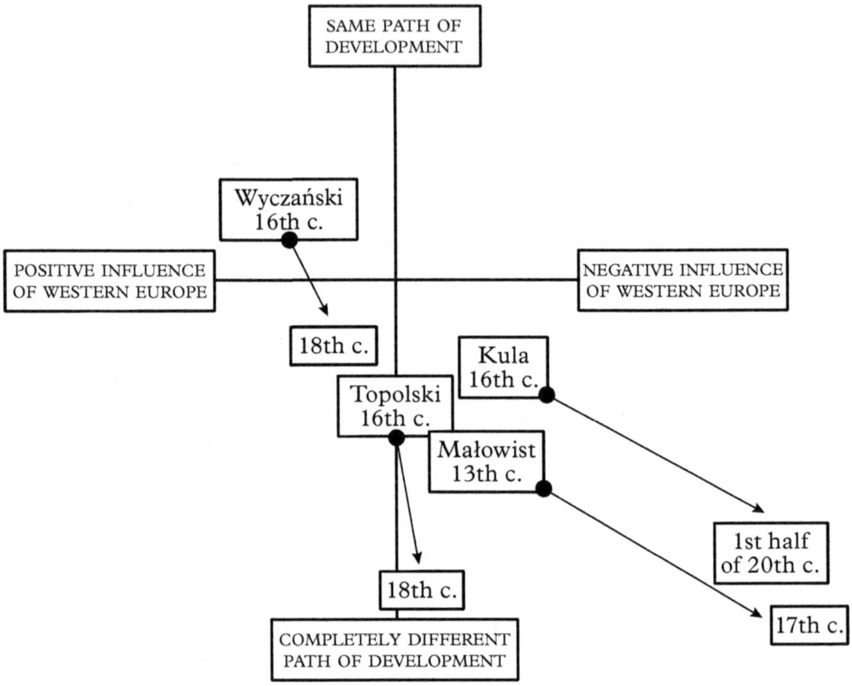

Figure 2. Models of Poland/Eastern Europe's development: perceived similarity to Western development (y-axis) and assessment of West European impacts (x-axis).

- diagnosis of the situation in the sixteenth century

⟶ Direction of development in subsequent centuries

role of external impacts on social change, are theoretical assumptions that are still being debated in the social sciences.

In Wyczański's model the unit of analysis was a national society, either the national society of Poland or of another country that represented the Central European form of development. The factors of social change or its absence were located within the society, but positive stimuli for change could arise through the imitation of developed societies. This is how Wyczański's model took account of Western external impacts, but it conceptualized them in a more abstract way compared to the other models—as the existence of a paradigm of economic, social, political, and cultural organization. In each case this paradigm was determined by societies considered to be the most

	The role of the economic impact of Western Europe on the process of change in the 16th century:		
Level of analysis:	**Minor**		**Major**
National	Wyczański: *catching up*	Topolski: *relatively independent development (historical coincidence)*	Kula: *hybrid development*
Transnational / Global			Małowist: *complementary and dependent (colonial) development*

Table 1. Conceptualization of the relationship between East European and West European development

advanced. In Topolski's model the unit of analysis was an economic system not greater than a national economy together with its social determinants. Topolski did not exclude external impacts, including international trade, as possible factors of economic and social change or its absence. However, in relation to Eastern Europe between the sixteenth and eighteenth centuries he regarded external impacts to be limited; at most, they were one of many factors of stagnation or growth. Topolski described external impacts primarily in terms of mentalities. They took the form of contacts with other cultures through the medium of travel, education, and literature. Kula's model combined analysis at the national level with elements of analysis at the global level, and presented external impacts in terms of their internal conditions and implications for national social structures. In relation to the sixteenth to eighteenth centuries, Kula conceptualized these impacts in Eastern Europe as the terms of trade. In relation to subsequent periods, the list of external impacts was increased to include:

- patterns of consumption and production (in that order) adopted by the elites of backward societies and adapted to their needs,
- international competition between national economies,

- the penetration of foreign capital (in relation to the twentieth century and to modernization under the conditions of economic liberalism),
- the possibility to transfer profits abroad.

Małowist's model took as its unit of analysis the European economy (trade and manufacturing). It presented external impacts as international trade relations and attached greater importance to them. The attitude of the national elites to those trade relations created long-lasting social and economic structures.

CHAPTER 5

Rentiers and Victims of Backwardness, and Pioneers of Progress: Images of Polish Society

The aim of this chapter is to present competing images of the groups and institutions in Polish society that featured in the debate on Eastern European economic backwardness. I am interested in the role particular actors played in (re)producing backwardness, bearing its burden, or contributing to economic development. The first group of social actors are the eponymous rentiers of backwardness; the second, victims of backwardness; and the third, pioneers of progress. The terms "rentier of backwardness" and "pioneer of progress" originate from Kula's works; the former is based on a paradox, the latter is ironic.[1] My own term, "victim of backwardness," stands in direct opposition to Kula's "rentier of backwardness." I have decided not to analyze the category of "victim of progress," because although a conservative might wish to interpret in this way the image of the nineteenth-century Polish peasant as proposed by postwar historiography, scholars of the day would have regarded the term as an oxymoron. It is also important to identify what distinguished Polish society from the model Western societies of the period.

---

[1] Kula wrote: "The independent variable of alterations in the 'terms of trade' rendered the noble *a rentier* of the initial stage of the process of the country's economic retardation," that is, backwardness (the term that the translator of *The Problems* avoided). *The Problems and Methods*, 578.

In this area, more so than in other areas, the four schools in the East European debate focused mainly on Polish issues, which is why I analyze the image of Polish society only. In studies of this kind—limited to the society of the Kingdom of Poland—Kula's school was at the forefront. The modernization of the Wielkopolska region was investigated by Topolski. The development of the modern Polish nation was also examined by Łepkowski. And the issue of modernization was tackled in the general works of Zientara, Ihnatowicz, Mączak, and others.[2]

I focus on the disputes around social stratification during watershed periods of history. The section entitled "Lords, Peasants, and Newcomers from the West" gives an account of the disputes over rentiers and victims of backwardness and pioneers of progress in the early modern era (sixteenth century). The section entitled "Origins of the Modern Transformation" presents the disputes around the social consequences of the transformation in the nineteenth century. All the protagonists of this book participated in the "folwark debate," which dealt with the period between the sixteenth and eighteenth centuries; the arguments over this period were even more heated. It was principally Kula's school, but also Ihnatowicz and Łepkowski, who researched the social consequences of the modern transformation in the nineteenth century. Although Polish society between the two world wars—and even Polish society today, as I argue in the Conclusion—can be analyzed in light of the social consequences of the manorial economy, the lively disputes over the situation of the peasantry in the nineteenth and twentieth centuries concerned different issues than when analyzing sixteenth to eighteenth centuries.[3]

These disputes did not just take place between scholars but also appeared in the narratives of individual scholars themselves. The most

---

[2] The formation of East European nation-states was the subject of the research conducted by Jerzy Tomaszewski (Kula's student) as well as by scholars from the Department of Polish History in the nineteenth and twentieth centuries at the Institute of History of the Polish Academy of Sciences. Żarnowski, *Struktura społeczna inteligencji*, Żarnowski, *Społeczeństwo Drugiej Rzeczypospolitej*, Żarnowski, *Dyktatury w Europie środkowo-wschodniej*, Balcerak, *"Ład wersalski,"* Balcerak, *Powstanie państw*.

[3] Kochanowicz, *Spór o teorię*, introduction.

impassioned arguments concerned the extent to which Polish society could be considered a special case. Some researchers considered Polish specificity to be a cause or symptom of backwardness, while others took the opposite view.

If we compare the work of the participants of the debate on East European economic backwardness with similarly ambitious contemporary studies, what is striking is the class reductionism of the former. The dominance—assumed but never challenged—of materialist criteria such as demography, ownership of the means of production, and share in social income, as well as the primacy of class conflict analysis, is especially apparent in works up to the 1970s. Polish socioeconomic historiography of that period paid little heed to the influence of the state and legal system on the class structure (an exception being the works of Karol Modzelewski and Antoni Mączak). At the same time it was blind to the impact of religion and culture on economic and social attitudes, as highlighted by Weber and contemporary mainstream scholars from Huntington to Inglehart.[4]

Lords, Peasants, and Newcomers from the West? The Folwark Debate and Interpretations of Social Stratification in the Early Modern Era

The early modern period is regarded by some as the moment when the development paths of Eastern and Western Europe ultimately diverged, and by others as the golden age of Polish history. The key aspects of the folwark debate were:

- the social role of the folwark as an institution,
- the situation of peasant serfs,
- economic attitudes, especially the consumer attitudes of the szlachta,

[4] The following works from the 1960s and 1970s focused on the influence of political structures on economic ones: Modzelewski, *Organizacja gospodarcza*, Mączak, *U źródeł nowożytnej gospodarki.* Weber's classic essay on the influence of religion and belief: *The Protestant Ethic.* See also: Landes, *The Wealth and Poverty.*

- the situation of towns and their inhabitants, and
- the role played by newcomers from the West, particularly merchants who mediated between the folwarks and West European markets.

Małowist and Wyczański were the main opponents in the debate. To put it simply, Małowist viewed the szlachta and Western newcomers as rentiers of backwardness and the peasants and town population as victims of backwardness. Wyczański was inclined to present the sixteenth-century folwark and serfdom as corporatist or paternalistic institutions. At the same time he stressed the active role of the local town population, the assimilationist tendencies of foreigners who had settled in the Polish–Lithuanian Commonwealth, and the flourishing of towns in the sixteenth century. In this dispute, Kula's position was close to Małowist's. Topolski, on the other hand, while generally negative about the economic role of the folwark and serfdom, distinguished pro- and anti- development groups among the szlachta. He believed that the impact of Western newcomers was insignificant, and associated the decline of towns with the seventeenth rather than the sixteenth century.

THE FOLWARK: AGENT OF BACKWARDNESS OR CORPORATIST INSTITUTION?

In the writings of Kula, Małowist, Mączak, and also of Topolski, the folwark and the manor were presented as system-building institutions that reproduced social and political structures. The suggestiveness of this image is evidenced by the fact that in world literature the grain-producing Polish folwark became a symbol of East European social systems. The folwark, which relied on the labor of peasant serfs, and the manor with its distinctive way of life and production methods, were seen as key to explaining East European backwardness. Similarly, a free peasantry, independent towns, and an absolutist state were seen in world historiography to be, in the long term, the social basis of the economic rise of Western Europe.

Polish historiography presented the folwark as the principal economic institution, one that produced and distributed social income; a huge landed estate, cultivated for free by peasant serfs who belonged to the manor. Topolski, although the most circumspect when equating the folwark with the way in which production was organized in early modern Poland, wrote: "Despite the fact that [folwarks] accounted for roughly one quarter of the country's arable land at most, they contributed to a gradual reduction in the productive capacity of peasant farms."[5] The development of this type of economy was accompanied by the szlachta's unique system of political power, which removed royal prerogatives and, through patronage, subordinated the lower-ranking szlachta to the great landowning magnates. As emphasized in particular by Małowist and Kula, and among Western historical sociologists by Perry Anderson, this system was characterized by despotism in social relations with the peasantry. By law the szlachta exercised total economic and political authority over the peasants and had significant control over their personal lives too.[6]

The folwark was also portrayed as the principal means by which the polarized rural structure of society was reproduced. At one extreme were the lords—people with legal personality who populated the legislative and judicial institutions. At the other extreme were the peasants—people without legal personality who were tied to the land yet not allowed to own it. In the social models advanced by Małowist, Kula, Topolski, and their followers, the folwark played the role of a system-building institution. It maintained the rural character of societies by prohibiting in law the geographical mobility of peasants, including their migration to the towns. Through serfdom it perpetuated a feudal hierarchical structure and prevented social mobility. According to Mączak, this system meant that "society was far more socially polarized . . . in terms of income than most European countries."[7]

The folwark also deprived both towns of their economic and cultural functions and the state of its social, legal, administrative, military,

---

[5] Topolski, *Polska w czasach nowożytnych*, 14.

[6] Małowist, "The Economic and Social Development," 188, Kula, *An Economic Theory*, Anderson *Lineages*, 264. This opinion has been recently criticized by demographic historians, e.g., Guzowski, "Village Court Records," Wiślicz, *Upodobanie*, Wiślicz, "Weddings, Christenings."

[7] Ihnatowicz, Mączak, and Zientara, *Społeczeństwo polskie X–XX*, 424. See also: Kamler, *Folwark szlachecki.*

and diplomatic functions. According to Kula, the autonomous, sovereign administrative functions of the magnatial court in the eighteenth century relied on the "efforts of the magnates to standardize weights and measures within their 'realm'" and "to ensure that these were different . . . from the weights and measures applicable elsewhere."[8] Perversely, they imitated in this way the behavior of bureaucracies in states governed by enlightened absolutism. The political functions of the folwark were due to the magnates possessing their own armies as well as extensive diplomatic contacts.[9] This allowed them to absorb the local minor szlachta into their clientelist networks. The effect was to decentralize political power across the country at a time when bureaucracies in Western Europe were being centralized. Clienteles were also important for the social status of magnate-patrons and the political power of their manors.[10] In his book *Clientage* (Klientela), Mączak wrote:

> The manor, along with the administrative apparatus of the vast estate, performed numerous roles in the lives of the Polish and Lithuanian gentry. In that period [sixteenth to eighteenth centuries], but in other countries, those roles were already being performed by the towns. . . . Thus, by replacing the town (or, rather, by being shielded from its competition), the court of a Polish or Lithuanian magnate offered that which royal courts offered in other countries: a monopoly over the life opportunities of those who attended. Such opportunities included education, advance-

[8] Kula, *Measures and Men.*

[9] Kula, *Początki układu kapitalistycznego*, Kula, *An Economic Theory*, Kula, "Rządzący i rządzeni.."

[10] The "pessimistic" Polish political historiography tradition established in the nineteenth century by the Kraków School of History links the decline of the Commonwealth to its inability to create efficient central government at a time when neighboring absolutist military states were growing stronger. Bobrzyński, *Dzieje Polski w zarysie*, Jasienica, *Polska anarchia*. Contrary to this tradition, Mączak describes the phenomenon of clientage not in opposition to the centralization of power and creation of a loyal bureaucracy, but as a typical form of organizing and distributing power in political systems based on the privileges accorded by social status. In his approach, a "clientelist attitude" is the basis of the central bureaucratic network.

ment in public life (public offices, military commissions), higher prestige . . . but also the chance to acquire wealth.[11]

In Mączak's view, the development of magnatial clienteles and private offices meant that in the sixteenth and seventeenth centuries "no one apart from the king and a small group of top officials identified with the state (and in the case of those royal officials, this was by no means guaranteed)."[12]

For Topolski, it was the expansionist, large-scale, export-oriented folwarks, usually located in the Vistula river basin, that played a negative role. He juxtaposed these with the autonomous folwark, a smaller entity that produced for the local market and was economically prudent and rational. Topolski's negative assessment also concerned a shorter period than Małowist's or Kula's: the mid-seventeenth until the mid-eighteenth century. He argued that in the sixteenth century, when the manorial system based on the second serfdom was first introduced, the folwark "was the main means by which the East European szlachta became directly involved in economic life."[13] Topolski saw this as a positive phenomenon. It was not the folwark as such, but rather its historical, specific Polish form, related to non-economic factors, that led to catastrophic results.

Wyczański opposed treating the folwark and serfdom solely as exploitative institutions that reproduced backwardness. Contrary to the dominant interpretation, he did not view the creation of folwarks and the introduction of the second serfdom in the sixteenth century as the key moment in the divergence of Polish and Western social structures. Instead he suggested that the desire to create larger, more market-oriented farms should be acknowledged as "a common trend that occurred both in Poland and in neighboring countries as well as in the West."[14] Wyczański portrayed the folwark as a paternalistic institution where lords and serfs lived in harmony, exchanging protection and guidance for service and obedience. Defending the folwark system, he argued that the expansion of serfdom brought with it mutual benefits:

---

11 Mączak, *Klientela*, 293–94.

12 Mączak in Ihnatowicz et al., *Społeczeństwo polskie*, 225.

13 Topolski, *Polska w czasach nowożytnych*, 23.

14 Wyczański, *Polska w Europie*, 37.

> one must assume, therefore, that the gradual strengthening of serfdom occurred through a degree of consent, through an agreement between the respective parties that was to some extent real. At that time the peasant was relatively willing to accept a greater burden, since he perhaps preferred to offer a little more of his labor than to lose money [to pay the rent], especially as the rising profitability of the peasant economy more than rewarded his increasing workload. . . . The landowner, in turn, was keen to retain the prosperous and hard-working peasant. He also granted him hereditary possession of his farm, protected him from mistreatment by his neighbors, and helped him in moments of crisis.[15]

Wyczański argued that the folwark—through the intensification, commoditization, and specialization of the economy—was an institution conducive to economic growth, at least in the sixteenth century.[16] The size of folwarks increased thanks to the cultivation of barren land, and not, as Kula argued, due to the confiscation of peasant land. "For a folwark owner, serfdom was a means of securing unpaid labor, thus increasing production and income. For this reason, unlike in the West, landowners had no interest in depriving peasants of their farms and absorbing their land into the folwark."[17]

Wyczański also emphasized that due to the manorial system based on the second serfdom, the lower social classes in Poland avoided the hardships experienced by "vagabonds and dispossessed people" in early modern Western Europe.[18] Consequently, he did not consider the folwark as an institution crucial for social stratification. It neither impacted on the decline of local trade and crafts, nor of the towns, nor in the sixteenth century did it cause the disappearance of wealthy peasants and hired labor. Aside from performing a paternalistic role characteristic of feudal society, the folwark was an independent, rela-

---

[15] Wyczański, *Dogonić Europę*, 13. There is a striking similarity between Wyczański's interpretation of the *folwark* and feudalism, and the interpretation of the plantation slavery system in the South of the United States. Compare with Genovese, *Roll, Jordan, Roll.*

[16] Wyczański, *Studia nad folwarkiem*, 247–60.

[17] Wyczański, *Dogonić Europę*, 13.

[18] Ibid., 15.

tively efficient, modern productive entity. The relative innovativeness of the folwark lay in the commercialization of its production and in the employment of paid servants, who in the sixteenth century constituted an important group in the social division of labor. What also emerges from Wyczański's research is an image—quite different to that proposed by the other three authors—of the power relationship between the manor and the state. The former is seen as too weak in the sixteenth century to assume the functions of the state, while the sixteenth-century state is deemed to be much more capable of creating a protonational solidarity. Wyczański emphasized the standardization of language and the creation of a pro-state consciousness that went beyond attachment to a royal dynasty.[19] An interesting difference between Wyczański and Kula was their use of data on the system of weights and measures applied in Poland. Both authors employed that data to demonstrate either the strength or weakness of the state vis-à-vis the manor. Wyczański argued that weights and measures became standardized in the sixteenth-century Commonwealth, while Kula claimed that they were completely arbitrary, even in the royal demesnes.[20]

"DID THE PEASANTS SUFFER?"

The discussion over class relations within the manorial-serf system contributed a moral dimension to the East European debate. In analysis of the situation of peasant serfs, it even took precedence over the economic and social dimensions of the debate.

Kula and Kochanowicz portrayed peasants as producers striving for independence who were endowed with a kind of economic rationality that was appropriate to the conditions, over which they had little influence. The economic freedom of peasants was limited to passive forms of resistance to the economic decisions of their masters: sabotage; "concealment" of the true size of production; retention of a greater part of their crop than was allowed; and a struggle for access to the market and the possibility to sell their goods. The peasant economy operated according to subsistence and survival.[21]

---

[19] Wyczański, *Polska—Rzeczą Pospolitą*, 150.

[20] Ibid., 155, Kula, *Measures and Men.*

[21] Kula, *An Economic Theory*, Kochanowicz, *Spór o teorię.*

The depiction of peasant serfs as autonomous economic players, however, was the exception not the rule. The dominant image was that peasants were the victims of increasing exploitation by the szlachta and the main contributors to a system that undermined their thriftiness and instilled bad habits. Kula, Małowist, and to a lesser extent Topolski, presented various processes that were under way in the sixteenth to eighteenth centuries as detrimental to the peasantry. These included: the increasing workload under serfdom; the gradual absorption of peasant land; the prevention of market access for peasant farms; the introduction in the eighteenth century of the szlachta's monopoly on the production and sale of alcohol; and finally an obligation to purchase products from the szlachta's distilleries and manufactories. Accompanying all this was poverty, hunger, and the restriction of liberty. Małowist wrote that the intensification of serfdom was a "painful" process. "That period [the fifteenth century] was marked by the introduction of a system of peasant service known as the second serfdom. This painful process lasted for more than a century, but viewed from a longer perspective, most peasants were ruined by it."[22] Kula, in turn, described the social cost of Polish grain exports: "Polish grain was cheap for the West for the same reason that yields in Poland were low: because it was produced using unpaid, coerced labor performed by undernourished peasant serfs."[23]

Both the sociological and moral dimension were present in descriptions of the working and living conditions of peasant families presented by the authors who specifically dealt with the peasant economy, that is, Kula and Kochanowicz.[24] Kula's portrayal of manorial interference in the daily life of the peasantry, in particular, emphasized the way peasants were objectified and denied privacy. Control over marriage and the permitted number of offspring determined a manor's demographic policy, the aim of which was to create an optimal model of the working peasant family. The problem of vodka consumption and peasant drunkenness, which Kula tackled in *The Manor and the Peasant Family* (Dwór a rodzina chłopska) and in numerous other

---

22 Małowist, "The Problem of the Inequality," 27.

23 Kula, "Czynniki gospodarcze w polskim procesie dziejowym," 164–65.

24 Kula, *An Economic Theory*, Kula and Kochanowicz, *Chłopstwo*, Kochanowicz, *Spór o teorię*, Kochanowicz, *Pańszczyźniane gospodarstwo*.

works, turned out to be a consequence of the szlachta's desire to divest its subjects of their cash. Particularly astonishing were the figures relating to the amount of vodka that peasants were forced to buy on family occasions—from baptisms to marriages and funerals.[25]

Mączak, in language that was more sociological than it was sententious (albeit not free of judgement), emphasized that "for European opinion at the end of the sixteenth century, and even more so in subsequent centuries, the legal status of the town population, and in particular the enslavement of the peasantry, were a major burden on the Commonwealth."[26] Elsewhere, using a different research convention and writing in 1998, Mączak cited the diary entry of an eighteenth-century German traveller, J. E. Biester, who attributed the peasantry's low level of hygiene to their humiliating social position. The fragment is very vivid, and Mączak rightly treated it as an expression of sophisticated sociological insight free of national prejudice: "And now a few words about the charge made so commonly and so vociferously against the Poles—that they are unclean. In good homes in Warsaw there undoubtedly prevails great order and cleanliness, but the lowest classes are marked by dirt in their dwellings, food, attire, and so on. Yet does this arise because they are Poles or rather because they are paupers and slaves? . . . That same misfortune which so demeans the simple Pole that he wretchedly kisses his master's feet . . . leads him also to show indifference toward dirt."[27] Presenting the changes in social stratification during the early modern era, Mączak described the steady degradation of non-szlachta groups, especially the peasantry. "Social degradation was most evident among the peasantry; it had a clear dimension, measured by terms such as *kmieć*, *półkmieć*, and *zagrodnik*, and by the size of landholdings. But the notion as to how much a *kmieć* (a wealthy peasant) should possess changed; at the beginning of the sixteenth century it was a fief; in the second half of the sixteenth century Anselm Gostomski[28] wanted the *kmieć* to be a half-fief-holder

25 Kula, "Doświadczenia i nadzieje," 486–90, Kula and Kochanowicz, *Chłopstwo*.

26 Mączak in Ihnatowicz et al., *Społeczeństwo polskie*, 241–42.

27 Mączak, *Travel in Early Modern Europe*.

28 Anselm Gostomski was an author of *Gospodarstwo*, a guide for the *szlachta* on how to run a landed estate. It was originally published in Kraków in 1588.

(*półkmieć*); and by the eighteenth century the *kmieć* was a quarter-fief-holder in many areas, whereas two hundred years earlier he would have been referred to as a *zagrodnik* (poor farmer)."[29]

Wyczański, too, admitted that in the context of Europe the peasantry occupied a specific place in the social structure of the Polish–Lithuanian Commonwealth. However, unlike other authors, in answer to the question: "Did peasants have a bad life in the sixteenth century?"—the title of one of his articles—his response was "no."[30] Similarly to Topolski, he believed that peasant income was still rising in the sixteenth century; its collapse was caused by the wars of the seventeenth century and not by the policies of the szlachta. In Wyczański's interpretation, serfdom was a kind of voluntary contract comparable to tenant farming or sharecropping in Western Europe at that time. Serfdom seemed to Wyczański beneficial and appropriate for peasants given Poland's demographic situation. "The biggest differences between the social structure of Western countries and Poland concerned the situation of the peasantry. Whereas in the West, as early as in the sixteenth century, there was more available labor than there was land under cultivation, which led to the confiscation of peasant land and vagrancy, the opposite was true in Poland: labor was in short supply and landowners tried to keep peasants in the countryside."[31] The surplus of land relative to the workforce meant that the sixteenth-century peasant had a choice: either risk farming his own land, which could end in bankruptcy, or enter into a serfdom contract with the local landowner. "In early sixteenth-century Poland, work was easier to find, labor was precious, and there were often vacant farms to be had. In the West, the opposite was the case: the peasant—poor, debt-ridden, often ruined by excessive rent, taxes, or natural disasters—had to abandon the land to seek his fortune in the city, often as a 'lazy' vagabond pursued by the law, with no hope of extricating himself from poverty."[32]

In contrast to other authors, Wyczański stressed the similarity between the situation of free peasants in Western Europe and peasant serfs in Poland. "Above all, in Western countries as in Poland, the land

[29] Mączak in Ihnatowicz et al., *Społeczeństwo polskie*, 305.
[30] Wyczański, "Czy chłopu."
[31] Wyczański, *Dogonić Europę*, 14.
[32] Ibid., 15.

generally belonged to feudal lords—the nobility, the church, and the monarch—and full ownership of land by peasants was very rare; it could be found in some areas of England and Sweden as a legacy of earlier medieval arrangements."[33] The difference in the social position of peasantry in the West and in the East was, according to Wyczański, purely formal and not real, especially in the way it was perceived by the peasants themselves. While land-based serfdom dominated in the West, in the East, personal serfdom was the rule. "In practice the attachment of peasants to the land in the sixteenth century was quite weak."[34] The law did not therefore, according to Wyczański, restrict the geographical mobility of peasants. "For the conditions of the time, the percentage of people who left the countryside was greater in the West; it was slightly smaller in Poland but present nonetheless."[35]

One of Wyczański's main arguments in support of the claim that the Polish peasantry enjoyed a good life was that, unlike other countries, Poland experienced no peasant revolts or protests.[36] This problem became one of the biggest mysteries for the participants of the debate over Polish society during the era of the manorial–serf economy. As Mączak wrote,

> If one discounts individual prewar researchers mainly connected with peasant parties, historians only began to take an interest in these issues after the Second World War. . . . Although they complied a rich and valuable body of source material, many researchers had a tendency to reduce virtually every aspect of rural life to the class struggle of the peasantry. Beginning in 1956, this led to another extreme: a complete lack of interest in the issue and an escape into the realm of rural economics and the grain trade. Yet the class struggle of the peasantry in the Commonwealth is an interesting topic, if only because it differed from the situation both in Russia . . . and in the West.[37]

33 Wyczański, *Polska w Europie*, 35.

34 Ibid., 100.

35 Ibid., 110.

36 Wyczański, *Dogonić Europę*, 13–15.

37 Mączak in Ihnatowicz et al., *Społeczeństwo polskie*, 378. Compare with Kochanowicz, *Spór o teorię*, 124–25.

The most popular hypothesis about the lack of active resistance to serfdom and the confiscation of peasant land—one advocated by Topolski, Kula, and Kochanowicz, as well as by Małowist and Mączak—was that these processes were slow and gradual. Małowist and Mączak showed that in the sixteenth century, when the processes commenced, the situation of some peasants was good.[38] They emphasized that in later centuries, when the situation of peasant farms had significantly deteriorated, revolts were no longer organizationally feasible. Małowist, who did not fundamentally differ from Kula or Topolski in this regard, expressed it thus:

> The high prices of the agricultural products and the ease of shipping them were favorable for the peasants, especially the well-to-do ones, who profited from rising prices. What is more, the well-to-do peasants often managed to throw their losses on to the poorer peasants. They forced these latter into debt and then made them pay a part of the rent to the lord. The practical result was that the peasants of the Baltic countries hardly took part in the peasants' wars of 1525 at all. Equally, the peasants played no part in the religious struggles which were so violent in the Baltic towns during the first half of the sixteenth century. From the middle of the sixteenth century, when the nobles began to appropriate peasant property at an ever increasing speed and thus ruin the mass of the peasants, all resistance by the peasants had already become impossible. . . . The towns could no longer help the peasants, either politically or economically.[39]

Kula and Kochanowicz identified numerous "other forms of resistance [i.e., other than revolts], sometimes referred to as 'passive' or 'hidden' resistance," which were evident in the mature, decadent phase of the period.[40] In his summary of trends during the age of the manorial–serf economy, Kula categorized peasant resistance as a game whose purpose was to acquire "at whatever cost, a commercial surplus and to develop

[38] Mączak, "Folwark pańszczyźniany," 377.

[39] Małowist, "The Economic and Social," 188. See also Kula, *An Economic Theory*, 142–43, Topolski, *Polska w czasach nowożytnych*, 37–46.

[40] Kochanowicz, *Spór o teorię*, 125.

a market relationship": the sale of even the tiniest portion of production that the peasant was due and thus the possibility to make purchases.[41] Peasants "without even being organized, without agreeing on a common plan, nevertheless constantly acted in the same direction, taking advantage of even the slightest existing possibilities. . . . Only thus could they improve their condition in some small way."[42] Kula saw these and other illegal activities as an expression of the class struggle. Similarly to Mączak and Kochanowicz, he included among these activities: "clandestine expansion of the area under cultivation . . . more intensive farming by means of greater investment of labor per unit of surface area; underfeeding of the farm animals, which were primarily to satisfy the needs of the demesne; use of surplus manpower on the peasant plot for fruit gardens, raising pigs, and poultry, and for activities related to transport and craft; an extreme cutback on peasant family consumption"[43] as well as "the ongoing struggle over the system of weights and measures . . . that was used to make tributes in kind to the manor,"[44] establish land surface area, or calculate the volume of transported goods, etc. Kochanowicz, for whom such activities were tantamount to a resistance economy rather than to the class struggle, presented, similarly to Mączak, a list that included more peasant failures than efforts, thanks to which his image of the peasant was less heroic than Kula's: "The basic form of resistance to serfdom was to be negligent in its performance," while passive resistance "manifested itself in sluggish work, pretending not to understand orders, playing the fool," or finally desertion.[45] Polish authors considered the last of these forms of resistance to be more available to the Polish or Russian peasant than to his West European counterpart. This was mainly due to lower population density, the sheer size of the relatively uncontrolled areas these countries acquired in the sixteenth and seventeenth centuries, and the demand for labor in other folwarks.[46]

---

[41] Kula, *An Economic Theory*, 119.

[42] Ibid., 134.

[43] Ibid., 135.

[44] Kula, *Measures and Men*, 226.

[45] Kochanowicz, *Spór o teorię*, 127–29, Mączak in Ihnatowicz et al., *Społeczeństwo polskie*, 383.

[46] Małowist, "Poland, Russia and Western Trade," Topolski, *Polska w czasach nowożytnych.*

THE SZLACHTA: LUXURY CONSUMERS OR PROTO-ENTREPRENEURS?

The numerical force and internal organization of the Polish szlachta aroused just as much interest among scholars as the subjugation and serfdom of the peasantry. Researchers sought to explain the origins of these phenomena and whether they represented an exception at the European level. The genesis and function of the minor szlachta was one of the major conundrums in the historical sociology of medieval Poland. Perry Anderson and Jenő Szűcs, and, among Polish researchers, Tymieniecki, Topolski, and Małowist, attributed the high numbers of Polish szlachta to the persistence of tribal structures. These took shape prior to Poland's adoption of Latin culture and were responsible for the underdevelopment of seigniorial relations typical of Western Europe. As the *drużyna,*[47] for a longer period than in the West, was more focused on war than on owning and inheriting land, the system based on the *drużyna* required the expansion of this group rather than the introduction of restrictions on the division of wealth.[48]

Among researchers of social stratification in Poland during the sixteenth to eighteenth centuries, the dispute concerned the extent to which the szlachta—diversified in term of wealth and accounting for approximately 7 to 10 percent of the country's total population—was unique in Europe, and whether it had any impact on backwardness. In his determination to demonstrate the similarity between Polish and Western social structures in the early modern period, Wyczański likened the numerous szlachta *zagrodowa* (i.e., members of the minor szlachta who owned only their own farm) and *szlachta jednowioskowa* (i.e., minor szlachta who owned only one village) to the free peasantry in Sweden or England. In the debate, Wyczański was alone in

---

47 In pre-Christian North European—Scandinavian, German, and Slavic—societies, the *drużyna* was a medieval military unit with members in principle equal to one another. It was composed of male heads of households and their families. Along with its military role, the *drużyna* played an extensive social role, being a combination of an association and a religious community. See: Modzelewski, *Barbarian Europe*.

48 Anderson, *The Lineages*, 279–98, Szűcs, "Three Historical Regions," Tymieniecki, *Kształtowanie się społeczeństwa średniowiecznego*, Topolski, *Polska w czasach nowożytnych*, 521–22.

making this argument. He wrote: "thus, in Poland, the abundance and diversity of the szlachta was more pronounced than in some European countries. However, this phenomenon was neither contrary to, nor especially different from, the process that was occurring in this regard in other countries of sixteenth-century Europe."[49] Other scholars of the sixteenth- to eighteenth-century Commonwealth regarded the szlachta, just as serfdom, to be a specifically Polish (or Central or East European) structural feature that impacted negatively on economic development.[50]

Both Wyczański and Topolski highlighted the fact that the impoverished minor nobility was spread very unevenly across Poland. In the Mazovia and Podlasie regions, the so-called *szlachta zagrodowa* accounted for roughly 20 percent of the population, while in Pomerania and Małopolska this figure was the lowest.[51] Wyczański used the data to argue that this was more a local exception for Poland rather than a national exception for Europe.

The dispute over the image of the szlachta, and in particular how it should be assessed, was less intense than the dispute over the situation of the peasants. Quite simply, the dominant view of the szlachta was that it was responsible for the country's backwardness and had a vested interest in maintaining it. What elicited greater controversy was whether to treat the numerous and financially disparate Polish szlachta as a single, negative social actor (as proposed by Małowist) or whether to make a distinction between the magnates and landless szlachta on the one hand, and the middle szlachta on the other (as did Wyczański and Topolski). In the latter model the owners of vast estates represented all the negative traits associated with the szlachta: the exploitation of the peasantry and ruin of the towns; ostentatiously dissolute lifestyles; and disloyalty toward the state and the economy through the consumption of luxury goods imported from the West. The landless szlachta, in turn, played the role of faithful assistants to the magnates,

---

49 Wyczański, *Polska w Europie*, 91–92.

50 Compare with Szűcs, "Three Historical Regions," Anderson, *The Lineages*, Mączak, *Klientela*, Małowist, "Polityka handlowa szlachty," Topolski, *Polska w czasach nowożytnych.*

51 Topolski, *Polska w czasach nowożytnych*, 76, Wyczański, *Polska w epoce Odrodzenia*, 139.

sharing their values but without their level of consumption or access to power. The owners of medium-sized folwarks, who produced for the domestic market rather than for export, represented the traits that were conducive to economic development. Wyczański strongly supported such an approach in relation to the sixteenth century, while Topolski advocated it in regard to the szlachta of the Wielkopolska region in the second half of the eighteenth century in particular. Kula, while appreciating the long-term differentiation of the szlachta and its nineteenth-century impact, nevertheless believed that the szlachta's feudal solidarity, which was anti-peasant, anti-town, and antistate, could explain the country's backwardness.

Małowist saw the position of the szlachta in legal terms. He argued that it should be treated as a single group with common privileges and interests that were contrary to the interests of other important local actors: peasants, artisans, and merchants, as well as central government. The szlachta's privileges were the reason for the steady decline of other social groups and the economy in general. According to Małowist, the particularly negative economic behavior of the szlachta included its preference for imported craft products, which were "better, albeit more expensive than Polish ones."[52] The szlachta's handsome revenues from exports from the sixteenth century onwards did not translate into investment and development: "the use [of cash flowing in from the West] for productive purposes was minimal; it was mainly earmarked for consumption."[53]

Małowist was the sharpest critic of the Polish szlachta not only in the 1950s, when he wrote that "feudal Poland was a state founded on the open and brutal dictatorship of the szlachta as a class,"[54] but also in 1987, by which time such statements could hardly be considered an example of communist-style political correctness.[55] The selfishness of the early modern elites and their lack of political imagination were, according to Małowist, the root cause of an economic policy that wrecked domestic crafts and trade, made Poland dependent on a stronger Western partner, and ensured the country's long-term back-

---

52 Małowist, *Z problematyki Polski feudalnej*, 16.
53 Małowist, *Wschód a Zachód*, 383.
54 Małowist, *Z problematyki Polski feudalnej*, 22.
55 Małowist, "Marian Małowist o historii."

wardness.[56] In less judgemental and more descriptive language, he linked backwardness to the ossification of the social structure caused by the "szlachta's monopoly" over politics and the economy. The late fifteenth and early sixteenth centuries were characterized by "the intrusion of the szlachta into trade and manufacturing while maintaining serfdom as the foundation of its economy," an "open door" policy for foreign imports and a focus on the "mass export . . . of raw materials," as well as the establishment of direct contact with "foreign" merchants, primarily in Gdańsk, to the exclusion of domestic merchants.[57] Kochanowicz, in verifying Małowist's claim about the relationship between Poland's backwardness and the country's dependence on the more developed countries of the West, argued that it was the position of the szlachta in relation to other social groups, and not international trade relations (although these perhaps played a secondary role), that determined the structure of the Polish, Czech, and Hungarian economies and prevented the development of capitalism. "The domination of the aristocracy over the bourgeoisie and the cities inhibited capitalist development, and that was critical."[58]

Wyczański proposed a different image of the early modern Polish szlachta, emphasizing its internal variation. He attributed less importance to the common privileges and interests of the szlachta as an estate in its relations with other social actors. Operating on the assumption that "besides legal status a greater role was sometimes played by property arrangements and real incomes, and in addition to material circumstances the issue of prestige was important for assessing the position of individuals and groups in society at that time," Wyczański was in favor of clearly distinguishing the szlachta *zagrodowa* (who owned only their own farm) and minor and middle szlachta (who owned one or several villages) from the extravagantly wealthy magnates.[59] On the basis of research on social stratification, which was reflected in national poll tax records, Wyczański identified seven main social strata at the beginning of the sixteenth century, rising to eight by the end of the century. Categories of szlachta in the legal sense

[56] Małowist, "Polityka handlowa," 94.
[57] Małowist, *Z problematyki Polski feudalnej*, 16–17.
[58] Kochanowicz, "The Polish Economy."
[59] Wyczański, *Uwarstwienie społeczne*, 5.

were absent only in the lowest (for 1520) or two lowest (for 1590) tax bands, and at least half the tax bands comprised a mixture of people belonging to various estates of feudal society, for example, the szlachta and peasantry.[60] This was meant to show that, contrary to the opinion of historians who held that the main line of division in early modern Polish society was between the szlachta and everyone else, non-feudal divisions due to wealth and prestige were more important or at least as important. Going on the assumption that the "picture of stratification . . . revealed to us through poll tax records . . . basically corresponds to the social reality at that time," Wyczański saw it as evidence of "huge differences, especially in property, between the extreme categories," including between categories of szlachta.[61] By comparing poll tax records at the beginning and end of the sixteenth century and analyzing the tax returns of szlachta in the Kraków province and peasants in the Korczyn *starostwo* (a territorial unit in the Polish–Lithuanian Commonwealth, a complex of Crown estates), Wyczański concluded that the trend toward differentiation within the szlachta, and toward social mobility, intensified during the period.[62]

The picture of the middle szlachta that emerges from Wyczański's and Topolski's work is of a group whose economic behavior at the turn of the fifteenth and sixteenth centuries contributed to the development of the country as a whole. The folwarks it founded, although based on serfdom, supposedly expressed the szlachta's new, post-medieval mentality and economic rationality. "The szlachta that came to play an active role was clearly no longer the medieval szlachta, which had embraced chivalry and martial skills and ignored the economy."[63] In Poland this role was performed by the "middle szlachta in the popular understanding of the term."[64] At that time "the entry of the szlachta into economic life was . . . a factor that revitalized the economy" and increased social income.[65] According to Topolski, the commercial activities of the sixteenth-century Polish writer, nobleman, and Calvinist, Mikolaj Rej,

60 Ibid., 234–36.
61 Ibid., 253.
62 Ibid., 249–50.
63 Topolski, *Polska w czasach nowożytnych*, 24.
64 Ibid.
65 Ibid.

were an example of the new economic rationality.[66] Although feudal in character since they were based on a belief in the advantages of serfdom, those activities nevertheless used commercial thinking to calculate investment outlays, income, and profit. Topolski considered Rej an exponent of the Protestant work ethic, a proto-entrepreneur similar in mentality to the new elites of England or the Netherlands. Interestingly, according to Małowist, the creative output of this sixteenth-century writer, as I mentioned in Chapter 4, was meant to express the noble ideal of a good life, which was compatible neither with investment risk nor with the country's economic development.[67]

Other scholars, too, emphasized the increasing stratification of the szlachta during the sixteenth century and particularly over the next two centuries. They typically associated this with the "rise in luxury consumption"[68] by the magnates. The social consequences of this phenomenon were referred to as "aristocratization," both with regard to the distribution of social income and political organization and in terms of the perceived values and ideals of a good life.[69] Paradoxically, in a country where "the magnates . . . had no formal means of subordinating the szlachta, such as through a seigniorial system," which "distinguished them . . . from the aristocracy in other countries,"[70] in reality they acquired a political position that was stronger than elsewhere in Europe. Scholars agreed about the origins of this phenomenon. The manorial-serf economy, which was oriented toward commodity production and export, became increasingly popular from the late fifteenth century onwards. Due to economies of scale it was more successful on larger folwarks, which were able to organize and cover the cost of transporting grain to Gdańsk. The development of this economy benefited larger landowners, who were better placed to import goods regarded as status symbols. "On account of their social status the magnates exhib-

---

66 Topolski, "Działalność gospodarcza Mikołaja Reja," 99–111.

67 Małowist, "Poland, Russia and Western Trade," 32–33.

68 Topolski, *Polska w czasach nowożytnych*, 522.

69 Anderson, *The Lineages*, Brenner, "Economic Backwardness," Małowist, *Wschód a Zachód*, 383–84, Mączak, *Klientela*, Sugar, "External and Domestic Roots," Tazbir, "Stosunek do obcych," Topolski, *Polska w czasach nowożytnych*, 521–22.

70 Wyczański, *Polska w epoce Odrodzenia*, 138.

ited a tendency to consume luxury goods," wrote Topolski of the seventeenth century.[71] In doing so, however, they also aroused a need for luxury consumption among the poorer szlachta. Mączak considered this fact to have long-term consequences. "Access to foreign goods was a measure of wealth and prestige (and in Poland this has always been the case)."[72] On smaller estates the effects of extensive farming with no possibility to expand into new areas were felt more quickly. "The seventeenth-century szlachta (in areas without easy access to ports or to Wrocław) became dependent on wealthy neighbors when it came to transporting elite consumer goods from the ports by raft."[73]

Małowist also attributed the impoverishment of the already poor szlachta to "the natural growth of this social group and the fragmentation of property,"[74] which was more acute on smaller estates. As I mentioned earlier, debt and the absorption of smaller estates by larger ones played an important role in the concentration of land after the crisis of the seventeenth century. This situation "obviously strengthened Central European aristocracy politically."[75] Kula noted that the difference in the terms of trade between a typical nobleman and a magnate, which rose during the sixteenth to eighteenth centuries, by the middle of the seventeenth century was greater than the difference in the terms of trade between a nobleman and a peasant.[76] On this understanding of the changes taking place within the szlachta, lower-ranking szlachta became victims of the system, albeit to a lesser extent than peasants and townspeople.

Mączak regarded the process of "aristocratization" on the one hand, and the impoverishment and fragmentation of the szlachta on the other, as the basis for long-term and rampant clientage. As Mączak demonstrated, this clientage developed—not at all paradoxically—within the Commonwealth's legally and rhetorically egalitarian szlachta estate.[77] Using anthropological theories of political organization, Mączak com-

[71] Topolski, "Założenia modelu gospodarki polskiej," 30.
[72] Mączak in Ihnatowicz et al., *Społeczeństwo polskie*, 424.
[73] Mączak, *Klientela*, 146.
[74] Małowist, *Wschód a Zachód*, 383–84.
[75] Ibid.
[76] Kula, *An Economic Theory*.
[77] Antoni Mączak, *Klientelsysteme im Europa*.

pared Poland's szlachta clientele with other such structures in Europe and found that it was especially similar to the clienteles that emerged in Mediterranean countries. In this way he stripped the system of the Commonwealth of its uniquely East European character, although he placed it within the context of other countries regarded as backward. Nearly forty years earlier, Kula had drawn attention to the paradoxical nature of the economically diverse szlachta—from the magnates with their vast properties in the East to the mass of lower-ranking, landless szlachta.[78] Due to their cherished membership of the szlachta class, many lower- and middle-ranking szlachta were forced to act against—as Kula put it—their own objective interests. Clientelist "factotums" managed their patrons' properties as a means of supporting themselves and often in order to repay the debts they had incurred from their masters. For the same reason, their property was often absorbed into the magnates' estates. These "factotums" performed a variety of functions that were for the most part economically useless and which only served to enhance the feudal splendour of their lords. They also acted as the magnates' political representatives vis-à-vis the central Crown authorities which, in Kula's view, could have provided a career path in the state administration.

The manufactories of the late eighteenth century, in the period preceding the Partitions of Polish–Lithuanian Commonwealth[79] were,

78 Kula, *Początki układu kapitalistycznego.*

79 The Polish–Lithuanian Commonwealth, also called The Commonwealth of the Two Nations, was a confederation created in 1386 and confirmed by the Union of Lublin in 1569. It consisted of the Kingdom of Poland (referred to as "the Crown") and the Grand Duchy of Lithuania. The subsequent partitions of 1772 and 1793 reduced the size of the country, and the Third Partition of 1795 annihilated it. Its territory was divided among the Russian and Habsburg Empires and Prussia. As a result of Napoleon's expansion in Europe, the Duchy of Warsaw was created in 1807 from part of the Prussian partition. The Duchy was a client state of France. Following Napoleon's defeat in Russia and the Congress of Vienna in 1815, the Russian Empire took control over most of the Duchy's territory. In 1815, the Kingdom of Poland (also referred to as "Congress Poland" or "the Congress Kingdom") was established as a puppet state tied by personal union with Russia. In 1831, the Kingdom of Poland was annexed by Russia in response to a failed anti-Russian uprising. However, it maintained its name within the Russian Empire until 1918 when the independent Second Republic of Poland was established at the Congress of Versailles.

according to Kula, another example of economic behavior by the magnates that had a negative impact on the country's economy. "A country that had experienced neither enlightened absolutism, nor a period of heightened primitive accumulation, nor a mercantilist policy typical of absolutism, became the setting for what one might call a grotesque phenomenon: magnatial mercantilism; the term itself smacks of a *contradictio in adjecto*. The weapon whose objective function was to accelerate the development of the bourgeoisie and undermine the feudal class system was instead captured by the feudal magnates and used to their advantage."[80] Topolski also emphasized that "the magnates' manufactories [were] a manifestation of a phenomenon that could be termed sham industrialization," mainly because it did not modernize the social structure in the slightest degree.[81]

For Topolski, the opposite trend, which was both economically healthy and progressive, was represented in the eighteenth century by the middle szlachta of the Wielkopolska region. Its folwarks were "autonomous," not reliant on exports and of medium size, and by the end of the seventeenth century it had become the leader among the Polish szlachta of pro-capitalist transformations in agriculture, spearheading the change from serfdom to rents.[82] In the eighteenth century, it displayed "a willingness to invest . . . that was alien to the feudal model," and took up new, development-oriented forms of management.[83] Topolski presented "the middle szlachta (which owned one, two, or several villages)" as the embodiment of healthy economic instinct. Conducive to the middle szlachta's success was the optimal size of its landed property—not too small to invest in and develop, but small enough to manage personally. Unable to "afford the luxury of entrusting direct management of its property to tenants or administrators, it had to run its own affairs by embracing rational economic thinking and action."[84] Not without significance for the nurturing of this entrepreneurial spirit was the fact that the Wielkopolska szlachta was geographically close to the West and far away from the corrupting

---

[80] Kula, *Początki układu kapitalistycznego*, 74.
[81] Topolski, *Polska w czasach nowożytnych*, 743–46.
[82] Ibid., 735.
[83] Topolski, "Model gospodarczy," 275.
[84] Ibid., 274.

influence of the magnates in the eastern borderlands. As a result, it could adopt the consumption patterns of the West European bourgeoisie and develop a "contractual consciousness" in its relations with the peasantry.[85] All these factors, according to Topolski, were conducive to the development of textiles and agriculture as well as urbanization.

TOWNS: PROSPERITY OR DECLINE?

Another contentious aspect of social stratification in the Polish–Lithuanian Commonwealth from the sixteenth to the eighteenth centuries was the position of the town population. The specific disputes concerned the impact of the manorial economy on domestic crafts and trade as well as the link between the development of the manorial economy and the political power of the towns. Małowist argued that Polish towns were already in decline in the sixteenth century, a view opposed by Wyczański. Detailed research on the history of towns and their inhabitants from this perspective was conducted by, among others, Małowist's students: Henryk Samsonowicz, Maria Bogucka, and Antoni Mączak. A secondary, less apparent dispute took place among economic historians over the ethnic make-up of the Commonwealth's more important towns, especially Gdańsk and Toruń, but also Kraków.

Of the works analyzed here, and in postwar historiography in general, it was Małowist and his school in particular that initiated and developed research on medieval and early modern towns as well as crafts and trade in Poland.[86] Researchers from Małowist's circle emphasized the centuries-old weakness of East European towns compared to the towns of Western Europe, especially those situated in the former territories of the Roman Empire. There were fewer towns in the East, and they played a smaller role in crafts and trade. Their political power and degree of autonomy could not compare with the gains that had been made by West European towns in the Middle Ages. Małowist's

---

85 Ibid., 274, 281.

86 Małowist, *Ryga i Gdańsk*, Małowist, "Tezy do dyskusji nad budową miasta," Małowist, "Rzemiosło miejskie," Małowist, "W sprawie badań nad historią," Małowist, "W sprawie historii handlu," Małowist, "Miasta w Polsce średniowiecznej," Małowist, "Rzemiosło polskie epoki Odrodzenia." See also the section on Małowist in Chapter 4 of this book.

school countered the claims of prewar German historiography, however, which in the words of Zientara stuck "doggedly to a legal definition of the town, such that its very existence could be regarded as a German achievement."[87] Małowist noted that "the East [before the so-called German colonization of the thirteenth century], had towns in the economic sense," representing "small agglomerations near the castles of princes and their officials."[88] Like Kazimierz Tymieniecki, he attributed the rapid growth of urban settlement, crafts, and domestic trade in the thirteenth and fourteenth centuries not just to the influx of German colonists but first and foremost to the introduction of advantageous German town law—which Małowist persistently called "Western" law—in Eastern Europe.[89]

Małowist argued that from the sixteenth century onwards, under the influence of the import and export policies of the folwarks, domestic craftsmen lost access to raw materials and had no hope of manufacturing products of a quality that the szlachta's luxurious lifestyles demanded. He wrote: "in the sixteenth century they [the szlachta] constantly complained about shortages of raw materials, which were being exported abroad in huge quantities. It should be remembered that in Poland their ability to accumulate capital was very limited; similarly, their political position was very weak."[90] According to Małowist, and also to Kula and Topolski, the segment of the craft market traditionally oriented toward the poorer szlachta and peasants began to disappear with the expansion of serfdom. Małowist was convinced that "the problem of the decline of Polish towns is inextricably linked to the consolidation of serfdom in the countryside, to the policy of the szlachta and the triumph of that policy."[91] This process, which affected all of Eastern Europe in the early modern era, took a particularly negative course in Poland. "Urban industry, which was undeveloped, struggled against the competition of foreign products and the difficulties caused by the smallness of interior markets and either

87 Zientara in Ihnatowicz et al., *Społeczeństwo polskie*, 100.

88 Małowist, "The Problem of the Inequality," 15–16.

89 Małowist, "Uwagi o roli kapitału," 221, 226, Tymieniecki, *Procesy twórcze formowania.*

90 Małowist, "A Certain Trade Technique," 116.

91 Małowist, *Z problematyki Polski feudalnej*, 19.

remained insignificant or, as in Poland, was destined to disappear."[92] The image conjured up by Małowist related more to the towns than to their inhabitants: victims of the szlachta's trade policy and Western competition, the towns—disappearing, fading, declining—were a testament to growing backwardness.

Wyczański offered a very different vision of towns in sixteenth-century Poland. He felt that Małowist's school was guilty of presentism and that its conclusions were based on legal documents rather than on an analysis of the reality at the time. He wrote:

> As regards the supposedly negative impact of the folwarks on the situation of the towns, there is no evidence that Polish towns were in decline in the sixteenth century, whereas there are clear signs that they were developing. The only question is whether the resolutions of the szlachta parliament that threatened the towns and their inhabitants did indeed hamper urban development. I am referring here first and foremost to the famous Sejm resolution of 1565, which prohibited Polish merchants from exporting their goods. That resolution has long evoked harsh criticism from the majority of historians, yet only the more astute have taken solace in the fact that it was a resolution that everyone basically ignored.[93]

Wyczański countered the dark vision of Polish towns and the degradation of town populations offered by Małowist's school with an image of steady urbanization and prosperity in sixteenth-century Poland. He argued that these phenomena were mainly related to the development of the internal market,[94] although he admitted that the Vistula towns—from Kraków in the south to Gdańsk in the north—prospered thanks to their participation in the export of grain by raft.[95]

Despite evidence that the Baltic ports and Vistula towns were flourishing, Małowist's counter-argument was that the success of Gdańsk and Toruń could not be put down to the state of the econ-

[92] Małowist, "The Problem of Inequality," 28.
[93] Wyczański, *Polska—Rzeczą Pospolitą*, 154.
[94] Wyczański, *Dogonić Europę*, 4, Wyczański, *Polska w Europie*.
[95] Wyczański, "Czy rzeczywiście czasy upadku?"

omy.[96] He saw the rise of Gdańsk as complementary to the decline of Polish towns. When "Gdańsk was experiencing its boom, especially in the late sixteenth and early seventeenth centuries," "the situation in Poland was very different."[97] It was during this period that "Gdańsk, which had earlier monopolized and exploited Polish agriculture and certain aspects of foreign trade, in all likelihood aided by capital from the Netherlands and even Antwerp, . . . became a dangerous industrial competitor for other towns in Poland."[98]

Małowist emphasized the Hanseatic and Prussian-Teutonic origins of Gdańsk's position in Baltic trade and, after 1466 when the port returned to Poland, the reliance of the Polish monarchy on loans from local townspeople and Gdańsk's common interests with Dutch merchants and Western markets rather than Polish ones.[99] Kula held a similar view in the debate over Polish towns in the early modern era. The urban economy supposedly declined under the control of the szlachta,[100] and the burgeoning Vistula towns represented—in a similarly dialectical manner to Małowist's vision—the future decline of the Polish economy. "The Vistula could perform its integrative role in the manorial system based on the second serfdom, but by helping to consolidate that system it became an 'accessory' to our historical backwardness. Let us not be deceived by the beautiful towns that adorn its banks, which grew rich on the grain trade, or by the stunning granaries we see today in the towns of Kazimierz, Toruń, and Bydgoszcz, for they foreshadowed Poland's future backwardness."[101]

Wyczański had a different view on the matter. For him, the splendour of sixteenth-century Gdańsk and the economic and political power of its inhabitants were sufficient evidence of the positive impact of foreign trade on Polish towns and the Polish economy in general. "The Vistula trade did not circumvent domestic buyers and eliminate

---

96 Małowist, "Podstawy gospodarcze przywrócenia."

97 Małowist, "A Certain Trade Technique," 116, Mączak, *Między Gdańskiem a Sundem*, 159–60.

98 Małowist, "Polska a przewrót cen," 318.

99 Małowist, "Poland, Russia and Western Trade," 30.

100 Kula, *An Economic Theory*, Kula, *Measures and Men*, especially ch. 19: The Struggle of the Nobility with the Bourgeoisie in the Urban Market.

101 Kula, *Wokół historii*, 511.

the towns. On the contrary, it concentrated large-scale grain trade in the hands of wealthy Gdańsk merchants and elevated Gdańsk's status."[102]

Małowist's school argued that economic interest tied the townspeople of Gdańsk to remote cities rather than to the court of the Polish monarch. Henryk Samsonowicz wrote that in the first half of the sixteenth century the political relationship between Gdańsk and Crown "was not too close." He asked rhetorically: "Was Gdańsk, which arose to become the premier Baltic port, proof of Poland's maritime presence . . . ?" To which he replied: "For [Dutch and English] relations with Gdańsk were more important than relations with the Polish monarchy. This state of affairs is important to understanding our country's place in Europe."[103]

Małowist emphasized that the political traditions of Polish towns from the end of the Middle Ages onwards were different to those in Western Europe. The towns' relationship with the state apparatus was looser than in the West, and their inhabitants, regardless of their ethnic origin, did not play a role in state building: "At the beginning of the fourteenth century the situation in Poland was different to other Western countries, particularly France, where the towns had helped the Capetian dynasty to create a strong, centralized feudal monarchy from the outset."[104]

A characteristic feature of Małowist's thinking about the role of towns, which partly explains the discrepancy in his assessment of Gdańsk and the Polish economy, was that he contrasted the situation of larger and smaller towns, at least in the early modern era. "Merchants in the larger towns managed to become involved in [overseas] trade, from which they drew considerable profits," but the increasing importance of international trade in sixteenth-century Poland "undermined crafts that were produced for the mass market."[105] According to Małowist, but in contrast to Braudel, the situation of small towns was crucial to the health of their surrounding economy. Braudel attrib-

---

102 Wyczański, *Dogonić Europę*, 4.

103 Samsonowicz, "Polska widziana przez Hanzę," 30. See also Samsonowicz, *Badania nad kapitałem*, 1960.

104 Małowist, *Z problematyki Polski feudalnej*, 5.

105 Małowist, "Poland, Russia and Western Trade," 32.

uted "the European miracle" to the fact that "cities enjoyed unparalleled freedom," metropolises "developed as autonomous worlds," and that "they managed to escape the tutelage of the territorial state, which [in the early modern era] had barely stabilized."[106] Małowist, on the other hand, pointed out that it was precisely crafts, often practised in small towns, and not the metropolises and foreign merchants, that had played a revolutionary role in the West in the late Middle Ages and early modern era.[107]

However, in a later work—*Tamerlane and His Times* (*Tamerlan i jego czasy*)—Małowist, like Braudel, emphasized the importance of the political freedom enjoyed by medieval European towns for the development of urban civilization, which was beneficial not just to the economy but also to society's capacity of self-government. He juxtaposed this model with the Asian model, in which towns "were completely subordinate to a despotic central authority, hence the lack of autonomy and underdevelopment of guilds. This did not inhibit the economic development of towns, which performed no worse in this regard than towns in Western Europe. However, their populations were at the mercy of a despotic ruler and had no opportunity to pursue their own organizational initiatives in public life."[108]

This complex vision of the relationship between the success of large towns and the strength of the patriciate on the one hand, and the socioeconomic development of the country in which they were situated on the other, can in my view be described as follows: essentially, the freedom and autonomy of the town population, which were characteristic of European medieval society, were a prerequisite of development in the early modern era. However, this model was dangerous for countries that were already backward and dominated by an anti-urban nobility. It afforded development opportunities to metropolises that were able to resist the policies of the nobility and which had links with cities abroad. Yet it was disastrous for small towns unable to survive competition from larger towns or oppose legal restrictions. Consequently, the model was detrimental to the overall economy of backward countries.

[106] Braudel, *Civilization and Capitalism*, vol. 3, 425.
[107] Małowist, review of Braudel, *Civilisation materielle*,.
[108] Małowist, *Tamerlan i jego czasy*, 119.

NEWCOMERS FROM THE WEST: INNOVATORS OR AGENTS OF ECONOMIC COLONIZATION?

The debate over the situation of towns also addressed the question of what role was played by foreign settlers and merchants in the early modern era. I refer to this group as "newcomers from the West," regardless of whether they settled in Poland for good or lived there only temporarily for business. The term reflects the attitude of historiography, which usually treated such people "separately." In the case of settlers it stressed their "arrival" and linguistic and cultural otherness, and in the case of merchants—their distinct interests.

It was Małowist's school that introduced this issue into the debate, but from then on all the scholars discussed here took account of foreign settlers. Mączak noted that although migration was "insignificant in terms of numbers," it was "of considerable social importance."[109] Dominant among the identified categories of foreign settlers were townspeople (artisans and merchants), hired peasants known as *olędrzy*, and professionals (artists, impresarios, practitioners of the liberal professions, teachers).[110] Between the thirteenth and seventeenth centuries the most controversial groups were considered to be townspeople of German origin and merchants of the Hanseatic League, followed by Dutch merchants.

Townspeople of German origin occupied a special place in Polish historiography. The group was seen as more controversial than settlers of other nationalities on account of its role in the country's development. This interpretation was, I believe, somewhat influenced by the anti-German sentiment of the war generation.

Resentment of Germany stemmed not just from the recent experience of occupation but also from historiographical tradition—German, Polish, and European alike. This treated nations in linguistic and ethnic terms and traced their origins to the Middle Ages. For this reason the judgements of historiography concerning even the very dis-

[109] Mączak in Ihnatowicz et al., *Społeczeństwo polskie*, 376.

[110] Ibid., 308, 376, Mączak, *Gospodarstwo chłopskie*, Wyczański, "Uwagi o ksenofobii," Zientara, "Cudzoziemcy w Polsce," Kula, *Początki układu kapitalistycznego*, Małowist, *Wschód z Zachód*, 148, 248–49, Małowist, "The Problem of Inequality."

tant past could be used as an argument in favor of the civilizational superiority of one nation over another. Consequently, Kazimierz Tymieniecki, and later Małowist, postulated that the importance of legal and formal innovations from the West, and not the settlers themselves, should be considered first and foremost.[111] Małowist was of the opinion that "population growth and the new legal code were hugely significant" for the growth of East European economies in the late Middle Ages.[112] He emphasized the importance of German law, rather than of newcomers. "German law was also used in various forms in areas where foreign settlement was limited or did not exist at all, for instance in the Mazovia region; it generally had very beneficial economic effects in the form of increased production and trade, etc."[113]

The debate over the role of foreign settlers in the early modern era was, therefore, more about ambivalence within individual works rather than disputes between researchers. On the one hand, scholars emphasized the innovative, pro-development function of newcomers: repopulation, the supply of capital, a more sophisticated work culture, and political self-organization. Małowist wrote that in the late Middle Ages "newcomers from Germany played an important role in Poland as entrepreneurs who organized urban and rural settlement on a leasehold basis, and many figured as investors in areas where there were lead and salt mines."[114] This group would become a symbol of class, ethnic, and religious divisions characteristic of dependent regions. Małowist's school was especially sensitive to this phenomenon.[115] Zientara noted that in the late Middle Ages, Germans, "due to their high numbers in certain areas (the Sudeten Foothills and many towns across Poland), formed close-knit communities that maintained their separateness. By assuming a preeminent role in trade and crafts, and thanks to their

---

[111] Tymieniecki proposed that the new law introduced in the Polish territories in the Middle Ages should be referred to as "Western law" rather than "German law." This practice has become a tradition in Polish historiography.

[112] Małowist, "Problems of the Growth," 325.

[113] Ibid.

[114] Małowist, "Uwagi o roli kapitału," 223–24. Compare with: Małowist, "Some Remarks on the Role," 85–100.

[115] Małowist, *Miejsce Polski w świecie feudalnym*, Małowist, *Z problematyki Polski feudalnej*, Zientara, *Cudzoziemcy w Polsce.*

influence at royal courts and in the Church, they became a factor shaping the fortunes of the Polish nation and state."[116]

Wyczański, in turn, argued that the attitude of Western settlers in the late Middle Ages and in the sixteenth century was precisely the opposite. According to his research, newcomers were more likely to go native than to cultivate their separateness. He wrote: "Masons and artists arrived from Italy, Germany, and other countries, followed in later years by apostles and exiles of the Reformation, . . . foreign merchants, especially from Silesia and Germany, settled in Poland, quickly acclimatizing themselves to the patriciate of the large towns and becoming polonized."[117]

Małowist and Zientara emphasized the analogy between German settlement in Poland in the Middle Ages and Polish settlement in Lithuania and Rus'. Zientara expressed it in terms of social consciousness. In the period after the union of Poland and Lithuania (the fifteenth century), "naturally the Poles saw themselves as a culturally more advanced society than the 'barbaric' Lithuanians and Ruthenians, just as two hundred years earlier the Germans had ridiculed the barbaric customs and wretched economy of the Poles."[118]

Scholars from Małowist's school stressed the fundamentally different nature of German settlement in the Middle Ages compared to the modern era (nineteenth and twentieth centuries). The former was spontaneous, prompted by the attractive conditions that prevailed in Poland; the latter was planned—a result of the nationalistic demographic and cultural policies of the Prussian and German state.[119] Topolski, too, drew attention to the uniqueness and premodern attractiveness of the Wielkopolska region for German newcomers.[120]

An issue especially important for Małowist, and then for Maria Bogucka, was "a certain trade technique" introduced in the Baltic

---

116 Zientara, "Cudzoziemcy w Polsce," 18, Małowist, *Z problematyki Polski*, 25–26.

117 Wyczański, "Uwagi o ksenofobii w Polsce," 70–71.

118 Zientara, "Cudzoziemcy w Polsce," 34, Zientara in Ihnatowicz et al., *Społeczeństwo polskie*, 102.

119 Zientara, "Z zagadnień terminologii," Małowist, "Problems of the Growth," 325.

120 Topolski, "Model gospodarczy," 275.

region by Hanseatic League traders. They offered credit to producers, thus securing a supply of future crops. "There was a certain risk involved in this for the merchant, but it made the seller well disposed toward him, and also made the seller more dependent on the merchant."[121] This technique reduced supply-side risk and gave merchants control over prices; it was also used by the Teutonic Knights and, from the sixteenth century onwards in particular, by merchants from Gdańsk and Western Europe in their dealings with Poland. Małowist highlighted the many links in the credit chain that existed outside the country. "[T]he merchants of Amsterdam, which was the main market for grain in Western Europe, more than once concluded with the merchants of Gdańsk the same kind of contracts that the Gdańsk merchants concluded with rest of Poland. The Gdańsk merchants received advance payments from the Dutch, and, as one may surmise from certain information, the latter sometimes collected for that purpose certain sums from merchants in Antwerp."[122] This trading system, argued Małowist, was beneficial to all the merchants involved in it as well as being beneficial for the local szlachta, who were at once the organizers of production, sellers, and political decision makers. Other social groups and the economy in general were presented as hostages and victims of this system. "The economic policy of the szlachta was most fully reflected in the famous Sejm resolution of 1565, which prohibited Polish merchants from exporting their goods or importing foreign goods, and which openly favored foreign merchants operating in Poland."[123]

Peasant settlers in the Żuławy region, who were mostly of Dutch origin, gained a decidedly more positive image in Polish historiography than did urban settlers, particularly merchants. According to source documents, they were referred to by the collective term *olędrzy*, which sounds very similar to "Holendrzy," the Polish word for inhabitants of the Netherlands. The region in which they settled, Żuławy Wiślane, lies below sea level at the mouth of the Vistula, and the Dutch settlers were expected to bring their skills in land reclamation to the Polish economy. Topolski described them as "experts in the cultivation of

[121] Małowist, "A Certain Trade Technique," 113.
[122] Ibid., 114.
[123] Małowist, "Polityka handlowa," 94, 96, Bogucka, "Obcy kupcy."

wetlands and floodplains."[124] Without mentioning the newcomers' Protestant work ethic, both Topolski and Mączak emphasized that the contractual nature of this migration, which assumed freedom for landowners and peasants alike, was important for social relations within Poland and promoted development. It was to set a new and more modern standard in rural social relations. Mączak, however, presented the settlers' role in the spirit of Małowist's colonial thesis. As shown by his research on farming by the *olędrzy* in the Żuławy region in the sixteenth and seventeenth centuries, the settlers represented a higher level of material culture (houses and furniture, for instance) and organization compared to local communities. They sought to maintain a separate, privileged legal and economic status.[125] Mączak considered this attitude to be typical of economies that were open to trade with more developed regions, such as those from which the settlers originated. Newcomers, whether they were colonizers or, as in this case, settlers, were interested in maintaining their distinct culture, which they felt to be superior to the local culture. Their communities became a permanent symbol of the economic disparity between the places from which they came and their adopted country, and the dependency of the latter on the former.

Origins of the Modern Transformation. Social Change and Continuity in Studies on Nineteenth-Century Society

It was Kula's team that first tried to answer the question about the extent and social consequences of the process whose equivalent in Western Europe is sometimes referred to as the modern transformation. Ireneusz Ihnatowicz, who joined the debate in the 1970s, wrote that "the studies initiated under the research program [of Kula's group] influenced many historians of the nineteenth century as regards the types of source materials used, the manner in which they were used, and in the way research hypotheses were formulated."[126]

[124] Topolski, *Polska w czasach nowożytnych*, 734.

[125] Mączak, *Gospodarstwo chłopskie.*

[126] Ihnatowicz, "Review of *Przemiany społeczne*," 392. See also: Żarnowski, *Historia społeczna*, 15–21.

It was in the 1950s that Kula and Janina Leskiewiczowa came up with the idea of creating a team that would research the structure of Polish society in the eighteenth and nineteenth centuries. The team investigated stratification and modern transformation, and their research resulted in the series entitled *The Polish Society of the Eighteenth and Nineteenth Centuries* (*Społeczeństwo polskie XVIII i XIX wieku*). Methodologically, it tried to mimic sociological studies produced in the 1970s. However, its approach went beyond a Marxist analysis of class conflict, which at that time was the norm, in several respects. It assumed that class divisions were a historical phenomenon restricted to the modern era rather than a universal one.[127] The category of "transition from feudalism to capitalism" was translated into the language of social studies as "the penetration of the old feudal structure by new class divisions." Second, the analysis also covered the Catholic Church hierarchy and clergy—a rare subject of inquiry during the communist era. The attitude of Catholic priests toward the national question was treated in this series as an indicator of social change: the increasing incorporation of peasants into the Polish Catholic clergy and, as a result, the extension of national consciousness to the lower strata of Polish society during the period of the Partitions. Third, the series contained articles by Arthur Eisenbach on Poland's Jewish community and its economic role, a subject much neglected in postwar historiography. Fourth, Jerzy Jedlicki also wrote about ideological divisions, notions of economic progress, and the social ideals of the period.[128] Fifth, the problem of participation in power, not necessarily in state structures, and the formation of the modern nation also found their way into the series.[129]

The image of both macrosocial issues and particular groups produced by Kula and Leskiewiczowa's team was ambivalent. The authors often presented their findings in the form of an internal dialogue, a set of sometimes competing hypotheses. Discussions about estates and classes, about new aspects of ethnic diversity and the creation of the

[127] The following publications were the result of a collaborative effort: *Społeczeństwo Królestwa Polskiego* and *Społeczeństwo polskie XVIII i XIX wieku*, vol. 1–8.

[128] Jedlicki, "Obozy ideowe," Jedlicki, *A Suburb of Europe*.

[129] Kula, "Udział we władzy," Chamerska, "Wspólnoty religijno-narodowe," Śliwowska, "Udział w ruchu niepodległościowym."

modern nation, and about the new role of the (partitioning) state in economic development, all took place within individual studies themselves. This internal dialogue involved, on the one hand, an interpretation that drew analogies with modern social transformations known from the history of the West and, on the other, an interpretation that focused on revealing the peculiarities and slow pace of change. Elements of both interpretations were present in virtually all of the studies. However, the first interpretation was largely embraced by Jedlicki and Ihnatowicz, and the second by Kula, Kaczyńska, and Kochanowicz.

The main aspects of this inner dialogue were those features of macrosocial change, especially the transformation of estates into classes, which were seen as either favoring or hindering development. Aside from this, what seems to me particularly interesting is the often discussed image of two new social groups: the bourgeoisie and the intelligentsia. These two strata—the first similar to its Western counterpart, the second uniquely East European—were suspected of playing the leading role in the modernization of the economy and society.

FEUDAL ESTATES: AMALGAMATION OR STRATIFICATION?

The macrosocial image of the first half of the nineteenth century presented by Kula's school suggested a society marked by slow and inconsistent changes. These changes did not progress along a single trajectory, nor did they cumulate, but rather consisted of a series of leaps that were sometimes conducive to development and at other times hindered it.

The articles in the series analyzed the birth of modern Polish society. In the preface to each volume the authors emphasized that the process took place—especially in the Kingdom of Poland—under the influence of a state-controlled industrial revolution and the top-down development of "capitalist relations" in the countryside, as well as in the absence of a market and nation-state, both of which were characteristic of Western modernity. This structural revolution entailed the decomposition of estates, that is, "old" social groups, reconfiguration, social "amalgamation" and, as a result, the creation of classes, that is, "new" social groups. The aim of the research was to describe mass processes, hence, in a move that was unprecedented in Polish historiography, the authors chose sources such as treasury and tax documents, parish records, notarial deeds, administrative documents, and legal regulations. The studies also included articles on how society perceived stratification, which were written with reference to popular literary works and journalism. Research on the basis of sources generated on a mass scale fulfilled Kula's ideal of studies of social change, that is to say, as he wrote in *An Economic Theory*, "singling out those continuous or recurring phenomena which, by having a cumulative effect, lead to structural transformations,"[130] and allow us to discover historical trends. "These tendencies consist . . . of countless facts which occur periodically or continuously and the course of which is irreversible. Their effects build up and bring about a change in structure. These tendencies express, at the same time, the contradictions inherent in the system, and particularly the class contradictions."[131]

What is most interesting about these studies, however, is that they went beyond the boundaries set both by the Marxist theory of transition from feudal to capitalist society and by classical sociological theories of transition from traditional to modern society. The ethnic diversity of Polish society, which could hardly be translated into the language of class divisions, as well as the presence of social classes not found in modern Western Europe and the absence a nation-state in an era of nationalism, made it necessary to modify well-known social theories.

The social structures research programme that Kula established at the Polish Academy of Sciences' Institute of History assumed that systems undergoing modernization included a greater number of key social groups compared to stable, mature systems. As Kula agued, only in relation to the latter, does fit a dichotomous Marxist vision of the class structure composed of proletariat and bourgeoisie. For Kula, premodern Polish society comprised the clergy, szlachta, peasants, and Jews (in the introduction to volume 1 of *The Society of the Kingdom of Poland*, Kula did not even mention townspeople), whereas during the modern transformation it comprised various classes and strata: landowners; the haute bourgeoisie; rural and municipal officials; state and private officials; the technical and creative intelligentsia; the petite

---

130 Kula, *An Economic Theory*, 112

131 Ibid., 118

bourgeoisie; artisans; the separate category of Jewish artisans and petite bourgeoisie; urban workers and domestics; peasant-workers; smallholders and wealthy peasants; and hired agricultural laborers.[132] The process of amalgamation, preceded by a period of intense social mobility, involved the estates becoming stratified in such a way that their various strata formed new social classes. Kula presented this process using the metaphor of a chemical reaction, in which various elements were joined to form new compounds. He defined amalgamation as "the mixing of society in a vast melting pot and the formation of new classes comprising people of the most diverse origins."[133] What the work of Kula's team actually described, however, was the stratification of estates along class lines rather than the mixing of different estates to form new classes. Estate-based structures proved very durable. "Areas where a process of amalgamation might have been expected . . . saw the restoration of barriers that were clearly rooted in the estates. Thus, schools, the military, the intelligentsia, and the clergy, instead of helping to transform traditional society, actually replicated it."[134]

THE SZLACHTA

Janina Leskiewiczowa, Jerzy Jedlicki, and Stanisław Grodziski, the main researchers of the nineteenth-century transformation of the szlachta, emphasized that after the fall of the Polish-Lithuanian Commonwealth, in accordance with the practice of absolutist monarchies, the szlachta as an estate lost its political rights, personal inviolability, and freedom of expression and assembly.[135] After the Partitions of Poland, the degradation of the szlachta was linked to the elimination of "traditional career paths and graces" in the institutions of noble republicanism and offices of the Polish-Lithuanian state.[136] The status of the Polish szlachta was changed in accordance with the rules of the partitioning powers (Austria, Prussia, and Russia). The new states distinguished the higher and more affluent groups of szlachta from the lower

132 Kula, introduction to *Społeczeństwo Królestwa Polskiego*, vol. 1, 5–18.
133 Kula, "Rozwój gospodarczy," 15.
134 Jedlicki and Kula, "Struktura społeczna Królestwa Polskiego," 43.
135 Jedlicki, *Przemiany społeczne*, 25–26.
136 Grodziski, "Schyłek stanu szlacheckiego," 98.

ones, the latter often being not recognized at all. The authors stressed the importance of the liberal principles of equality before the law, the inviolability of property, and freedom of economic activity, including the sale and purchase of land, which were introduced under the Constitution of the Duchy of Warsaw established by Napoleon in 1807. In the Kingdom of Poland, created in 1815 after Napoleon's failure and tied by personal union with Russia, feudal divisions were restored under a law of 1836 which distinguished szlachta families that had verified, registered, and paid for their titles. According to Jedlicki, such families accounted for approximately 15 percent of the pre-Partition szlachta. At the time, the szlachta was also differentiated according to wealth, source of income, and lifestyle to an even greater degree than in the eighteenth century. Besides the prosperous gentry and smallholding szlachta there appeared in the Kingdom of Poland new strata of landless szlachta, the early intelligentsia: clerks, hired administrators of large estates, and town dwellers.[137]

Emerging from among the gentry during the same period were elite groups of wealthy entrepreneurs and high-ranking officials, who were employed by the state and by important economic institutions such as the Land Credit Association (Towarzystwo Kredytowe Ziemskie) and the Polish Bank (Bank Polski). In addition, all the authors emphasized that in first half of the nineteenth century, with the possible exception of the Wielkopolska region, old szlachta enjoyed a monopoly of land ownership;[138] it also retained its traditional privileges and customs, which distinguished it from other feudal estates,[139] including those szlachta families that had not verified and registered their titles under the 1836 law. Jedlicki believed that "estate-based divisions lived on in customs even where they had no basis in law or property."[140] Leskiewiczowa noted that even after the abolition of

---

[137] Jedlicki, *Przemiany społeczne*, 47, Chamerska, "Struktura własności ziemskiej," Rzepniewska, "Wiejscy oficjaliści," Smoleńska, "Oficjaliści dóbr wilanowskich," Homola, "Inteligencja galicyjska," Czepulis, "Inteligencja warszawska," Czepulis, "Kształtowanie się inteligencji," Czepulis, "Lekarze urzędowi."

[138] Ihnatowicz et al., *Społeczeństwo polskie 1864–1914*, 520–22.

[139] Grodziski, "Schyłek stanu," 98.

[140] Jedlicki, *Przemiany społeczne*, 37.

serfdom, that is, the Emancipation Reform of 1864, old privileges such as the szlachta's monopoly on the production and sale of alcohol were translated into the language of new property rights. The landed aristocracy and high-ranking officials from the gentry's economic and financial institutions—the loyal part of the gentry that had not been deprived of its assets after the anti-Russian January Uprising of 1863—ruled "over the peasant from the position of the lowest level of state power."[141] Kula, too, stressed the continuity of the powerful elite in the Kingdom of Poland, which was unaffected by formal and discursive change. "The transition from feudalism to capitalism was in this case the transition from a system in which one did not whip the szlachta to a system in which one did not whip the landowners."[142]

The authors disagreed over the extent to which the partitioning powers entrenched feudal divisions and mentalities. Grodziski linked the post-Partition conservatism, insularity, and traditionalism of the szlachta to its discrimination by new state administrations and its loss of citizenhood. Jedlicki, who studied the Kingdom of Poland, and scholars who studied Galicia argued that, on the contrary, the rigidity of feudal divisions and the hegemony of the szlachta were a result of the conservative policies of the partitioning powers in the period between the two national uprisings (1831–64).[143]

THE PEASANTRY

According to Kula, the period between the two national uprisings was also key as regards the stratification of the peasantry. Although Kula was interested in this issue himself, "it rarely found its way into our studies," wrote Leskiewiczowa on behalf of the team.[144] It was Kochanowicz, Kula's student, who eventually presented a detailed picture of the transformation of the nineteenth-century peasantry in the Kingdom of Poland. His book, *The Peasantry. An Intellectual Problem*

---

141 Leskiewiczowa, "Ziemiaństwo" in *Przemiany społeczne*, 386. See also: Czepulis, "Urzędnicy Towarzystwa Kredytowego."

142 Kula, "Rządzący i rządzeni."

143 Jedlicki, *Przemiany społeczne*, 56. In reference to Galicia, similar conclusions were drawn by Kruczkowska, "Deputowani Koła Polskiego."

144 Leskiewiczowa, introduction to *Społeczeństwo polskie*, vol. 6, 5.

and Social Science Issue (*Chłopstwo. Problem intelektualny i zagadnienie nauk społecznych*), which he wrote together with Kula, as well as his independent work, *The Dispute over the Theory of the Peasant Economy* (*Spór o teorię gospodarki chłopskiej*), attempted to summarize the debate in Polish historiography on the "post-traditional" peasantry in the Polish lands.

That the team was not especially interested in the transformation of the peasantry in the mid-nineteenth century may have been due to the research programme itself, the aim of which was to study change. The peasantry, the most numerous social group both before the Partitions and right up until the 1960s, represented "the persistence of certain problems in the social structure of post-Partition Poland."[145] Kochanowicz wrote that in the nineteenth century the "rapid development of industry did not reduce the gap between the Kingdom and the West and . . . had very little impact on the rural population."[146] The latter, according to Leskiewiczowa's estimates, accounted for between 65 and 73 percent of the population of the Kingdom of Poland in the mid-nineteenth century, and agricultural areas included not just villages but also small towns. Kaczyńska estimated that "of the 450 towns, a significant proportion were tiny settlements, almost exclusively rural."[147]

The peasants were presented as victims both of old-style backwardness and of changes that had done nothing to overcome it. Researchers emphasized that in the period just prior to the abolition of serfdom the life of rural communities was characterized by the convergence of old and new burdens and the absence of old and new rights. Leskiewiczowa wrote that "the peasants were saddled . . . with elements of feudal serfdom while at the same time their customary rights, which had previously placed them under the patriarchal care of the manor, were being eliminated."[148] Other authors, too, pointed to the fact that obligatory military service was introduced in all three Partitions and that the separate and harsh judicial system for peasants was

---

145 Jedlicki, *Klejnot i bariery społeczne*, 449.

146 Kochanowicz, *Spór o teorię*, 159.

147 Leskiewiczowa, *Przemiany społeczne*, 61–62, Kaczyńska, *Przemiany społeczne*, 88.

148 Leskiewiczowa, *Przemiany społeczne*, 68.

maintained.[149] In the Kingdom of Poland, unlike in the other Partitions, the decision to exact feudal obligations in the form of money-rent or corvée depended entirely on the lord. The formal granting of personal freedom, which was not accompanied by the right to own land, "worsened the situation of the peasants: it imposed on them obligations toward the state while at the same time preserving their feudal burdens and constraints," noted Orzechowski.[150] Kochanowicz described the transformation of the peasantry in the first half of the nineteenth century as follows: "The peasant class paid for the modernization of the state and for state-led industrialization directly (through a higher taxes) and indirectly (through increased labor both on their own farms and when performing additional work)."[151]

The authors all agreed that the main transformation trends in the nineteenth and twentieth centuries, especially in the Kingdom of Poland and Galicia, included the stratification of the countryside and the formation of a post-traditional agrarian structure, overpopulation, hidden unemployment, and a predominance of small farms that were not run on market principles and operated on the basis of subsistence and survival. Stratification consisted in the formation of a group of farm owners, who were self-sufficient and used hired labor, and a group of landless farm workers and superfluous people who migrated to the towns. As Leskiewiczowa notes, in the mid-nineteenth century 40 percent of the peasantry was landless, of which 50 percent were hired laborers who worked on folwarks. Researchers of the late nineteenth and early twentieth centuries acknowledged that overpopulation and the economically unfavorable model of the peasant economy were typical of backward countries. Unlike in Western countries, non-agricultural sectors, especially industry, developed so slowly that they were not able to absorb even a relatively small number of "superfluous people."[152] Kochanowicz stressed the ingenious ways in which the overpopulated countryside found ways of earning a living and saving money: intensification, cultivation of wasteland, changes in reproductive habits and inheritance

149 Ibid., 69–70, Ihnatowicz in Ihnatowicz et al., *Społeczeństwo polskie*, 493.
150 Orzechowski, "Pozostałości przedziałów stanowych," 87.
151 Kochanowicz, *Spór o teorię*, 159.
152 Ibid., 160.

patterns, seasonal emigration or non-agricultural activities, and finally, especially in Galicia—foreign emigration.[153]

Ireneusz Ihnatowicz presented a somewhat different image of peasants in the nineteenth and twentieth centuries that focused on other aspects of their life and not just their victim status. He believed that after the Emancipation Reform, living conditions in the countryside improved and the marketable yield of peasant farms increased, as did their access to industrial goods.[154] According to Ihnatowicz, "where serfdom was abolished . . . part of the population left the countryside," and this was followed by "a sudden increase in peasant mobility after emancipation."[155] Accepting this hypothesis, Kochanowicz linked the increase in consumption to the fact that agricultural production corresponded better to the size of the population. He also noted that "these changes, however, took place more slowly than in richer countries and were not accompanied by depopulation of the countryside, which was characteristic of [countries] at the core of the capitalist world-system."[156]

Ihnatowicz stressed the persistence of feudal (as opposed to class) consciousness among peasants at the beginning of the twentieth century, despite real changes in the distribution of social income and social mobility of the peasantry. "The relics of the old system persisted not in institutions but in ways of thinking." Writing about the rise of peasant parties in Galicia during the period of autonomy, he emphasized the discursive dominance of old social categories over new capitalist ones: "the creation of some political parties included an element of opposition to the szlachta—not to large estates or landowners, but precisely to the szlachta." Ihnatowicz argued that the way in which the intelligentsia perceived the peasantry likewise reflected a feudal mentality. The protagonists of literary works and political writings were "peas-

---

[153] Ibid., 161–63. See also: Jezierski, *Problemy rozwoju gospodarczego*, Styś, *Rozdrobnienie gruntów*, Styś, *Wpływ uprzemysłowienia*, Styś, *Drogi postępu gospodarczego*, Mieszczankowski, *Struktura agrarna*, Styś, *Rolnictwo II Rzeczpospolitej*, Roszkowski, *Land Reforms*.

[154] Ihnatowicz in Ihnatowicz et al., *Społeczeństwo polskie*, 439–45.

[155] Ibid., 432–33, 448.

[156] Kochanowicz, *Spór o teorię*, 164.

ants, not farmers or villagers; the peasant estate was ever-present . . . regardless of the economic structure."[157]

Among the old social groups, it was the Jewish population that was most geographically and socially mobile during the nineteenth century. Arthur Eisenbach notes that at the beginning of that century, Jews and peasants had a similar status. The former had been detached from the rest of society on the basis of individual or group contracts during the early modern period, but after the introduction of the principle of equality before the law and freedom of movement they were still not allowed to own land and had limited political rights.[158] However, in contrast to the peasantry, there emerged among the Jewish population a statistically small but—as researchers emphasized—structurally significant group that entered the ranks of the bourgeoisie in the Kingdom of Poland. Thanks to its new status and education, this group managed to overcome legal restrictions and become part of the intelligentsia and landowning elite.[159]

Researchers of Jewish and urban communities showed how the nineteenth century was a period of intense migration by the Jewish population to towns and cities which intensified as the century progressed. The territory of what would later become the Kingdom of Poland, especially Warsaw, was where Jews from Germany settled during the pre-Napoleonic period when much of the area was under the jurisdiction of Prussia. The Duchy of Warsaw, with its principle of personal freedom for all, prompted the next phase of migration to towns and cities. Following the demise of the Duchy in 1815, the geographical mobility of Jews was linked to the deteriorating economic situation on rural estates, previously their principal place of settlement. As a result, according to Kaczyńska's estimates, Jews on average accounted for 46.5 percent of the total urban population in the Kingdom of Poland after the 1863 uprising.[160] The overwhelming majority of Jews in the Kingdom were members of a new petit bourgeois class unconnected with the guild system. A smaller portion of

157 Ihnatowicz in Ihnatowicz et al., *Społeczeństwo polskie*, 493–94

158 Eisenbach, "Ludność żydowska."

159 Eisenbach, "Prawa obywatelskie i honorowe," Eisenbach, "Dobra ziemskie w posiadaniu Żydów," Kaczyńska, "Drobnomieszczaństwo polskie."

160 Kaczyńska, "Mieszczaństwo," 92.

the Jewish population, especially in the second half of the nineteenth century when cottage industries were being created, had the status of craftsmen or proletarians.[161] "In the towns and cities of the Kingdom of Poland [between 1815 and 1864], Jews constituted between 64 and 73 percent of the population engaged in trade and related activities."[162]

Both Eisenbach (investigating the fortunes of the Jewish population) and Kaczyńska and Ihnatowicz (investigating the bourgeoisie) indicated that in the mid-nineteenth century the Jewish population became more diverse, as did the urban population in general.[163] In his study of the origins and structure of the Warsaw bourgeoisie, Ihnatowicz claimed that in the late eighteenth century its nucleus comprised "thirty-one Jews and a few Christians."[164] He also estimated that during the industrial revolution's "third leap forward," as Kula termed it, in the years 1883–92, Jews accounted for approximately 33 percent of the Warsaw bourgeoisie. They were clearly dominant in banking and commerce and had a strong presence in the textile and paper industries.[165]

Researchers who studied the origins of the bourgeoisie in the Kingdom of Poland believed that the main factor in the stratification of the Jewish population was education and, indirectly, geographical origin. In the late eighteenth and early nineteenth centuries it was Jews from Prussia—polyglots educated in the new, pro-capitalist style in Prussian schools—who had the opportunity to form a new bourgeois elite. Access to foreign education and a predilection for Western habits and management methods were also important when it came to joining the ranks of the elite during the industrial booms of the 1830s and 1880s. Beginning in the mid-nineteenth century, Jews from bourgeois families could join the intelligentsia and—in exceptional cases—the landed gentry.[166]

---

[161] Kaczyńska, "Drobnomieszczaństwo polskie," Ihnatowicz, *Burżuazja warszawska*, 79, 203.

[162] Kaczyńska, "Mieszczaństwo," 94.

[163] Ibid., 104–05, Ihnatowicz, *Burżuazja warszawska*, 89–92.

[164] Ihnatowicz, *Burżuazja warszawska*, 43–46.

[165] Ibid., 199.

[166] Matejko, "Profesorowie uczelni warszawskich," Ihnatowicz, *Społeczeństwo polskie 1864–1914*, 31.

Eisenbach juxtaposed the circumstances of this small group with the situation of the Jewish population as a whole. He stressed that the majority of Jews whose families originated from the Kingdom of Poland became members of the impoverished petite bourgeoisie, who were restricted by semi-feudal laws and prejudices and cultivated the old customs and way of life.[167] An important element of the image of Jews was the emphasis on the fact that it was only through a combination of wealth, education, and even conversion to Christianity, that they could hope to be promoted to the intelligentsia or landowning elite. Kaczyńska and Eisenbach emphasized the uncertainty of this hope. Kaczyńska also pointed to the distinct and alternative customs of the new Jewish elite in the first half of the nineteenth century.[168] Ihnatowicz disagreed, perhaps because was writing about the second half of the century and about the Warsaw bourgeoisie. He emphasized lifestyles that were common to the entire bourgeoisie irrespective of their ethnic origin, whether Polish, Jewish, or German. He believed that "the rigid boundaries of custom that prevented assimilation separated" the elite not from the Jewish bourgeoisie but from the Jewish petite bourgeoisie and proletariat.[169]

The many new social categories identified by researchers derived from the stratification of old social groups. What was lacking in their image of the Kingdom of Poland were cohesive, new social groups—classes composed of people from different feudal estates. In the introduction to *Social Change in the Kingdom of Poland, 1815–1864*, Kula stressed that change had taken place slowly due to the failure of the industrial revolution and the forms of capitalism in the countryside, which were harmful to the peasants. He argued that feudal structures had not rapidly disintegrated or been replaced by Western-style, capitalist social structures. There had been no bourgeois revolution, and the industrial revolution had proceeded slowly, inconsistently, and under state control. Neither "the nobleman nor the peasant spontaneously invested during that period [1815–64]; or at least they did not invest money,

[167] Eisenbach, "Ludność żydowska," Rzepniewska, "Imigracja do Warszawy. Osiedleńcy spoza Królestwa."

[168] Ibid., Kaczyńska, "Burżuazja," 319–21.

[169] Ihnatowicz, *Burżuazja warszawska*, 203.

they did not invest in the market. No accumulation, whether in kind or in cash, took place at that time without the participation of the state."[170]

Among the new social groups, it was the lowest categories of the intelligentsia (primary school teachers[171] and railway officials[172]) that were an amalgam of feudal estates. This group brought together members of the impoverished szlachta and bourgeoisie. Another group was the petite bourgeoisie, comprising a few descendants of the old bourgeoisie and numerous poor Jews.[173] A third was, to a lesser degree, workers, especially skilled workers, where a population largely of peasant origin (albeit second generation) was joined by members of the old bourgeoisie that had been ruined by big industry.[174] Among the old social groups, the one most open to people of different backgrounds proved to be the Catholic clergy, although not in its upper echelons.[175]

The stratification of nineteenth-century Polish society was presented both as evidence of backwardness and its driving force. The most important features of stratification that shared these two qualities were rural character, with a dominant social division between lord and peasant, and the persistence of feudal divisions both in law and in mentality. In a work on the significance of noble titles in nineteenth-century Poland, Jedlicki wrote that "throughout the period of the Partitions, every few years someone would proclaim anew that feudal barriers were to be overthrown and the lower classes turned into citizens. . . . It was a period when steel and spinning mills were built, towns

[170] Kula, "Rozwój gospodarczy," 15.

[171] Matejko, "Nauczyciele szkół elementarnych," 134–35. The author claims that between 1831 and 1864 the ascribed status of the primary school teachers from the Lublin Province was as follows: registered szlachta: 5%, unregistered szlachta: 36%, townspeople: 46%, people listed as both townspeople and peasants: 11%, peasants: 2%.

[172] Rożenowa, "Pochodzenie społeczno-zawodowe." They belonged in equal proportions to three social groups: registered szlachta, unregistered szlachta, and townspeople. Ihnatowicz, "Urzędnicy galicyjscy w dobie autonomii," 220–21.

[173] Kaczyńska, "Drobnomieszczaństwo polskie," Kaczyńska, "Mieszczaństwo," Kowalska-Glikman, "Drobnomieszczaństwo."

[174] Kaczyńska, "Tkacze w Zduńskiej Woli," Kowalska, "Robotnicy."

[175] Chruszczewski, "Zakonnicy diecezji lubelskiej," Litak, "Duchowieństwo diecezji lubelskiej w okresie międzypowstaniowym," Olszewski, "Struktura społeczna duchowieństwa," Dylągowa, "Episkopat polski."

and roads were constructed, and banks and a stock exchange were opened; it witnessed the emergence of locomotives, the telegraph, and factory strikes. And yet the issue of nobility in all its aspects continued to absorb social thought, national literature, and politics."[176] What was novel in relation to the eighteenth century and which exacerbated backwardness in new ways was the fact that, in contrast to Western Europe, the modern Polish nation took shape in the absence of a national market, a bourgeoisie, and a nation-state. For the higher echelons of society—the szlachta followed by the intelligentsia—this meant far fewer career opportunities in the modern state administration. The Polish members of these groups either suffered discrimination at the hands of the partitioning powers' bureaucracies or were dismissed for taking part in patriotic activities against the state. In the Polish lands, state structures were regarded as being of low quality, and in the Kingdom of Poland this was reflected in the corruption and arbitrariness of the Czarist administration. In the Prussian and Austrian Partitions, prior to the period of autonomy, incompetence stemmed from the fact that in these territories—regarded as peripheral by the partitioning powers—bureaucracies were staffed by the worst sorts of officials, almost as a means of punishment.[177] Authors also pointed to the fact that relations between the state and its subjects remained feudal and were not conducive to the modern transformation of subjects into citizens. The specific form of stratification, the earlier ethnic differences that were deepened by the Partitions, also encouraged class and ethnic divisions to overlap in a damaging fashion, especially in the second half of the nineteenth century.

Ihnatowicz and Żarnowski offered a completely different view of Polish society to that of Kula and his research team. Their research focused on the late nineteenth and early twentieth centuries, not the mid-nineteenth century, and they portrayed an image of rapid urbanization and proletarianization. One might ask whether this can be put down to the differences between the periods studied. Ihnatowicz believed that the "explosion of modern industry" as well as geographical and social mobility did not significantly accelerate until after the

[176] Jedlicki, *Klejnot i bariery*, 449.
[177] Grodziski, "Schyłek stanu," 105. Szczepański, "Burmistrzowie miasteczek."

abolition of serfdom.[178] By contrast, Kula's team felt that it was the period between the establishment of the Kingdom of Poland in 1815 and the emancipation of the serfs in 1864, rather than the period after emancipation, that played the key role in shaping modern Polish society.[179] As a sociologist, I believe that Ihnatowicz was right in this instance: the fact that the peasantry was no longer tied to the land after 1864 was crucial for the transformation of the social structure.[180]

Ihnatowicz emphasized that social change in the late nineteenth and early twentieth centuries was more rapid and qualitatively different. It bore many of the characteristics we tend to associate with modernity—conflicts based on interests, social class, and occupational group rather than on sentiment or historical, regional, and feudal identity. "In the first half of the century there were virtually no class-based conspiracies, while in the last quarter [of the nineteenth century] they were a permanent fixture." This was accompanied by a decline in the popularity of armed, pro-independence activities.[181] Similarly, Magdalena Micińska, the intellectual granddaughter of Kula who researched the image of the national hero, argued that a fundamental change in consciousness did not occur until end of the nineteenth century. It was then that "the existing image of the noble or aristocratic hero took on egalitarian and urban features" and the "as yet non-existent image of the peasant hero began to emerge."[182]

In a sympathetic review of *Social Change in the Kingdom of Poland, 1815–1864*, Ihnatowicz noted that neither this book nor the earlier volumes of *The Society of the Kingdom of Poland* appreciated the role of "soft institutions" in reconfiguring society. He argued that these "integrative institutions" were not just the "external institutions" analyzed by Kula and his team but also included newspapers, the invention of the telegraph and telephones, and faster mass transport by sea and rail. According to Ihnatowicz, this methodological shortcoming of Kula's

178 Ihnatowicz, *Burżuazja warszawska*, 6, Ihnatowicz et al., *Społeczeństwo polskie*, 432–38.

179 Kula, *Kształtowanie się kapitalizmu*, 7–13, Kula, introduction to *Społeczeństwo Królestwa Polskiego*, vol. 1, 5–18.

180 Kula, "Rozwój gospodarczy."

181 Ihnatowicz, *Społeczeństwo polskie 1864–1914*, 26.

182 Micińska, *Między Królem Duchem a mieszczaninem*, 20–21.

study had influenced the image it presented of sluggish social change even before 1864. This change was dramatic, Ihnatowicz believed, particularly in the area of values and in the perception of social hierarchy. He presented his own view in an especially vivid way:

> In how many ways did the aspirations of immigrant artisans, carrying all their belongings on a cart pulled by a dog, overlap with the aspirations of increasingly wealthy peasants who observed these newcomers from behind their fences? During the period of the January Uprising of 1863, the former, if they had not gone bankrupt, had in some cases already become factory owners, while in the same period some of the latter had already lost their cottage, their horse, and their land. That is material change. But at what point did the former stop envying the latter and the reverse start to take place? It seems that if we were able to take into account all these cases, perhaps the process of unification of old and new—the creation of the amalgam—would appear stronger. Perhaps, also, the great anxieties that destroyed the quality of life during that period would reveal themselves more clearly.[183]

While acknowledging that Kula was right about the relative persistence of feudal identities, Ihnatowicz believed that, especially in the second half of the nineteenth century, "geographical mobility, clear changes in the structure, and the congruence of examined trends testified to the weakening of barriers . . . and to progress in the creation of a modern society."[184]

The hegemons of change: The bourgeoisie, intelligentsia, and enterprising landowners?

Even in the historiography of the communist period, the authors discussed here did not simply condemn the role of the bourgeoisie. The general trend, to put it in simple terms, was sympathy for the Western

---

[183] Ihnatowicz, review of *Przemiany społeczne*, 396–97.
[184] Ihnatowicz, "Urzędnicy galicyjscy," 223.

bourgeoisie and aversion to the Polish bourgeoisie. Researchers of the Kingdom of Poland, with Jedlicki and Kaczyńska at the fore, tried to find a positive influence similar to that which the bourgeoisie had exerted on Western modernity in the ideological, economic, and civic attitudes of the Polish intelligentsia.

A feature of the modern transformation common to both East and West was the key role of towns and cities and the urban atmosphere and lifestyles. Jedlicki compared the transformation of the town elites with the inertia of the rural elites. "In the towns and cities . . . there was a reconfiguration of elites in line with the development of capitalist civilization. In the countryside, which was still more important to the economy, if not to Polish culture, the elites became immobilized and social barriers remained."[185] This was significant because, as Ihnatowicz noted, at the beginning of the nineteenth century Polish towns and cities were still centers of a culture, including a material culture, that was almost entirely foreign and completely different from the autarkic world of country manors and peasant farms.[186]

THE BOURGEOISIE

Researchers of the Polish bourgeoisie presented it as a group that introduced new, Western methods of economic activity into society that were unknown to the traditional craft and merchant guilds. At the same time, it was marked by a lifestyle that was different to that of the bourgeoisie in the West.[187] Historians emphasized the absence of a "bourgeois morality" that had been associated with the rise of West European bourgeoisie. Following Maria Ossowska, Kaczyńska and Jedlicki identified bourgeois morality with modesty, prudence, reliability, compassion, honesty, education, and patriotism. Similarly to Ossowska in her polemic against Weber, they did not associate those values specifically with Protestantism.[188] The bourgeoisie of the Kingdom of Poland, unlike the West European but like the German

---

185 Jedlicki, introduction to *Przemiany społeczne*, 56.

186 Ihnatowicz, *Burżuazja warszawska*, 156–59.

187 Kaczyńska, "Mieszczaństwo," 97–99, "Burżuazja," 322, Ihnatowicz, *Burżuazja warszawska*, 45–46.

188 Kaczyńska, ibid., Jedlicki, *A Suburb of Europe*, Ossowska, *Bourgeois Morality*.

bourgeoisie, was seduced by the magic of nobility and its tendency to covet land ownership. Kaczyńska also linked these attitudes to the conspicuous consumption of luxury goods, which was regarded by contemporaries as tasteless and by researchers as not conducive to investment or development.[189]

Particularly detrimental were those economic methods and elements of morality and lifestyle that led to the formation of political capitalism, which was monopolistic and encouraged corruption. Kaczyńska wrote that "the bourgeoisie made their fortunes not under the conditions of free competition but of state protection, often using the privilege of exclusivity."[190] Jedlicki, Ihnatowicz, and independently of them Jan Kosim, painted a similar picture of industrialization and the birth of modern commerce. New fortunes were made thanks to state loans, government contracts, the leasing and monopolization of public services (often secured through bribes), as well as smuggling, financial scandals, deliberate insolvency, etc.[191] Kosim pointed to the pre-Partition origins of a business culture that was based on performing government contracts for the benefit of, for instance, future invading armies. During the period of the Duchy of Warsaw and the Kingdom of Poland "the close cooperation between private capital and the state's fiscal system, and the taking over of the latter's functions by representatives of trade and banking, was one of the major reasons why large fortunes were to be made."[192] For Jedlicki this business culture resulted from the very fact that the state was involved in investment and lending to industry. His book, *The Failed Attempt at Capitalist Industrialization* (*Nieudana próba kapitalistycznej industrializacji*), was a voice against state interventionism in the debate over the conditions of economic growth in backward countries. During the communist period it probably represented the most free-market economic thinking that was able to get past the censors.

The authors' reflections on the role of the bourgeoisie in modernizing the economy and society brought into focus the dispute over the

[189] Ihnatowicz, *Burżuazja warszawska*, 201–03.

[190] Kaczyńska, "Burżuazja," 316.

[191] Ihnatowicz, *Burżuazja warszawska*, 62–64, Jedlicki, *Nieudana próba*, Kosim, *Losy pewnej fortuny*.

[192] Kosim, *Losy pewnej fortuny*, 48.

origins of the bourgeoisie and capital in nineteenth-century Poland. Jedlicki and Łepkowski argued that the first members of the bourgeoisie were local and home grown and that foreign capital did not appear until the end of the century. Łepkowski, analyzing the problem from the point of view of the formation of the modern Polish nation, wrote:

> Here I touch upon a delicate and controversial issue: the role of industrialization in the development of the nation, in the formation of the "national" economy. Some have argued that industrialization was imported by foreign economic entities, foreign states, and foreigners in general. In brief, industry was allegedly based on foreign capital and on foreign technical cadres and workers in the service of markets far beyond the Polish lands. In fact, most of the decision-making centers of capital were not located abroad ("abroad" in inverted commas because for the better part of this period Poland as a whole had no national borders) and did not siphon profits away to foreign metropolises. "The Geyer and Scheibler families accumulated and managed their wealth primarily within Poland and strove for the greatest possible level of capitalist accumulation" (Kula). Polish production practices and technical cadres played an important role in technological progress, indeed a greater role than was admitted, particularly by the Germans. In addition, a certain proportion of the technical cadres became polonized and took root in the local society. . . . However, one should not deny the importance of certain foreign elements (the technical and to some extent the worker cadres) or the artificiality of the revolution in the manufactories, especially that this issue was—as we shall later see—echoed in the Polish national consciousness and Polish nationalism as well as in the Polish independence movement.[193]

Kaczyńska, Leskiewiczowa, and Czepulis tended to emphasize the different ethnicity of the bourgeoisie. Some researchers associated the predatory capitalism in the Kingdom with the fact that the bourgeoisie, "a group formed largely of immigrants," acted above and beyond the

[193] Łepkowski, *Polska—narodziny*, 98–99.

political community, was unfettered by custom, and was free of social or institutional control by public authorities other than the partitioning state.[194] "The new bourgeoisie," wrote Czepulis, was "set apart nationally and culturally," had no "established traditions," and was "poorly integrated with society at large."[195] Kaczyńska argued that "in the Kingdom of Poland the overlapping of ethnic, occupational, and social divisions was not as straightforward as in Silesia and Galicia, for instance. Despite this there were discernible patterns: the commercial and financial role of the Jews, the industrial role of the Germans, etc."[196] Ihnatowicz summed it up as follows: "the discussions around the involvement of foreign capital in industry in the Kingdom of Poland revealed that claims about the foreignness of capital often rested on equating the nationality of the entrepreneur with the origin of the capital itself. Entrepreneurs with foreign names were thus seen as bringing in foreign capital. . . . The bourgeoisie of the Kingdom of Poland was largely of urban and non-noble origin . . . foreign by nationality, and with capital it had accumulated on Polish soil."[197]

Eisenbach, Ihnatowicz, and Kaczyńska believed that the alienation of the bourgeoisie was a result of both politics and culture. They emphasized that the government of the Kingdom of Poland, contrary even to the recommendations of the Czarist authorities and the practices of the Russian Empire up to 1862, maintained a separate, feudal policy toward the Jewish population that enhanced its economic rights while restricting its political and civil rights.[198] Unlike in the West European model, the bourgeoisie in Poland had no opportunity for genuine civic assimilation (municipal government was non-existent or was subordinate to private or state administrations), or for national assimilation (the non-native ethnicity of Jews was accentuated by the old Polish elites, traditional Jewish institutions, and German organi-

[194] Leskiewiczowa, introduction to "Nowe klasy i warstwy" in *Przemiany społeczne*, 306. See also: Kaczyńska, "Mieszczaństwo," 95–96, and Kaczyńska, "Burżuazja," 319–20.

[195] Czepulis, "Inteligencja," 343.

[196] Kaczyńska, "Mieszczaństwo," 94.

[197] Ihnatowicz, *Społeczeństwo polskie*, 37.

[198] Ihnatowicz, *Burżuazja warszawska*, 206, Eisenbach, "Ludność żydowska," 108, 110–12, 115–16.

zations alike).[199] Instead, the bourgeoisie, about which "there is no doubt . . . that . . . it was, firstly, for the most part of foreign origin and, secondly, that it was not descended from the old bourgeoisie and was formed only after the creation of the Kingdom of Poland . . . harboured an attitude of self-interested loyalty toward the (partitioning) state."[200] Ihnatowicz emphasized the different political sentiments of the bourgeoisie (or their absence). "In the January Uprising [of 1863] and in the Positivist movement, the Polish bourgeoisie, and the Warsaw bourgeoisie in particular, remained on the sidelines to a much greater extent than its economic position would have suggested."[201]

THE INTELLIGENTSIA

In the historiography analyzed here, the image of the intelligentsia was apologetic. Much beloved by researchers, the enlightened groups "sometimes unconsciously, or even against their deepest wishes, undermined the centuries-old social order . . . and thus contributed to the modernization of society as a whole."[202] The intelligentsia supposedly embodied the values of the West European bourgeoisie, which the Polish bourgeoisie lacked and which could further the cause of social and economic progress: a modest lifestyle, integrity, respect for education and systematic work, and a willingness to sacrifice oneself for the common good. "It was the Positivists who attempted, albeit late, to create a surrogate [of the middle class ideology of asceticism and prudence] that indeed sprang from the intelligentsia and not the bourgeoisie."[203]

The "flower of society," as Irena Homola termed the intelligentsia, was apparently responsible for what I could describe (on the basis of the image presented by the authors) as a modernization of the mind, which occurred independently of economic modernization.[204] Tomasz

---

199 Eisenbach, "Ludność żydowska," 110–12, Kaczyńska, "Mieszczaństwo," 192–93, Ihnatowicz, *Burżuazja warszawska*, 209.
200 Kaczyńska, "Burżuazja," 311.
201 Ihnatowicz, *Burżuazja warszawska*, 211.
202 Hass, "Warstwa oświecona," 20, Czepulis, "Inteligencja," 343.
203 Jedlicki, "Polskie nurty ideowe," 193.
204 Homola, *Kwiat społeczeństwa*.

Kizwalter argued that it was the elites who led the way in the reception of modern ideas and technology in the Kingdom of Poland in the mid-nineteenth century. The assimilation of ideas through publications was more successful than the acquisition of technology. "In a country peripheral in terms of development, but whose elites remained in constant contact with the West, people took advantage of this influx of goods whenever they could—they travelled by rail and read about humanity becoming united through inventions. . . . Among the 'enlightened classes,' modernization made for a popular . . . topic of reading material."[205]

Researchers also emphasized that while in the early days of the Kingdom (1815–30), the growing importance of education was related to the requirements of the administration, later on, after the November Uprising (1830–31), education became a value in itself. It no doubt served a social purpose, allowing entry into a new social elite. Usually, however, it was not associated with participation in economic life or in state governance.[206] The increasing popularity of humanities education compared to engineering, medicine, or science is another argument in favor of the idea that what was taking place was an imitative modernization of the mind, of ideas and culture, rather than of the economy and lifestyles. Joanna Matejko showed that in the period between the two national uprisings (1831–54), the majority of university professors were trained in the liberal arts or languages, and almost half had been educated abroad.[207] Łepkowski wrote about a "kind of social empowerment and elevation of the intelligentsia in Poland (a process not especially unique in the countries of Central and Eastern Europe)" in the second half of the nineteenth century. He associated this with the intelligentsia's self-identification as a class that mediated between the world of high culture and the masses, a class whose role was to modernize society.[208]

205 Kitzwalter, "*Nowatorstwo i rutyny*," 179.
206 Jedlicki, introduction to *Przemiany społeczne*, 36.
207 Matejko, "Profesorowie uczelni," 189.
208 Łepkowski, *Polska—narodziny*, 228.

THE ENTERPRISING GENTRY

Social historians of the Wielkopolska region were inclined to ascribe a similar role to the landed gentry. According to Witold Molik, in the late nineteenth and early twentieth centuries the educated and enterprising gentry was at the forefront of change. Not as rich as the gentry in other Partitions, it faced competition from the local bourgeoisie (in the 1860s, fifty-nine of the seventy biggest entrepreneurs were German) as well as denationalizing pressure from the state.[209] Topolski characterized Wielkopolska in the late eighteenth and early nineteenth centuries as a more urbanized region than the other Polish lands; its szlachta was fewer in number but owned medium-sized folwarks. This fact ostensibly accounted for the lesser importance of the intelligentsia in the nineteenth century. The associations created at that time according to the Prussian model, such as savings and loans companies, agricultural cooperatives, trade unions, educational societies, and self-help organizations encompassed all groups in society, proving that "the gentry did not close ranks within its own estate . . . This was the first attempt at public patronage in the history of Poland; it aimed to create elites that did not only originate from the gentry estate."[210]

The gentry-innovators and gentry-industrialists of Wielkopolska were seen to represent the ethos of the Western bourgeoisie favored by scholars, with diligence and patriotism at the fore, as well as an ethos previously associated with the intelligentsia in the Kingdom of Poland—bringing education to the masses.

After 1989, the view that landowning agricultural entrepreneurs had been modernizers also gained popularity among researchers of the Kingdom of Poland. In a new style and language (e.g., the term "bourgeoisie" was replaced with "economic entrepreneurs"), Wiesław Caban and Tomasz Kizwalter argued that in the Kingdom of Poland too, in the mid-nineteenth century, gentry-industrialists "tried to combine their modernizing efforts with political activity" in a manner characteristic of the "periphery of civilization at that time."[211]

---

209 Molik, "Wzór osobowy ziemianina," 73.

210 Ibid., 76.

211 Kizwalter, "*Nowatorstwo i rutyny*," 179–80. Caban, "Ziemianie przemysłowcy."

In the picture presented by Kula's team, the bourgeois-landowning elite and the partitioning state rivalled each other as the principal rentiers of backwardness in the Kingdom of Poland. In works written before 1989, regardless of which Partition they concerned, the concept of the developmental (capitalist) state did not feature at all. The state was instead seen as an exploiter, a source of corruption among officials and entrepreneurs, a source of injustice and discrimination, both social and national. It was also blamed for the poor level of education. Even the period of autonomy under Austrian rule was depicted, following Franciszek Bujak, as a "treacherous gift" (*Timeo Danaos)*, for by granting the Polish elite access to parliamentary and local government posts, it consolidated the gentry's strong position and burdened "Galician society with a disastrous irony of fate."[212]

The example of the Prussian-German state was not seen in a positive light in works by the older generation of scholars; it appeared in Kochanowicz's book of 1992.[213] The economic picture of Wielkopolska presented by researchers from Poznań was more favorable than that of other Polish regions, but this was not due to a belief in the positive impact of the Prussian legacy; rather, it was attributed to growth trends in the pre-Partition era.[214] Topolski's interpretation corresponded more to the "self-modernization" model proposed by his university colleagues in 1999 "in relation to nations deprived of statehood that wished to maintain or regain their national identity through economic, social, and cultural activity that aimed to establish a capitalist society."[215] Modernization (the term used in the 1990s to describe capitalist transformation), undertaken by the Polish elites themselves, was surprisingly juxtaposed with "enforced modernization and pressure to integrate" with the German state.

212 Kruczkowska, "Deputowani Koła Polskiego," 219.

213 Kochanowicz, *Spór o teorię*, 149–153.

214 Topolski, "Społeczeństwo wielkopolskie," 845, Hahn, "Przymus modernizacyjny."

215 Trzeciakowski and Markowski, *Samomodernizacja społeczeństw*, 7.

Conclusion

An analysis of the debate on East European economic backwardness does not elicit a particular image of the region that has to be accepted in the way that a theory is accepted on the basis of empirical tests. Like most studies in the humanities, my work is interpretive. However, it does allow me to consider some propositions of a sociological nature:

- backwardness is a *longue durée* structure, hence it merits being conceptualized in historical terms,
- when trying to conceptualize the problem of backwardness in sociological terms, it is worth referring to competing historical and economic models,
- the attempts to overcome backwardness, and thus, indirectly, backwardness itself, are elements which have determined the continuity of East European societies in the socioeconomic sphere, in how they are perceived by the West, and in their perception of themselves.

Eastern Europe and the Europe of Serfdom

The models I discuss here are encumbered by presentism. By that, I mean that they project the criteria of a Europe divided by the Iron Curtain onto the societies of previous epochs. These models are not unique in this respect. Presentism is the main intellectual danger faced by historical sociology. After all, scholars seek historical explanations of precisely those aspects of the current situation that they consider to be the most important. With this comes a tendency to focus on past phenomena that foreshadow the present and to ignore those that do not. The danger of this is that it creates a teleological image not only of the past but also of the future. Yet we have no certainty that an element which seems important today will survive in the future.

EASTERN EUROPE

In the authors' conceptions of Eastern Europe, the historical region was identified—openly by Małowist, indirectly by Kula, and not very obviously by Topolski—with the post-Yalta communist bloc. Małowist and Topolski did this by demarcating the geographical boundaries of the region; Kula did it indirectly. He included Eastern Europe within the prewar community of shared backwardness and simultaneously made a sharp distinction between the state of the region's economy after the socialist changes and the persistent backwardness of capitalist Southern Europe and Latin America. One may suspect, therefore, that the conceptions which identified Soviet bloc countries with an already underdeveloped Eastern Europe were to some extent a projection of contemporary conditions onto the past. Despite this, however, I think that it is worth retaining the idea of Eastern Europe. The economic consequences of the introduction of socialism in Eastern Europe after the Second World War, and the ease with which the West abandoned its influence in the region after Yalta, seem to be more understandable in the context of the region's earlier underdevelopment. Soviet socialism, which was designed for predominantly peasant societies, can be seen as yet another costly and unsuccessful attempt to extricate those societies from backwardness.

I believe that it is still appropriate to employ the concept of Eastern Europe—the region situated between Germany and Russia and between the Baltic Sea and the Aegean. It is a region whose Europeanness is sometimes questioned; a region whose rural legacy and non-participation in overseas colonial conquest link it to Scandinavia, Russia, and Germany. Though geographically European, it was excluded from the "European miracle" of industrial capitalism, and in this respect it is similar to Southern Europe (Greece, Spain, Portugal, the south of Italy) and Russia. Eastern Europe was also a periphery of one or another of the modern empires, an experience it shares with the southern islands of present-day Italy. This last feature distinguishes the countries of Eastern Europe from Russia, Germany, Austria, and Turkey, all of which were imperial powers. With those four countries Eastern Europe shares social and political characteristics as well as a tradition of combating peripheral status, whether economic or cultural, in relation to Western Europe seen as a model. One can surmise that these circumstances gave rise to the traditional modernization dilemma in Eastern Europe: whether to opt for an anti-imperial, nationalist, or socialist project or, alternatively, a liberal project entailing openness toward the great economic powers.

I also think that it is worth retaining the concept of Eastern Europe due to the latter's ties with Western Europe, primarily cultural and political ties, but also economic ones, over which the protagonists of my book argued. From the point of view of demarcating the region's boundaries, which would be sociologically significant, the issue is not only and not so much whether the economies of Eastern Europe developed through dependency or imitation or by catching up with Western Europe. What is telling is that this problem—as Jerzy Jedlicki noted—occupied the imagination of East European intellectuals and still plays an important role in the collective political consciousness.

Regardless of whether we accept Larry Wolff's contention that the backwardness of Eastern Europe was for two centuries a hegemonic construct of the Western elites, or whether we believe the historical sociologists discussed in this book that backwardness was an economic fact, it is worth considering Eastern Europe as a community whose Europeanness was questioned—precisely and primarily on account of its economic weakness.

THE EUROPE OF SERFDOM

I am convinced—following Topolski, Kula, and Małowist—that in economic terms, the Europe of serfdom also constituted a region. It encompassed the countries east of the Elbe (from eastern Germany to Russia), south of the Baltic, and north of the Danube. Its borders only partially overlapped with the borders of Eastern Europe as defined here; it included Russia but not the Balkans. The social structures that governed economic behavior were different than in the Balkans. The Europe of serfdom was characterized by a legacy of social and cultural polarization between the nobility on the one hand, and peasants and Jews on the other; it was also marked by the virtual enslavement of the peasantry, who made up the majority of the population. Structurally, the Europe of serfdom differed from Western Europe in terms of its weaker bourgeois and farmer traditions, and compared to the Balkans it had weaker folk and tribal traditions and stronger feudal ones.

The propensity to create and accept profound economic disparities is stronger in the former serf societies of Eastern Europe than in the Balkan countries, which are poorer or similar according to macroeconomic data. It would be worth looking for analogies to this phenomenon in postcolonial or post-slave societies, such as in Latin America, where social relations were based on sharp feudal, ethnic, or class divisions.

Within the Europe of serfdom one should further distinguish societies such as Poland, Hungary, Russia, and Romania, which—despite the loss in the twentieth century of their Jewish, German, aristocratic, and bourgeois populations and the forced migrations of other groups—preserved the duality of peasant versus noble culture, from those such as Belarus, Ukraine, Slovakia, and Lithuania, which, as a result of those losses and migrations, became completely peasant or post-peasant societies that were culturally egalitarian. The countries in the first group have stronger traditions stemming from the nobility and intelligentsia, and the divisions (at least imagined) between the elite and the masses are more resilient. Such societies are more internally differentiated in terms of social capital, acquiescence and adaptability to capitalist rules, and patterns of investment, saving, and consumption. I believe that in this case, too, one can look for analogies between the Europe of serfdom and other postcolonial and post-slave societies that differ according to the extent to which the old masters are members of the current economic elite.

Finally, it is worth considering Central Europe not as a region "hijacked" by Communism and restored to the West after 1989, but as a subregion of the Europe of serfdom and Eastern Europe with political and cultural traditions that set it apart from its neighbors. The separateness of those traditions may be associated with the dominance of a Catholicism based on law and hierarchy, with more clearly articulated and codified organizing principles compared to Christian Orthodoxy and—more importantly, I think—with a greater influence of Western social and political thought. It seems to me, however, that what is key to the identity of Central Europe is simply the impact of the region's geographical proximity to the West. I treat Central Europe as a region characterized by a particular tension between the poverty of the masses and economic backwardness on the one hand, and Westernized elites on the other.

Hybrid development from a global perspective and critical pessimism

Among the models of East European backwardness presented here, Kula's seems the most conceptually interesting. His model took into account three types of factors that influenced economic development:

- The universal features of societies undergoing modernization: industrialization and urbanization.
- The typical characteristics of backward countries, that is, countries attempting to modernize in a situation where other countries modernized earlier. In Kula's day these included the export of raw materials, economies dominated by agriculture, the peasantry as the largest social stratum, and international labor migration from less developed to more developed regions. More recently, cheap labor has become the main "raw material" exported from or provided in underdeveloped countries. International labor migration, which until the mid-twentieth century had been a part of the experience of people from Southern and Eastern Europe, Latin America, and the Caribbean, had by the end of the twentieth century become a common experience for people in underdeveloped countries globally. At the same time, a large share of industrial production was shifted from the most developed countries to countries with a cheaper and more obedient workforce. This has become a typical characteristic of all backward countries.
- The particular characteristics of a region undergoing modernization. In Eastern Europe, these resulted from the fact that modernization occurred in a context of geographical proximity and close

economic ties (and I would add cultural ties, which Kula ignored) with more developed countries.

In other words, like Topolski, Kula considered the impact of universal economic mechanisms and of economic mechanisms specific to a region, which resulted from local social conditions. In contrast to Topolski, however, and similarly to Małowist, Kula's model left room for social and economic mechanisms arising from contact and competition with a stronger partner. At the same time, unlike Małowist, he did not consider these to be the only important mechanisms. For this reason, Kula's model fared better when confronted with empirical (historical, sociological, economic) evidence. The findings of subsequent research could be incorporated into the model simply by altering the weight assigned to different groups of factors that influenced the shape and performance of the economic system. Kula's model was the most universal. It could be applied not just to Eastern Europe but also to other underdeveloped regions, with different local conditions, at different historical junctures, and subject to different levels of influence from more developed countries. His model thus provided greater opportunities for comparison.

Kula's model shared with the colonial development model a pessimism about the prospects for overcoming backwardness, especially if attempts to overcome it were not accompanied by radical social change and transnational change in economic dependencies. In the sphere of economy, society, and culture, such change was represented by state-socialist industrialization, or so Kula believed in the 1960s. Socialist industrialization was to create a modern human being who was urban and industrial, educated, and able to form a variety of civic groups beyond the realm of the family. It would also ensure that everyone received at least a minimum of bread and freedom. From today's perspective the biggest shortcoming of Kula's model was that it juxtaposed the backwardness of Greece, Spain, and Portugal in the 1960s with the development of Eastern Europe, and in so doing attempted to prove that while under capitalism backwardness persisted, under socialism it was being conquered. By the 1970s and 1980s Kula was aware of this shortcoming. It is somewhat surprising that he did not consider integration with the European Economic Community as a radical change for those backward countries of Southern Europe. He must have known in the 1970s how much southern Italy had benefited from integration with the European Economic Community. He might have considered a similar scenario for Greece, Spain, and Portugal. However, in the face of the profound economic crisis in Southern Europe in the second decade of the twenty-first century, one can see that history matters and that the old divisions between the less developed and more developed regions of Europe are re-emerging.

What is useful in Kula's model, therefore, is its conceptual readiness for another failed attempt to overcome Eastern European backwardness, namely, integration with the European Union. Elements of Kula and Małowist's visions of capitalism as a mechanism, which, even if it brings real economic growth, distributes the social costs and benefits of that growth very unevenly, are likewise worth retaining. Their focus on the structural barriers to growth and sustainable development, and especially to the elimination of backwardness, seems valuable. At the time a large group of East European countries acceded to the European Union in May 2004, Greece and Portugal, after several decades of membership, and despite enormous investment, were the least prosperous members of the European Union. The burdens of history and the limited impact of the institutional solutions adopted are evidenced by the fact that GDP per capita in those poorest countries of the European Union was the same as in postcommunist Slovenia, which received no foreign assistance prior to 2004, was not a destination for foreign direct investment, and did not allow its economy to be privatized.

Also worth preserving is Kula's idea that hybridity requires hybrid solutions and not the imitation of more advanced countries. His model removed the need to describe a development path exclusively in terms of success or failure. If elements didn't fit the classic Western model, this meant searching for a new type of economic rationality.

After decades of globalization, the conditions of which have only been apparent to social science for a quarter of a century, Małowist's (and less obviously Kula's) proposal to adopt a transnational unit of socioeconomic analysis, particularly in relation to a distant epoch, seems surprisingly astute. Such a consistently global perspective would be a good complement to the hybrid model.

Social Structures and Economic Development

A HISTORICAL CANON FOR SOCIAL RESEARCHERS?

The debate on East European economic backwardness is important for social researchers, including sociologists, economists, and anthropologists, for two reasons. First, it offers general proposals on how to interpret the relationship between the social structure and the possibility of sustainable economic development. I analyzed this in detail in Chapter 5.

Second, it reveals to social researchers investigating changes in stratification and social mobility which elements of historical stratification were disputed and which were generally accepted. It reveals historians' views about the extent to which East European societies were a special case and which elements of their structures were sometimes regarded to be analogous to Western European structures. Social researchers need this knowledge in order to be able to choose more freely between models of development and social change that, like Marxism or Weberism, were usually elaborated in relations to non-East European societies, and in order to be able to modify or reject those models. This knowledge allows sociologists to understand the successive changes that took place prior to the current state of affairs.

What indisputably belongs to the historical canon is the conviction that the following had very long-term consequences for Polish society: the rural legacy, folwarks, the dominance of the szlachta and magnates, serfdom, the commencement of modernization later than in the West, and the existence of an intelligentsia—a stratum unique to Eastern Europe. Elements often added to this list, but that remain controversial, include: the overlapping of feudal and class divisions with ethnic and religious ones, the foreign nature of towns, urban culture and capitalism, and the presence of clientage with a propensity for corruption and ostentatious consumption.

THE STATE AND IDEOLOGY

In the images of society presented here (especially those produced up until the mid-1980s), the idea of the state as simply the superstructure should, I believe, be rejected. Indeed, none of the presented models allowed for the possibility of a capitalist state that was even relatively independent of the interests of the upper strata of society and that could initiate and successfully oversee modernization. Kula regarded the development of interwar Germany and Japan, countries well-known for such development, as necessarily linked to fascism. He therefore considered the path to prosperity taken by those countries as unacceptable. Their nationalist ideologies, argued Kula, obscured internal class conflict and directed its associated aggression against other nationalities and ethnic groups. Małowist, in turn, emphasized the positive nature of the Japanese example. He attributed the country's economic success to the attitude of its nineteenth-century elites, which had played a leading role in the reconstruction of the Japanese state.

However, in light of the twentieth-century economic success of countries in Southeast Asia on the one hand, and the relative success of Southern Europe and Ireland on the other, one must concede that Kula was right in this respect too, namely, that top-down modernization requires an aggressive ideology. Such an ideology relies on divisions that are not based on class but on ethnicity, territory, or culture, thereby eliminating, at the level of consciousness, competition, conflict, and the stressful effects of modernization within a country or region, and directing them outwards instead. The nationalism of Germany and Japan in the late nineteenth and early twentieth centuries, which Kula analyzed, has its modern equivalent in the ideology of Europeanism in post-1989 Eastern Europe. A consequence of the ongoing project to Europeanize Eastern Europe through top-down modernization may be greater public aversion to nations outside the EU or to nations lower down the EU hierarchy as established by EU decision makers (such as crisis-ridden Greece since 2010).

THE ETHNIC DIVISION OF LABOR

An important difference between Eastern and Western Europe seems to be ethnic diversity and the ethnic division of labor, which persisted in Eastern Europe at least up until the Second World War. This problem was addressed by Małowist and his students and by Kula's collaborators. The weakness of Marxist historiography is that it denies the autonomy of ethnic divisions, which it regards as important only in so far as they coincide with feudal or class divisions. This is particularly jarring nowadays given that East European nationalism and the creation of nation-states—more than any issue except the fall of Communism—have become the subject of numerous academic studies. I think it would be worth examining economic attitudes in today's societies of Eastern Europe in terms of the dominant role played by their (symbolic) ethnic or national precursors in the social division of labor during the multinational empires of the sixteenth to nineteenth centuries. The starting point for such studies could be the observations made by the historians presented in this book about the overlapping of feudal, social class, ethnic, and religious divisions in Poland's multinational society. In the twenty-first century these observations have been developed in the work of Jacek Kochanowicz.

What demands serious consideration, I believe, are Małowist and Kula's insights into the traditionally specific and economically unfavorable long-term links between the domestic East European political elites and the West European economic elites, and Małowist's remarks about the unequal competition between less efficient domestic enterprises and their stronger Western counterparts. Regardless of the findings of economist-practitioners, what is important to social researchers is that the social perception of these phenomena is such that it has led, throughout the modern period, to the creation of political parties whose manifestos are based on economic nationalism and on protest against economic domination by foreigners. Among the youngest parties in this tradition, which stretches back to the nineteenth century, are Hungary's Fidesz party led by Viktor Orbán and Poland's Law and Justice Party led by Jarosław Kaczyński.

INTERESTS AND SUSTAINABLE DEVELOPMENT

The language used by my protagonists treated economics as part of the social sciences and not (only) as a collection of mathematical and objective models. Describing economic policies not just in terms of efficiency and financial stability but also in terms of group interests and the conflicts between those interests and the interests of other groups is, I believe, something that is worth keeping. Analytically, it is also necessary to distinguish between sustainable development and a situation where economic growth significantly improves the quality of life of certain groups and worsens it for others.

I am persuaded by Małowist's argument that only durable, legally guaranteed, balanced social stratification, that is, where different occupational and income groups are equipped with a balanced system of social privileges and obligations, makes sustainable development possible. Such a statement need not comply, especially in the short term, with the assumptions of classical economics. However, it does concur with the knowledge in social science that, in an era of mass society, social polarization causes social tensions that undermine the conditions necessary for sustainable development: peace, security, and a sense of social cohesion and solidarity.

The current concept of sustainable development emphasizes the link between a successful economy and a relatively egalitarian social structure. By this measure, it is European countries rather than the oil-rich countries of the Middle East that are considered to be developed, despite the fact that their GDP per capita is similar. Małowist's reflections on the relationship between the social structure and opportunities for development inclines me to the view that the political planning of development paths, and the way these are described by social science, should emerge from existing social structures and from prevailing ideas about what a good, equitable structure should look like. A project likely to lead to sustainable development would therefore have to be one that was relatively innovative and constructed on the basis of thorough knowledge about the social structure and values of a given society and the way they are perceived. Furthermore, the project would have to be relative in character: not composed of clearly defined features (only "the balance-sheet would have to tally," as Kula said) but adapted to the existing social structure.

Biblilography

Abrams, Philip. "History, Sociology and Historical Sociology." *Past and Present* 87 (1980): 3–16.

Althusser, Louis, and Etienne Balibar. *Reading "Capital."* Translated by B. Brewster. New York: New Left Books, 1970.

Amin, Samir. *Unequal Development. An Essay on the Social Formation of Peripheral Capitalism.* New York: Monthly Review Press, 1976.

Anderson, Benedict. *Imagined Communities. Reflections of the Origin and Spread of Nationalism.* London: Verso, 1983.

Anderson, Jeffrey L. *Explaining Long-Term Economic Change.* Cambridge: Cambridge University Press, 1995.

Anderson, Perry. "Portugal and the End of Ultra-Colonialism." *New Left Review* 17, 1962.

———. *The Lineages of the Absolutist State.* London: New Left Books, 1974.

———. *Passages from Antiquity to Feudalism.* London: New Left Books, 1974.

Aparicio, Frances R., and Cándida Jáquez. *Musical Migrations: Transnationalism and Cultural Hybridity in Latin(o) America.* Philadelphia: Temple University Press, 2001.

Assorodobraj-Kula, Nina. *Początki klasy robotniczej: problem rąk roboczych w przemyśle polskim epoki stanisławowskiej* [Beginnings of the working class: the problem of labor in Polish industry in the era of the king Stanislaus August Poniatowski]. Warsaw: Czytelnik, 1946.

Balcerak, Wiesław. "Czynniki integrujące i osłabiające 'ład wersalski' w Europie Środkowo-Wschodniej (1919–1939)" [Integrating and disintegrating factors of the Versailles order in Central-Eastern Europe (1919–1939)]. In *Ład wersalski w Europie Środkowej* [The 'Versailles order' in Central Europe], edited by Wiesław Balcerak, 35–64. Wrocław: Ossolineum, 1971.

———, ed. *"Ład wersalski" w Europie Środkowej* [The post-Versailles political order in Central Europe]. Wrocław: Ossolineum, 1971.

———. *Powstanie państw narodowych w Europie Środkowo-Wschodniej* [The formation of nation-states in Central-Eastern Europe]. Warsaw: PWN, 1974.

Batou, Jean, and Henryk Szlajfer, eds. *Western Europe, Eastern Europe and World Development, 13th to 18th Centuries. A Collection of Essays of Marian Małowist.* Leiden: Brill, 2010.

Batygin, Gennady S., and Inna F. Deviatko. "The Metamorphoses of Russian Sociology." In *Eastern Europe in Transformation. Impact on Sociology*, edited by Mike Keen and Janusz Mucha, 11–24. Westport, Conn.: Greenwood Press, 2003.

Bauman, Zygmunt. Review of *Teoria ekonomiczna ustroju feudalnego* [An economic theory of the feudal system, by Witold Kula. *Studia Socjologiczne* 3 (1963): 219–28.

———. *Modernity and Ambivalence.* Ithaca, New York: Cornell University Press, 1991.

Bendix, Reinhard. *Work and Authority in Industry: Ideologies of Management in the Course of Industrialization.* Berkeley: University of California Press, 1974.

———. *Nation-Building and Citizenship: Studies in Our Changing Social Order.* Berkeley: University of California Press, 1977.

Berend, Iván T. *Central and Eastern Europe 1944–1993: Detour from the Periphery to the Periphery.* Cambridge: Cambridge University Press, 1996.

Berend, Iván, and György Ránki. *The European Periphery and Industrialization 1780–1914.* Cambridge: Cambridge University Press, 1982.

Bibó, István. "The Distress of the East European Small States." In *Democracy, Revolution, Self-Determination. Selected Writings*, edited by Karol Nagy, 13–86. New York: Columbia University Press, 1991.

Bidlo, Jaroslav. "Ce qu'est l'histoire de l'Orient Europeen, quelle en est l'importance, et quelles furent ses etapes." *Bulletin* VI:1–2 (1934): 74–81.

Bieżuńska-Małowist, Iza, and Marian Małowist. *Niewolnictwo* [Slavery]. Warsaw: Czytelnik, 1987.

Bhaba, Homi K., ed. *The Nation and Narration.* London: Routledge, 1990.

Bloch, Marc. *Feudal Society.* Chicago: University of Chicago Press, 1964.

Bobrzyński, Michał. *Dzieje Polski w zarysie* [An outline of the history of Poland]. Warsaw: PIW, 1986.

Bogalska-Czajkowska, E. "Od Antwerpii do San Salwador. O źródłach, mechanizmach i efektach europejskiej ekspansji zamorskiej w pracach Mariana Małowista" [From Antwerp to San Salvador. On the origins, mechanisms, and results of the European overseas expansion in the works of Marian Małowist]. In *Interdyscyplinarne studia nad genezą kapitalizmu* [Interdisciplinary studies on the origins of capitalism], edited by Adama Czarnota and Andrzej Zybertowicz, vol. 2, 55–68. Toruń: Uniwersytet im. Mikołaja Kopernika, 1993.

Bogucka, Maria. "Les dernieres recherches sur l'histoire de la Baltique." *Acta Poloniae Historica* 7 (1962): 103–22.

———. "Merchant's Profits in Gdansk Foreign Trade in the First Half of the Seventeenth Century." *Acta Poloniae Historica* 23 (1971): 73–90.

———. "Handel bałtycki w życiu Polski i Europy XVI–XVII wieku" [The Baltic trade in the life of Poland and Europe in the 16th–17th century]. *Kultura i Społeczeństwo* 1 (1972): 71–76.

———. "Obcy kupcy osiadli w Gdańsku w pierwszej połowie XVII wieku" [Foreign merchants settling in Gdansk in the first half of the XVII century]. *Zapiski Historyczne* 34: 2 (1972): 59–82.

———, ed. *Warszawa w latach 1526–1795* [Warsaw in the years 1526–1795]. Warsaw: PWN, 1984.

———, ed. *Studia nad dziejami miast i mieszczaństwa w średniowieczu* [Study on the history of towns and townspeople in the Middle Ages]. Toruń: Uniwersytet im. Mikołaja Kopernika, 1996.

Bogucka, Maria, and Henryk Samsonowicz. *Dzieje miast i mieszczaństwa w Polsce przedrozbiorowej* [The history of towns and townspeole in Poland before the Partitions]. Wrocław: Ossolineum, 1986.

Bottomore, Tom B., and Michael J. Mulkay, eds. *Controversies in Sociology*, vol. 10. London: Allen&Unwin, 1980.

Bourdieu, Pierre. *Language and Symbolic Power*, edited by John Thompson, translated by Gino Raymond and Matthew Adamson. Cambridge, Mass.: Harvard University Press, 1991.

Brah, Avtar, and Annie Coombes. *Hybridity and Its Discontents. Politics, Science, Culture.* London: Routledge, 2000.

Braudel, Fernand. *Civilization and Capitalism, 15th–18th Century*, vol. 1–3. Berkeley: University of California Press, 1992.

———. Preface to Szűcs, *Trzy Europy* [The three Europes], 9–11. Lublin: Instytut Europy Środkowo-Wschodniej, 1995.

Brenner, Robert. "Agrarian Class Structure and Economic Development in Pre-Industrial Europe." *Past and Present* 70 (1976): 30–75.

———. "The Origins of Capitalist Development. A Critique of Neo-Smithian Marxism." *New Left Review* 104 (1977): 25–92.

———. The Agrarian Roots of European Capitalism." In *The Brenner Debate: Agrarian Class Structure and Economic Development in Pre-Industrial Europe*, edited by Trevor H. Aston and Charles H.E. Philpin, 213–28. Cambridge: Cambridge University Press, 1985.

———. "Economic Backwardness in Eastern Europe in Light of Developments in the West." In *The Origins of Backwardness in Eastern Europe. Economics and Politics from the Middle Ages Until the Early Twentieth Century*, edited by Daniel Chirot, 15–52. Berkeley: University of California Press, 1989.

Brubaker, Rogers. *Nationalism Reframed. Nationhood and the National Question in the New Europe.* Los Angeles: University of California Press, 1996.

Brzechczyn, Krzysztof. *Odrębność historyczna Europy Środkowej. Studium metodologiczne* [The historical separateness of Central Europe. A methodological study]. Poznań: Fundacja Humaniora, 1998.

Burke, Peter. "The Differentiation of History and Theory." In Peter Burke, *History and Social Theory*, 3–9. Ithaca: Cornell University Press, 2005.

Burke, Peter, Antoni Mączak, and Henryk Samsonowicz, eds. *East-Central Europe in Transition: XIV–XVII Century*. Cambridge: Cambridge University Press, 1985.

Caban, Wiesław. "Ziemianie przemysłowcy w Królestwie Polskim (1832–1864)" Land-owning industrialists in the Kingdom of Poland 1832–1864]. In *Image przedsiębiorcy gospodarczego w Polsce w XIX i XX wieku* [The image of an entrepreneur in Poland in the 19th and 20th century], edited by Ryszard Kolodziejczyk, 73–83. Warsaw: Instytut Historyczny Uniwersytetu Warszawskiego, 1993.

Cardoso, Fernando H. "Associated-Dependent Development: Theoretical and Practical Implications." In *Authoritarian Brazil,* edited by Alfred Stephen. 142–78. New Haven: Yale University Press, 1973.

Cardoso, Fernando H., and Enzo Faletto. *Dependency and Development in Latin America.* Berkeley: University of California Press, 1978.

Chałasiński, Józef. *Drogi awansu społecznego robotnika. Studium oparte na autobiografiach robotników* [Paths of worker's upward mobility. A study based on workers' autobiographies]. Poznań: Drukarnia Rolnicza, 1931.

———. "Emigracja jako zjawisko społeczne" [Emmigration as a social phenomenon]. *Przegląd Socjologiczny* 8 (1936): 495–501.

———. "Związek z parafią a świadomość narodowa emigranta" [The connection with the parish and the national consciousness of emigrants]. *Przegląd Socjologiczny* 8 (1936): 547–49.

———. *Młode pokolenie chłopów. Procesy i zagadnienia kształtowania się warstwy chłopskiej w Polsce* [Young generation of peasants. Processes and problems of the formation of peasantry in Poland]. Warsaw: Państwowy Instytut Kultury Spółdzielnia Wydawnicza "Pomoc Oświatowa," 1938.

———. *Społeczna genealogia inteligencji polskiej* [Social genealogy of the Polish intelligentsia]. Warsaw: Ludowa Spółdzielnia Wydawnicza, 1946.

———. *Rewolucja młodości. Studia o awansie młodego pokolenia i integracji narodu polskiego* [The youth revolution. Study on the upward mobility of the young generation and the integration of the Polish nation]. Warsaw: Czytelnik, 1969.

Chamerska, Halina. "Struktura własności ziemskiej w podlaskich powiatach guberni lubelskiej (1832–1863)" [The structure of landproperty in the Podlasie districts in Lublin county (1832–1863)]. In *Społeczeństwo polskie XVIII i XIX wieku. Studia o uwarstwieniu i ruchliwości społecznej* [Polish society in the 18th and 19th century. Study on social stratification and mobility], edited by Witold Kula and Janina Leskiewiczowa, Vol. 5, 9–23. Warsaw: PWN, 1970–1980.

———. "Wspólnoty religijno-narodowe a społeczeństwo polskie" [Ethno-religious communities and Polish society]. In *Przemiany społeczne w Królestwie Polskim 1815–1864* [Social changes in the Kingdom of Poland 1815–1864], edited by Witold Kula and Janina Leskiewiczowowa, 283–304. Wrocław: Ossolineum, 1979.

Chirot, Daniel. "The Social and Historical Landscape of Marc Bloch." In *Vision and Method in Historical Sociology*, edited by Theda Skocpol, 22–46. Cambridge: Cambridge University Press, 1984.

———. "Causes and Consequences of Backwardness." In *The Origins of Backwardness in Eastern Europe. Economies and Politics from the Middle Ages until the Early Twentieth Century*, edited by Daniel Chirot, 1–14. Berkeley: University of California Press, 1989.

———. *Social Change in the Modern Era.* New York: Harcourt Brace Jovanovich Publishers, 1986.

———. *How Societies Change.* Thousand Oaks: Pine Forge Press, 1994.

Chruszczewski, Adam. "Zakonnicy diecezji lubelskiej w świetle spisu z 1835 roku" [The monks of the Lublin diocese according to the 1835 census]. In *Społeczeństwo Królestwa Polskiego. Studia o uwarstwieniu i ruchliwości społecznej* [The society of the Kingdom of Poland. Study on social stratification and mobility], Vol.3, edited by Witold Kula, 165–99. Warsaw: PWN, 1968.

Czepulis-Rastenis, Ryszarda. "Urzędnicy Towarzystwa Kredytowego Ziemskiego w Królestwie Polskim" [The officials of the Credit Association for Agriculture in the Kingdom of Poland]. In *Społeczeństwo Królestwa Polskiego. Studia o uwarstwieniu i ruchliwości społecznej* [The society of the Kingdom of Poland. Study on social stratification and mobility], edited by Witold Kula, Vol. 2, 155–75. Warsaw: PWN, 1965–1968.

———. "Lekarze urzędowi 1832–1862" [Doctors in the government sector 1832–1862]. In *Społeczeństwo Królestwa Polskiego XVIII i XIX. Studia o uwarstwieniu i ruchliwości społecznej* [Polish society in the 18h and 19th century. Study on social stratification and mobility], edited by Witold Kula and Janina Leskiewiczowa, Vol. 3, 47–88. Warsaw: PWN, 1968.

———. "Inteligencja warszawska przed powstaniem styczniowym" [Warsaw intelligentsia before the uprising of January 1863]. In *Społeczeństwo polskie XVIII i XIX wieku. Studia o uwarstwieniu i ruchliwości społecznej* [Polish society in the 18th and 19th century. Study on social stratification and mobility], Vol. 5, edited by Witold Kula and Janina Leskiewiczowa, 141–58. Warsaw: PWN, 1972.

———. "Kształtowanie się inteligencji technicznej w Królestwie Polskim" [Formation of the Polish technical intelligentsia in the Kingdom of Poland]. In *Społeczeństwo polskie XVIII i XIX wieku. Studia o uwarstwieniu i ruchliwości społecznej* [Polish society in the 18th and 19th century. Study on social stratification and mobility], edited by Witold Kula and Janina Leskiewiczowa, Vol. 4, 69–120. Warsaw: PWN, 1970.

Delanty, Gerard. *Inventing Europe. Idea, Identity, Reality.* London: Macmillan, 1995.

———. "Discussion of Kula's *An Economic Theory*." *Kwartalnik Historyczny* 3 (1963): 690–96.

Dobb Maurice. *Studies in the Development in Capitalism.* New York: International Publishers, 1963.

Domański, Henryk. *On the Verge of Convergence. Social Stratification in Eastern Europe.* Budapest–New York: Central European University Press, 2000.

Dos Santos, Theotonio. "The Crisis of Development Theory and the Problem of Dependence in Latin America." In *Underdevelopment and Development*, edited by Henry Bernstein, 57–80. London: Penguin, 1973.

Drozdowski, Marian. "Od badań regionalnych do syntez dziejów narodowych i historii powszechnej" [From regional studies to national and world history]. In *Między historią a teorią: refleksje nad problematyką dziejów i wiedzy historycznej. Prace ofiarowane Jerzemu Topolskiemu* [Between history and theory: reflections upon the problems of the past and the historical knowledge. Works dedicated to Jerzy Topolski], edited by Marian Drozdowski, 6–20. Warsaw–Poznań: PWN, 1988.

Dutkiewicz, Józef, and Krystyna Średniowska. *Zarys historii historiografii polskiej* [An outline of the history of the Polish historiography], Vol. 3: *1900–1939*. Łódź: PWN, 1959.

Dyląngowa, Hanna. "Episkopat polski w latach 1795–1830" [Polish episcopate 1795–1830]. In *Społeczeństwo polskie XVIII i XIX wieku. Studia o grupach elitarnych* [Polish society in the 18th and 19th centuries. Study of the elite groups], edited by Janina Leskiewiczowa, Vol.7. Warsaw: PWN, 1982.

Eisenbach, Artur. "Dobra ziemskie w posiadaniu Żydów" [Land properties owned by Jews]. In *Społeczeństwo Królestwa Polskiego. Studia o uwarstwieniu i ruchliwości społecznej* [The society of the Kingdom of Poland. Study on social stratification and mobility], edited by Witold Kula, Vol. 3, 201–94. Warsaw: PWN, 1968.

———. "Ludność żydowska" [Jewish population]. In *Przemiany społeczne w Królestwie Polskim 1815–1864* [Social change in the Kingdom of Poland 1815–1864], edited by Witold Kula and Janina Leskiewiczowa, 107–36. Warsaw: Ossolineum, 1979.

———. "Prawa obywatelskie i honorowe Żydów (1790–1861)" [Civil and tradition based rights of the Jews (1790–1861)]. In *Społeczeństwo Królestwa Polskiego. Studia o uwarstwieniu i ruchliwości społecznej* [The society of the Kingdom of Poland. Study on social stratification and mobility], edited by Witold Kula, Vol. 1, 237–300. Warsaw: PWN, 1965.

Eisenstadt, Shmuel N. *The Political Systems of Empires*. New York: Free Press, 1963.

Evans, Peter B., Dietrich Rueschemayer, and Theda Skocpol, eds. *Bringing the State Back In*. Cambridge: Cambridge University Press, 1985.

Evans, Peter, and John D. Stephens. "Development and the World-Economy." In *Handbook of Economic Sociology*, edited by Neil Smelser, 739–73. London: Sage, 1988.

Feagin, Joe R., Charles Tilly, and Constance W. Williams. *Subsidizing the Poor: A Boston Housing Experiment*. Lexington, Mass: Lexington Books, 1972.

Fehér, Ferenc. "On Making Central Europe." *Eastern European Politics and Society* 3, 3 (1989): 414–48.

Foster-Carter, Aidan. "The Modes of Production Controversy." *New Left Review* 107 (1978): 47–77.

Foucault, Michel. *Archaeology of Knowledge*, translated by A. M. Sheridan Smith. London: Routledge, 2002.

Frank, Andre G. *Capitalism and Underdevelopment in Latin America.* New York: Monthly Review Press, 1967.

Fukuyama, Francis. *The End of History and the Last Man.* New York: Free Press, 1992.

Fulbrook, Mary, and Theda Skocpol. "Destined Pathways: The Historical Sociology of Perry Anderson." In *Vision and Method in Historical Sociology*, edited by Theda Skocpol, 170–210. Cambridge: Cambridge University Press, 1984.

Furtado, Celso. *Development and Underdevelopment.* Berkeley: University of California Press, 1964.

———. *The Economic Growth of Brazil: A Survey from Colonial to Modern Times,* translated by Ricardo W. de Aguiar and Eric Charles Drysdale. Berkeley: University of California Press, 1971.

———. *The Myth of Economic Development and the Future of the Third World.* Cambridge: Center of Latin American Studies, University of Cambridge, 1974.

Gellner, Ernest. *Thought and Change.* London: Weidenfeld and Nicolson, 1964.

———. *Nations and Nationalism.* Ithaca, NY: Cornell University Press, 1983.

Genovese, Eugene D. *Roll, Jordan, Roll. The World the Slaves Made.* New York: Vintage Books, 1972.

Gerschenkron, Alexander. *Economic Backwardness in Historical Perspective. A Book of Essays.* Cambridge: Harvard University Press, 1962.

Giddens, Anthony. *Capitalism and Modern Social Theory.* Cambridge: Cambridge University Press, 1971.

———. *The Consequences of Modernity.* Stanford: Stanford University Press, 1990.

Godelier, Maurice. "Objet et methode de l'anthropologie economique." *L'homme* 5, 2 (1965): 32–91.

Grabski, Andrzej E. *Zarys historii historiografii polskiej* [An outline of the history of Polish historiography]. Poznań: Wydawnictwo Poznańskie, 2000.

Gramsci, Antonio. *Selection from the Prison Notebooks*, edited and translated by Quintin Hoare and Geoffrey Noel Smith. New York: International Publishers, 1971.

Greenfeld, Liah. *Nationalism: Five Roads to Modernity.* Cambridge, Mass.: Harvard University Press, 1992.

Grinberg, Daniel. "Problematyka przemocy związanej z tzw. erą przemysłową w perspektywie nowej historii społecznej oraz socjologii historycznej" [The issues of violence related to the so-called industrial age in the perspective of the new social history and historical sociology]. In *Człowiek i agresja. Głos o nienawiści. Ujęcie interdyscyplinarne* [Human being. Voice about hatred. An interdisciplinary approach], 154–72. Warsaw: Sic!, 2002.

Grodecki, Roman. *Powstanie polskiej świadomości narodowej* [The emergence of the Polish national consciousness]. Katowice: Wydawnictwa Instytutu Śląskiego, 1946.

Grodziski, Stanisław. "Schyłek stanu szlacheckiego" [The end of the nobility estate]. In *Społeczeństwo polskie XVIII i XIX wieku. Studia o aktywności spo-*

łecznej oraz jej politycznym uwarunkowaniu [Polish society in the 18th and 19th century. A study on the social activity and its political background], edited by Janina Leskiewiczowa, Vol. 8, 95–108. Warsaw: PWN, 1987.

Guzowski, Piotr. "Village Court Records and Peasant Credit in Fifteenth- and Sixteenth-Century Poland." *Continuity and Change* 29:1 (2014): 115–42.

Habermas, Jürgen. *The Structural Transformation of the Public Sphere. An Inquiry into a Category of Bourgeois Society.* Boston: MIT Press, 1991.

Hahn, Hans. "Przymus modernizacyjny i nacisk integracyjny – rola państwa w kształtowaniu mentalności politycznej Polaków w drugiej połowie XIX w." [Coerced to modernize and pressured to integrate. The role of the state in the formation of the political mentality of the Poles in the second half of the 19th century]. In *Ideologie, poglądy i mity w dziejach Polski i Europy* [Ideologies, views, and myths in the history of Poland and Europe], edited by Jerzy Topolski, 289–96. Poznań: UAM, 1991.

Halecki, Oskar. "L'histoire de L'Europe orientale. Sa division en époques, son milieu géographique et ses problèmes fondamentaux." In *La Pologne au Vè Congrès International des Sciences Historiques.* Brussels–Warsaw, 1923–1924.

———. "Qu'est que l'Europe Orientale." *Bulletin* 1–2 (1934): 81–93.

———. "Europa Środkowa" [Central Europe]. In *Encyklopedia nauk politycznych* [Encyclopedia of political sciences], Vol. 2. Warsaw: Instytut Społeczny, 1937.

———. "East Central Europe in Postwar Organization." *The Annals of the American Academy of Political and Social Science.* Philadelphia, July 1943.

———. "The historical role of Central-Eastern Europe." *The Annals of the American Academy of Political and Social Science.* Philadelphia, March 1944.

———. *The Limits and Divisions of European History.* London: Sheed and Ward, 1950.

Handelsman, Marceli. "Quelques remarques sur la definition de l'histoire de l'Europe Orientale." *Bulletin* 1–2 (1934): 74–81.

Hass, Ludwik. "Warstwa oświecona na ziemiach centralnej Polski" [The enlightened stratum of central Poland]. In *Społeczeństwo polskie XVIII i XIX wieku. Studia o grupach elitarnych* [Polish society in the 18th and 19th century. A study on elite groups], Vol. 7, edited by Janina Leskiewiczowa, 19–66. Warsaw: PWN, 1982.

Herling-Bianco, Marta. "Jedno- i wielokierunkowość rozwoju: przejście od feudalizmu do kapitalizmu w dziele Witolda Kuli" [One and multi-directional development: the passage from feudalism to capitalism in the work of Witold Kula]. In *Interdyscyplinarne studia nad genezą kapitalizmu* [Interdisciplinary studies on the rise of capitalism], edited by Adam Czarnota and Andrzej Zybertowicz, Vol. 2, 39–54. Toruń: Uniwersytet im. Mikołaja Kopernika, 1993.

Hirschman, Albert O. *Journeys toward Progress. Studies of Economic Policy-Making.* New York: Twentieth Century Fund, 1963.

———. *Underdevelopment and Dependence: The Fundamental Connections.* Cambridge: Cambridge University Press, 1974.

———. *National Power and the Structure of Foreign Trade.* Berkeley: University of California Press, 1980 [1945].

———. *Essays in Trespassing. Economics to Politics and Beyond.* Cambridge: Cambridge University Press, 1981.

———. "A Dissenter's Confession: 'The Strategy of Economic Development' revisited." In *Pioneers in Development*, edited by Gerald Meire and Dudley Seers, 87–111. Oxford: Oxford University Press, 1984.

Hirszowicz, Maria. "Socjologia na Wydziale Filozoficznym UW w latach sześćdziesiątych" [Sociology in the Philosophy department of the University of Warsaw in the 1960s]. *Kultura i Społeczeństwo* 1 (1998): 189–95.

Hobsbawm, Eric. *Nations and Nationalism since 1780: Programme, Myth, Reality.* Cambridge: Cambridge University Press, 1990.

———. *The Age of Extremes: The Short Twentieth Century, 1914–1991.* London: Michael Joseph, 1994.

Hobsbawm, Eric, and Terence Ranger, eds. *The Invention of Tradition.* Cambridge: Cambridge University Press, 1983.

Homola, Irena. "Inteligencja galicyjska w połowie XIX wieku. Próba charakterystyki" [Galician intelligentsia in the mid-19th century. An attempt at a portrait]. In *Społeczeństwo polskie XVIII i XIX wieku. Studia o uwarstwieniu i ruchliwości społecznej* [Polish society in the 18th and 19th century. Studies on social stratification and mobility], edited by Witold Kula and Janina Leskiewiczowa, Vol. 5, 103–40. Warsaw: PWN, 1972.

———. *Kwiat społeczeństwa. Struktura społeczna i rys położenia inteligencji krakowskiej w latach 1860–1894* [The flower of society. The social structure and characteristics of the situation of the Cracow intelligentsia in the years 1860–1894]. Kraków: Wydawnictwo Literackie, 1984.

Hopkins, Terence K., and Immanuel Wallerstein. *The Age of Transition: Trajectory of The World-System 1945–2025.* London: Zed Books, 1996.

Huntington, Samuel. *The Clash of Civilizations and the Remaking of World Order.* New York: Simon & Schuster, 1996

Ihnatowicz, Ireneusz. *Burżuazja warszawska* [The Warsaw Bourgeoisie]. Warsaw: PWN, 1972.

———. Review of *Przemiany społeczne* [Social changes], by Witold Kula and Janina Leskieczowa. *Przegląd Historyczny* 2 (1980): 391–97.

———. "Urzędnicy galicyjscy w dobie autonomii" [Galician government officials during the period of autonomy in the late 19th century]. In *Społeczeństwo polskie XVIII i XIX wieku. Studia o uwarstwieniu i ruchliwości społecznej* [Polish society in the 18th and 19th century. Study on social stratification and mobility], Vol. 6, edited by Witold Kula and Janina Leskiewiczowa, 205–23. Warsaw: PWN, 1980.

———. *Społeczeństwo polskie 1864–1914* [Polish society 1864–1914]. Warsaw: KAW, 1988

Ihnatowicz, Ireneusz, Antoni Mączak, and Benedykt Zientara, eds. *Społeczeństwo polskie od X do XX wieku* [Polish society from the 10th to the 20th century]. Warsaw: KiW, 1979.

Janos, Andrew C. *East Central Europe in the Modern World. The Politics of the Borderlands from Pre- to Post Communism.* Stanford: Stanford University Press, 2000.

———. *Politics and Paradigms. Changing Theories of Change in Social Science.* Stanford: Stanford University Press, 1986.

———. *The Politics of Backwardness in Hungary, 1825–1945.* Princeton: Princeton University Press, 1982.

———. "The Politics of Backwardness in Continental Europe, 1780–1945." *World Politics* vol. 41, no. 3 (1989): 325–58.

Jasienica, Paweł. *Polska anarchia* [Polish anarchy].Warsaw: Czytelnik, 1993.

Jedlicki, Jerzy. *Nieudana próba kapitalistycznej industrializacji. Analiza państwowego gospodarstwa przemysłowego w Królestwie Polskim XIX w.* [Unsuccessful attempt at capitalist industrialization. Analysis of the industrial economy in the Kingdom of Poland in the 19th century]. Warsaw: KiW, 1964.

———. Introduction to *Przemiany społeczne w Królestwie Polskim.*

———. *Klejnot i bariery społeczne. Przeobrażenia szlachectwa polskiego w schyłkowym okresie feudalizmu* [The jewel of nobility and social barriers. Transformations of the Polish nobility in the late period of feudalism]. Warsaw: PWN, 1968.

———. "Polskie nurty ideowe wobec cywilizacji Zachodu (1790–1863)" [Polish ideological currents regarding the Western civilization (1790–1863)]. In *Swojskość i cudzoziemszczyzna w dziejach kultury polskiej* [Familiarity and foreigness in the history of the Polish culture], edited by Zofia Stefanowska, 186–231. Warsaw: PWN, 1973.

———. "W sprawie automatycznego krachu feudalizmu" [On the automatic crash of feudalism]. In *Między feudalizmem a kapitalizmem. Studia z dziejów gospodarczych i społecznych. Prace ofiarowane Witoldowi Kuli* [Between feudalism and capitalism. Study on economic and social history. Works dedicated to Witold Kula], edited by Ryszarda Czepulis-Rastenis, et al., 230–37. Wrocław: Ossolineum, 1976.

———. "Obozy ideowe w Królestwie Polskim wobec zmian społecznych" [The ideological camps in the Kingdom of Poland in regard to the social changes]. In *Przemiany społeczne w Królestwie Polskim 1815–1864* [Social changes in the Kingdom of Poland 1815–1864], edited by Witold Kula and Janina Leskiewiczowa, 463–96. Wrocław: Ossolineum, 1979.

———. "Witold Kula jako historyk cywilizacji" [Witold Kula as historian of the civilization]. In *Dziedzictwo Witolda Kuli, referaty wygłoszone podczas konferencji zorganizowanej 13 i 14 lutego 1989 r. przez Zarząd Główny Polskiego Towarzystwa Historycznego* [The legacy of Witold Kula, papers read during the conference organized on February 13th and 14th, 1989 by the Main Board of the Polish Historical Society], edited by Marcin Kula, 87–104. Warsaw: Uniwersytet Warszawski, 1990.

———. *A Suburb of Europe. Nineteenth-Century Polish Approaches to Western Civilization.* Budapest–New York: CEU Press, 1999.

Jedlicki, Jerzy, and Witold Kula. "Struktura społeczna Królestwa Polskiego w przededniu powstania styczniowego" [The social structure of the Kingdom of Poland on the eve of the uprising of January 1863]. In *IX Powszechny Zjazd Historyków Polskich* [The 9th general congress of the Polish historians], Vol. 2, edited by Stefan Kieniewicz, 7–35. Warsaw: PWN, 1964.

Jezierski, Andrzej. *Problemy rozwoju gospodarczego ziem polskich XIX i XX w.* [Problems of the industrial development of the Polish lands in the 19th and 20th century]. Warsaw: KiW, 1984.

Jędruszczak, Tadeusz. "Europa środkowa w przededniu II wojny światowej" [Central Europe on the eve of the World War II.] *Dzieje Najnowsze* 2 (1971): 5–51.

Jones, Eric L. *The European Miracle. Environments, Economies, and Geopolitics in the History of Europe and Asia.* Cambridge: Cambridge University Press, 1987.

Judt, Tony. *A Grand Illusion? An Essay on Europe.* New York: New York University Press, 2011.

Kaczyńska, Elżbieta. "Tkacze w Zduńskiej Woli i Turku w końcu XIX wieku" [Weavers in Zduńska Wola and Turek in the late 19th century]. In *Społeczeństwo Królestwa Polskiego. Studia o uwarstwieniu i ruchliwości społecznej* [The society of the Kingdom of Poland. Study on social stratification and mobility], Vol. 3, edited by Witold Kula, 337–94. Warsaw: PWN, 1968.

———. "Drobnomieszczaństwo polskie w XIX i na początku XX wieku. Problemy dyskusyjne i trudności badawcze" [Polish petite bourgeoisie in the 19th and the beginning of the 20th century. Problems for discussion and research difficulties]. In *Społeczeństwo polskie XVIII i XIX wieku. Studia o uwarstwieniu i ruchliwości społecznej* [Polish society in the 18th and 19th century. Study on social stratification and mobility], edited by Witold Kula and Janina Leskiewiczowa, Vol. 5, 235–71. Warsaw: PWN, 1972.

———. "Mieszczaństwo" [Bourgeoisie]. In *Przemiany społeczne w Królestwie Polskim 1815–1864* [Social changes in the Kingdom of Poland 1815–1864], edited by Witold Kula and Janina Leskiewiczowa. Wrocław: Ossolineum, 1979.

———. "In Memoriam: Witold Kula." *Kwartalnik Historyczny* 3 (1989): 302–303.

Kamler, Marcin. *Folwark szlachecki w Wielkopolsce w latach 1580–1655* [Manorial estate in Wielkopolska region in the years 1580–1655]. Warsaw: PWN, 1976.

Karpiński, Jakub. *Nie być w myśleniu posłusznym. Ossowscy, socjologia, filozofia* [Not to be obedient while thinking. The Ossowskis, sociology, philosophy]. London: Polonia Book Fund, 1989.

Katznelson, Ira, and Aristide Zolberg. *City Trenches: Urban Politics and the Patterning of Class in the United States.* New York: Pantheon Books, 1981.

Keen, Mike, and Janusz Mucha, eds. *Socjologia Europy Środkowo-Wschodniej 1956–1990* [Sociology of Central-Eastern Europe 1956–1990]. Translated by Lucyna Stetkiewicz and Janusz Mucha. Warsaw: Instytut Filozofii i Socjologu PAN, 1995.

Kiciński, Krzysztof. "Popaździernikowa socjologia" [Post-October 1956 sociology]. *Kultura i Społeczeństwo*, 1 (1998): 197–204.

Kizwalter, Tomasz. "*Nowatorstwo i rutyny.*" *Społeczeństwo Królestwa Polskiego wobec procesów modernizacji (1840–1863)* [Innovation and routines. The society of the Kingdom of Poland regarding the process of modernization (1840–1863)]. Warsaw: PWN, 1991.

Kłoczowski, Jerzy. "Wstęp" [Introduction]. In *Historia Europy – jej granice i podziały* [Limits and divisions of Europe], by Oskar Halecki, translated by Jan Maria Kloczowski, 7–10. Lublin: Instytut Europy Środkowo-Wschodniej, 1994.

———. *East Central Europe in the Historiography of the Countries of the Region.* Lublin: Institute of East Central Europe, 1995.

———. *Młodsza Europa. Europa Środkowo-Wschodnia w kręgu cywilizacji chrześcijańskiej średniowiecza* [Younger Europe. Central-Eastern Europe within the sphere of medieval Christian civilization]. Warsaw: PIW, 1998.

Kochanowicz, Jacek. *Pańszczyźniane gospodarstwo chłopskie w Królestwie Polskim w pierwszej połowie XIX wieku* [Peasant economy under serfdom in the Kingdom of Poland in the first half of the 19th century]. Warsaw: Wydawnictwo Uniwersytetu Warszawskiego, 1981.

———. "'Teoria ekonomiczna' W. Kuli w oczach krytyków" [Witold Kula's "An Economic Theory" in the eyes of his critics]. In Witold Kula, *Teoria ekonomiczna ustroju feudalnego* [An Economic theory of the feudal system]. Warsaw: KiW, 1983.

———. "Badania historyczno-porównawcze" [Historical-comparative research]. In *Encyklopedia socjologii* [Encyclopedia of sociology], Vol. 1, 58–60. Warsaw: Oficyna Naukowa, 1998.

———. "Czy tylko historia gospodarcza? Jubileusz Witolda Kuli" [Is it only economic history? Anniversary of Witold Kula]. *Kronika Warszawy* 1–2 (1985): 129–46.

———. "The Polish Economy and the Evolution of Dependency." In *The Origins of Backwardness in Eastern Europe. Economies and Politics from the Middle Ages Until the Early Twentieth Century*, edited by Daniel Chirot, 92–130. Berkeley: University of California Press, 1989.

———. *Spór o teorię gospodarki chłopskiej. Gospodarstwo chłopskie w teorii ekonomii i w historii gospodarczej* [The dispute over the theory of peasant economy. Peasant economy in the economic theory and economic history]. Warsaw: Wydawnictwo Uniwersytetu Warszawskiego, 1992.

———. "Twórca i dzieło" [The author and his work]. In *Kultura materialna, gospodarka i kapitalizm XV–XVIII wiek* [Civilization and capitalism, 15th–18th century], Vol. 1, edited by Fernand Braudel, translated by Maria Ochab and Piotr Graff. Warsaw: PIH 1992.

———. "Teoria systemu światowego" [Theory of the world system]. In *Encyklopedia socjologii* [Encyclopedia of sociology], Vol. 4, 207–11. Warsaw: Oficyna Naukowa, 2002.

———. *Backwardness and Modernization. Poland and Eastern Europe in the 16th–20th century.* Aldershot: Ashgate, 2006.

———. "Duch kapitalizmu na polskiej peryferii: perspektywa historyczna" [Spirit of capitalism in the Polish periphery: historical perspective]. In *Kul-*

tura i gospodarka, edited by Jacek Kochanowicz and Mirosława Marody, 21–51. Warsaw: Wydawnictwo Naukowe Scholar 2010.

Kosim, Jan. *Losy pewnej fortuny. Z dziejów burżuazji warszawskiej w latach 1807–1830* [The fate of certain financial success. From the history of the Warsaw bourgeoisie in the years 1807–1830]. Wrocław–Warsaw: Ossolineum–Instytut Historii PAN, 1972.

Kovács, János M. "Praising the Hybrids. Notes on Economic Thought Ten Years After." *East European Politics and Societies* 2 (1999): 313–22.

Kowalska, Stefania. "Robotnicy" [Workers]. In *Przemiany społeczne w Królestwie Polskim 1815–1864* [Social changes in the Kingdom of Poland 1815–1864], edited by Witold Kula and Janina Leskiewiczowa, 345–70. Wrocław: Ossolineum, 1979.

Kowalska, Stefania, Jerzy Jedlicki, and Andrzej Jezierski. *Ekonomika górnictwa i hutnictwa w Królestwie Polskim 1831–1864* [The effectiveness of mining and metallurgy in the Kingdom of Poland 1831–1864]. Warsaw: PWN, 1958.

Kowalska-Glikman, Stefania. "Drobnomieszczaństwo polskie w warunkach rozwoju kapitalizmu (XIX wiek-lata międzywojenne)" [Polish petite bourgeoisie in the conditions of development of capitalism (between the 19th century and the interwar years)]. In *Metamorfozy społeczne. Badania nad dziejami społeczeństwa polskiego XIX i XX wieku* [Social metamorphosis. Research on the history of the Polish society in the 19th and 20th century], edited by Janusz Żarnowski, 79–107. Warsaw: Instytut Historii PAN, 1997.

Kruczkowska, Maria. "Deputowani Koła Polskiego w Wiedniu w latach 1865–1879" [The representatives of the Polish Association in Vienna in the years 1865–1879]. In *Społeczeństwo polskie XVIII i XIX wieku. Studia o grupach elitarnych* [Polish society in the 18th and 19th century. Study on the elite groups], edited by Janina Leskiewiczowa, Vol. 7, 219–34. Warsaw: PWN, 1982.

Krzemiński, Ireneusz. "Metodologia jako filozofia pozytywistycznej równowagi. Ćwierć wieku w Instytucie Socjologii Uniwersytetu Warszawskiego" [Methodology as a philosophy of positivist balance. A quarter of a century in the Institute of Sociology of Warsaw University]. *Kultura i Społeczeństwo* 4 (1998): 103–19

Kuklo, Cezary. *Rodzina* w *osiemnastowiecznej Warszawie* [The family in 18th-century Warsaw]. Białystok: Wydawnictwo Uniwersyteckie, 1991.

———. *Kobieta samotna w społeczeństwie miejskim u schyłku Rzeczypospolitej szlacheckiej: studium demograficzno-społeczne* [The single woman in the urban society at the dawn of the Polish-Lithuanian Commonwealth: a socio-demographic study]. Białystok: Wydawnictwo Uniwersyteckie, 1998.

———. "Profesor Andrzej Wyczański doktorem Honoris Causa Uniwersytetu w Białymstoku" [A honoris causa degree for Professor Andrzej Wyczański in the Białystok University]. *Kwartalnik Historyczny* 57: 1 (2000): 156–57.

———, ed. *Między polityką a kulturą. Studia ofiarowane A. Wyczańskiemu w 75-lecie urodzin i 50-lecie pracy naukowej* [Between politics and culture. Studies dedicated to A. Wyczański on his 75th birthday and the 50th anniversary of his academic work]. Białystok–Warsaw: PWN, 1999.

Kula, Marcin. *Początki czarnego niewolnictwa w Brazylii* [The beginnings of black slavery in Brazil]. Wrocław: Ossolineum, 1970.

——— ed. *Zamachy stanu, przewroty, rewolucje. Ameryka Łacińska w XX wieku.* [Coup d'états, upheavels, and revolutions. Latin America in the 20th century]. Warsaw: Czytelnik, 1983.

Kula, Witold. "Włościański przemysł domowy tkacki w Królestwie Polskim w latach 1846–1865" [Peasant homeworkers in the textile industry in Kingdom of Poland 1846–1865]. *Przegląd Socjologiczny* 1–2 (1938): 166–224.

———. *Historia gospodarcza Polski w dobie popowstaniowej 1864–1918* [The economic history of Poland in the post-uprising period 1864–1918].Warsaw: Wiedza, 1947.

———. "Manufaktura sukienna Radziwiłłów w Nieświeżu" [The Radziwiłłs' Textile Manufactory in Nieśwież]. *Roczniki Dziejów Społecznych i Gospodarczych*, 1–39, 1947.

———. "Rozwój kapitalizmu w rolnictwie w Polsce (1864–1900)" [The formation of capitalism in agriculture in Poland (1864–1900)]. *Wieś* 49 and 50 (1950).

———. "Począ*tki układu kapitalistycznego w Polsce XVIII wieku*" [The beginnings of capitalist system in 18th-century Poland]. *Przegląd Historyczny* 42, (1951): 36–81.

———. "Karol Marks—przyjaciel i obrońca Polski" [Karl Marx—a friend and advocate of Poland]. *Nowe Drogi* 4 (1953): 60–73.

———. "Marks a sprawa polska" [Marx and the Polish question]. *Życie Warszawy*, 24 March, (1953): 3.

———. "O nowy, marksistowski uniwersytecki podręcznik historii Polski" [A new, Marxist college handbook of Polish history is needed]. *Kwartalnik Historyczny* 1 (1953): 279–88.

———. "Huta szklana w Cudnowie. Przenikanie kapitału handlowego do feudalnej manufaktury" [The glass factory in Cudnow. The penetration of commercial capital into the feudal manufactory]. *Kwartalnik Historii Kultury Materialnej* 4 (1954): 676–90, 830.

———. *Kształtowanie się kapitalizmu w Polsce* [The formation of capitalism in Poland]. Warsaw: PWN, 1955.

———. "Przemysł włókienniczy w Królestwie Polskim (1831–1865). Materiały dotyczące dynamiki jego rozwoju" [Textile industry in the Kingdom of Poland (1831–1865). Evidence of the growth dynamic]. *Kwartalnik Historyczny* 4–5 (1956): 180–99.

———. *Szkice o manufakturach w Polsce XVIII wieku* [Sketches of manufactories in 18th-century Poland], vol. 1–2: 1720–1780, vol. 3: 1780–1795. Warsaw: PWN, 1956.

———. "Wstęp" [Introduction]. In *Studia z dziejów wsi polskiej XVI–XVIII w.* [Studies in 16th–18th-century Polish countryside], by Jan Rutkowski, 5-61. Warsaw: PWN, 1956.

———. "Some Observations on the Industrial Revolution in Eastern European Countries." *Kwartalnik Historii Kultury Materialnej* 1–2 (1958): 239–48

———, ed. *Społeczeństwo Królestwa Polskiego. Studia o uwarstwieniu i ruchliwości społecznej* [The society of the Kingdom of Poland. Study on social stratification and mobility], Vol. 1–3. Warsaw: PWN, 1965–1968.
———. "Ekonomia a społeczeństwo. Antropologiczny punkt widzenia" [Economy and society. An anthropological point of view]. In *O gospodarce mieszanej w krajach 'trzeciego świata'* [On the mixed economy in Third World countries], 22–58. Warsaw: PWN 1967.
———. "Doświadczenia i nadzieje" [Experiences and hopes]. In *Wokół historii* [Around history], 486–90. Warsaw: PWN, 1988.
———. "Rządzący i rządzeni" [The rulers and the ruled]. In *Wiek XVIII. Polska i świat. Księga poświęcona Bogusławowi Leśnodorskiemu* [Eighteenth-century Poland and the world. A book dedicated to Bogusław Leśnodorski], 399–414. Warsaw: PIW 1974.
———. *An Economic Theory of the Feudal System. Toward a Model of the Polish Economy 1500–1800*, translated by Lawrence Garner. London: New Left Books, 1976.
———. "Rozwój gospodarczy w warunkach rosnącego zacofania" [Economic development under condition of increasining backwardness]. In *Przemiany społeczne w Królestwie Polskim 1815–1864* [Social privilege and economic porgress], edited by Witold Kula and Janina Leskiewiczowa, 11–23. Wrocław: Ossolineum, 1979.
———. "Udział we władzy" [Participation in political power]. In *Przemiany społeczne w Królestwie Polskin 1815–1864* [Social privilege and economic porgress], edited by Witold Kula and Janina Leskiewiczowa, 405–19. Wrocław: Ossolineum, 1979.
———. "Przywilej społeczny a postęp gospodarczy" [Social priviledge and economic progress]. In *Historia, zacofanie, rozwój*, 22–63. Warsaw: PIW, 1983.
———. Podział dochodu społecznego" [Division of the national income]. In *Historia, zacofanie, rozwój*, 11–21. Warsaw: PIW, 1983.
———. *Historia, zacofanie, rozwój* [History, backwardness, development]. Warsaw: PIW, 1983.
———. *Wokół historii* [Around history]. Warsaw: PWN, 1988.
———. *Rozdziałki* [Short chapters]. Warsaw: Wydawnictwo TRIO, 1996.
———. *Dziennik czasu okupacji* [Diary from the times of the Nazi occupation]. Warsaw: PIW, 1997.
———. *The Problems and Methods of Economic History*, translated by Richard Szreter. Aldershot: Ashgate, 2001.
———. *Measures and Men*, translated by Richard Szreter. Princeton: Princeton University Press, 2014.
———. *Rozważania o historii* [Reflections on history]. Warsaw: PWN, 1958.
———. *Teoria ekonomiczna ustroju feudalnego. Próba modelu*. Warsaw: PWN, 1962. Translated by L. Garner as *An Economic Theory of the Feudal System. Towards a Model of the Polish Economy, 1500–1800*. London: Verso Books, 1976. Translated by G. Calaforra as *Teoria econòmica del sistema feudal*. València: Universitat de València, 2009. Translated by S. Zembrzuski as *Teoría económica del sistema feudal*. Buenos Aires: Siglo Veintiuno

Editores–Torino: G. Einaudi, 1972. Translated by K. Żaboklicki and B. Bravo as *Teoria economica del sistema feudale: proposta di un modello.* Torino: G. Einaudi, 1976. Translated by M. do Carmo as *Teoría económica do sistema feudal.* Lisboa Edit. Presença; Sao Paulo: Livraria M. Fontes, 1979. Translated by István D. Molnár as *A feudális rendszer gazdasági elmélete.* Budapest: Gondolat, 1985. Translated as *Théorie économique du système féodal: pour un modèle de l'économie polonaise 16e–18e siècles.* Paris, Mouton: de Gruyter, 1970.

Kula, Witold, and Nina Assorodobraj-Kula. *Writing Home. Letters from Immigrants in Brazil and the United States 1890–1891,* translated, edited, and annotated by Josephine Wtulich. New York: Columbia University Press, 1986.

Kula, Witold, and Bronisław Geremek. "Wstęp" [Introduction]. In Fernand Braudel, *Historia i trwanie* [History and longue durée], translated by Bronisław Geremek, 5–19. Warsaw: Czytelnik, 1971.

Kula, Witold, and Jacek Kochanowicz. *Chłopstwo. Problem intelektualny i zagadnienie nauk społecznych* [Peasantry. An intellectual problem and an issue of the social sciences]. Warsaw: Wydział Nauk Ekonomicznych Uniwersytetu Warszawskiego, 1981.

Kula, Witold, and Janina Leskiewiczowa, eds. *Społeczeństwo polskie XVIII i XIX wieku.* [Polish society in the 18th and 19th century]. Vol. 8 *Studia o aktywności społecznej oraz jej politycznym uwarunkowaniu* [Studies in social activities and their political conditions]. Warsaw: IH PAN, 1987.

———. *Społeczeństwo polskie XVIII i XIX wieku. Studia o uwarstwieniu i ruchliwości społecznej* [Polish society in the 18th and 19th century. Studies in social stratification and mobility], vol. 4–7. Warsaw: PWN, 1970–1982.

———. *Przemiany społeczne w Królestwie Polskim 1815–1864.* Warsaw: Ossolineum, 1979.

Kula, Witold, Andrzej Jezierski, and Elżbieta Kaczyńska. "Zagłębie Dąbrowskie" [Zagłębie Dąbrowskie area]. In *Źródła do dziejów klasy robotniczej na ziemiach polskich* [Primary sources on the working class in Polish lands], edited by Natalia Gąsiorowska, Vol. 1:2 *Królestwo Polskie i Białostocczyzna 1864–1900* [Kingdom of Poland and Białystok area], 445–633. Warsaw: PWN, 1962.

Kundera, Milan. "The Tragedy of Central Europe." *New York Review of Books* 31, 7 (1984): 33–38.

Landes, David S. *The Wealth and Poverty of Nations. Why Some Are So Rich and Some So Poor.* New York: W. W. Norton, 1998.

Lenin, Vladimir I. *The Development of Capitalism in Russia.* Collected Works, Vol. 3. Moscow: Progress Publishers, 1964.

Leskiewiczowa, Janina. "Program badania struktur społecznych" [The social stratification research project]. In *Dziedzictwo Witolda Kuli* [Legacy of Witold Kula], papers presented at the conference organized by the Main Board of the Polish Historical Society, 13–14 February, 1989, edited by Marcin Kula. Warsaw: Uniwersytet Warszawski, 1990.

Lewis, W Arthur. "Economic Development with Unlimited Supplies of Labor." *Manchester School.* May, 1954.

———. *The Theory of Economic Growth.* London: Allen & Unwin, 1955.

Litak, Stanisław, "Duchowieństwo diecezji lubelskiej w okresie międzypowstaniowym (1835–1864)" [The clergy in the Lublin diocese in the period between the uprisings (1835–1864)]. In *Społeczeństwo Królestwa Polskiego. Studia o uwarstwieniu i ruchliwości społecznej* [Society of the Kingdom of Poland. Studies on stratification and social mobility], edited by Witold Kula, Vol. 3, 89–164. Warsaw: PWN, 1968.

Łepkowski, Tadeusz. *Polska–narodziny nowoczesnego narodu: 1764–1870* [Poland. The birth of the modern nation 1764–1870]. Warsaw: PWN, 1967.

———. "Słowo końcowe" [Epilogue]. In *Chłopstwo w życiu politycznym Trzeciego Świata. Z rozważań porównawczych nad dziejami ruchów chłopskich* [Peasantry in the political life of the Third World countries. The comparative approach to history of peasant movements], edited by Tadeusz Łepkowski, 184–92. Wrocław: Ossolineum, 1976.

———. *Historia Meksyku* [History of Mexico]. Wrocław: Ossolineum, 1986.

———. "Wątki trzecioświatowe w twórczości Witolda Kuli" [The Third World motifs in the works of Witold Kula]. In *Dziedzictwo Witolda Kuli* [Legacy of Witold Kula], papers presented at the conference organized by the Main Board of the Polish Historical Society on February 13–14, 1989, edited by Marcin Kula, 195–209. Warsaw: Uniwersytet Warszawski, 1990.

Luxemburg, Rosa. *The Industrial Development of Poland*, translated from German by Tessa DeCarlo. New York: Campaigner Publications, 1977.

Małecki, Jan. *Studia nad rynkiem regionalnym Krakowa w XVI wieku* [Studies on regional market in Kraków in the 16th century]. Warsaw: PWN, 1963.

———. *Związki handlowe miast polskich z Gdańskiem w XVI i pierwszej połowie XVII w.* [Trade relations of Polish towns with Gdańsk in the 16th and the first half of the 17th century]. Wrocław: Ossolineum, 1968.

Małowist, Marian. "Kwestia bałtycka w. XVI i XVII w świetle nowszej literatury szwedzkiej." [The Baltic question in the 16th and 17th century according to the newest Swedish literature]. *Przegląd Historyczny* 30 (1932/1933): 104–22.

———. "Handel zagraniczny Sztokholmu i polityka zewnętrzna Szwecji w latach 1470–1503" [Foreign trade of Stockholm and the foreign policy of Sweden in years 1470–1503]. Warsaw: Rozprawy Historyczne Towarzystwa Naukowego Warszawskiego, 1935.

———. "The Baltic and the Black Sea in Medieval Trade." *Baltic and Scandinavian Countries* 3 (1937): 36–42.

———. "Baltic Affairs in the Sixteenth and Seventeenth Centuries in the Light of Historical Literature." *Baltic and Scandinavian Countries* 3 (1937): 417–27.

———. "Bałtyk i Morze Czarne w handlu średniowiecznym" [Baltic Sea and Black Sea in the trade in the Middle Age]. *Jantar* 1 (1937): 69–74.

———. "Polish–Flemish Trade in the Middle Ages." *Baltic and Scandinavian Countries* 4 (1938): 1–9.

———. "Riga und Danzig vom Ausbruch des Dreizehnjahrigen Krieges bis zum Ende des XVI Jahrhunderts." In *Prima Baltijas Veslurnieku Konference.* Riga 1938.

———. "Ryga i Gdańsk. Od wybuchu wojny 13-letniej do końca XVI stulecia" [Riga and Gdansk. From the outbreak of the Thirteen Years War to the end of the 16th century]. In *Polska a Inflanty: praca zbiorowa* [Poland and the Inflants. A collection of essays], 123–38. Gdynia: Instytut Bałtycki, 1939.

———. "Historia gospodarcza Szwecji w świetle najnowszych badań" [Economic history of Sweden according to the newest research]. *Roczniki Dziejów Społecznych i Gospodarczych* 9 (1947): 107–28.

———. *Kaffa—kolonia genueńska na Krymie i problem wschodni w latach 1453–1475* [Kaffa—a Genovese colony on Crimea and the Eastern Problem in the years 1453–1475]. Warsaw: Prace Instytutu Historycznego Uniwersytetu Warszawskiego, 1947.

———. "Z problematyki dziejów gospodarczych strefy bałtyckiej we wczesnym średniowieczu" [On the economic history of the Baltic sphere in the early Middle Ages]. *Roczniki Dziejów Społecznych i Gospodarczych* 10 (1948): 81–120.

———. "Rzemiosło miejskie w średniowieczu" [Urban craftsmanship in the Middle Ages]. *Wiedza i Życie* 18 (1951): 53–66.

———. "Tezy do dyskusji nad budową miasta średniowiecznego" [Theses for discussion on the structure of a medieval town]. Warsaw: Prace Instytutu Urbanistyki i Architektury, 1950.

———. "Miejsce Polski w świecie feudalnym na tle tworzenia się państw wielonarodowych. Tezy" [The place of Poland in the feudal world and the creation of the multinational states. Theses]. In *Materiały z Pierwszej Konferencji Metodologicznej w Otwocku* [Materials from the First Methodological Conference in Otwock]. Warsaw: Instytut Historyczny Uniwersytetu Warszawskiego, 1951.

———. "W sprawie badań nad historią rzemiosła miejskiego w średniowiecznej Polsce" [On researching urban craftsmanship in medieval Poland]. *Roczniki Dziejów Społecznych i Gospodarczych* 13 (1951): 1–22.

———. "W sprawie historii handlu średniowiecznego" [On the history of trade in the Middle Ages]. *Przegląd Historyczny* 42 (1951): 405–12.

———. "Miasta w Polsce średniowiecznej" [Towns in medieval Poland]. *Wiedza i Życie* (1952): 222–32.

———. "Rzemiosło polskie epoki Odrodzenia" [Polish craftsmanship during the Renaissance]. Materials for discussion in PAN for the academic session on the Renaissance 32. Warsaw: PAN, 1953.

———. "Podstawy gospodarcze przywrócenia jedności państwowej Pomorza Gdańskiego z Polską w XV wieku" [Economic base for the restoration of the state's unity of Gdansk maritime region with Poland in the 15th century]. *Przegląd Historyczny* 45:2–3 (1954): 141–87.

———. "Rzemiosło polskie w okresie Odrodzenia" [Polish craftsmanship in the period of the Renaissance]. From the works of the academic session *Renaissance in Poland.* Warsaw: PIW, 1954.

———. *Studia z dziejów rzemiosła w okresie kryzysu feudalizmu w zachodniej Europie w XIV i XV wieku* [Studies on the history of craftsmanship in the period of crisis of feudalism in Western Europe in the 14th and 15th century]. Warsaw: PWN, 1954.

———. "Poland, Russia and Western Trade in the Fifteenth and Sixteenth Centuries." *Past and Present* 13 (1958): 26–41.

———. *Z problematyki Polski feudalnej XIV–XV11 wieku* [On the feudal Poland of the 14th–17th centuries]. Unpublished manuscript. University of Warsaw, 1958.

———. "The Economic and Social Development of the Baltic Countries 15–17th centuries." *The Economic History Review* 12 (1959): 177–89.

———. "Z zagadnień popytu na produkty krajów nadbałtyckich w Europie Zachodniej w XVI wieku" [On the Western European demand for products from the Baltic sphere]. *Przegląd Historyczny* 50 (1959): 720–52.

———. "A Certain Trade Technique in the Baltic Countries in the 15th to 17th Centuries." In *Poland at the 11th International Congress of Historical Sciences*, 103–16. Warsaw: Instytut Historii PAN, 1960.

———. "O niektórych cechach rozwoju gospodarczo-społecznego krajów nadbałtycluch w XV–XVII w." [About some characteristics of the social-economic development of the Baltic countries in the 15th–17th century]. In *VIII Powszechny Zjazd Historyków Polskich* [8th General Congress of the Polish Historians], Vol. 6, 81–104. Warsaw: PAN, 1960.

———. "Polska a przewrót cen w Europie w XVI i XVII w." [Poland and the change of the prices in Europe in the 16th and 17th century]. *Kwartalnik Historyczny* 68 (1961): 315–19.

———. "O społecznych aspektach wczesnej ekspansji kolonialnej" [On the social aspects of the early colonial expansion]. *Przegląd Historyczny* 54:1 (1963): 20–38

———. *Wielkie państwa Sudanu Zachodniego w późnym średniowieczu* [The great countries of Western Sudan in the late Middle Ages]. Warsaw: PWN, 1964.

———. "Uwagi o roli kapitału kupieckiego w Europie Wschodniej" [Remarks on the role of commercial capital in Eastern Europe]. *Przegląd Historyczny* 56:2 (1965): 220–31.

———. "The Problem of the Inequality of Economic Development in Europe in the Later Middle Ages." *The Economic History Review* 19 (1966): 15–28.

———. Review of *Civilisation materiélle, économie et capitalisme, XV–XVIII siècle* by F. Baudel. *Przegląd Historyczny* 58 (1967): 691–96.

———. *Europa a Afryka Zachodnia w dobie wczesnej ekspansji kolonialnej* [Europe and West Africa in the era of early colonial expansion]. Warsaw: PWN, 1969.

———. "Górnictwo w średniowiecznej Europie Środkowej i Wschódniej jako element struktur społeczno-gospodarczych w XII–XV w." [Mining in East Central Europe in the Middle Ages as an element of the socioeconomic structures in the 12th to 15th century]. *Przegląd Historyczny* 63 (1972): 589–604.

———. *Wschód a zachód Europy w XIII–XVI wieku. Konfrontacja struktur społeczno-gospodarczych* [East and West of Europe in the 13th to 16th centuries. Confrontation of social and economic structures]. Warsaw: PWN, 1973.

———. “Problems of the Growth of the National Economy of Central-Eastern Europe in the Late Middle Ages and the Beginning of the Sixteenth Century.” *The Journal of European Economic History* 3 (1974): 319–57.
———. *Konkwistadorzy portugalscy* [Portuguese conquistadors]. Warsaw: PIW, 1976.
———. “Z zagadnień wzrostu i upadku miast Imperium Mongolskiego od XIII do XV wieku” [On the growth and decline of the Mongolian Empire's towns in the 13th to 15th centuries]. *Przegląd Historyczny* 67 (1976): 537–63.
———. *Tamerlan i jego czasy* [Tamerlan and his times]. Warsaw: PIW, 1985.
———. “Podziały gospodarcze i polityczne w Europie w średniowieczu i w dobie wczesnej nowożytnej” [Economic and political divisions in medieval and early modern Europe]. *Przegląd Historyczny* 82 (1991): 233–44.
——— *Europa i jej ekspansja X1V–XV1I w.* [Europe and its expansion in the 14th to 17th centuries]. Warsaw: PWN, 1993.
———. “Some Remarks on the Role of Merchant Capital in Eastern Europe in the Late Middle Ages.” In *Western Europe, Eastern Europe and World Development, 13th to 18th Centuries. A Collection of Essays of Marian Małowist*, edited by Henryk Szlajfer and Jean Batou, 85–100. Leiden–Boston: Brill, 2010.
———. “Commercial Capitalism and Agriculture.” In *Western Europe, Eastern Europe and World Development, 13th to 18th Centuries. A Collection of Essays of Marian Małowist*, edited by Henryk Szlajfer and Jean Batou, 15–71. Leiden–Boston: Brill, 2010.
———. “Kaffa. The Genovese Colony in the Crimea and the Eastern Question (1453–1475).” In *Western Europe, Eastern Europe and World Development, 13th to 18th Centuries. A Collection of Essays of Marian Małowist*, edited by Henryk Szlajfer and Jean Batou, 101–32. Leiden–Boston: Brill, 2010.
———. “East and West Europe in the Thirteenth–Sixteenth Centuries. Confrontation of Social and Economic Structures.” In *Western Europe, Eastern Europe and World Development, 13th to 18th Centuries. A Collection of Essays of Marian Małowist*, edited by Henryk Szlajfer and Jean Batou, 215–28. Leiden–Boston: Brill, 2010.
———. “Problems of the Growth of the National Economy of Central-Eastern Europe in the Late Middle Ages.” In *Western Europe, Eastern Europe and World Development, 13th to 18th Centuries. A Collection of Essays of Marian Małowist*, edited by Henryk Szlajfer and Jean Batou, 161–79. Leiden–Boston: Brill, 2010.
———. “Economic and Political Divisions in Medieval and Early Modern Europe.” In *Western Europe, Eastern Europe and World Development, 13th to 18th Centuries. A Collection of Essays of Marian Małowist*, edited by Henryk Szlajfer and Jean Batou, 229–45. Leiden–Boston: Brill, 2010.
———. “Marian Małowist o historii i historykach” [Marian Małowist on history and historians]. *Res Publica* 7 (1988): 49–50.
Mann, Michael. *The Sources of Social Power*. 2 vols. Cambridge: Cambridge University Press, 1986–93.
Martin, Dominique. “Modernization in the Crisis: From Talcott Parsons to Jürgen Habermas.” In *System Change and Modernization. East-West in Com-*

parative Perspective, edited by W. Adamski. Warsaw: Instytut Filozofii i Socjologii, 1999.

Martinussen, John. *Society, State and Market. A Guide to Competing Theories of Development.* London: Zed Books, 1997.

Matejko Joanna. "Nauczyciele szkół elementarnych na Lubelszczyźnie i Podlasiu w okresie międzypowstaniowym" [Primary school teachers in Lublin and Podlasie areas in the period between 1831 and 1863]. In *Społeczeństwo Królestwa Polskiego. Studia o uwarstwieniu i ruchliwości społecznej* [The society of the Kingdom of Poland. Study on social stratification and mobility], edited by Witold Kula, Vol. 2, 111–53. Warsaw: PWN, 1965.

———. "Profesorowie uczelni warszawskich (1836–1864)" [University professors in Warsaw (1836–1864)]. In *Społeczeństwo Królestwa Polskiego. Studia o uwarstwieniu i ruchliwości społecznej* [The society of the Kingdom of Poland. Study on social stratification and mobility], edited by Witold Kula, Vol. 173–98. Warsaw: PWN, 1965.

Mączak, Antoni. *Sukiennictwo wielkopolskie. XIV–XVII wiek* [Textile industry in the Wielkopolska region, 14th–17th century]. Warsaw: PWN 1955.

———. "Folwark pańszczyźniany a wieś w Prusach Królewskich w XVI/XVII wieku" [Serf-manorial estate and village in Royal Prussia in the sixteenth and the seventeenth centuries]. *Przegląd Historyczny* 47:2 (1956): 353–92.

———. "O przydatności modeli ekonomicznych na przykładzie badań wiejskiej gospodarki feudalnej" *Kwartalnik Historyczny* 3 (1963): 675–96.

———. *Gospodarstwo chłopskie na Żuławach Malborskich w początkach XVII wieku* [Peasant farm in the Malbork Żuławy in the beginning of the 17th century]. Warsaw: PWN, 1962.

———. *U źródeł nowożytnej gospodarki europejskiej* [Origins of the modern European economy]. Warsaw: Wiedza Powszechna, 1967.

———. *Klientela. Nieformalne systemy władzy w Polsce i Europie XVI–XVIII wieku* [Clientage. Informal systems of power in Poland and Europe, 16th–18th century]. Warsaw: Semper, 1994.

———. *Między Gdańskiem a Sundem. Studia nad handlem bałtyckim od połowy XVI do połowy XVII wieku* [Between Gdansk and Öresund. Study on the Baltic trade from the mid-16th until the mid-17th century]. Warsaw: PWN, 1972.

———. *Klientelsysteme im Europa der Fruhen Neuzeit (Schriften des Historischen Kollegs)*. Munich: R. Oldenbourg, 1988.

———. Introduction to *Europa i jej ekspansja XIV–XVII w.* [Europe and its expansion 14th–17th centuries], 5–12. Warsaw: PWN, 1993.

———. *Money, Prices and Power in Poland. 16th and 17th Centuries. A Comparative Approach.* London: Routledge, 1995.

———. *Travel in Early Modern Europe*, translated by Ursula Phillips. London: Polity, 1995.

———. *Odkrywanie Europy* [Discovering Europe]. Warsaw: Novus Orbis, 1998.

Mączak, Antoni, and Henryk Samsonowicz. "La zone baltique; L'un des éléments du marché Européen." *Acta Poloniae Historica* 11 (1965): 71–99.

Mączak, Antoni, and Wojciech Tygielski. *Latem w Tocznabieli* [Summer in Tocznabiel]. Warsaw: Biblioteka Więzi, 2000.

Micińska, Magdalena. *Między Królem Duchem a mieszczaninem. Obraz bohatera narodowego w piśmiennictwie polskim przełomu XIX i XX w. (1890–1914)* [Between the King Spirit and the townsman. The image of the national hero in the Polish literature at the turn of the 19th and 20th century (1890–1914)]. Wrocław: Fundacja na Rzecz Nauki Polskiej, 1995.

Mieszczankowski, Mieczysław. *Struktura agrarna Polski międzywojennej* [The agrarian structure of the interwar Poland]. Warsaw: PWN, 1960.

———. "O naszej Europie" [About our Europe]. *Kultura* 4 (1986): 3–12.

Miłosz, Czesław. *The Captive Mind*. Vintage Books, 1990.

Modzelewski, Karol. *Organizacja gospodarcza państwa piastowskiego X–XIII wiek* [The economic organization of the state of the Piast dynasty from the 10th to the 13th century]. Wrocław: Ossolineum, 1975.

———. *Barbarian Europe*, translated by Ewa Macura. Hamburg: Peter Lang Internationaler Verlag der Wissenschaften, 2015.

Molenda, Danuta. *Górnictwo kruszcowe na terenie złóż śląsko-krakowskich do połowy XVI w.* [Ore mining on the terrains of the Silesian-Cracowian motherlodes until the mid-16th century]. Wrocław: Ossolineum, 1963.

———. "Miasta górnicze Europy środkowo-wschodniej w epoce feudalnej" [Mining towns in Central-Eastern Europe in the feudal epoch]. In *Miasta doby feudalnej w Europie Środkowo-Wschodniej. Przemiany społeczne a układy przestrzenne* [The towns in feudal era in Central-Eastern Europe. Social changes and spatial order], edited by Aleksander Gieysztor and Tadeusz Rosłanowski, 189–215. Warsaw: PWN, 1976.

Molik, Witold. "Wzór osobowy ziemianina w Wielkim Księstwie Poznańskim w drugiej połowie XIX i początkach XX w." [An ideal of a landowner in the Great Duchy of Poznań in the second half of the 19th century]. In *Ziemiaństwo polskie 1795–1945. Zbiór prac o dziejach warstwy i ludzi* [Polish landed gentry 1795–1945. Collection of works about the history of social stratum and individuals], edited by Janina Leskiewiczowa, 121–46. Warsaw: PWN, 1985.

Moore, Barrington, Jr. *Social Origins of Democracy and Dictatorship. Lord and Peasant in the Making of the Modern World*. Boston: Beacon Press, 1966.

Morawska, Ewa. Foreword to "Historical and Comparative Sociology Section." American Sociological Association, Newsletter 12 (1999): 1–4.

Morawski, Witold. *Socjologia ekonomiczna: problemy, teoria, empiria* [Economic sociology: problems, theory, facts]. Warsaw: PWN, 2001.

Naumann, Friedrich. *Mitteleuropa*. Berlin: Reimer, 1915.

Neumann, Iver B. "Russia as Central Europe's Constituting Other." *Eastern European Politics and Society* 7:2 (1993): 349–69.

———. "European Identity, EU Expansion and the Integration/Exclusion Nexus." *Alternatives* 23:3 (1998): 397–416.

———. "Forgetting the Central Europe of the 1980s." In *Central Europe: Core or Periphery*, edited by Christopher Lord. Copenhagen: Copenhagen Business School Press, 2000.

Nicholson, Linda J. *Gender and History: The Limits of Social Theory in the Age of the Family*. New York: Columbia University Press, 1986.
North, Douglass C. *Institutions, Institutional Change and Economic Performance*. Cambridge: Cambridge University Press, 1990.
———. *Structure and Change in Economic History*. New York: Norton, 1981.
North, Douglass C., and Robert R. Thomas. *The Rise of the Western World. A New Economic History*. Cambridge: Cambridge University Press, 1973.
Nowicka, Ewa. "Dyfuzja kulturowa" [Cultural diffusion]. In *Encyklopedia socjologii* [Encyclopedia of sociology]. Vol. 1. Warsaw: Oficyna Naukowa, 1998.
Olszewski, Daniel. "Struktura społeczna duchowieństwa diecezji kielecko-krakowskiej (1835–1864)" [The social structure of the clergy in the Kielce–Cracow diocese (1835–1864). In *Społeczeństwo polskie XVIII i XIX wieku. Studia o uwarstwieniu i ruchliwości społecznej* [Polish society in the 18th and 19th century. Study on social stratification and mobility], edited by Witold Kula and Janina Leskiewiczowa, Vol. 6, 250. Warsaw: PWN, 1980.
Orczyk, Józef. "Conditions and Extent of Evolution in Agrarian Structure in the Interwar Poland against Comparative Background." *Studia Historiae Oeconomica* 11 (1976): 241–50.
Orzechowski, Kazimierz. "Pozostałości przedziałów stanowych w kapitalizmie. Chłopi" [The vestiges of the estate social divisions in capitalism. The peasants]. In *Społeczeństwo polskie XVIII i XIX wieku. Studia o aktywności społecznej oraz jej politycznym uwarunkowaniu* [Polish society in the 18th and 19th century. Study on social activity and its political bacground], edited by Janina Leskiewiczowa, Vol. 8, 85–94. Warsaw: PWN, 1987.
Ossowska, Maria. *Ethos rycerski i jego odmiany* [Chivalric ethos and its variants]. Warsaw: PWN, 1973.
———. *Bourgeois Morality*. London: Routledge & Kegan Paul, 1986.
———. *Social Determinants of Moral Ideas*. Philadelphia: University of Pennsylvania Press, 1971.
Ostrowski, Marian, and Zdzisław Sadowski. *Wyzwania rozwojowe* [Developmental challenges]. Warsaw: PWE 1978.
Palma, J. Gabriel. "Dependency." In *The New Palgrave Dictionary of Economics,* edited by John Eatwell, Murray Milgate and Peter Newman. London: Macmillan Press, 1988, http://www.dictionaryofeconomics.com/article?id=pde2008_D000077 (accessed on 25 July 2017).
Parsons, Talcott. *Societies. Evolutionary and Comparative Perspective*. Englewood Cliff, NJ: Prentice Hall. 1966.
———. *The System of Modern Societies*. Englewood Cliff, NJ: Prentice Hall, 1971.
———. "The Industrial Revolution and Asynchronism in Social Development." *Studia Historiae Oeconomicae* 11 (1976): 101–18.
———, ed. *Gospodarka przemysłowa i początki cywilizacji technicznej w rolniczych krajach Europy* [Industrial economy and the beginnings of the technical civilization in the European agricultural countries]. Wrocław: Ossolineum, 1977.
Polanyi, Karl. *The Great Transformation*. Boston: Beacon Press, 1957.

Pomorski, Jan. *Historyk i metodologia* [The historian and methodology]. Lublin: Uniwersytet im. Marii Curie-Sklodowskiej, 1991.

Popper, Karl. *The Poverty of Historicism.* London: Routledge, 1969.

———. *The Open Society and its Enemies.* London: Routledge, 2011.

Prebisch, Raul. *Change and Development: Latin America's Great Task; Report Submitted to the Inter-American Development Bank.* New York: Praeger, 1971.

Ragin, Charles, and Daniel Chirot. "The World System of Immanuel Wallerstein: Sociology and Politics as History." In *Vision and Method in Historical Sociology,* edited by Theda Skocpol, 276–312. Cambridge: Cambridge University Press, 1984.

Rostow, Walt W. *The Stages of Economic Growth. A Non-Communist Manifesto.* Cambridge: Cambridge University Press, 1960.

———, ed. *The Economics of Take-Off into Sustained Growth. Proceedings of a Conference Held by the International Economics Association.* London: Macmillan, 1964.

Roszkowski, Wojciech. *Land Reforms in East Central Europe after World War One.* Warsaw: Instytut Studiów Politycznych PAN, 1995.

Rożenowa, Halina. "Pochodzenie społeczno-zawodowe funkcjonariuszy drogi żelaznej warszawsko-wiedeńskiej" [Social and professional origins of the officials of the Warsaw-Vienna railway]. In *Społeczeństwo Królestwa Polskiego. Studia o uwarstwieniu i ruchliwości społecznej* [Society of the Kingdom of Poland. Study on social stratification and mobility], edited by Witold Kula, Vol. 3, 295–336. Warsaw: PWN, 1968.

Rueschemeyer, Dietrich, and Theda Skocpol. *States, Social Knowledge, and the Origins of Modern Social Policies.* Princeton: Princeton University Press, 1996.

Rusiński, Władysław. "W sprawie struktury gospodarstw chłopskich i związków rolnictwa z przemysłem w końcu XVIII w." [On the structure of the peasants' farms and the connections of agriculture with industry at the end of the 18th century]. *Roczniki Dziejów Społecznych i Gospodarczych* 37 (1976): 103–12.

Rutkowski, Jan. "La genèse du régime de la corvée dans l'Europe Centrale depuis la fin du Moyen Âge." In *La Pologne au sixième Congrès International des Sciences Historiques,* Oslo: 1928, Warsaw-Lviv: 1930.

———. *Badania nad podziałem dochodów w Polsce w czasach nowożytnych* [Research on the income divison in Poland in modern era]. Kraków: PAU, 1938.

———. *Studia z dziejów wsi polskiej XVI–XVIII w.* [Study on the history of the Polish countryside in the 16th and 17th century], selection and introduction by Witold Kula, 87. Warsaw: PWN, 1956

———. *Wokół teorii ustroju feudalnego: prace historyczne* [Around the theory of the feudal system: historical works]. Warsaw: PIW, 1982.

———. *Wieś europejska późnego feudalizmu (XVI–XVIII w)* [The European countryside in the late feudalism (16th–18th century)]. Warsaw: PWN, 1986.

Rychard, Andrzej. *Reforms Adaptation and Breakthrough. The Sources of and Limits to Institutional Changes in Poland.* Translated by Katarzyna Niżnik. Warsaw: Instytut Filozofii i Socjologii PAN, 1994.

Rzepniewska, Danuta. "Imigracja do Warszawy" [Immigration in Warsaw]. In *Społeczeństwo Królestwa Polskiego. Studia o uwarstwieniu i ruchliwości społecznej* [The society of the Kingdom of Poland. Studies on social stratification and mobility], edited by Witold Kula, Vol. I, 123–72. Warsaw: PWN, 1965.

———. "Wiejscy oficjaliści" [Village officials]. In *Społeczeństwo Królestwa Polskiego. Studia o uwarstwieniu i ruchliwości społecznej* [Society of the Kingdom of Poland. Study on social stratification and mobility], vol.1, edited by Witold Kula, 199–236. Warsaw: PWN, 1965.

Said, Edward W. *Orientalism.* New York: Vintage Books, 1977.

Samsonowicz, Henryk. *Rzemiosło wiejskie w Polsce X1V–XVI w.* [Rural craftsmanship in Poland, 14–16th century]. Warsaw: PWN, 1954.

———. *Badania nad kapitałem mieszczańskim Gdańska w drugiej połowie XV wieku* [Research on bourgeois capital in Gdańsk in the second half of the 15th century]. Warsaw: PWN 1960.

———. "Polska widziana przez Hanzę w I połowie XVI wieku" [Poland as seen by the Hanseatic League in the first half of the 16th century]. In *Między polityką a kulturą. Studia ofiarowane A. Wyczańskiemu w 75-lecie urodzin i 50-lecie pracy naukowej* [Between politics and culture. Studies dedicated to A. Wyczański on his 75th birthday and the 50th anniversary of his academic work], edited by Cezary Kuklo, 27–30. Białystok–Warsaw: PWN, 1999.

———. *Późne średniowiecze miast nadbałtyckich. Studia nad dziejami Hanzy nad Bałtykiem w XIV–XV w.* [The late Middle Ages of the Baltic towns. Study on the history of the Hanseatic League on the Baltic Sea in the 14th and 15th century]. Warsaw: PWN, 1968.

———. "Recherches polonaises sur l'histoire de la Baltique au declin du Moyen Age (XIVe–XVe siècle)." *Acta Poloniae Historica* 23 (1971): 150–62.

——— "In Memoriam: Marian Małowist." *Kwartalnik Historyczny* 3 (1988): 297–300.

Schöpflin, George, and Nancy Wood, eds. *In Search of Central Europe.* Cambridge: Polity Press, 1989.

Seton-Watson, Hugh. *Nations and States.* London: Methuen, 1977.

Singer, Hans W. *Growth, Development, and Trade. Selected Essays of Hans W. Singer.* Northampton, MA: 1998.

Singer, Hans W, and Sumit Roy. *Economic Progress and Prospects in the Third World. Lessons of Development Experience since 1945.* Brookfield, VT.: Edward Elgar, 1993.

Skocpol, Theda. *Social Revolutions in the Modern World.* Cambridge–New York: Cambridge University Press, 1994.

———. "Sociology's Historical Imagination." In *Vision and Method in Historical Sociology,* edited by Theda Skocpol, 1–21. Cambridge: Cambridge University Press, 1984.

———. *States and Social Revolutions. A Comparative Analysis of France, Russia, and China.* Cambridge: Cambridge University Press, 1979.

Smith, Anthony D. *The Ethnic Revival.* Cambridge: Cambridge University Press, 1981.

———. *The Ethnic Origins of Nations*. Oxford: Blackwell, 1986.

Smith, Dennis. *The Rise of Historical Sociology*. Philadelphia: Temple University Press, 1991.

Smoleńska, Barbara. "Oficjaliści dóbr wilanowskich (1800–1854)" [The officials of the Wilanow possessions]. In *Społeczeństwo polskie XVIII i XIX wieku. Studia o uwarstwieniu i ruchliwości społecznej* [Polish society in the 18th and 19th century. Study on social stratification and mobility], edited by Witold Kula and Janina Leskiewiczowa, Vol. 4, 121–86. Warsaw: PWN, 1970.

So, Alvin. *Social Change and Development. Modernization, Dependency and World-System Theories*. London: Sage, 1990.

Sosnowska, Anna. "Tu, Tam—pomieszanie" [Here, there—confusion], *Studia Socjologiczne* 4 (1997): 61–86.

———. "Teorie zmiany i rozwoju społecznego a zmiany w Europie Wschodniej po 1989 roku. O potrzebie perspektywy globalnej" [Theories of change and social development and the changes in Eastern Europe after 1989. About the need for a global perspective]. *Kultura i Społeczeństwo* 1 (1998): 61–72.

———. "Europa Środkowo-Wschodnia a orientalizm" [Central-Eastern Europe and the orientalism]. *Studia Socjologiczne* 2 (1999): 101–109.

———. "Searching for a Theoretical Framework for Eastern Europe: Interpretations in Social Theory." *Sisyphus* 12 (1999): 51–63.

———. "Acquiescent versus Humiliated Periphery. Global Attitudes, Political Ideologies and Economic Interests in Polish Politics." In *Regional Issues in Polish Politics*, edited by Tomasz Zarycki and George Kolankiewicz. London: School of Slavonic and Eastern European Studies, 2003.

Srinivasan, T.N. "Introduction." In *Handbook of Developmental Economics*, by H. Chenery and T.N. Srinivasan, 61–72. Amsterdam: Elsevier Science Publishers, 1988.

Steinmetz, George. "Ideas in Exile. Refugees from Nazi Germany and the Failure to Transplant Historical Sociology into the United States." *International Journal of Culture Politics and Society* (2009): 1–27.

Stemplowski, Ryszard, ed. *Ameryka Łacińska. Dyskusja o rozwoju* [Latin America. Debate on development], translated by Izabela Budzyńska and others. Warsaw: Czytelnik, 1987.

Stobiecki, Rafał. *Historia pod nadzorem. Spory o nowy model historii w Polsce (II połowa lat czterdziestych-początek pięćdziesiątych)* [History under supervision. Disputes about the new model of historiography in Poland (second half of the 1940s and early 1950s)]. Łódź: Wydawnictwo Uniwersytetu Łódzkiego, 1993.

Styś, Wincenty. *Rozdrobnienie gruntów chłopskich w byłym zaborze austriackim w latach 1787–1931* [Fragmentation of the peasants' plots in the former Austrian partition in the years 1787–1931]. Lviv: Gebethner i Wolf, 1934.

———. *Wpływ uprzemysłowienia na ustrój rolny* [The influence of industrialization on the agrarian system]. Lviv: Towarzystwo Nauk, 1936.

———. *Drogi postępu gospodarczego wsi. Studium szczegółowe na przykładzie zbiorowości próbnej wsi Husowa* [The roads of economic progress of the countryside. Detailed study on the example of the sample community of the village Husowa]. Wrocław: Wrocławskie Towarzystwo Naukowe, 1947.

Sugar, Peter F., ed. *Ethnic Diversity and Conflict in Eastern Europe.* Santa Barbara: ABC-Ctio, 1980.

Sugar, Peter F., and Ivo J. Lederer, eds. *Nationalism in Eastern Europe.* Seattle: University of Washington Press, 1969.

Szacki, Jerzy. *History of Sociological Thought,* Vol. 2. Westport, Conn.: Greenwood Press, 1979.

Szczepański, Jan. "Burmistrzowie miasteczek Królestwa Polskiego 1815–1866 (na przykładzie guberni radomskiej)" [The mayors of the small towns in the Kingdom of Poland 1815–1866 (on the example of the Radom province)]. In *Społeczeństwo polskie XVIII i XIX wieku. Studia o grupach elitarnych* [Polish society in the 18th and 19th century. Studies on the elite groups], vol. 7, edited by Janina Leskiewiczowa, 199–218. Warsaw: PWN, 1982.

Szlajfer, Henryk. *Modernizacja zależności. Kapitalizm i rozwój w Ameryce Łacińskiej* [Modernization of dependency. Capitalism and the development in Latin America]. Wrocław: Ossolineum, 1985.

Sztompka, Piotr. *The Sociology of Social Change.* Oxford: Blackwell, 1993.

Szűcs, Jenő. "The Three Historical Regions of Europe: An outline." *Acta Historica Academiae Scientiarum Hungaricae,* Vol. 29, No. 2/4, Budapest: Institute of History, Research Center for Humanities, Hungarian Academy of Sciences, 1983.

———. *Trzy Europy.* Lublin: Instytut Europy Środkowo-Wschodniej, 1994.

Śliwowska, Wiktoria. "Udział w ruchu niepodległościowym" [Participation in the independence movement]. In *Przemiany społeczne w Królestwie Polskim 1815–1864* [Social changes in the Kingdom of Poland 1815–1864], edited by Witold Kula and Janina Leskiewiczowa, 421–62. Wrocław: Ossolineum, 1979.

Tajerowa, Stefania. *O gospodarce mieszanej w krajach "trzeciego świata"* [About the mixed economy in Third-World countries]. Warsaw: PWN, 1967.

Taylor, John G. *From Modernization to Modes of Production. A Critique of the Sociologies of Development and Underdevelopment.* London: Macmillan, 1979.

Tazbir, Janusz. "Stosunek do obcych w dobie baroku" [Attitude toward foreigners in the Baroque period]. In *Swojskość i cudzoziemszczyzna w dziejach kultury polskiej* [Familiarity and foreignness in the history of Polish culture], edited by Zofia Stefanowska, 80–112. Warsaw: PWN, 1973.

Thompson, Edward R. *The Making of the English Working Class.* New York: Pantheon Books, 1963.

———. *As Sociology Meets History.* New York: Academic Press, 1981.

———. *Big Structures, Large Processes, Huge Comparisons.* New York: Russel Sage Foundation, 1984.

———. *Coercion, Capital, and European States, AD 990–1990.* Cambridge: Blackwell Publishers, 1990.

Tilly, Charles, Louise Tilly, and Richard Tilly. *The Rebellious Century (1830–1930).* Cambridge, Mass.: Harvard University Press, 1975.

Todorova, Maria. *Imagining the Balkans*. Oxford: Oxford University Press, 1997.

Tomaszewski, Jerzy. "Rewolucja w Europie środkowej i wschodniej (1917–1919)" [Revolution in Central and Eastern Europe (1917–1919)]. *Człowiek i Światopogląd* 9 (1974): 134–47.

———. "Gospodarka krajów Europy środkowej i południowo-wschodniej w latach międzywojennych" [The economy in the countries of Central and southeastern Europe during the interwar years]. In *Dyktatury w Europie Środkowowschodniej 1918–1939. Konferencja naukowa w Instytucie Historii PAN, 2–3 grudnia 1971* [Dictatorships in Central-Eastern Europe 1918–1939. Academic conference in the Institute of History PAN, 2–3 Dec. 1971], edited by Janusz Żarnowski, 63–82. Wrocław: Ossolineum-PAN, 1983.

Topolska, Maria. "Bibliografia prac profesora Jerzego Topolskiego za lata 1951–1987" [Bibliography of professor Jerzy Topolski's works for the years 1951–1987]. In *Między polityką a kulturą. Studia ofiarowane A. Wyczańskiemu w 75-lecie urodzin i 50-lecie pracy naukowej* [Between politics and culture. Studies dedicated to A. Wyczański on his 75th birthday and the 50th anniversary of his academic work], edited by Cezary Kuklo. Białystok–Warsaw: PWN, 1999.

———. *Rozwój latyfundium arcybiskupstwa gnieźnieńskiego od XVI do XVIII wieku* [Development of the demesne of the Gniezno Archbishopric from the 16th to the 18th century]. Poznań: PWN, 1955.

———. *Gospodarstwo wiejskie w dobrach arcybiskupstwa gnieźnieńskiego od XVI do XVIII wieku* [The peasant economy in the demesne of the Gniezno Archbishopric from the 16th to the 18th century]. Poznań: PWN, 1958.

———. "Teoria ekonomiczna ustroju feudalnego. Na marginesie kiążki Witolda Kuli" [An economic theory of the feudal system. On the margins of Witold Kula's book]. *Ekonomista* 1 (1964): 137–44.

———, ed. *Dzieje Gniezna* [History of Gniezno].Warsaw: PWN, 1965.

———. *Narodziny kapitalizmu w Europie w XIV–XVII wieku* [The birth of capitalism in Europe from the 14th to the 17th century]. Warsaw: PWN, 1965.

———, ed. *Żnin. 700 lat dziejów miasta* [Znin. 700 years of the town's history]. Bydgoszcz: PWN, 1965.

———. "Causes of Dualism in the Economic Development of Modern Europe (A Tentative New Theory)." *Studia Historiae Oeconomicae* 3 (1968): 3–12.

———, ed. *Dzieje Wielkopolski* [The history of the Wielkopolska region], vol. 1. Poznań: Wydaw. Pozn., 1969.

———. *Świat bez historii* [A World without history]. Warsaw: Wiedza Powszechna, 1972.

———. "Economic Decline in Poland from the Sixteenth to the Eighteenth Centuries." In *Essays in European Economic History 1500–1800*, edited by Peter Marle, 127–42. Oxford: Clarendon Press, 1974.

———. "The Manorial–Serf Economy in Central and Eastern Europe in the 16th and 17th Centuries." *Agricultural History* 48: 3 (1974): 341–52.

———. *Methodology of History*. Warsaw: PWN, 1976.

———. *Gospodarka polska a europejska w XVI–XVII wieku* [Polish and European economy in the 16th–17th centuries]. Poznań: Wydawnictwo Poznańskie, 1977.
———. "Działalność gospodarcza Mikołaja Reja. Przykład aktywizacji szlachty." In *Gospodarka polska w XVI–XVII wieku*, 99–111.
———. "Model gospodarczy Wielkopolski w XVIII wieku: Przykład regionu rozwijającego się" [Economic model of the 18th-century Wielkopolska region. An example of developing region]. In *Gospodarka polska a europejska w XVI–XVII wieku*, 267–81.
———. "Wielki przewrót w gospodarce europejskiej w XVI wieku: przyczyny rozwoju i struktura gospodarki folwarczno-pańszczyźnianej" [The great turn in the European economy of the 16th century: Origins of development and structure of the serf–manorial economy]. In *Gospodarka polska a europejska w XVI–XVII wieku*, 71–84.
———. "Założenia modelu gospodarki polskiej XVI–XVIII wieku" [A model of the Polish economy in the 16th–18th century]. In *Gospodarka polska a europejska w XVI–XVII wieku*, 9–46.
———. *Marksizm i historia* [Marxism and history]. Warsaw: PIW, 1977.
———. *Nowe idee współczesnej historiografii: o roli teorii w badaniach historycznych* [New ideas in the historiography: on the role of theory in the historical research]. Poznań: Wydawnictwo Poznańskie, 1980.
———. *Prawda i model w historiografii* [The truth and the model in historiography]. Łódź: Wydawnictwo Łódzkie, 1982.
———. "Modele teoretyczne i historyczne w interpretacji rozwoju feudalizmu w Europie Wschodniej (X–XVIII w.)" [Theoretical and historical models and interpreting the Eastern European feudalism (10th–18th century)]. In *Prawda i model w historiografii* [Truth and modeling in historiography], 267–334. Łódź: Wydawnictwo Łódzkie 1982.
———. *Zarys dziejów Polski.* [Brief history of Poland]. Warsaw: Interpress, 1982.
———. *Teoria wiedzy historycznej* [Theory of historical knowledge]. Poznań: Wydawnictwo Poznańskie, 1983.
———. *Metodologia historii* [Methodology of history]. Warsaw: PWN, 1984.
———. "Podział dochodu narodowego jako oś syntezy historycznej. Koncepcja Jana Rutkowskiego" [The division of the national income as an axis of the historical interpretation. The concept of Jan Rutkowski]. *Ekonomista* 4–5 (1985): 791–806.
———. *Jan Rutkowski (1886–1949): o nowy model historii* [Jan Rutkowski (1886–1949): a new model of historical research]. Warsaw: PWN, 1986.
———. *Dzieje Pleszewa* [History of Pleszew]. Kalisz: Pleszewskie Towarzystwo Kulturalne, 1989.
———. "Kierunek rozwoju nauki historycznej w Wielkopolsce" [The direction of development of the historical science in Wielkopolska region]. In *Wybitni historycy wielkopolscy* [Prominent historians of Wielkopolska region], edited by Jerzy Strzelczyk, 11–28. Poznań: Wydawnictwo Naukowe Uniwersytetu im. Adama Mickiewicza, 1989.

———, ed. *Narration and Explanation. Contributions to the Methodology of the Historical Research.* Amsterdam: Brill, 1990.

———, ed. *Historiography between Modernism and Postmodernism: Contributions to the Methodology of Historical Research.* Amsterdam: Brill, 1994.

———. *Polska w czasach nowożytnych. Od środkowoeuropejskiej potęgi do utraty niepodległości (1501–1795)* [Poland in modern times. From regional power to the loss of sovereignty (1501–1795)]. Poznań: Wydawnictwo Naukowe Uniwersytetu im. Adama Mickiewicza, 1994.

———. "Cywilizacje i kultury V–XX wieku" [Civilizations and cultures from the 5th to the 20th century]. In *Wielka encyklopedia geografii świata* [Great encyclopedia of the world's geography], Vol. 10. Poznań: Kurpisz, 1998.

Topolski, Jerzy. *Położenie i walka klasowa chłopów w XVIII w. w dobrach arcybiskupstwa gnieźnieńskiego* [The life conditions and the class struggle of the peasants in the demesne of the Gniezno Archbishopric in the 18th century]. Warsaw: PWN, 1956.

Topolski, Jerzy, and Cezary Kuklo, eds. *Studia nad gospodarką, społeczeństwem i rodziną w Europie późnofeudalnej. Księga ofiarowana Profesorowi Andrzejowi Wyczańskiemu w 60-lecie urodzin i 40-lecie pracy naukowej* [Studies on the economy, society and family in late feudal Europe. The book dedicated to Professor Andrzej Wyczański on the 60th birthday and 40th anniversary of his academic work]. Lublin: Wydawnictwo Lubelskie, 1987.

———, eds. *Między polityką a kulturą. Studia ofiarowane A. Wyczańskiemu w 75-lecie urodzin i 50-lecie pracy naukowej* [Between the politics and culture. Studies dedicated to A. Wyczański on his 75th birthday and the 50th anniversary of his academic work]. Białystok/Warsaw: PWN, 1999.

Topolski, Jerzy, Ewa Domańska, and Wojciech Wrzosek. *Między modernizmem a postmodernizmem. Historiografia wobec zmian w filozofii historii* [Between modernism and postmodernism. Historiography toward the changes in the philosophy of history]. Poznań: Uniwersytet im. Adama Mickiewicza, 1994.

Topolski, Jerzy, and Antoni Gąsiorowski, eds. *Wielkopolski słownik biograficzny* [Who is who in the Wielkapolska region]. Poznań: PWN, 1981.

Topolski, Jerzy, Zbigniew Drozdowicz, and Wojciech Wrzosek. *Swoistość poznania historycznego* [The peculiarity of the historical cognition]. Poznań: Wydawnictwo Naukowe Uniwersytetu im. Adama Mickiewicza, 1990.

Trimberger, Ellen K. "E.P. Thomposon: Understanding the Process of History." In *Vision and Method in Historical Sociology,* edited by Theda Skocpol, 211–43. Cambridge: Cambridge University Press, 1984.

Tymieniecki, Kazimierz. "L'histoire sociale de l'Europe orientale au Moyen Âge. Les problemes foundamentaux." In *La Pologne au VIe Congrès Internationales des Sciences Historiques.* Oslo (1928): 233–48.

———. *Procesy twórcze formowania się społeczeństwa polskiego w wiekach średnich* [The formation processes of the Polish society in the Middle Ages]. Warsaw: E. Wende, 1921.

———. *Kształtowanie się społeczeństwa średniowiecznego (Polska na tle Słowiańszczyzny zachodniej)* [Formation of the medieval society (Poland and the Western Slavs)]. Poznań: Wydawnictwo Poznańskie, 1996.

Trzeciakowski, Lech, and Krzysztof Markowski, eds. *Samomodernizacja społeczeństw w XIX wieku: Irlandczycy, Czesi, Polacy* [Self-modernization of the societies in the 19th century: The Irish, Czechs, Poles]. Poznań: Instytut Historii Uniwersytetu im. Adama Mickiewicza, 1999.

Urwanowicz, Jerzy, ed. *Władza i prestiż. Magnateria Rzeczypospolitej w XVI–XVIII wieku* [Power and prestige. Magnates of the Polish-Lithuanian Commonwealth from the 16th to the 18th century]. Białystok: Wydawnictwo Uniwersytetu w Białymstoku, 2003.

Walicki, Andrzej. *A History of Russian Thought from the Enlightenment to Marxism.* Stanford: Stanford University Press, 1979.

Wallerstein, Immanuel. *The Modern World System. Capitalist Agriculture and the Origins of the European World Economy in the Sixteenth Century.* New York: Academic Press, 1974.

———. *The Capitalist World Economy: Essays.* Cambridge: Cambridge University Press, 1979.

———. "Economic Theories and Historical Disparities of Development." In *Economic Theory and History*, edited by J. Kocka and Gy. Ránki, 17–26. Budapest: Akadémiai Kiadó, 1985.

———. "Development: Lodestar or Illusion." *Economic and Political Weekly*, September 24th, 1991.

———. *Geopolitics and Geoculture.* Cambridge–Paris: Cambridge University Press–Editions de la Maison des Sciences de l'Homme, 1991.

———. *Unthinking Social Science. The Limits of Nineteenth-Century Paradigms.* Cambridge, Mass.: Polity Press, 1991.

———. *After Liberalism.* New York: New Press, 1995.

Wandycz, Piotr S. *The Price of Freedom: A History of East Central Europe from the Middle Ages to the Present.* London: Routledge, 1992.

———. "Polska" [Poland]. In *Historiografia krajów Europy Środkowo-Wschodniej: Polska, Czechosłowacja, Węgry, Rumunia, była Jugosławia, Bułgaria* [Historiography of the Central-Eastern European countries: Poland, Czechoslovakia, Hungary, Romania, former Yugoslavia, Bulgaria], edited by Jerzy Kłoczowski and Paweł Kras, 21–45. Lublin: Instytut Europy Środkowo-Wschodniej, 1997.

Weber, Max. *Economy and Society. An Outline of Interpretive Sociology*, vol. 1–2. Berkeley: University Of California Press, 1978.

———. *The Protestant Ethic and the Spirit of Capitalism, and Other Writings.* London: Penguin, 2002.

Webster, Andrew. *Introduction to the Sociology of Development.* Atlantic Highlands, NJ: Humanities Press International, 1990.

Werbner, Pniny, and Tariq Modood. *Debating Cultural Hybridity: Multi-Cultural Identities and the Politics of Anti-Racism.* London: Zed Books, 1997.

Wiślicz, Tomasz. "Weddings, Christenings and Funerals in the Sixteenth–Eighteenth Centuries. Life and Death Culture." *Acta Poloniae Historica* 83 (2001): 263–64.

———. *Upodobanie: Małżeństwo i związki nieformalne na wsi polskiej XVII–XVIII wieku. Wyobrażenia społeczne i jednostkowe doświadczenia* [Marriage and informal relationships in the Polsih countryside in the 17th and the 18th centuries]. Wrocław: Chronicon, 2012.

Wnuk-Lipiński, Edmund. "Is a Theory of Post-Communist Transformation Possible?" In *After Communism: A Multidisciplinary Approach to Radical Social Change,* edited by Edmund Wnuk-Lipiński, 5–18. Warsaw: ISP PAN, 1995.

Wolff, Larry. *Inventing Eastern Europe. The Map of Civilization on the Mind of Enlightenment.* Stanford: Stanford University Press, 1994.

Wyczański, Andrzej. "Zastosowanie mikrofilmu w organizacji bibliotek i pracy naukowej" [Using of microfilm in libraries and academic research]. *Przegląd Biblioteczny* 3–4 (1950): 234–46.

———. "Mikrofilm. Mały zwitek mikrofilmu zastępuje kilkusetstronicową książkę" [Microfilm. A small roll of microfilm replaces a book of hundreds of pages]. *Problemy* 8 (1951): 540–43.

———. "Z dziejów reform skarbowo-wojskowych za Zygmunta 1. Próby relucji pospolitego ruszenia" [From the history of king Zigmunt I's reforms of the treasury and military. Attempts to replace the noble military service with taxes]. *Przegląd Historyczny* 43: 2 (1952): 287–304.

———. "Rozdawnictwo dóbr królewskich za Zygmunta I" [The free distribution of royal demesnes during the reign of the king Zigmunt I]. *Przegląd Historyczny* 44: 3 (1953): 281–308.

———. *Francja wobec państw jagiellońskich w latach 1515–1529. Studium z dziejów francuskiej polityki zagranicznej epoki Odrodzenia* [France and the Jagiellonian countries in the period 1515–1529. A study on the history of French foreign policy during the Renaissance]. Wrocław: Ossolineum, 1954.

———. "O folwarku szlacheckim w Polsce XVI stulecia. (Uwagi dyskusyjne)" [About the Polish noble folwark in 16th-century Poland. (Remarks for discussion)]. *Kwartalnik Historyczny* 61: 4 (1954): 169–91.

———. *Historia Polski* [History of Poland], edited by Tadeusz Manteuffel, Vol. 1, part 2. Warsaw: 1957.

———. "O francuskich badaniach powojennych nad historią wsi w XV-XVIII w." [About the French postwar historical research on the countryside in the 15th through the 18th century]. *Kwartalnik Historyczny* 64: 3 (1957): 252-61.

———. "Polska w stosunkach politycznych Europy I połowy XVI w." [Poland in the European political relations in the first half of the 16th century]. In *Pamiętnik VIII Powszechnego Zjazdu Historyków Polskich w Krakowie, 14–17 IX 1958 r.* [Diary of the 8th General Congress of the Polish Historians in Cracow, 14–17 September 1958]. Warsaw: Polskie Towarzystwo Historyczne, 1958.

———. *Studia nad folwarkiem szlacheckim w Polsce w latach 1500–1580* [Studies on the Polish folwark 1500–1580]. Warsaw: PWN, 1960.

———. "Uwagi o konsumpcji żywności w Polsce XVI w." [Remarks about the food consumption in Poland in the 16th century]." *Kwartalnik Historii Kultury Materialnej* 8:1 (1960): 15–42.

———. "Plony zbóż w folwarkach królewskich województwa lubelskiego w 1564" [Grain crops in the royal folwarks of the Lublin voivodship in 1564]. *Studia z dziejów gospodarstwa wiejskiego* [Studies on the history of the rural economy], edited by Janina Leskiewiczowa, Vol. 4, no. 1 [the entire issue] Warsaw: PWN, 1961.
———. "Rola Uniwersytetu Jagiellońskiego w pierwszej połowie XVI w." [The role of the Jagiellonian University in the first half of the 16th century]. *Kwartalnik Historyczny* 71 (1964): 3–16.
———. *Studia nad gospodarką starostwa korczyńskiego 1500–1660* [Studies on the economy of the Korczyn district office 1500–1660]. Warsaw: PWN, 1964.
———. "Uniwersytet Krakowski w czasach Złotego Wieku" [Krakow University during the golden age]. In *Dzieje Uniwersytetu Jagiellońskiego w latach 1364–1764* [The history of the Jagiellonian University, 1364–1764], vol. 1, edited by Kazimierz Lepszy, 221–52. Kraków: PWN, 1964.
———. "Kultura polskiego Odrodzenia. Próba określenia historycznego mentalności" [The culture of the Polish Renaissance. An attempt at historical description of mentality]. *Odrodzenie i Reformacja w Polsce* 10 (1965): 11–52.
———. *Polska–Rzeczą Pospolitą szlachecką 1454–1764* [Poland: a res publica of the nobility 1454–1764]. Warsaw: PWN, 1965.
———. "Czy rzeczywiście czasy upadku?" [Was it really the time of the fall (of the Polish-Lithuanian Commowealth)?]. *Tygodnik Demokratyczny* 27 (1966): 3 and 7.
———. "Polska służba dyplomatyczna w latach 1506–1530" [Polish diplomatic sevice in the period 1506–1530]. In *Polska służba dyplomatyczna XVI–XVI11 w.* [Polish diplomatic service, 16–18th century], edited by Zbigniew Wojak, 11–79. Warsaw: Instytut Historii PAN, 1966.
———. "Przedmurze? Czy rzeczywiście? (głos w dyskusji)" [Murale Christianis? Was (Poland) really this? (A voice in the discussion)]. *Wiedza i Życie* 4 (1966): 2–8.
———. "W sprawie oceny gospodarki europejskiej w XIV–XVII wieku" [On the assesment of the European economy from the 14th to the 17th century]. Review of *The Birth of Capitalism* by Jerzy Topolski. *Kwartalnik Historyczny* 73:3 (1966): 618.
———. "Polska na tle Europy w XVI stuleciu" [Poland and Europe in the 16th century]. In *Dziejów Polski blaski i cienie* [The lights and the shadows of the Polish history], edited by Marian Turski, 147–73. Warsaw: Wiedza Powszechna, 1968.
———, ed. *Wieś polskiego Odrodzenia* [The countryside of the Polish Renaissance]. Warsaw: KiW, 1969.
———, ed. *La Pologne au XlIIe Congrès International des Sciences Historiques a Moscou. P. 1. La recherche historique en Pologne 1945–1968.* Warsaw: PWN 1970.
———. "Obraz Polski w historiografii obcej (a voice in the discussion)" [The image of Poland in foreign historiography]. *Kwartalnik Historyczny* 78, no. 2 (1970): 331–53.

———, ed. *Polska w epoce Odrodzenia. Państwo–społeczeństwo–kultura* [Poland during the Renaissance. State, society, culture]. Warsaw: Wiedza Powszechna, 1970.

———. "Czy istnieje polska szkoła historyczna?" [Does a Polish school of historiography exist?]. *Polityka* 13 (1973): 15.

———. *Polska w Europie XVI stulecia* [Poland in Europe in the 16th century]. Warsaw: Wiedza Powszechna, 1973.

———. "The Social Groups of the Polish Society." In *Poland. The Land of Copernicus*, edited by Bogdan Suchodolski, 55–73. Wrocław: Ossolineum, 1973.

———. "Uwagi o ksenofobii w Polsce XVI w." [Remarks on xenophobia in 16th-century Poland]. In *Swojskość i cudzoziemszczyzna w dziejach kultury polskiej* [Familiarity and foreigness in the history of the Polish culture], edited by Zofia Stefanowska, 68–79. Warsaw: PWN, 1973.

———. "Przemiany organizacji wielkiej własności ziemskiej w Polsce XV i XVI w. (Uwagi dyskusyjne)" [Changes in the organization of the large demesnes in Poland in the 15th and 16th century. (Remarks for discussion)]. In *Społeczeństwo, gospodarka, kultura. Studia ofiarowane Marianowi Małowistowi w czterdziestolecie pracy naukowej* [Society, economy, culture. Studies dedicated to Marian Małowist on the 40th anniversary of his academic work], edited by Stanisław Herbst, 407-12, Warsaw: PWN, 1974.

———. "Polityka w Polsce XVI stulecia" [Politics in Poland in the 16th century]. *Człowiek i Światopogląd* 14: 2 (1975): 23-42.

———. "Oświata a pozycja społeczna w Polsce XVI stulecia. Próba oceny umiejętności pisania szlachty województwa krakowskiego w drugiej połowie XVI w." [Education and social position in 16th-century Poland. An attempt at evaluation the writing skills of the nobility in the Krakow voivodshiop in the second half of the 16th century]. In *Społeczeństwo staropolskie. Studia i szkice* [Early modern Polish society. Studies and sketches], edited by Andrzej Wyczański, Vol. 1, 27–55. Warsaw: PWN, 1976.

———, ed. *Społeczeństwo staropolskie. Studia i szkice* [Early modern Polish society. Studies and sketches] Vol. 1–4. Warsaw: PWN, 1976–1986.

———. *Uwarstwienie społeczne w Polsce XVI wieku. Studia* [Social stratification in Poland in the 16th century. Studies.]. Wrocław: Ossolineum, 1977.

———. "Czy chłopu było źle w Polsce w XVI wieku?" [Did the peasants suffer in 16th-century Poland?]. *Kwartalnik Historyczny* 85:3 (1978): 627–41.

———. "Die Frau in der Gesellschaft Polens im 16. jh. Versuch einer Sondierung." *Jahrbuch für Geschichte* 23 (1981).

———. "The Adjustment of the Polish Economy to Economic Checks in the XVIIth Century." *Journal of European Economic History* 10: 1 (1981): 207–12.

———. "Parallélisme des structures socio-économiques au XVle siècle." In *La Pologne et la Hongrie aux XVIe–XVIIIe siécles*, edited by Vera Zimányi. Budapest: Akadémiai Kiadó, 1981.

———. *Zygmunt Stary* [King Zigmund I the Old]. Warsaw: Zamek Królewski w Warszawie, 1985.

———. *Dogonić Europę, czyli Polska w czasach Zygmunta I (1506–1548)* [Catching up with Europe. Poland in the times of the king Zigmunt I (1506–1548)]. Kraków: KAW, 1987.

———. *Między kulturą a polityką: sekretarze królewscy Zygmunta Starego (1506–1548)* [Between culture and politics: the secretaries of the king Zigmunt I the Old (1506–1548). Warsaw: PWN, 1990.

———. "In Memoriam: Jerzy Topolski." *Kwartalnik Historyczny* 2 (1999): 139–42.

———. *Wschód i Zachód Europy w początkach doby nowożytnej*. Warsaw: Semper, 2003.

———. "Polska na tle Europy XVI stulecia." In *Dziejów Polski blaski i cienie*, edited by Marian Turski, 147–73. Warsaw: Wiedza Powszechna, 1968.

———. *Studia nad konsumpcją żywności w Polsce w XVI i pierwszej XVII w.* [Studies on the food consumption in Poland in the 16th and the first half of the 17th century]. Warsaw: PWN, 1969.

Wyczański, Andrzej, Krzysztof Groniowski, Janina Leskiewiczowa, and Henryk Samsonowicz. "Warszawskie środowisko historyczne. Uniwersytet Warszawski, IH PAN, IHKM PAN" [Warsaw historical milieu. Warsaw University, Institute of History Polish Academy of Science, Institute of History of Material Culture Polish Academy of Science]. *Kwartalnik Historyczny* 66: 3 (1959): 960–85.

Wyczański, Andrzej, and Antoni Mączak. "Folwark" [Manor/Folwark]. In *Wielka encyklopedia powszechna* [Great general encyclopedia], vol. 3, 751–52. Warsaw: PWN, 1964.

Wyczański, Andrzej, and Jerzy Topolski. "Badania historyczne w Polsce w latach 1945–1970" [Historical research in Poland in the years 1945–1970]. *Nauka Polska* 19, no. 2 (1971): 20–46.

———. "Peasant Economy Before and During the First Stage of Industrialization." In *Sixième Congrès International d'Histoire Economique*. Copenhagen, 1974.

Wyrobisz, Andrzej. "Zagadnienie upadku rzemiosła i kryzysu gospodarczego miast w Polsce – wiek XVI czy XVII?" [On the decline of the craft and the economic crisis of towns in Poland: did it happen in the 16th or the 17th century?] *Przegląd Historyczny* 58:1 (1967): 132–38.

Young, Robert. *Colonial Desire: Hybridity in Theory, Culture and Race*. London: Routledge, 1995.

Zalejko, Gwidon, and Andrzej Zybertowicz. "Gospodarcza aktywność szlachty jako czynnik przesądzający o narodzinach kapitalizmu: prezentacja i analiza koncepcji Jerzego Topolskiego" [The economic activity of the nobility as a decisive factor of the birth of capitalism: presentation and analysis of Jerzy Topolski's ideas]. In *Interdyscyplinarne studia nad genezą kapitalizmu* [Interdisciplinary studies on the origins of capitalism], vol. 2, edited by Adam Czarnota and Andrzej Zybertowicz, 69–83. Toruń: Uniwersytet im. Mikołaja Kopernika, 1993.

Zarifian, Philippe. *L'émergence d'un peuple monde*. Paris: Presses Universitaires de France, 1999.

Zarycki, Tomasz. "Class Analysis in Conditions of a Dual-Stratification Order." *East European Politics & Societies* 29, 3 (2015): 711–18.

Zientara, Benedykt. *Dzieje małopolskiego hutnictwa żelaznego XIV–XVII w.* [History of the iron industry in Małopolska region, 14th–17th century]. Warsaw: PWN, 1954.

———. "Cudzoziemcy w Polsce X–XV wieku: ich rola w zwierciadle polskiej opinii średniowiecznej" [Foreigners in Poland from the 10th to the 15th century: their role according to the Polish opinions in the Middle Ages]. In *Swojskość i cudzoziemszczyzna w dziejach kultury polskiej* [Familiarity and foreignness in the history of Polish culture], edited by Zofia Stefanowska, 9–37. Warsaw: PWN, 1973.

———. "Z zagadnień terminologii historycznej *Drang nach Osten*" [On the historical terminology *Drang nach Osten*]. In *Społeczeństwo, gospodarka, kultura. Studia ofiarowane Marianowi Małowistowi w czterdziestolecie pracy naukowej* [Society, economy, culture. Studies dedicated to Marian Małowist on the 40th anniversary of his academic work], edited by Stanisław Herbst, 425–34. Warsaw: PWN, 1974.

Zins, Henryk. *Anglia a Bałtyk w drugiej połowie XVI wieku. Bałtycki handel kupców angielskich z Polską w epoce elżbietańskiej i Kompania Wschodnia* [England and the Baltic in the second half of the 16th century. The Baltic trade of the English merchants in Poland in the times of Elizabeth I, and the Eastland Company]. Wrocław: Ossolineum, 1967.

Zinsser, Judith P. *History & Feminism. A Glass Half Full.* New York: Twayne Publishers, 1993.

Ziółkowski, Marek. "O różnorodności teraźniejszości (Pomiędzy tradycją, spuścizną socjalizmu, nowoczesnością a ponowoczesności)" [About the variety of the present (Between tradition, the legacy of socialism, modernity, and postmodernity)]. *Kultura i Społeczeństwo*, 4 (1997): 19–48.

Zybertowicz, Andrzej. "Materializm historyczny jako program badawczy" [Historical materialism as a research program]. In *Między historią a teorią: refleksje nad problematyką dziejów i wiedzy historycznej. Prace ofiarowane Jerzemu Topolskiemu* [Between history and theory: reflections on the past and historical knowledge. Works dedicated to Jerzy Topolski], edited by Marian Drozdowski, 39–49. Warsaw–Poznań: PWN, 1988.

Żamowski, Janusz, ed. *Metamorfozy społeczne. Badania nad dziejami społeczeństwa polskiego XIX i XX wieku* [Social metamorphosis. Research on the history of 19th- and 20th-century Polish society]. Warsaw: Instytut Historii PAN, 1997.

Żarnowski, Janusz. *Struktura społeczna inteligencji w Polsce 1918–1939* [The social structure of the intelligentsia in Poland 1918–1939]. Warsaw: PWN, 1964.

———. "Stan i perspektywy polskich prac badawczych nad najnowszą historią Europy Środkowej i Południowo-Wschodniej" [The condition and the perspectives of the Polish research projects on the newest history of Central and southeastern Europe]. *Przegląd Historyczny* 61, no. 2 (1970): 297–306.

———. "W sprawie genezy systemu państw narodowych w Europie środkowej i południowo-wschodniej po 1918 r." [About the genesis of the system of nation-states in Central and South East Europe after 1918]. *Kwartalnik Historyczny* 77 (1970): 585–603.

———. *Społeczeństwo Drugiej Rzeczypospolitej 1918–1939* [The society of Poland 1918–1939]. Warsaw: PWN, 1973.

———. "Historia społeczna: nadzieje, rozczarowania, perspektywy" [Social history: Hopes, disappointments and prospects]. In *Metamorfozy społeczne. Badania nad dziejami społeczeństwa polskiego XIX i XX wieku* [Social metamorphoses. Research on the history of Polish society in the 19th and 20th century], edited by Janusz Żarnowski, 9–34. Warsaw: Instytut Historii PAN, 1997.

———. "Kryzys i perspektywy historii społecznej" [The crisis and the perspectives of social history]. In *Między polityką a kulturą. Studia ofiarowane A. Wyczańskiemu w 75-lecie urodzin i 50-lecie pracy naukowej* [Between politics and culture. Studies dedicated to A. Wyczański on his 75th birthday and the 50th anniversary of his academic work], edited by Cezary Kuklo, 383–92. Białystok–Warsaw: PWN, 1999.

———, ed. *Dyktatury w Europie Środkowowschodniej 1918–1939. Konferencja naukowa w Instytucie Historii PAN* [Dictatorships in Central Eastern Europe 1918–1939. Academic conference in the Institute of history of the Polish Academy of Sciences]. Wrocław: Ossolineum, 1983.

Żytkowicz, Leonid, "W sprawie badań porównawczych nad genezą i rozwojem folwarku pańszczyźnianego" [On the comparative research on the origins and development of the serf manor]. In *Społeczeństwo-Gospodarka-Kultura. Studia ofiarowane Marianowi Małowistowi w czterdziestolecie pracy naukowej* [Society, economy, culture. Studies dedicated to Marian Małowist on the 40th anniversary of his academic work]. Warsaw: PWN, 1974.

———. "Directions of Agrarian Development in Southeastern Europe in the Sixteenth to Eighteenth Centuries." *Acta Poloniae Historica* 43 (1981): 31–74.

Index

F

G

H

I

J

L

S

T

Index of names

For Product Safety Concerns and Information please contact our EU representative GPSR@taylorandfrancis.com Taylor & Francis Verlag GmbH, Kaufingerstraße 24, 80331 München, Germany

Batch number: 10725853

Printed by Printforce, the Netherlands